# Jewish and Christian Liturgy and Worship

## New Insights into its History and Interaction

*Edited by*

Albert Gerhards & Clemens Leonhard

BRILL

LEIDEN · BOSTON

2007

This book is printed on acid-free paper.

**Library of Congress Cataloging-in-Publication Data**

A C.I.P. record for this book is available from the Library of Congress

BM
660
.J47
2007

ISSN 1388-2074
ISBN 978 90 04 16201 3

PRINTED IN THE NETHERLANDS

Jewish and Christian Liturgy and Worship

# Jewish and Christian Perspectives Series

VOLUME 15

# CONTENTS

PART ONE

# INTRODUCTION

# INTRODUCTION

*Albert Gerhards and Clemens Leonhard*
Rheinische Friedrich-Wilhelms-Universität Bonn, Germany
Westfälische Wilhelms-Universität Münster, Germany

More than 25 years ago, Jakob J. Petuchowski suggested establishing an international center for the study of Jewish and comparative liturgy (1980, 124f). It was designed to foster the interdisciplinary dialogue of scholars studying liturgies and rituals and to provide students with the opportunity of receiving special training in these fields. Jakob Petuchowski's idea never materialized in the broad scheme in which it was conceived. Yet, his concern did not lose its appeal. It remains of vital interest for the study of the history of Jewish and Christian liturgies today. The Aachen symposium was convened in commemoration of this great Jewish liturgist and his concern about liturgical studies as a common interest of Jewish and Christian scholars. It assessed the thriving branches of the study of Jewish and Christian liturgies and looked for common interests and challenges that required the combined efforts of both disciplines in the future.

The later 20th century witnessed an enormous increase in data available for the study of Jewish liturgy, especially due to a rising interest in the treasures of the Cairo Genizah. Fortunately, this trend continues unabatedly, as new texts continue to be published while comprehensive studies are being composed that will allow a wider audience to participate in the assessment of the meaning of those texts. Some decades earlier, the study of Christian liturgies (conducted during the first half of the 20th cent.) enjoyed tremendous success in the Catholic church which based large parts of its reform of the liturgy on findings relating to its history. 'Liturgical studies' was established as an academic subject. In the Aachen symposium and the following papers, scholars of two expanding disciplines explore the need for—and the benefits of—scientific cooperation.

The following book was created by scholars studying Judaism and/or Christianity who accepted Albert Gerhard's and Hans Hermann Henrix's invitation to a symposium that was convened in Aachen in November 2003. The participants were invited to present papers about topics that were of interest to the whole group and to do this in a way that facilitated the access of non-specialists to the data. They were asked, to refrain from reducing the degree of sophistication and intricacy of their subject, although they were asked to open the specialized discussion to all participants. The papers published in this book reflect this methodological approach of the symposium regarding thriving areas of research that deserve and require the attention of scholars of both Judaism and Christianity.

The symposium and the present publication were generously supported by the Deutsche Forschungsgemeinschaft, the GEFFRUB foundation of the Rheinische Friedrich Wilhelms-Universität Bonn, the Fritz Thyssen-Stiftung, and the Catholic Episcopal Academy in Aachen.

The first two papers by Hans-Hermann Henrix and Albert Gerhards introduce the occasion and the scope of the symposium and the volume. Hans-Hermann Henrix presents Jakob J. Petuchowski as a person and as a scholar. Jakob Petuchowski's achievements have provided the study of Jewish and Christian liturgies with a high scientific and theological standard. Albert Gerhards takes the meanings and interrelationship of the Christian Sanctus and the Jewish Kedusha as an example that elucidates the historical and theological questions which are at stake in this interdisciplinary approach. Studying the intricate relationship between historical and theological research, he supports a realistic assessment of the relationship between Judaism and Christianity—an academic activity that will also have a positive effect on an interreligious dialogue.

The second section concentrates on Jewish liturgical poetry including a glimpse of Christian poetic texts. Thus, Ruth Langer discusses the way in which Jewish prayer texts use the Bible. While it is evident that prayer texts are worded in 'biblical language', the relationship between liturgical and biblical texts requires a more complex explanation when compared in a scientific way. From the analysis of the remains of a piyyut by the famous payyetan Elazar birabbi Qallir, Elisabeth Hollender proceeds to a description of the Ashkenazi Jews' approach to the biblical laws of tithes and their implication for eschatology as well as the practice of giving part of one's income to the poor. Avi Shmidman reads birkhot ha-mazon of the Cairo Geniza and discusses the influence of the poetical additions to the standard text. Michael Rand compares Aramaic lament poems with the Qalliri's Hebrew poetry for the 9th of Av and provides among other results a tentative explanation for the eventual demise of the Aramaic poetry. In the same epoch, Jacob of Serugh composed poetic texts in Syriac. Thus, Andrew Palmer's paper provides one of the Christian counterparts to Jewish liturgical poetry. This section is introduced by Stefan Reif, who describes the implications of the renewed interest in the treasures of the Genizah for current research.

In the third section, Stephan Wahle takes up the theological discussion that was opened by Albert Gerhards in his introduction to the book. Martin Lang and Reinhard Meßner present a synthesis of historical, philological, and theological approaches to a Eucharistic prayer. Harald Buchinger collects and analyzes what can be learned about the Eucharist in Origen's time from that author's vast oeuvre. Wolfram Kinzig follows similar lines in an historical assessment of Christian liturgies, analyzing the creed and its use in the liturgy. The study of the use of the creed enhances its understanding in performances of the liturgy today.

The fourth section turns towards rabbinic Judaism and its relationship to the Christians of that day. Uri Ehrlich discusses the question of the role of Israel's ancestors in prayer. Marcel Poorthuis and Daniel Stökl-Ben Ezra investigate contacts between Christians and (rabbinic) Jews in regard to the understanding of biblical texts (Ps 72 and 24) and the interpretation of liturgies (Pentecost and Shavuot). Both scholars discover traces of such contacts and instances of reactions to the respective 'others' way of thinking. In their field of interest, a careful reading of the texts leads to the suggestion of important parallels. Gerard Rouwhorst and Clemens Leonhard discuss questions of the early history of the Eucharist and the prayers performed during Christian symposia in late Antiquity. They call into question earlier assumptions of contacts between Judaism and Christianity that could be used as ways of understanding the similarities and differences between Jewish and Christian prayers in the context of meals. Gerard Rouwhorst also discusses the role of customs of Hellenistic symposia in the process of the shaping of Jewish and Christian religious acts at meals. Thus, the third section of the book provides examples for the patterns of describing Judaism and Christianity in the first centuries of the common era. While some groups of data lead to strong structural parallels or even to traces of a real discourse about the understanding of texts and liturgies, others must be explained as independent developments in both religions despite some more or less superficial similarities.

'Five things are one-sixtieth [of something else], and these are they: fire, honey, the Sabbath, sleeping, and dreaming. Fire is one-sixtieth of Gehenna. Honey is one-sixtieth of manna. The Sabbath is one-sixtieth of the world to come. Sleep is one-sixtieth of death. Dreaming is one-sixtieth of prophecy' (Ber 57b, translated by Jacob Neusner). If the Aachen Symposium and the present collection of articles is one-sixtieth of Jakob Petuchowski's International Institute for Jewish and Comparative Liturgy, it is a worthy contribution to its inventor's honor and testifies to his lasting and stimulating impact on the subject which was the focus of his scholarly life.

## LITERATURE

The abbreviations follow Siegfried M. Schwertner, *IATG²; Internationales Abkürzungsverzeichnis für Theologie und Grenzgebiete; International Glossary of Abbreviations for Theology and Related Subjects* [..., 2nd ed.]. Berlin—New York 1992.
Petuchowski, J.J., 'Entwurf zu einem internationalen Institut für jüdische und vergleichende Liturgie', *LJ* 30.

# JAKOB J. PETUCHOWSKI (1925–1991): RABBI, SCHOLAR, ECUMENIST

*Hans Hermann Henrix*
Bischöfliche Akademie des Bistums Aachen, Germany

## 1 A BIOGRAPHICAL SKETCH

Understanding Jakob J. Petuchowski through his biography and point of origin corresponds to his own self-understanding.[1] In his *summa*, he recalls the view of his teacher, Leo Baeck, to the effect that as a genre, 'Confessions' are 'not very much at home in Judaism' (MS v), whereas they have their place within Christianity, e.g., the Confessions of St. Augustine or those of Kierkegaard. Differing from his teacher in emphasis, however, Jakob J. Petuchowski stresses that today, it is no longer possible to present religion as something purely abstract; for the sake of credibility, Judaism as a religion needed to be presented in terms of today's lives. Drawing from the sources of Jewish tradition, a modern Jew who would present Judaism, would have to report 'how, when and why' he reached the views he tried to present. The *summa*, then, contained something of a *confessio* (1992, 9–17).

Petuchowski here regarded himself as contemporary with the end of the 20th century. While at the beginning of that century both Jews and Christians endeavoured to define Judaism and, respectively, Christianity by means of the guiding principle ('essence'), events and developments in the course of that century made the word 'essence', as a guiding principle, problematical for both these religious traditions, and '[philosophical] changes [...] redirected our focus from "essence" to "existence"' (MS 2). However, understanding that 'existence' meant a form of expression, reflection, or documentation of an 'essence', Petuchowski does not endorse a splitting of Judaism into 'Judaisms'. He

---

[1] Hans Hermann Henrix's quotations from Petuchowski 1992 are here either translated into English (cited as 1992), or bring wording from the opening pages of an unpublished English manuscript 'My Judaism' (cited as MS) which antedated the German book and only the opening of which corresponds to the published German version.

will rather 'speak of Judaism in [...] terms which emerge from one's own existential condition and personal choices' (MS 6).

It was part of Jakob J. Petuchowski's self-understanding to be from a family of orthodox Jews living in Berlin. For orthodox Judaism in Berlin, Dr. Markus Petuchowski, Jakob's paternal grandfather, was a remarkable rabbi who led those High Holiday services in 1913 which proved pivotal for Franz Rosenzweig as he discovered the powerful fact of his Jewishness. Rabbi Dr. Petuchowski died in 1926, and already two years later his son, Samuel Meir Sigmund, Jakob's father, followed him in death. Jakob J. Petuchowski was therefore too young to have any conscious memory of them which he could have taken with him into his own life. 'I was born in 1925[2]. It was my mother of blessed memory who saw to it that I received a good general and a good Jewish education. She also made sure that I was introduced to the family tradition. In that, she was on occasion assisted by several uncles and other relatives who were in the German [and Czech] Orthodox rabbinate. [...] Also, although we were not members of the separatist Orthodox community, I was sent to the school—both grade school and high school—of its Adath Israel Congregation, because it had the reputation of offering the best and most intensive Jewish education of any of the Jewish schools, communal or private, in Berlin. To graduate from the high school, a student was expected to have attained sufficient mastery of the Talmud and its related literature to be able to deal with, i.e., to read, translate [from the Aramaic] and interpret, two pages of the Talmud at sight, taken from anywhere among the many volumes of the Talmud, and to explain Rashi's [1040–1105] commentary to that passage as well as the comments made by the later casuists' (MS 23–24).

The normal and at the same time ambitious school instruction enjoyed by Jakob J. Petuchowski was, in his case, supplemented and deepened. For, in addition, he took part in religious instruction for the community, which, though conducted in the building of a liberal congregation, was taught by the Petuchowski family's orthodox rabbi. Furthermore, Petuchowski joined a 'group of boys who volunteered for some more instruction given by the rabbi in his private home' (MS 26). Jakob spoke of this rabbi with great respect. It was no less a personage than Alexander Altmann (1906–1987), who, over and above

---

[2] The exact date of birth is July 25, 1925, or: 9th of Av, 5685, cf. A.M. Petuchowski 1993.

acting as communal rabbi, taught as Professor of Jewish Philosophy at Berlin's orthodox rabbinical seminary since 1931 and who left Berlin for England one day after Jakob's bar mitzvah in August 1938. He was communal rabbi in Manchester until, in 1959, he became Professor of Jewish Philosophy at Brandeis University and one of the top experts on Mendelssohn.[3]

Looking back on his childhood and his education, Petuchowski mused: 'If I try, after more than fifty years, to analyze what German Orthodox Judaism meant to me at the time, I come up with feelings of both deep satisfaction and intellectual excitement. Notwithstanding the ever increasing threat under which we Jews in Nazi Germany lived at the time, it felt good to be Jewish. The way we lived our Jewish lives was also aesthetically pleasing. It was a privilege to serve in our synagogue choir. The manner in which we performed the many rituals of the Jewish tradition was imbued with a certain dignity and a sense of beauty' (MS 27). Here Jakob J. Petuchowski apparently touches on a personal center which, in spite of all the distress from living in national-socialist Germany, formed his identity and stayed with him throughout his life. His aesthetic sense always remained vital—in his rabbinic functions as well as in his scholarly work. And in liturgy, he went beyond aesthetics, reaching a poetic dimension, and this meant going beyond prose, or: adding to the logic of prose by going beyond it, for prayers are not simple prose. In prayers, and in liturgy in general, a sense of the poetic testifies to a reality which, if expressed in prose, would not be sayable, or perhaps even believable. Conversely, in the poetic dimension, things can be left unsaid because more is implied than said. Jakob J. Petuchowski regarded this poetic dimension highly.[4]

A harsh fate awaited the young student, thus schooled in an elect Jewishness. In May, 1939, he left Germany with a children's transport— his mother would be murdered in the Shoa—and, with one year of English instruction at his Berlin school, he arrived in Scotland.[5] At age sixteen, he became a student at the Glasgow Rabbinical College. The name may be misleading because this institution was 'really an old-time yeshiva in the East European style recreated on Scottish soil, with

---

[3] Cf. Hyman (1974, 779).

[4] Cf. Petuchowski (1978, esp. 3). Significantly, the book bears the dedication: 'In memory of my dear Mother, who taught me the poetry of faith.'

[5] Elizabeth Petuchowski (2004) draws attention, in this connection, to Jakob J. Petuchowski (1990a, 242–244).

hardly any awareness that it was located in Scotland and that it was the twentieth century' (MS 28). In these sentences, one can still feel the disappointment that the young Petuchowski underwent in this learning experience in Glasgow. Rabbi Samson Raphael Hirsch's Neo-orthodoxy had managed to combine a life led in strict accordance with Torah and Halachah with a solid secular education and participation in worldly culture. Instead of such a 'neo-orthodox' union of traditional Jewish observance and western culture, Glasgow taught Talmud and nothing but Talmud, and it was studied from morning to night. Petuchowski speaks with admiration and gratitude about the personal and financial commitment on the part of the east-European Jewish community of Glasgow which supported the college, and provided lodging and meals for the students in individual families.

Petuchowski wanted to become a rabbi already at the time he attended the Glasgow College, which was not for the training of rabbis. It was for training in Torah study *lishmah*, 'for its own sake', not to make a living from it. He admits that his Talmud study there stood him in good stead: 'I would never have become an Assistant Professor of Rabbinics at a rabbinical seminary at the age of 31, advancing to the rank of Associate Professor and then full Professor in rapid succession thereafter, if it had not been for the knowledge which I was able to acquire at the Glasgow Rabbinical College' (MS 31–32). But before his academic career as a teacher of Rabbinics could take off, Jakob J. Petuchowski had to proceed with his Jewish and secular education. He was able to do that with the support of Rabbi Dr. Harold Reinhart (1891–1969) in London, who advised him to study not Semitic languages and literature, but to major in Psychology. His subsidiary was Philosophy, in addition to Latin, Roman history, Logic and English literature. Petuchowski attained a B.A. (Honours) degree from the University of London in 1947.

He continued his studies privately—with Rabbi Dr. Arthur Loewenstamm (1881–1965), Rabbi Dr. Benno Jacob (1862–1945), Professor Dr. Isaac Markon (1875–1949) or Rabbi Dr. Bruno Italiener (1881–1956). Petuchowski attributes to Rabbi Loewenstamm (1992, 51) the fact that he could reduce the usual course of study at the Hebrew Union College from twelve semesters to seven. However, of most consequential importance while studying for his B.A., and thereafter, while he took Semitic language courses at University College London, was Rabbi Dr. Leo Baeck.

Upon his release from the concentration camp in Theresienstadt, Leo Baeck came to London where, every Monday, he lectured to an invited group of rabbis and scholars, heirs of Wissenschaft des Judentums, and Petuchowski had leave to attend. Moreover, Baeck became his private teacher in Baeck's area of specialization: the Midrash. It was also Leo Baeck who advised Jakob J. Petuchowski, upon receiving his University degree from the University of London, that he needed Rabbinic Ordination from a recognized rabbinical seminary, and therefore made contact on his behalf with both the Conservative Jewish Theological Seminary in New York and the Reform Hebrew Union College in Cincinnati, the latter founded by Isaac Mayer Wise in 1875. Petuchowski decided in favour of Cincinnati because Leo Baeck had accepted an invitation to the Hebrew Union College in Cincinnati (1992, 60–61) and, in October 1948, joined the faculty as guest professor for winter semesters. Thus, Jakob could continue studying with him. On October 1, 1948, Jakob flew to the United States to become a student at the Hebrew Union College. He had married Elizabeth Mayer from Bochum on November 28, 1946, who travelled with him, and they would later have three sons, Samuel, Aaron, and Jonathan.

Among other faculty members who profoundly influenced Jakob was Samuel S. Cohon (1888–1959) who taught Jewish Theology and Liturgy. 'I would later become his successor in both subjects at the Hebrew Union College' (1992, 61). In addition to Cohon's scholarly achievements in the field of Rabbinic theology and Jewish religious thought, Petuchowski appreciated the fact that his teacher, though an enthusiastic representative of 'Reform', was a person who, at the same time, sought to express his own enlightened piety in the forms of ancient sacred Jewish tradition, of course in accordance with twentieth-century rational and aesthetic sensibilities. Although Cohon stressed 'the institutional loyalties of Reform Judaism' more than did Leo Baeck, he was, like Baeck, 'concerned with Jews and Judaism as a whole' (MS 49), a way of thinking that coincided with Jakob J. Petuchowski's. It may also have been Cohon's influence which made Jakob reject a certain Jewish self-description according to which Judaism has no theology, nor could it ever have one. Instead, Petuchowski of course stood for an interpretation of Jewish teaching which, pursued methodically, yielded Jewish theology. He liked to cite Cohon, also in conversations: 'Theology is to religion what grammar is to speech.' The nature of theology as a discipline allowed for distinguishing between authentic religious experience and its interpretation, as he had also learned from Cohon: 'Religion, supplying the data of theological investigation, naturally precedes theology, even as flowers precede botany, or as health precedes hygiene or medicine'.

The training Jakob J. Petuchowski received enabled him, as he functioned as rabbi, scholar and ecumenist, to combine well grounded Jewish knowledge with the purpose transmitting the great heritage of Judaism as a habitable house of life for Jewish men and women of the 20th century and to make Christian men and women aware of Judaism as an independent tradition. The track for an astonishing course of life had been laid. After he was ordained and received his Master's degree in 1952, he found himself placed in a definite position within the religious and multifarious world of Judaism. His Ph.D. (1954) dissertation dealt with David Nieto (1654–1728) as defender of the Jewish tradition (1954, 1970a). Petuchowski served as rabbi in Welch, W. Va., on a bi-weekly basis between 1949 and 1955.[6] He was full-time rabbi in Washington, Pennsylvania, from 1955 to 1956.[7] In response to objections at the Hebrew Union College in Cincinnati, that such a talented scholar had been let go, Jakob was recalled in 1956. From that year on, he travelled every year to the small Jewish community in Laredo, Texas, to officiate as rabbi for the High Holidays at the B'nai Israel Temple, and to perform pastoral and liturgical functions.[8] His

---

[6] Letter from Jakob J. Petuchowski to Rabbi Abraham J. Shindeling, Feb. 14, 1957, in the American Jewish Archives, Cincinnati. See also (A.M. Petuchowski 1993, 29–32), where the cited period excludes Petuchowski's pre-ordination years in Welch.

[7] 'The congregation was nominally orthodox, had built a handsome modern synagogue and probably wanted a modern rabbi to go with it. The year turned out to be unbelievably full and active, with the introduction of an organ, a volunteer choir and sermons, and with classes on a Jewish subject almost every evening for smaller or larger groups': Elizabeth Petuchowski to the author in a letter of January 7, 2005.

[8] A few weeks before his death, the Laredo congregation tendered a celebration in honor of the 35th year of Petuchowski's ministry on the annual High Holidays. In Jakob's last letter to the author, dated October 1, 1991, he wrote about this: 'In Laredo, my 35th year there for the High Holidays was celebrated very beautifully with a dinner at the Country Club and with pleasant speeches. The chief address was given by Rabbi Samuel Stahl from the "neighboring" congregation in San Antonio ("only" 150 miles away from Laredo, which is not considered a great distance in Texas). Years earlier, Stahl had written both his master's thesis and his doctoral dissertation with me. The congregation had invited Elizabeth to come, too. But the chief surprise for me (everyone else seems to have known it) was that it had also invited Rabbi Aaron Petuchowski from Roslyn Heights, New York, to say a few fitting words that festive evening. It surely could not have been easy for the Senior Rabbi of a large congregation to undertake the long flight to the Mexican border and to make himself available for two days just

teaching in Cincinnati had started as Assistant Professor of Rabbinic Studies. Already in his early courses he dealt with Rabbinic texts as apologetic and polemic source material, a counterpart to Paulinian Christianity, the Church Fathers and Gnosticism. During the academic year 1963–1964, he was rabbi and founding director of Judaic Studies at the newly established Jerusalem branch of the Hebrew Union College. There, in addition to other tasks, he was invited to give a lecture to the Jerusalem B'nai B'rith Lodge about the different trends of American Judaism—in German!—and this turned out to be an external impetus to turn to his German mother tongue which had become estranged (see 1992, 136–138). The fifties and sixties were a period for numerous publications (1966a, 1979a [3rd ed.] and 1968). From 1974 to 1981, he was Research Professor of Jewish Theology and Liturgy, and from 1981, the Sol and Arlene Bronstein Professor of Judaeo-Christian Studies at Hebrew Union College-Jewish Institute of Religion in Cincinnati. Beginning with 1973, when the first official invitation from the Oratio Dominica Foundation of the Herder Verlag, publishers in Freiburg, brought him back to his former homeland, he visited Germany again and again. Movingly he wrote about the inner resistance he had to overcome (1992, 135–145). After crossing that threshold, he began to appear ever more frequently in Germany in response to invitations and to feel welcome there during his visits (see 1985a, 64–67).

Petuchowski, the scholar, was effective over a wide radius, recognized by, a.o., Maimonides College, Winnipeg (1959), the Albertus-Magnus University, Cologne, in 1978, and Brown University in Providence, R.I., in 1979. Numerous guest professorships, among them Antioch College in Oxford, Ohio, Tel Aviv, Oxford (England), Lucerne, Freiburg, Cologne, Denver, CO; Cambridge, MA; and Tempe, AZ, enabled him to teach an international audience. Several fellowships were expressions of the collegial esteem of peers. When he died on November 12, 1991, after heart surgery, an abundance of eulogies lauded his personality and rabbinic activity, his charisma as professor, and his merits in connection with the Jewish-Christian dialogue on a scholarly level (cf. among German eulogies Anon. 1991, 29; Henrix 1991a, 26; 1991b, 3; Walter 1991, 396; Strolz 1992, 52f).

---

between Rosh ha-Shanah and Yom Kippur. The whole evening was such an outpouring of great love, and now, three weeks later, I am still under its impact [...]'

## 2  JUDAISM DOES HAVE THEOLOGY—PETUCHOWSKI
### AS AN ACADEMIC THEOLOGIAN

The scholar carried about—or rather: internalized—by Jakob J. Petuchowski, the rabbi, was plainly the theologian. He granted: 'The religious world of Judaism which I entered in 1952 as rabbi and in 1956
as academic theologian was and is no monolithic bloc' (1992, 64). As
an academic theologian, ever mindful of the great religious varieties
within Judaism, he has always insisted that Judaism does have theology.
With this, he has always contradicted Jews who think that 'theology
is not even a "Jewish subject".' He considered this view wrong. 'Jews
probably did not always do theology the way Christians do—although
this did happen in the Middle Ages and in modern times—but they did
theology, nevertheless' (1981a; 204–215, here 205; cf. 1980a, 231–234
as an earlier version, and 1987a, 41–52 for a slightly differing English
version. Cf. also 1979b, English 1982a, and 1980b; as well as 1981b,
1981c, and 1982b).

Petuchowski's defense of theology went beyond contradicting those
who held that Judaism had no theology. He also contended with those
who conceded that Judaism had a theological element, but denied that
Judaism established dogmas or had a systematic theology (1980c). In
inner-Jewish discussions of this position he warned against an inherent
'simplification and generalization', and is close to his teacher Samuel
S. Cohon who says: 'Rabbinic Judaism could not manage totally without
a structure of dogmas. [...] The Mishnah, for one, denies a portion in
the world-to-come to those who repudiate belief in Resurrection and
Revelation (Sanhedrin 10,1), similarly to the Apiqores (whatever the
word may have signified). [...] That surely means that these people were
not included among the community of believers sub specie aeternita-
tis—which must certainly be regarded as one of the chief functions of
an establishment of dogmas. Furthermore, one should bear in mind that
Judaism did not constantly stick to this alleged lack of system in Rabbinic theology. Saadya Gaon in the tenth century and Maimonides in
the twelfth century [...] have, for all their ties to the sources of Rabbinic
Judaism, systematized quite masterfully. And Hermann Cohen's Religion
der Vernunft aus den Quellen des Judentums, and Franz Rosenzweig's
Das neue Denken would have been impossible without the intellectual
impetus of a Kant or a Schelling' (1981f; 154–162, here 154–155).
The Rabbis 'thought, as it were, "concretely," and not in the abstract.
Sharply disagreeing views are often peaceably juxtaposed without an

effort to harmonize them or to arrange them into an overarching system. Rabbinic theology always refers to life' (1980b, 11f).

There are two focal points in Jakob J. Petuchowski's summa of his Jewishness, in his 'confessing a specific faith', as he sets out to give reasons for his belief both for himself and for others, and he does that by searching for a model on which to orient himself, a basic structure, as he says (1992, 84–85). Jewish tradition is familiar with attempts to condense the chief issues of the Torah and its interpretation. Maimonides's Thirteen Principles of the Faith are well known and were taken into the Jewish prayer book. If thirteen principles are deemed too many for a presentation [of basic principles], says Petuchowski, the Zohar, chief work of Jewish mysticism from the thirteenth century, offers a three-point version: '[In the Zohar] it is said that God, Torah, and Israel are connected to one another. [...] And with the aid of these three themes I will make my Jewishness clear theologically' (1992, 85).

In all of his work, a great breadth of individual theological subjects is apparent, though this does not preclude a certain preference, in his theology, for the triad Creation, Revelation, and Redemption. He repeatedly returns to the triad (1981c, 15; 1979a, 30–31; 1979c; 66–76, here 71–72; 1979d, 309–315; 1987b, 28–32; *et passim*). Even so, the theme Revelation predominates.[9] As to his perception of Revelation,[10] Jakob J. Petuchowski wants to dialogue with those for whom—not necessarily the idea of God, but—the idea of Revelation is very foreign, and he draws a line from biblical understanding to modern understanding: 'A deep gulf gapes between human beings and the transcendent God of the Hebrew Bible. God is God, and human beings are human beings. God's ways are not human ways, and God's thoughts are not human thoughts, just as the heavens are high above the earth (Isa 55:8–9). Even so, this biblical spiritual concept could never have become biblical *religion* had the acknowledgment of this gulf's existence not been accompanied by the certainty that this gulf could be bridged—nay, by the [historical] experience that it has on occasion *been* bridged. This metaphor should not be misunderstood. Judaism never obliterates the

---

[9] For Petuchowski's understanding of Creation and Redemption, cf. 1979d ; 1980d; 136–151, here 140–142; 1981c, 59–66 (Creation), 76–82 (Redemption); 1984, 70–81; 1985b, 9– 18.

[10] See the essays, articles, sermons or chapters: 1959, 212–239, most readily available in 1998, 101–112; 1961, 23–27; 1979a, 66–83; 1965, 29–50; 1966c, 4–11; 1976a, 61–74, English: 1987c, 45–54 (not identical with the 1959 essay with a similar title); 1981d, 72–86; 1983; 1989, 267–272.

boundary between God and human beings. There is no apotheosis of man, and no incarnation of God. But God, who remains God, reveals himself to human beings who remain human beings. Theologically, this is known as Revelation' (1976a, 61 = 1987c, 45).

For Petuchowski, there can be no real conflict between Revelation and reason. And he regards Reform Judaism as better equipped to deal with the challenge of reason and science than orthodox Judaism because Reform Judaism could, for instance, develop a positive attitude towards historical Bible criticism as it arose in the context of modern Christian Biblical criticism. Franz Rosenzweig essentially contributed to Jakob J. Petuchowski's equanimity regarding biblical criticism. He had shown a new way for Jewish understanding of the Torah. As Rosenzweig's disciple, Jakob J. Petuchowski establishes a belief in Revelation which does not have to rely on the scholarly historical reconstruction of ancient Hebrew literature, but looks for God's word in the human word.[11]

### 3   Judaism as a Liturgical Religion—Petuchowski as Scholar of the Liturgy

Not without reason could one call Jakob J. Petuchowski a Revelation theologian—and one would not even have touched upon the center of his scholarly work, namely the exploration of liturgy. One would, of course, have brought to light the most important theological presuppositions—he was Professor for Jewish Theology and Liturgy at HUC–JIR in Cincinnati from 1974 to 1981. 'Jewish liturgy has its being at a point where it intersects with *Aggadah* and *Halakhah; Aggadah*—because the contents of liturgy and its ideological presuppositions are of course theological, that is, "*aggadic*". Liturgy involves the belief in God who hears prayer, who has redeemed Israel from Egypt, who forgives sin and heals diseases, who offers consolation and lets sprout messianic salvation, etc., etc. [...] All this is Jewish theology, or, in rabbinic terms, *Aggadah*' (1987b, 29). Thus, liturgy presupposes the Revelation of God who participates in history, redeems Israel from Egypt, is close to his people and promises messianic salvation, or Redemption. This theology, then, 'which has become part of the liturgy, can be regarded as generally accepted theology' (1987b, 30–31).

---

[11]   On this topic see Petuchowski's fundamental explanations in 'Theologisches Fazit: Gotteswort und Menschenwort', the final chapter in 1982b, 120–138.

Petuchowski's interest in the study of liturgy contained, at its core, his interest in theology. He saw liturgy, or the act of prayer, at a place between religion—linked to experience, that is, primary and immediate—and theology, that is, an educed, secondary and interpretative delineation of religious experience: '[...] there is the phenomenon of prayer itself, the act of man's addressing himself to God. This is both a datum of religious experience and a task for theological understanding. Moreover, since man [...] is never man in the abstract, but a concrete, specific individual, who stands within a concrete, specific religious tradition, there is room for an investigation of how the Jew is experiencing Jewish prayer, and of what the Jewish theological tradition has to say on the subject' (1972, vii; 1976b, 7). Prayer, liturgy, is a religious act and religious experience, and as such, a subject for theology, or conversely, theology has an impact on prayer and on liturgy. Liturgy both comes before theology and is in turn influenced by it. In a certain, and admittedly limited way one could call it a primordial, original, pre-reflective theology in progress. The study of liturgy as a unit of the study of theology is, then, secondary and reflective, in the sense that it reflects on what happens in liturgy, or in the act of praying.

Jakob J. Petuchowski devoted great parts of his work to reflection on liturgy. He researched the development of Jewish liturgy, but not in the manner of a general history of Jewish liturgy. And John D. Rayner, for one, regretted (Rayner 1992, 1) that there was no work from the pen of Jakob J. Petuchowski that followed up on the corresponding fundamental work of an Ismar Elbogen (Elbogen 1931). His monograph of more than 400 pages, 'Prayerbook Reform in Europe. The Liturgy of European Liberal and Reform Judaism' (1968) deals with the modern history of Jewish liturgy, in particular the innovations made by the European reformers, their theological conceptions or errors (1991, 170–187). Jules Harlow, Conservative Rabbi, has rightly assumed that this volume, dedicated to the author's three sons, is also a book of remembrance, a memorial to the pioneers of Liberal and Reform Judaism in Europe (Harlow 1993; 22, 27).

'Prayerbook Reform in Europe' offers a characterization of Jewish liturgy: 'There is, first of all, the very fact that we can speak of something as definite as a "Jewish Liturgy". Judaism, in other words, is a liturgical religion. Herein Judaism differs from some other religions which rely on hymns and ex tempore prayer exclusively. Judaism has its prayerbook. It, too, knows of the free outpourings of the pious heart, of the prayer uttered by the individual in his joy and in his anguish. But, in addition

to those private expressions of devotion, Judaism has, for use in both
synagogue and home, the fixed liturgy which is known as the siddur.
The name itself (meaning "order") indicates that Jewish prayer follows a
definite and established order or arrangement' (1968, 22f). The siddur
is the result of a development over many generations. It is open to local
customs and yet maintains the one common basic structure of Jewish
prayer, beyond differences between ashkenazi and sephardi rites and
individual congregations. Up to the time of nineteenth-century Reform
Judaism, change always meant addition. Prayers which had started off
as private and personal, found their way into the communal service.
Thus arose a tension between the *keva*-aspect—fixed times and fixed
liturgy—and *kavvana*-aspect—inwardness and spontaneity. A dialectic
arose which became the subject of one of several liturgical laws that
Petuchowski saw at work: 'One generation's expression of kavvanah
becomes the next generation's qebha'.[12]

Jakob J. Petuchowski's major scholarly volume greatly enhanced his
reputation (Harlow 1993, 21f). He added numerous books, articles
and studies showing his understanding of the liturgy as the central
and dependable expression of Jewish belief.[13] He asked that the set
liturgy be respected, and he criticized those who treated the liturgical
tradition too freely no less than those who seemed to regard it as an
unyielding armor. Although he was in the camp of liturgical reform,
and thus of Reform Judaism, he sometimes created the impression of
being an outsider there and of feeling more at home in conservative
Judaism. His scholarly writings on liturgy have influence even after his

---

[12] 1968, 24. Petuchowski's studies discovered something like a pattern in the development of the Jewish liturgy, and he mentioned these 'laws' on many occasions. Cf.
Petuchowski 1985c, 312–326, also in: 1998, 153–168. He enumerates and explains these
laws here: 1) One generation's spontaneity becomes another generation's routine. 2)
When the choice is between one or more versions of a prayer, the usual decision is to
say them all. 3) Talmudic liturgical requirements are predicated on the non-existence
of written prayerbooks; but this fact is ignored by later authorities. 4) Concern with
the need not to 'bother the congregation' has atrophied in the course of the millennia.
5) The 'Conservative' and the 'Reformer' are perennial types in the history of Jewish
Liturgy. 6) The ultimate authority in matters liturgical is the printer. 7) There is, and
there is not, such a thing as 'the' traditional Jewish Prayerbook.

[13] See Petuchowski as editor and co-editor of works on liturgy—this listing does not
aim to be exhaustive: 1970b; 1974; 1975; 1981e; 1988a; 1990b. For works on liturgy
authored by Petuchowski, see, e.g.1966b 175–189; 1969/1970, 299–324, also in 1998,
193–219; 1976b; 1978 (repr. 2000); 1979c, 13–32, 66–76, 77–88, 103–110, 111–121;
1981e, 45–54, also in 1998, 183–191; 1981c; 1982c, 119–123; 1984; 1985d, 99–107;
1987b, 28–32; 1988b, 13–33; 'Einleitung' in: 1988a, 5–10; the article 'Liturgie 1,
Jüdisch', 1989, 222–227; 1994, 407–462.

death. They continue to be taken into consideration especially among women and men in the field of Christian theology and here particularly in the study of the liturgy. The liturgist Jakob J. Petuchowski makes up a large part of Jakob J. Petuchowski, the ecumenist.

## 4   THE ECUMENIST

For Jakob J. Petuchowski, ecumenism did not start in 1984 upon his appointment to the Sol and Arlene Bronstein Chair for Judaeo-Christian Studies at the Hebrew Union College in Cincinnati. In April 1962, he took one of the greatest representatives of twentieth-century Protestant theology by surprise. Karl Barth had been visiting the United States for several weeks, and in Chicago, one of his dialogue partners during a round-table discussion before an audience of more than 2000 was, among others, Jakob who amazed his listeners with both his Jewish self assurance and his engagement in dialogue. Barth reminisced full of appreciation: 'The discussion was quite open, and the differences which inevitably emerged were neither disguised nor exaggerated, but were tackled passionately and yet pertinently'.[14]

The ecumenist Petuchowski became better known to a wider circle in Germany in 1971 through an 'Introduction' ('Zum Geleit') to a small monograph by Johannes Oesterreicher who had inspired efforts towards convening a Vatican council. Oesterreicher here pleaded for under-standing and acceptance of the Conciliar Statement 'Nostra Aetate' (Oesterreicher 1971 German and Engl. ed.). In an 'Introduction' to this booklet, Jakob paid tribute to a recently more 'objective' understanding, on both sides, of their respective religious literatures, which he deemed to be only 'a beginning, not the end of mutual understanding'. He called for going beyond literary criticism and philological knowledge: 'We have to bring back the theological dimension—with full awareness of (and protection against) the dangers which, in the past, infested that dimension. We need, in other words, a Jewish theology of Christianity

---

[14] Busch (1976), 459: 'Here [in Chicago], too, under the chairmanship of Professor Jaroslav Pelikan, on two evenings he [Karl Barth] joined in a public discussion: an open "round table" conference with a Jesuit, a Jewish Rabbi, a liberal Protestant, an orthodox Protestant, and a layman, the lawyer William Stringfellow, whom he held in high esteem.' Photo of participants during the discussion, 452. Cf. also Klappert 1980, 28.

and a Christian theology of Judaism.'[15] The two theologies face one
another and have to be developed with respect for one another, and
Jakob thought of them in terms of categories of interpretation. ' "Interpretation" is a weighty matter in our respective religious traditions; it is
a process in which the Holy Spirit has its share. The New Testament
is an "interpretation" of the Hebrew Bible, and the Patristic literature
is an "interpretation" of the New Testament. The Talmud is another
"interpretation" of the Hebrew Bible, an "interpretation" of which the
dynamics are the life-blood of Judaism to this very day. But the Talmud
is more than one interpretation. It is a collection of "interpretations",
of conflicting interpretations' (in: Oesterreicher 1971, 13). Jakob's
speaking about the twofold interpretation of the Hebrew Bible lays out
in nuce a position strengthened [on the Christian side] by the Papal
Bible Commission in its document 'The Jewish People and its Holy
Scripture in the Christian Bible', dated May 24, 2001. With its several
statements and passages, the document has drawn attention, because
of its basic thesis that there are a Jewish and a Christian tradition of
interpretation and way of reading the Old Testament, which must not
be a matter of contention (cf. for details Dohmen 2003).

   Jakob broadened his programmatic formulation, 'a Jewish Theology of Christianity', with further motifs and categories. He dealt with
an asymmetry, namely that 'Christianity needed a Christian theology
of Judaism much more than Judaism needed a Jewish theology of
Christianity'. Whereas Christianity claimed legitimacy in part with
reference to the Old Testament, Judaism had its own sources and did
not base its legitimacy on the sacred writings of any other religion. But
'because the God of Israel is also the God of all humankind, it should
be of some theological importance for Jews to ponder how the God
whose covenant they received at Sinai is disposed towards the rest of
humankind' (Petuchowski 1981a, 206); hence there is a need, on the
part of Jews, to evince interest in a Jewish theology of Christianity. The
ancient Rabbis already manifested such an interest: Judaism recognizes
that there are righteous persons among the non-Jewish peoples who
have, as the Rabbis put it, 'a share in the World-to-Come'. But this
concept, created by the ancient rabbis, did not allot a special status to

---

[15] 'Zum Geleit' Oesterreicher 1971, 14–20, German 17 English 9–13. Petuchowski
had laid out the basics of his position in 1963a, 373–384, republished as 1970c, 141–159
and 1985e, 141–159; translated into German as 1963b, 453–468, without, however,
using the programmatic formulation 'Jewish theology of Christianity'.

Christians, as part of the divine plan for salvation. 'The issue is that out of the commonly held Bible—ordained by God—there developed two different legitimate religions, Judaism and Christianity, who ought not to contend with one another for their justification to exist—indeed, they should, on the contrary, become aware of their inextricable connection in the divine plan in time and eternity' (1981a, 210f). According to Petuchowski, the aim of a Jewish theology of Christianity, as outlined by Rosenzweig,[16] and of the analogous Christian theology of Judaism, is respect for, and theological recognition of, the legitimacy of both religions, and of the difference between them.

Jakob J. Petuchowski provided outlines for his vision of a Jewish theology of Christianity; he understood its completion as a future matter. He wanted to work toward what was still in the distance by means of an academic project to which he devoted himself especially during his last years. The project concerned Christian-Jewish studies, for the implementation of which he was given the Sol and Arlene Bronstein-Chair at the Hebrew Union College as a mandate. He was eager to keep misunderstandings away from his vision of Jewish-Christian studies. The adjectival compound 'Judaeo-Christian' was not to describe the Jews of the first century, nor those of the first three centuries who connected their inherited faith with the acceptance of belief in Jesus and whose heirs today would be 'Hebrew Christians' or 'Messianic Jews'. Nor did he want this adjective misunderstood as simply a diplomatic formula. 'It remains a desideratum of modern scholarship to work out in detail what may actually be considered to be a part of a common "Judaeo-Christian" tradition, and what remains part of a distinctively Jewish and a distinctively Christian tradition. And this presupposes that we are, in fact, dealing with three different traditions, which have co-existed for almost two thousand years: a Jewish one, Christian one, and a tradition which is common to both Jews and Christians ('The

---

[16] Jakob J. Petuchowski saw himself as following Rosenzweig also in another respect: 'One should not be totally absorbed by "Dialogue". That is to say: one has to keep one's reputation also in other areas within Judaism, lest one ceases to be regarded as representative by one's own people. A Franz Rosenzweig, for instance, could afford to develop a Jewish theology of Christianity as part of his Star of Redemption. And with this theology Rosenzweig, as a Jew, went to meet Christianity more closely than any Jew before him. But after all, he had translated the Tanakh together with Martin Buber, and he made a translation of Judah Halevi's poems, complete with commentary. His Judaism did not consist solely of '"Dialogue" with Christianity', as Petuchowski wrote to the author in a letter of Oct. 16, 1981.

Aims and Objectives of Judaeo-Christian Studies. A Jewish View' in: *Defining a Discipline* 15–28 here 17). Petuchowski was eager to avoid 'syncretistic wishy-washiness'. 'What, then, do we mean when we speak of "Judaeo-Christian" Studies? We mean, in the first place, the study of Jewish beliefs, Jewish practices, Jewish documents and Jewish history, undertaken by Christian scholars; and we mean the study of Christian beliefs, Christian practices, Christian documents and Christian history, undertaken by Jewish scholars' (18). He was acquainted with such studies from the past, but 'they were all engaged in the "battle of the proof texts", trying to establish the truth of their own faith and to demolish the truth claims of the other side' (19). But beyond the purely philological-anthropological-sociological approach, more was involved because, unlike some ancient civilizations that are objects of archaeological research, Judaism and Christianity, are 'not dead and gone', but are 'contemporary and living traditions' (22). Therefore it is important to learn to Jewish the other religion not only via an academic study of its historical development, but as beliefs sincerely held.

It was 'important to know what the Birth Narrative means to the believing Christian today—and what it has meant to all the believing Christians before. It is no less important to know the significance of the Eucharist to the practicing Catholic and the practicing Protestant of today than it is to find a solution to the problem of whether or not the Last Supper originated in a Passover seder. And it is certainly no less important to discover the existential meaning which the doctrine of the Trinity has for the contemporary Christian than it is to determine with precision how and when the Trinitarian doctrine became an essential component of the Christian faith' (21). Similarly, the Christian Old Testament scholar with exegetical knowledge of the Pentateuch may not 'have insight into the feelings of a truly orthodox Jew today [...] who prays thrice daily for the restoration of the sacrificial cult' (21). This is how Jakob described the relationship between theory and practice: '[W]e mean to say that purely objective scholarship, delving into the remote past, may have to show more recognition than it has shown thus far of the fact that Judaism and Christianity are not only phenomena of Antiquity, but also contemporary and living religious traditions. In other words, Rezeptionsgeschichte and present-day realities should be considered every bit as important as the study of historical origins' (22). Judaeo-Christian Studies of this kind call for scholars who stand within their own inherited tradition and at the same time have a deep appreciation for the values of the other tradition.

It was no longer granted to Jakob J. Petuchowski to stake out further his vision of a projected discipline, 'Judaeo-Christian Studies'. Together with Clemens Thoma, he exemplarily demonstrated it in the 'Lexikon der jüdisch-christlichen Begegnung' (1989). From the start of the idea to the end of its execution, the lexicon is a Jewish-Christian co-operative work. It provides solid, objectively scholarly information on important topics of contemporary Jewish-Christian dialogue, and formulates a theological position of the respective existential religion. In this, it corresponds to the basic requirements of the Judaeo-Christian Studies Jakob had striven for. Beyond that, one can notice a farther reaching effect of his vision.

As for the German-speaking area, the continuing effect of Jakob J. Petuchowski's vision is not so much the creation of institutional structures as a remarkably intensive and enduring interest on the part of, precisely, Christian liturgists in pursuing studies and research initiated by Jakob (cf. Gerhards, Doeker, & Ebenbauer 2003, Gerhards & Henrix 2004, Gerhards & Wahle 2004). There, the interest in Jewish prayers and prayer services, which Jakob aroused among Christian liturgists in the 1970's, has not faded: it has steadily grown. And if a symposium, titled 'Transitions and Transformations', is devoted to deepening the understanding of relationships between the Jewish and the Christian liturgies, and is taking place in the German city of Aachen in the year 2005, thus a reminder of Jakob J. Petuchowski's 80th birthday, then this shows an extraordinary appreciation on the part of the next generation of Christian liturgists for Jakob J. Petuchowski the rabbi, scholar and ecumenist whom most of them could no longer have known personally. For a Christian theologian who could know Jakob and experience him for almost two decades as teacher, friend, dialogue partner and companion, this was one of the greatest enrichments of his life as human being, Christian and theologian. Mindful of this experience he recalls a berakhah which is recited, according to Jewish tradition, upon seeing a famous Torah scholar: *Barukh atta adonai, elohenu melekh ha'olam, shehalaq mehokhmato lire'av*, 'Praised are You, Lord our God, ruler of the universe, who has imparted His wisdom to those who fear Him' (Sidur Sefat Emet 292).

Translated by Elisabeth Petuchowski

LITERATURE

Anonymous, 'Der Rabbi von Berlin. Jakob J. Petuchowski gestorben', *Frankfurter Allgemeine Zeitung* No. 267 (November 16, 1991).

Busch, E., *Karl Barth*; *His Life from Letters and Autobiographical Texts*, Grand Rapids, Michigan 1976.

Dohmen, C. (ed.), *In Gottes Volk eingebunden*; *Christlich-jüdische Blickpunkte zum Dokument der Päpstlichen Bibelkommission 'Das jüdische Volk und seine Heilige Schrift in der christlichen Bibel'*, Stuttgart 2003.

Elbogen, I., *Der jüdische Gottesdienst in seiner geschichtlichen Entwicklung* [3rd ed.], Frankfurt/Main 1931 [repr. Hildesheim 1967].

Gerhards, A.; A. Doeker, & P. Ebenbauer (eds), *Identität durch Gebet*; *Zur gemeinschaftsbildenden Funktion institutionalisierten Betens in Judentum und Christentum*, Paderborn 2003.

———, & H.H. Henrix (eds), *Dialog oder Monolog? Zur liturgischen Beziehung zwischen Judentum und Christentum* (QD 208), Freiburg 2004.

———, & St. Wahle (eds), *Kontinuität und Unterbrechung*; *Gottesdienst und Gebet in Judentum und Christentum*, Paderborn 2004.

Harlow, J., 'Jakob J. Petuchowski, Liturgist, Zikhrono Libhrakhah', in: A.M. Petuchowski 1993.

Henrix, H.H., 'Arbeiter in demselben Weinberg. Zum Tod des jüdischen Theologen Jakob J. Petuchowski', *Kirchenzeitung für das Bistum Aachen* No. 47 (November 24, 1991) [quoted as 1991a].

———, 'Gegen die Überfrachtung des theologischen Dialogs. Zum Tod des großen Rabbiners Jakob J. Petuchowski', *Allgemeine Jüdische Wochenzeitung* No. 48 (November 28, 1991) [quoted as 1991b].

Hyman, A., 'Altmann, Alexander', *Encyclopaedia Judaica* 2 (1974).

Klappert, B., *Israel und die Kirche*; *Erwägungen zur Israellehre Karl Barths* (TEH 207), Munich 1980.

Oesterreicher, J.M., *Die Wiederentdeckung des Judentums durch die Kirche*; *Eine neue Zusammenschau der Konzilserklärung über die Juden*, Meitingen 1971; English edition (quoted above): *The Rediscovery of Judaism*; *A Re-Examination of the Conciliar Statement on the Jews*, South Orange, N.J. 1971.

Petuchowski, A.M. (ed.), *Memorial Tributes to Jakob Josef Petuchowski*, Roslyn Heights, N.Y. 1993.

Petuchowski, E., *New to America. New to Cincinnati* (Max Kade Occasional Papers in German-American Studies University of Cincinnati 14), Cincinnati 2004.

Petuchowski, J.J., 'Ansätze zu einer jüdischen Theologie des Christentums', *Orien.* 44/21 (November 15, 1980) [quoted as 1980a; republished in updated forms in 1981a and 1987a].

———, 'The Aims and Objectives of Judaeo-Christian Studies. A Jewish View', in: J.J. Petuchowski (ed.), *Defining a Discipline* [typescript, Cincinnaty 1984].

———, '"Arbeiter in demselben Weinberg". Ansätze zu einer jüdischen Theologie des Christentums ["'Workers in the Same Vineyard', Towards a Jewish Theology of Christianity'], in: H.H. Henrix (ed.), *Unter dem Bogen des Bundes. Beiträge aus jüdischer und christlicher Existenz*, Aachen 1981 [quoted as 1981a].

———, *Beten im Judentum*, Stuttgart 1976 [quoted as 1976b].

———, 'British Museum, Bloom's, and Charlie Chaplin', in: B. Leverton & Sh. Lowensohn (eds), *I Came Alone*; *The Stories of the Kindertransports*, Lewes 1990 [quoted as 1990a].

———, *Contributions to the Scientific Study of Jewish Liturgy*, New York 1970 [quoted as 1970b].

———, 'Das "Höre Israel",' in: H.H. Henrix (ed.), *Jüdische Liturgie*; *Geschichte—Struktur—Wesen* (QD 86), Freiburg 1979 [quoted as 1979c].

——, [together with M. Brocke & W. Strolz] *Das Vaterunser; Gemeinsames Beten von Juden und Christen*, Freiburg 1974.

——, 'Der Offenbarungsglaube im neuzeitlichen Judentum', in: A. Falaturi, J.J. Petuchowski, & W. Strolz (eds), *Drei Wege zu dem einen Gott; Glaubenserfahrung in den monotheistischen Religionen*, Freiburg 1976 [quoted as 1976a, English version: 1987c].

——, 'Die Geschichte des synagogalen Gottesdienstes [trsl. E.R. Petuchowski]' in: G. Mayer (ed.), *Das Judentum*, Stuttgart—Berlin—Cologne 1994.

——, 'Die Liturgie als Thema der jüdischen Theologie', in: K. Richter (ed.), *Liturgie— ein vergessenes Thema der Theologie?* (QD 107), Freiburg 1987 [quoted as 1987b].

——, *Die Stimme vom Sinai; Ein rabbinisches Lesebuch zu den zehn Geboten [The Voice from Sinai; A Rabbinic Reader about the Ten Commandments]*, Freiburg 1981 [quoted as 1981b].

——, 'Drei Stadien im christlich-jüdischen Gespräch', in: *Orient.* 49 (1985) [quoted as 1985a].

——, 'Erlösung—Sünde—Vergebung; Eine dialogische Erkundung christlich-jüdischer Konvergenzen und Widersprüche', in: H.H. Henrix & W. Licharz (eds), *Welches Judentum steht welchem Christentum gegenüber?*, Frankfurt 1985 [quoted as 1985b].

——, *Es lehrten unsere Meister [...]; Rabbinische Geschichten*, Freiburg 1979 [quoted as 1979b].

——, *Ever Since Sinai; A Modern View of Torah* [3rd ed.], Milwaukee 1979 [quoted as 1979a].

——, *Feiertage des Herrn; Die Welt der jüdischen Feste und Bräuche*, Freiburg 1984.

——, *Ferner lehrten unsere Meister [...]; Neue rabbinische Geschichten*, Freiburg 1980 [quoted as 1980b].

——, 'From Censorship Prevention to Theological Reform. A Study in the Modern Jewish Prayerbook', in: *Hebrew Union College Annual* 40/41 (1969/1970).

——, 'Gibt es Dogmen im Judentum? [*Does Judaism have dogmas?*]' in: *ThQ* 160 (1980) [quoted as 1980c].

——, *Gottesdienst des Herzens; Eine Auswahl aus dem Gebetsschatz des Judentums [Service of the Heart; A Selection from the Treasury of Jewish Prayers]*, Freiburg 1981 [quoted as 1981c].

——, 'Judentum und Christentum in jüdischer Sicht', in: *CGG* 26 (1980) [quoted as 1980d].

——, 'Jüdische Liturgie?', in: *Judaica* 41 (1985) [quoted as 1985d].

——, *Le'ovdekha be'emet—Dass wir Dir in Wahrheit dienen; Ein jüdischer Gottesdienst für den Sabbatmorgen; Mit einem Nachwort von Hans Hermann Henrix*, Aachen 1988a [quoted as 1988a].

——, 'Liberal Halakhah and Liturgy', in: W. Jacob (ed.), in: *Liberal Judaism and Halakhah*, Pittsburgh 1988 [quoted as 1988b].

——, [together with J. Heinemann], *Literature of the Synagogue*, New York 1975.

——, *Mein Judesein; Wege und Erfahrungen eines deutschen Rabbiners*, Freiburg 1992.

——, *Prayerbook Reform in Europe; The Liturgy of European Liberal and Reform Judaism*, New York 1968.

——, 'Offenbarung', in: J.J. Petuchowski & C. Thoma (eds), *Lexikon der jüdisch-christlichen Begegnung*, Freiburg 1989 [new ed. 1997].

——, *Our Masters Taught*, New York 1982 [quoted as 1982a, English version of 1979b].

——, '"Rabbinische" und "dogmatische" Struktur theologischer Aussage', in: M. Stöhr (ed.), *Jüdische Existenz und die Erneuerung der christlichen Theologie; Versuch einer Bilanz des christlich-jüdischen Dialogs für die Systematische Theologie*, Munich 1981 [quoted as 1981f].

——, 'Reflections on Revelation', in: *CCAR Journal* 13/6 (1966) [quoted as 1966c].

——, 'Reform Benedictions for Rabbinic Ordinances', in: *HUCA* 37 (1966) [quoted as 1966b].

—— 'Revelation and the Modern Jew', in: *JR* 41 (1961).

————, 'Revelation—What Have We Been Told?' [A Rosh Hashanah Sermon 5744/1983 (manuscript)].

————, 'Some Laws of Jewish Liturgical Development', in: *Judaism* 34 (1985) [quoted as 1985c].

————, *Studies in Modern Theology and Prayer* [ed. by E. Petuchowski & A.M. Petuchowski], Philadelphia 1998.

————, [together with E. Fleischer], *Studies in Aggadah, Targum and Jewish Liturgy; In Memory of Joseph Heinemann*, Jerusalem and Cincinnati 1981e.

————, 'The Concept of Revelation in Modern Judaism', in: A. Falaturi, J.J. Petuchowski, & W. Strolz (eds), *Three Ways to the One God; The Faith Experience in Judaism, Christianity and Islam*, Tunbridge Wells 1987 [quoted as 1987c, English version of 1976a].

————, 'The Concept of Revelation in Reform Judaism', in: *CCAR.YB* 69 (1959).

————, 'The Creation in Jewish Liturgy', in: *Judaism* 28 (1979) [quoted as 1979d].

————, 'The Development and Design of a German-Jewish Prayerbook', in: M. Rischin & R. Asher (eds), *The Jewish Legacy and the German Conscience; Essays in Memory of Rabbi Joseph Asher*, Berkeley, Ca 1991.

————, 'The Dialectics of Reason and Revelation', in: A.J. Wolf (ed.), *Rediscovering Judaism*, Chicago 1965.

————, 'The Christian-Jewish Dialogue', in: *Lutheran World* 10 (1963) [quoted as 1963a], republished in: *Heirs of the Pharisees*, New York—London 1970 [quoted as 1970c] and: *Heirs of the Pharisees*, (Brown Classics in Judaica), Lanham, MD—London 1985 [quoted as 1985e], translated as 'Der christlich-jüdische Dialog aus jüdischer Sicht', in: *Lutherische Rundschau* 13 (1963) [quoted as 1963b].

————, *The Theology of Haham David Nieto; An Eighteenth-Century Defense of the Jewish Tradition* [Ph. D. Dissertation 1954], repr. New York 1970 [quoted as 1970a].

————, *Theology and Poetry; Studies in the Medieval* Piyyut, London 1978 [repr. Cincinnati 2000].

————, 'Toward a Jewish Theology of Christianity', in: V.A. McInnes (ed.), *Renewing the Judaeo-Christian Wellsprings*, New York 1987 [quoted as 1987a].

————, *Understanding Jewish Prayer*, New York 1972.

————, [together with H. Heinz & K. Kienzler], *Versöhnung in der jüdischen und christlichen Liturgie* (QD 124), Freiburg 1990 [quoted as 1990b].

————, *Wie unsere Meister die Schrift erklären; Beispielhafte Bibelauslegung aus dem Judentum* [*How Our Masters interpret Scripture; Samples of Jewish Bible Commentaries*], Freiburg 1982 [quoted as 1982b].

————, *Zion Reconsidered*, New York 1966 [quoted as 1966a].

————, 'Zur Geschichte der jüdischen Liturgie', in the same vol. as 1979c.

————, 'Zur rabbinischen Interpretation des Offenbarungsglaubens', in: J.J. Petuchowski & Walter Strolz (eds), *Offenbarung im jüdischen und christlichen Glaubensverständnis* (QD 92), Freiburg 1981 [quoted as 1981d].

————, 'Zur vermeintlichen jüdischen Vorlage eines christlichen Kindergebetes', in: *LJ* 32 (1982) [quoted as 1982c].

Rayner, J.D., 'Prayerbook Reform in Europe since 1966 as seen by Jakob J. Petuchowski (1925–1991)' [Leo Baeck College, May 26, 1992 (manuscript)].

Sanders, J.A., 'Words by Heart', in: see A.M. Petuchowski 1993.

*Sidur Sefat Emet; Mit deutscher Übersetzung von Rabbiner Dr. S. Bamberger*, Basel 1987.

Strolz, W., 'Ein glaubender und glaubwürdiger Brückenbauer. Jakob J. Petuchowski zum Gedächtnis (1925–1991)', in: *Anzeiger der Seelsorge* (1992, fasc. 2).

Walter, R., 'Es lehrten unsere Meister. Zum Gedenken an Jakob J. Petuchowski', in: *Christ in der Gegenwart* No. 48 [December 11, 1991].

# CROSSING BORDERS
## THE KEDUSHA AND THE SANCTUS: A CASE STUDY OF THE CONVERGENCE OF JEWISH AND CHRISTIAN LITURGY

*Albert Gerhards*
Rheinische Friedrich-Wilhelms-Universität Bonn, Germany

## INTRODUCTION

In recent times there has been much talk of a 'religious revival'. What is meant by this is that following an extended, involuntary absence, religion is once again back in the media. Although it is not that long ago since some in the West believed that the issue of religion would in time disappear of its own accord, religion is increasingly making headline news again as a result of fundamentalist currents and political and military developments around the world. Admittedly, this reawakening of interest is motivated less by the essence of religion itself and more by sensationalism and the desire to play with people's fear of the irrational. However, it cannot be denied that the rediscovery of the ritual in many western societies is widespread. In view of the increasing complexity of human life and humankind's estrangement from institutions that contribute to a sense of identity, the organising and healing power of the ritual is being recognised, valued, and commercially exploited by many parties. But there is so much more to religion than this. Its rituals target the totality of mankind and the world. This applies in particular to the dimension of lending meaning to life through retrospection, recollection, and orientation towards what is yet to come in both verbal and non-verbal rituals that are conducted in a community setting. This dimension, which is inherent in both the Jewish and Christian faiths, is not a feature of many other world religions. In this respect, one can really only speak of a liturgy, in the truest sense of the word, with regard to these two religions (cf. Gerhards 2001, 25–44). However, Judaism and (western) Christianity have a long tradition of enlightenment, which also plays a role in shaping their respective philosophy of religion and theology. Moreover, these two religions generally find themselves in an environment that is increasingly shaped by atheism. This in turn leads to counter-currents in both religions that seek their salvation in a rejection of all forms of dialogue by completely cutting themselves off from the 'world'. Such trends are also evident within Christian ecumenism and it is possible that they will also put a strain on the dialogue between Jews and Christians. In order to counteract this development, interest in getting to know not only one's own tradition, but also the traditions of other denominations should be fostered at all levels. In other words, it is first and foremost a question of understanding another tradition—not only another tradition within one's own Christian or Jewish community, but another tradition in the biblical religion to which one does not oneself belong (Gerhards 2003, 183–211 esp. 202f).

The focus here is not, however, on the question of the dialogue of the religions, which, by implication, always plays a role. It is instead a matter of how liturgical studies can help us better understand the interrelations or non-existent relations between the religions, i.e. it is a matter of conducting an appropriate comparative exploration of the liturgical traditions of Judaism and Christianity. In this regard, both Jews and Christians alike naturally assume a degree of presuppositional knowledge, a fact of which one must be aware. It is only on the basis of the hermeneutics of another liturgy (cf. Lurz 1999, 273–290) that one can academically address the question of comparable dimensions or even transitions. Recent studies of sources have rendered rash judgements about dependencies, parallels, and identities obsolete (cf. Leonhard 2006). On the other hand, the close study of the relevant texts and their literary, cultural, and historical contexts throws up new questions that might help make the nature of liturgical activities and the relevance of their exploration plausible outside the small circle of specialists and enthusiasts.

The intention is to illustrate this point using an example from Christian liturgy, namely the Sanctus in the Eucharistic Prayer, which is taken from Isa 6:3. Although no new findings are to be expected, it is hoped that this illustration will raise some new issues for discussion.

The text of the liturgical Sanctus:

| Greek text (Jakobusanaphora, Hänggi & Pahl 1968, 246 l. 25–27) | Latin text (Liturgia Romana, Hänggi & Pahl 1968, 427 l. 14–16) | English text (The roman missal. Order of mass: 416) |
|---|---|---|
| ἅγιος ἅγιος ἅγιος | Sanctus, sanctus, sanctus | Holy, holy, holy |
| κύριος σαβαώθ | Dominus Deus sabaoth | Lord, God of power and might, |
| πλήρης ὁ οὐρανὸς καὶ ἡ γῆ τῆς δόξης σου | Pleni sunt caeli et terra gloria tua | heaven and earth are full of your glory. |
| ὡσαννὰ ἐν τοῖς ὑψίστοις | Hosanna in excelsis. | Hosanna in the highest. |
| εὐλογημένος ὁ ἐλθὼν | Benedictus, qui venit | Blessed is he who comes |
| καὶ ἐρχόμενος ἐν ὀνόματι κυρίου | in nomine Domini. | in the name of the Lord. |
| ὡσαννὰ ἐν τοῖς ὑψίστοις. | Hosanna in excelsis. | Hosanna in the highest. |

## On the State of Research

Since Anton Baumstark's 1923 article 'Trishagion und Queduscha' (18–32) at the latest, the connection between the various Christian variants of the Trishagion and forms of Jewish prayer has been a subject of academic discourse. The widespread consensus reached in the aftermath of this discourse was that the Sanctus of the Christian liturgy was modelled on Jewish prayers, especially the Kedusha of morning prayer (cf., for example, Kretschmar 1962, 75–86 esp. 83f and 86: 'Von einer christlichen Qeduscha im Morgengebet führen Linien zur Verwendung des Seraphenrufes in die Osterliturgie'). In recent years, a variety of significant works have been published on this issue (Spinks 1991; Taft 1999; Winkler 2002; Meßner 2005, 3–41). Gabriele Winkler provides a summary of the current state of research (Winkler 2001, 78–90; 2002; 2005, 535–549; Budde 2004, 240–244, 263–265).

Only a rudimentary cross-section of the detailed discussion of this complex issue can be given here. Gabriele Winkler has delved into the prehistory and early history of the Christian Sanctus and gave a paper on the liturgical links between Judaism and Christianity at a conference in Aachen in 2002 (Gerhards & Henrix 2004, 8; Winkler 2002; 2003a,

213–238; 2003b, 111–131; compare with Ethiopian sources: Brakmann [forthcoming]). This paper illustrated the methodological difficulties inherent in assigning dependencies and dates to Christian prayer texts (in this case from Ethiopia), which are very hard to date, on the basis of literary parallels with Jewish sources. This raises the fundamental question as to how historical liturgical sources should be treated as literary testimony: are they the result of an explicitly written process, or only the more or less coincidental written record of moments in a living, evolving tradition that is, consequently, in a state of flux (Budde 2001, 127–141)? The question of 'transition' therefore relates not only to transitions between biblical and liturgical traditions or between Jewish liturgical and Christian liturgical traditions (or vice versa), but also to transitions within each tradition. In this respect, for example, the problem of the point at which the 'Holy, Holy, Holy' was first included in the Eucharistic Prayer, is of secondary importance. The question here is how the more or less literal quotation from Isa 6:3 (Sanctus) with its additions (Benedictus/Hosanna) must be understood within its context. Reinhard Meßner and Martin Lang provided an unequivocal explanation of eastern Syrian tradition and Jewish parallels at a conference in Bonn in 2001 and proved the programmatic significance of the Sanctus for the anaphora of Addai and Mari (Meßner & Lang 2003, 371–411). The following considerations are based on the Roman Catholic tradition, but also refer to other liturgical traditions.

## The Sanctus in the Roman Tradition

In the Roman liturgy, the actual Sanctus comes after the Preface, the wording of which changes throughout the church year, and which is introduced by a dialogue. The last line of this dialogue, 'Dignum et iustum est' (it is right to give Him thanks and praise) links up to the text, in this case the 'praefatio communis', which up to and including the Tridentine missal was used on weekdays (Hänggi & Pahl 1968, 427 l. 7–16).

1. Vere dignum et iustum est, aequum et salutare,
2. nos tibi semper et ubique gratias agere:
3. Domine sancte, Pater omnipotens, aeterne Deus:
4. Per Christum, Dominum nostrum.
5. Per quem maiestatem tuam laudant Angeli,

6. adorant Dominationes,
7. tremunt Potestates.
8. Caeli caelorumque Virtutes
9. ac beata Seraphim
10. socia exultatione concelebrant.
11. Cum quibus et nostras voces ut admitti jubeas, deprecamur,
12. supplici confessione dicentes:
13. Sanctus, sanctus, sanctus
14. Dominus Deus Sabaoth.
15. Pleni sunt caeli et terra gloria tua.
16. Hosanna in excelsis.
17. Benedictus, qui venit in nomine Domini.
18. Hosanna in excelsis.

Initially, the text (cf. Jungmann 1962 II, 156–161) pleonastically refers to the appropriateness of giving thanks (1–2) and then addresses God in three forms (3): Dominus, Pater, Deus. God is not addressed directly, but through an intermediary who is also God: Jesus Christ (4). This is followed by proclamations of glory made by the classes of angels, proclamations which also reach God through Christ (5–10). The classes of angels are listed on several occasions in the New Testament, for example in Eph 1:20–21 or Col 1:16. In addition to the angelic classes witnessed by Paul, there are also the Seraphim. The Seraphim are closely linked to the Sanctus (Isa 6:1–4). As heavenly creatures, the Seraphim (= 'the flaming creatures') are part of God's royal court and are described as creatures of serpentine form with faces, hands, and wings. In terms of religious history, it is difficult to pinpoint their origin. It is most probable that they are of Assyrian origin (Schart 2000, 35–69 esp. 48ff). By calling out to each other, the Seraphim bear witness to the fact that the 'Lord of Hosts' is the most holy one of all whose glory proclaims his greatness and power. In Isaiah, however, these seraphim do not belong to the celestial realm, but to the earthy sphere: the entire scene takes place in the temple in Jerusalem! Moreover, they have nothing to do with celebratory liturgy: the sound of their cries makes the foundation of the temple shake and smoke hides God from view, making him invisible and unapproachable for the impure Israel (Isa 6:4). The Seraphim are chimerical beings that act as wardens of God's throne (cf. Beuken 2003, 158–173).

But how did the Seraphim get into heaven? In the context of Isaiah's vision, they belong to the earthly sphere. God is proclaimed here as the 'Lord of Hosts', which corresponds to the Old Testament image of God in an age in which monotheism was asserting itself over polytheism. It was only with the passing of time that these hosts mutated into purely spiritual beings. If one examines the Sanctus closely, it becomes evident that the liturgy (and not only the Roman liturgy!) made two characteristic changes to the text of the Sanctus (13–14): firstly, the proclamation is transformed into an acclamation (gloria *tua*); secondly, not only the earth is filled with God's glory, *heaven* and earth are now full of His glory.

In his famous work *The Angels and the Liturgy* (1935), theologian and historian of religion Erik Peterson addressed this issue. He found a plausible explanation: as stated in the prologue to John's Gospel (John 1:14), when God became man, the glory (Hebrew: *kavod*; Greek: *doxa*) of God came into the world. When Jesus ascended into heaven, the *doxa* returned to its place of origin, albeit mingled with the transfigured nature of humankind. This means that heaven and earth are now indissolubly linked to one other. The link in the chain that binds heaven and earth is the intermediary between God and humankind, Jesus Christ. It is through him that the celestial praise occurs. This is why the text of the preface can ask that the praise of the Church be accepted (per Christum): Christ already provides the link between the earthly praise and the celestial praise, thereby anticipating the participation in the 'celestial liturgy'. We also find this same prayer structure in the old Church's Gloria (cf. Gerhards 2006, 89–105 esp. 99–101).

## On the Concept of Heaven and Earth Praising God together in Jewish and Christian Sources

Of course, the concept of heaven and earth praising God together is not alien to Judaism either. It is also mentioned in the Old Testament (e.g. Ps 148). The same also applies to later Jewish liturgy. In one of the congregational versions of the Amidah, the third benediction reads as follows:

> You are holy and Your Name is holy, and Your holy ones will daily praise You. Blessed are You, Eternal One, the holy God.
> [During public repetition:]
> Let us sanctify Your name in this world, just as they sanctify it in the high heavens, as it is written by Your prophet: They call one to another and say, 'Holy, holy, holy, is the Eternal of Hosts, the entire earth is filled with His glory.'

> Responding in blessing they say, 'Blessed is the glory of the Eternal One from His place'.
> And in Your Holy Scripture it is written, saying, 'The Eternal will reign forever, Your God, Zion, from generation to generation, Halleluyah.'
> From generation to generation, we will speak of Your greatness, and to all eternity we will sanctify Your holiness; and Your praise, our God, will never cease from our lips, for You are a great and holy Sovereign God. Blessed are You, Eternal One, the holy God (translation: Langer 2003, 127–156 esp. 151f).

Here too, the scene clearly takes place in heaven. Julie Kirchberg comments on this text as follows: 'Accordingly, the prayer of sanctification said by the congregation is considered to be an earthly copy of the celestial liturgy: the responsorial dialogue between the prayer leader and the congregation corresponds to the Trishagion which, according to the prophetic vision, is struck up by the seraphim and to which, according to traditional interpretation (from Ezek 3:12), the other heavenly creatures respond. "Heaven" and "earth"—angels and humans—unite in a cosmic liturgy which, in accordance with the words of the benediction in the second form, represents a coronation ceremony ["The crown, O Lord, our God, the angels, the throngs on high, offer to Thee; also Thy people Israel, who are gathered below; all of them, as one, sound the 'Thrice Holy' to Thee, as it is written,"]. The themes mentioned here put the Kedusha in the context of the Merkabah (throne chariot) mysticism, which influenced the temple cult in the early Jewish era and was subsequently integrated into religious worship in the synagogue' (Kirchberg 1991, 215).

As established by Günter Stemberger, the concept of heaven and earth praising God together was originally repressed in the rabbinical tradition and only gradually came into the conceptual world of Jewish liturgy by means of popular piety (Stemberger 2004, 92–102). Jewish sources differ in one respect from Christian sources: 'It is not a joint acclamation, but a responsorial dialogue between choirs,' (Kretschmar 1962, 83). However, the Christian adaptation is certainly not homogenous. The introductions to the Sanctus (and the links to the Sanctus) of the Orthodox Church's anaphora contain a variety of different ways in which the angels and the Church perform the Sanctus (cf. Gerhards 1984, 168–175; Budde 2004, 260–262; Winkler 2005, 452–525).

Apart from the aforementioned modification of the liturgical texts from the biblical model on which they were based, there is—with the exception of the genuinely Egyptian liturgy—one conspicuous addition to the Sanctus in the Roman liturgy and most other liturgies:

the addition of the Hosanna and the so-called 'Benedictus' (17–18),
which was based on Ps 118:25 and was an allusion to the acclamation
of the accounts of Palm Sunday (Matt 21:8f par.; cf. Winkler 2005,
526–549). It is likely that this addition was first made in Syria. Of
course, the psalm in question is not about 'celestial liturgy', but a liturgy
of thanks in the temple on the occasion of the Feast of Tabernacles.
In the Christian (patristic) interpretation of what happened on Palm
Sunday, the scene is relocated to heaven. According to Anton Baumstark, the combination of Kedusha and benediction first came about in
Christianity as a result of the aforementioned theology of the accounts
of the ascension; as a matter of fact, homilies on the ascension dating
from the patristic era transfer the song of the children of Jerusalem
during the triumphant entrance of the ascended Christ to the mouths
of the angels (Gerhards 1984, 220).

But as the quotation above illustrates, an acclamation was also added
to the Jewish Kedusha and transferred into celestial spheres. It has not
yet been clarified to what extent there is a direct relation between or
even a 'mutual permeation' of the Jewish and Christian traditions in
this regard (Winkler 2002; 2005, 357–418). The acclamation 'Hosanna
to the Son of David!' can be found in a Christian context, albeit without the Sanctus, as far back as the Didache (10.6). With the addition
of the words of praise 'Blessed is he who comes in the name of the
Lord' and the choral division, the Sanctus/Benedictus became a song
of victory (*epinikios*)—as some of the oriental anaphorae and Greek
fathers of the Church call the song—in the later tradition. A prayer
of thanksgiving that appears to be entirely Jewish, in the style of the
birkat ha-mazon, in the *Apostolic Constitutions* (VII 35.3) describes the
liturgically amended acclamation of Isa 6:3 (albeit without the addition) as an *epinikios ode*. This text reads 'But Israel, Thy Church on
earth, taken out of the Gentiles', thereby speaking of an Israel that
emulates the heavenly powers (cf. Gerhards 1984, 219–221; Winkler
2005, 517–525). In this context, there emerged a body of literature that
focussed on the competition between heaven and earth when praising
God (cf. Gerhards 1984, 220).

Erik Peterson interpreted the Christian adoption in terms of the substitution theory: 'It is only out of the life of the Church, which praises
God with the angels and the entire cosmos, that the glorification can
grow; a glorification that bears witness to the fact in both cult and the
mystic life of grace that heaven and earth are full of the glory of God

since the glory of God escaped from the temple of Jerusalem to take up residence in the temple that is the body of Christ in the Jerusalem that has become the 'highest' of all our mothers' (Peterson 1953, 65f).

The consequences of such considerations, which were already widespread in the early years of patristics, are well known (cf. Gerhards 2001). In reality, the Christian liturgy acknowledged Judaism, albeit negatively, as a contemporary entity; the Roman liturgy primarily in the prayers of intercession on Good Friday (cf. Gerhards & Wahle 2005).

However, the words of the Roman preface do not convey in any way the assurance of salvation that is discernable in Peterson's text. This is illustrated by a request that was added to the preface. After the portrayal of the angels' hymn of praise, we read: 'With these we pray thee join our voices also, while we say with lowly praise' (Cum quibus et nostras voces ut admitti jubeas, deprecamur, supplici confessione dicentes).

The 'participation' of the Church in the liturgy is not a matter of course; instead, like in the anaphora of Egyptian provenance (cf. Gerhards 1984, 169–173), permission to participate must first be asked. The Roman liturgy, however, acknowledges not only the purely heavenly song of praise, but also the fact that the Church naturally joins in the angels' unending hymn of praise, for example in the preface of the Solemnity of the Epiphany of the Lord (Et ideo cum angelis…hymnum gloriae tuae canimus, sine fine dicentes [And therefore with the angels…we sing a hymn to thy glory, saying without ceasing]; Deshusses 1971–82, 89). In a homily, John Chrysostom provides the theological grounds for the singing of God's praises in unison: 'Do you recognise this voice? Is it your voice or that of the seraphim? Is it your voice *and* that of the seraphim, on account of Christ, who destroyed the wall of separation and brought about peace between the heavenly and the earthly, on account of Him, who made the two one?' (Chrysostom, in *Vidi Dominum*, Homily 1.1: SC 277, 214; cf. Gerhards 1984, 173). Here, all differences are abolished. The 'earthly' liturgy and the 'heavenly' liturgy appear to be identical. In this way, however, Christianity is laying claim to an exclusiveness that rejects the concept of a Jewish way.

### THE AMBIVALENCE OF THE RELATIONSHIP BETWEEN 'HEAVENLY' AND 'EARTHLY' LITURGY AS A THEOLOGICAL PROBLEM

How does Christian theology deal with this ambivalence of hopeful expectation and triumphant certainty? In other words, how can the substance of Christian soteriology be maintained without ignoring or even negating the Jewish way? Let us recall at this point Franz Rosenzweig, 'who chose to perceive the fundamental affiliation of Christianity and Judaism in their very incongruity' (Wohlmuth 2005, 159). Both religions—Judaism and Christianity—have an organised celebrational structure. According to Rosenzweig, however, the forms of these celebrations differ significantly as a result of the fundamental difference in each religion's time structure, which fall into the categories 'eternal life' and 'eternal way'. The difference in the *memoria* is the fact that the constitution of Judaism is not defined by feasts, but that they are merely an expression of what the Jews already are, namely the chosen people (Rosenzweig 1996, 360). In Christianity, however, Jesus is the eternal beginning. Only Judgement Day will bring Christianity and all the other converted peoples to the place where Judaism already is.

Josef Wohlmuth, however, calls Rosenzweig's hermeneutic comparison of Christian and Jewish liturgies into question. There is also an intrusion of transcendence into the liturgical celebration of the Christian sacrament. In his study of the works of Emmanuel Levinas, Wohlmuth discovered an anthropological basis that is common to both Judaism and Christianity, up to and including the experience of eternity in time: 'The people celebrating are brought before that unrecallable and unattainable dimension in which God Himself in His faith creates anew.' Wohlmuth sees indications of this in the Eucharistic epiclesis: the divine mental power sweeps the three synthesising time modi into the 'interface' at which the *memoria* is exposed to the unattainable beginning of creation and the *exspectatio* to the unavailable end; in this way, the moment in between breaths becomes the gateway to a transformation that we can no longer describe in words' (Wohlmuth 2005, 165; cf. Wahle 2006, 445–447).

In reality, Christianity is increasingly being forced to justify itself. How can redemption be in the present in view of the 'real existing' world? Wohlmuth provides the following solution: the Christian celebration of the 'new and eternal covenant' roots the *memoria passionis et resurrectionis* in the covenant of Mount Sinai and its prophetic promise of renewal by interiorization of the Tora and radical forgiveness of sins (Wohlmuth

2005, 174). In this way, the Eucharistic celebration not only relates to the intervening period between Jesus' birth and Judgement Day, 'but extends the *memoria* to the covenant with the chosen people and its pledge, indeed to creation and fulfilment.' In this way, the Christian celebration is integrated into the time of revelation between creation and fulfilment.'

According to Rosenzweig, the experience of time is a linguistic phenomenon. 'Dialoguous simultaneity' occurs when we speak. The 'history of language' begins with the silence that does not yet have words and ends with the silence that no longer needs words (Görtz 1992, 73).

From the above, we can conclude that Christianity cannot exist without the connection to Judaism, and without the real existence of Jewish life, the Jewish faith, and the Jewish celebrations, (cf. Deeg & Mildenberger 2006): the voice of the peoples is only allowed to join in the hymn of praise sung by the heavenly creatures together with the voice of the people of Israel, which has been admitted to do so since it was chosen as God's people, whereby the voices are still singing independently of one another, although they are increasingly acknowledging each other in anticipation of the end of the world.

If these observations are correct, Jewish and Christian prayers are not as irreconcilable as they would appear in Rosenzweig's works. If this is indeed the case, then the Christian liturgy is not merely a anamnestic update of the original events of the history of salvation, but also the anticipation of redemption (the Messianic future), the celebration of the eternal covenant in the here and now (Wohlmuth 2005, 175).

In any case, it is an eschatological reservation that brings Jews and Christians closer together. For Rosenzweig there is a serious difference between the western culture, where 'no-one comes to the Father, except through Christ' and the Jewish people, which 'no longer needs to come to the Father, because it is already with Him'. Judaism and Christianity remain 'two original methods of being in the world while waiting for redemption' (ibid.). However, can the experience of waiting together—which is increasingly becoming a necessity for Christians in the 'post-Christian era'—possibly lead to mutual recognition of the different forms of 'being-in-the-world' through the joint exploration of both traditions of prayer and spirituality and nevertheless to the knowledge that the state of 'being-for-yourself' is already dissolved in the eternity of God?

The Consequences for the Historical Exploration of Liturgy
within the Boundaries of Interreligious Dialogue

Generally speaking, historical and philological research must not be influenced by direct interests. This statement is particularly relevant with regard to the exploration of the origins of Judaism and Christianity because in the course of recent decades, a positive bias has frequently clouded the judgement of Christian researchers investigating the differences between Jewish and Christian texts and ritual institutions (cf. Gerhards & Wahle 2005). Indirectly, however, such research can be of social and interreligious relevance insofar as it contributes to a more differentiated view of the relationships between the religions. For example, research has made it clear that different origins do not necessarily lead to permanent divergence, but can at least lead to a reconciled coexistence, even though convergence may only be expected to take place in the extra-temporal eschaton. The centre of studies planned by Jakob J. Petuchowski certainly had such a political purpose. The prerequisites for a continuative interreligious dialogue are disproportionately better with regard to the relationship between Judaism and Christianity than they are with regard to the relationship between each of the two religions and Islam. Naturally, it is inevitable that there will at some stage be a different relationship between these religions than that of the 'war of symbols' (cf. Meyer-Blanck & Hasselhoff 2006, 229–238). The road that must be travelled in order to arrive at this relationship will be just as long as that travelled in researching the historical, liturgical, and theological relationships between Judaism and Christianity (cf. Gerhards & Henrix 2004). The experience gathered and methodological conclusions arrived at in this area can, however, contribute to hermeneutics that are appropriate to the relationships of each religion with Islam. This would constitute a decisive step towards the aforementioned task of hermeneutics regarding another religion; hermeneutics that constitute an important prerequisite for successful religious interaction and, therefore, for the integration of religions and society.

## LITERATURE

Baumstark, A., 'Trishagion und Qeduscha', *JLW* 3 (1923).
Beuken, W., *Jesaja 1–12; Herders theologischer Kommentar zum Alten Testament*, Freiburg i.Br. 2003.
Brakmann, H. [forthcoming in OrChr 2007].
Budde, A., 'Improvisation im Eucharistiegebet. Zur Technik freien Betens in der Alten Kirche', *JAC* 44 (2001).
———, *Die Ägyptische Basilios-Anaphora; Text—Kommentar—Geschichte* (Jerusalemer Theologisches Forum 7), Münster 2004.
Deeg, A. & I. Mildenberger, '…*dass er euch auch erwählt hat'; Liturgie feiern im Horizont des Judentums* (Beiträge zu Liturgie und Spiritualität 16), Leipzig 2006.
Deshusses, J., *Le Sacramentaire Grégorien; Ses principales formes d'après les plus anciens manuscrits* [3 vols] (SpicFri 16, 24, 28), Fribourg 1971–1982.
Gerhards, A., *Die Griechische Gregoriosanaphora; Ein Beitrag zur Geschichte des Eucharistischen Hochgebets* (LQF 65), Münster, Westfalen 1984.
———, 'Kraft aus der Wurzel. Zum Verhältnis christlicher Liturgie gegenüber dem Jüdischen: Fortschreibung oder struktureller Neubeginn?', *KuI* 16 (2001).
———, 'Impulse des christlich-jüdischen Dialogs für die Liturgiewissenschaft', P. Hünermann & Th. Söding (eds), *Methodische Erneuerung der Theologie: Konsequenzen der wiederentdeckten jüdisch-christlichen Gemeinsamkeiten* (QD 200), Freiburg 2003.
———, '"Ehre sei dem Vater…" Wie monotheistisch betet die Kirche? Zur Frage des Adressaten christlichen Betens', in: A. Deeg & I. Mildenberger 2006.
——— & H.H. Henrix (eds), *Dialog oder Monolog? Zur liturgischen Beziehung zwischen Judentum und Christentum* (QD 208), Freiburg 2004.
——— & S. Wahle (eds), *Kontinuität und Unterbrechung; Gottesdienst und Gebet in Judentum und Christentum* (Studien zu Judentum und Christentum), Paderborn et al. 2005.
Görtz, H.-J., *Franz Rosenzweigs neues Denken; Eine Einführung aus der Perspektive christlicher Theologie*, Würzburg 1992.
Hänggi, A. & I. Pahl (eds), *Prex Eucharistica; Textus e Variis Liturgiis Antiquioribus Selecti* (SpicFri 12), Fribourg Suisse 1968.
Jungmann, J.A., *Missarum Sollemnia; Eine genetische Erklärung der römischen Messe* [2 vols], Wien et al. 5th ed. 1962.
Kirchberg, J., *Theo-logie in der Anrede als Weg zur Verständigung zwischen Juden und Christen* (IThS 31), Innsbruck—Wien 1991.
Kretschmar, G., 'Neue Arbeiten zur Geschichte des Ostergottesdienstes II. Die Einführung des Sanctus in die lateinische Messliturgie' *JLH* 7 (1962).
Langer, R. 'The 'Amida as Formative Rabbinic Prayer', in: A. Gerhards, A. Doeker, P. Ebenbauer (eds), *Identität durch Gebet; Zur gemeinschaftsbildenden Funktion institutionalisierten Betens in Judentum und Christentum* (Studien zu Judentum und Christentum). Paderborn et al. 2003.
Leonhard, C., *The Jewish Pesach and the Origins of the Christian Easter: Open Questions in Current Research* (SJ 35), Berlin—New York 2006.
Lilienfeld, F.v., *Chrysostomus; Die göttliche Liturgie des hl. Johannes Chrysostomus mit den besonderen Gebeten der Basilius-Liturgie im Anhang* (Oikonomia, Quellen und Studien zur orthodoxen Theologie 2, A–C), Erlangen 2nd ed. 1986.
Lurz, F., 'Für eine ökumenische Liturgiewissenschaft', *TThZ* 108 (1999).
———, *Erlebte Liturgie; Autobiografische Schriften als liturgiewissenschaftliche Quellen* (Ästhetik—Theologie—Liturgik), Münster 2003.
Meßner, R., 'Grundlinien der Entwicklung des eucharistischen Gebets in der frühen Kirche', in: Gerhards, A. et al. (eds), *Prex Eucharistica III; Studia; Pars prima; Ecclesia antiqua et occidentalis* (SpicFri 42), Fribourg 2005.

———— & M. Lang, 'Die Freiheit zum Lobpreis des Namens. Identitätsstiftung im eucharistischen Hochgebet und in verwandten jüdischen Gebeten', in: see Langer 2003.

Meyer-Blanck, M. & G.K. Hasselhoff (eds), *Krieg der Zeichen? Zur Interaktion von Religion* (Politik und Kultur = Studien des Bonner Zentrums für Religion und Gesellschaft 1), Würzburg 2006.

Peterson, E., *Das Buch von den Engeln; Stellung und Bedeutung der Heiligen Engel im Kultus*, München 1935.

*The roman missal, revised by Decree of the Second Vatican Ecumenical Council and Published by Authority of Pope Paul VI. The Sacramentary. Approved for Use in the Dioceses of the United States of America by the National Conference of Catholic Bishops and Confirmed by the Apostolic See. English Translation Prepared by the International Committee on English in the Liturgy*, Collegeville 1974.

Rosenzweig, F., *Der Stern der Erlösung; Mit einer Einführung von Reinhold Mayer und einer Gedenkrede von Gershom Scholem*, Frankfurt 5th ed. 1996.

Schart, A., 'Der Engelglaube in der biblischen Tradition mit Ausblicken in die Religionsgeschichte', in: Herzog M. (ed.), *Die Wiederkunft der Engel; Beiträge zur Kunst und Kultur der Moderne* (Irseer Dialoge: Kultur und Wissenschaft interdisziplinär 2), Stuttgart et al. 2000.

Spinks, B.D., *The Sanctus in the Eucharistic Prayer*, Cambridge et al. 1991.

Stemberger, G., '"Himmlische" und "irdische" Liturgie in rabbinischer Zeit', in: A. Gerhards & H.H. Henrix (eds), *Dialog oder Monolog? Zur liturgischen Beziehung zwischen Judentum und Christentum* (QD 208), Freiburg 2004.

Taft, R., *Il Sanctus nell'anafora; Un riesame della questione*, Roma 1999.

Wahle, S., *Gottes-Gedenken; Untersuchungen zum anamnetischen Gehalt christlicher und jüdischer Liturgie* [Diss. Bonn] (IThS 73), Innsbruck et al. 2006.

Winkler, G., *Das Sanctus; Über den Ursprung und die Anfänge des Sanctus und sein Fortwirken* (OCA 267), Roma 2002.

————, 'Übernahme und Adaption alttestamentlicher Bestandteile in den christlichen Riten. Das Sanctus (Ein Arbeitsbericht)', in: W. Groß (ed.), *Das Judentum—Eine bleibende Herausforderung christlicher Identität*, Mainz 2001.

————, 'Beobachtungen zu den im "ante Sanctus" angeführten Engeln und ihre Bedeutung', *ThQ* 183 (2003) [quoted as Winkler 2003a].

————, 'The Sanctus: Some Observations with Regard to its Origins and Theological Significance', *Liturgy and Life* (Prayer and Spirituality in the Early Church Liturgy 3), Everton Park, Queensland 2003 [quoted as Winkler 2003b].

————, *Die Basilius-Anaphora; Edition der beiden armenischen Redanktionen und der relevanten Fragmente, Übersetzung und Zusammenschau aller Versionen im Licht der orientalischen Überlieferung* (Anaphorae Orientales 2, Anaphorae Armeniacae 2), Rom 2005.

Wohlmuth, J., *Mysterium der Verwandlung; Eine Eschatologie aus katholischer Perspektive im Gespräch mit jüdischem Denken der Gegenwart* (Studien zu Judentum und Christentum), Paderborn et al. 2005.

PART TWO

LITURGICAL POETRY

# THE MEANING OF THE CAIRO GENIZAH FOR STUDENTS OF EARLY JEWISH AND CHRISTIAN LITURGY

*Stefan C. Reif*
University of Cambridge, United Kingdom

## INTRODUCTION

The topic which I am here invited to address is a vast one, covering extensive literature over a period of at least a thousand years. It should therefore be treated in a complete monograph and not be the subject of one brief conference lecture. How then to proceed? Fortunately for me—and hopefully also for those destined to absorb these remarks—I am in the final process of compiling a liturgical volume to complement the one that I published a dozen years ago and this assists me with the dilemma just posed. That volume is essentially a summary of most of my liturgical research over the course of the past twelve years and I have therefore thought it useful in the present context to derive from there some of the points that are essential for the topic here in hand. Much of the research I have done relates directly to Genizah manuscripts and is self-evidently of relevance to the present discussion.

But even when that research is concerned with pre-Genizah periods of, say, the late second temple period to the early geonic era, the Genizah evidence stands quietly at the rear waiting to be summoned. This is because it knows that the researcher must ultimately decide how to date, characterize and conceptualize its contents and how to explain where it varies significantly from what became, or is regarded (rightly or wrongly) as having become, the standard rabbinic liturgy sanctioned by the Iraqi authorities from the ninth to the eleventh centuries. My aim is then to utilize specific parts of my new volume to offer some guidance to those treating the subject of early Jewish and Christian liturgies. I shall summarize some of my findings, sound a few warning notes, cite the evidence from Qumran and Ben Sira in order to contextualize the developments of the first two Christian centuries, and then turn to specific prayers and liturgical themes that are highly illuminated by the precious fragments from the Cairo Genizah. I shall then draw some broad conclusions.

## EARLIER FINDINGS

Since my newest liturgical book, soon to be published, sets out from where my earlier one left off, let me briefly recall what I had to say about the Genizah evidence in that earlier publication. I made the point that just as it is now beyond doubt that standard and authoritative versions of midrashic and targumic material are a product only of the later geonic period, so it is possible to argue convincingly a similar case in the matter of liturgy. Pluralism, multiformity, and variation were characteristic of the late talmudic and early geonic periods, although it is not yet clear whether they represent a continuation of, or a reaction against, the notions of the earlier rabbinic teachers. That very much depends on whether one subscribes to the view that such notions and such teachers were or were not already themselves wholly authoritative. Be that as it may, I listed the types of liturgical non-conformity to be found among the Genizah texts, including novel benedictions, some of them disapproved by some talmudic and post-talmudic teachers, and alternative versions of such central prayer-texts as the *amidah*, the *kaddish* and the grace after meals.

I also drew attention to the uses made of biblical texts that are unfamiliar or unacceptable in the dominant versions, or had been thought to have disappeared at an earlier stage, such as the liturgical recitation of the Decalogue. What had also emerged from the Genizah source were messianic, pietistic and mystical renderings of central parts of the liturgy, otherwise lost or eliminated, and clear indications not only of what appeared to be hybrid rites but also of a lack of liturgical unanimity even in specific areas and communities. Aramaic and Arabic were sometimes used where the later standard had opted exclusively for Hebrew and the vast numbers of liturgical poems newly discovered testified to the fact that such a literary genre had almost ousted the regular and simpler forms of prayer from their central place. Indeed, according to Ezra Fleischer's interpretation of the liturgical history of the geonic period, the Genizah variants do not reflect an earlier lack of unanimity among the talmudic authorities but a revolutionary displacement of their versions with those of the later liturgical poets.

## SCHOLARLY CONTROVERSY

Since Fleischer's interpretation was an important part of the scholarly discussion of the early 1990s, it is important to make further reference to it in the present context and to the reactions it spawned. Fleischer was adamant that there was no obligatory Jewish prayer in any communal contexts during the Second Temple Period; that the apocryphal, hellenistic and early Christian sources said nothing of such prayer; and that the customs adopted and practised at Qumran were those of sectarians. Only at Yavneh was the novel idea introduced of praying thrice daily and Rabban Gamliel laid down a clear formulation of the prayers. This was closely followed in the Babylonian centres and the liturgical traditions of those communities are consequently closer to the original than those of Eretz Israel which are the product of later poetic tendencies.

Although agreeing with the overall argument that the communal prayers of the tannaitic rabbis, *as they came to be formulated and legislated in the second century*, were not recited in earlier synagogues, I was troubled by what appeared to me to be the anachronisms, generalizations and dogmatic conclusions in some of Fleischer's informed but controversial presentation. I did not wish to rule out completely the possibility that when Jews came together in communal contexts they might have prayed, as well as studying and providing communal facilities, and I felt that the definition of the Qumranic material as sectarian, and therefore somehow irrelevant to the early development of rabbinic liturgical practice, was misleading. Other sources did hint at communal Jewish prayer and Palestinian texts were, in my view, just as likely, if not more likely than Babylonian ones, to be original and authentic. Similar patterns of liturgical development, however differently expressed, could be detected for each generation and were a more impressive interpretation of historical change than a theory of unrelated revolutions led by bombastic individuals. A synchronic approach to the talmudic sources was still dictated by the lack of definitive criteria for establishing a reliable diachronic analysis.

What then has to be added on the basis of the work of the last fifteen years to this argument about the late Second Temple and early rabbinic and Christian periods? Firstly, given the increased evidence of the dynamic religious variety of that time, and the attendant stresses and strains, one must be wary, in the matter of methodology, of assuming that sects, philosophies and religious practices can be clearly and categorically defined or that credit can be given to a few outstanding individuals for major developments. The critical historian should, rather, be on the lookout for the degree to which religious traditions were mutually influential, overlapping and multifarious and for the manner in which individuals might be championing notions that have evolved in their own, or in other environments. As Moshe Greenberg and Lee Levine have forcefully and convincingly argued, the growing importance and formality of what had started out life as individual prayer, as well as the evolution of the synagogue as a centre of worship, may represent tendencies towards the democratic, egalitarian and popular, as against the oligarchic, elitist and exclusivist values of the temple and the priesthood.

## QUMRAN AND BEN SIRA

The evidence from the Dead Sea manuscripts points to the regular recitation at stipulated times or occasions of communal prayers, although there is no overall consistency of formulation or context. Some parts of such prayers are reminiscent of what was formulated by the tannaitic rabbis but, as in other cases of similarity between their religious traditions, it is not clear if there was a direct line of transmission or whether the medium was an oral or written one. While the material familiar from Qumran makes a re-appearance in rabbinic liturgy, the format, the vocabulary and the usage have all taken on a distinctive character that reflects the ideology of early talmudic Judaism. There was clearly more than one provenance for the development of hymns and prayers during the Second Temple period. Among the sources from which the early rabbis apparently drew their liturgical inspiration (perhaps in some cases indirectly) were the Temple and its priesthood, contemporary circles of pietists and mystics, proto-synagogal gatherings such as the *ma'amadot*, and local custom. There is ample evidence in the talmudic and geonic eras that this process of liturgical innovation, adaptation and adjustment did not come to an end in the second century so that it hardly seems valid to extrapolate backwards from the late geonic period to the early talmudic one in an effort to reconstruct precisely what constituted the earliest rabbinic formulations.

If we now offer a three-way comparison between Ben Sira, Qumran and the Rabbis, it has to be acknowledged that the apocryphal book has less in common with the other two sources than the latter two have with each other. To cite some examples, Ben Sira has no mention of regular prayers at specific times, of poetic formulations for special occasions, or of a special liturgical role for sabbaths and festivals and there is little stress in his book on angels, apocalyptic notions and the end of time. On the other hand, like the Rabbis after him, Ben Sira clearly sees the possibility of worshipping God in a variety of ways and contexts, including the educational and the intellectual, and has the greatest respect for the Jerusalem Temple—he perhaps more practically and the Rabbis more theoretically.

The use of hymns, prayers and benedictions, as well as of biblical words and phrases to which fresh meanings have been given, is common to all three sources. They also all include as central themes in their entreaties the election of Israel, the status of Zion, the holiness of Jerusalem, the return of the Davidic dynasty, and the manifestation of God's great power now and in the future. Ben Sira undoubtedly takes the matter of worship beyond that of most of the Hebrew Bible but does not reflect the same liturgical intensity as that found at Qumran. He thus sets the tone for some rabbinic developments but is apparently not the source for various others.

## Shema

I recently completed a close study of the early history and development of the *shema* as a Jewish liturgical text and it will again be useful to refer to the broader conclusions that I was able to reach.

At the axial age, one encounters the broader use of one paragraph, and maybe even two paragraphs, of the *shema*, or at least parts of these two passages, as well as of the Decalogue. There is a particular awareness of, and affection for, such passages and they are regarded as bearing a special theological message. They are consequently used as amulets, phylacteries or simply as sacred texts. What emerges from New Testament texts is that there also existed a tendency (perhaps inspired by hellenistic, philosophical notions) to see the whole religious message summarized in one brief biblical text, as interpreted by tradition, be it from the Decalogue, the *shema*, or what current scholarship knows as the Holiness Code.

The *shema* developed among the early rabbis as a declaration of their acceptance of the kingdom of God, rather than any other kingdom (such as that of Rome), and of all the commandments of the Torah. The devotion required in the light of such a declaration was interpreted as relating to all aspects of human nature, as demanding martyrdom when necessary, and as requiring a total acceptance of God's ultimate justice and the use of all one's assets. According to some halakhic midrashim, the messages carried by the *shema* are that Israel has a special role and that its special devotion to God may be traced back to the Patriarchs. Israel's constant loyalty is a form of martyrdom and the first paragraph of the *shema* is liturgically superior to the Decalogue and to the other two passages, given its special message of God's kingship and the yoke of its acceptance by Israel. What has therefore happened is that a biblical source, or set of sources, has been hijacked and used as a banner to proclaim some central but broad religious messages and then gradually employed more particularistically as the liturgical expression of Israel's special role as understood in rabbinic theology.

## BIBLICAL TEXTS

By the time that the talmudic rabbis of the early Christian centuries were debating the matter of the inclusion of biblical verses and chapters in their standard prayers for daily, sabbath and festival use, there were a number of these that were well established by popular tradition within the liturgical context. Minor examples are the sets of verses, included in the *musaf* ('additional') *amidah* for New Year and illustrating the three themes of kingship, remembrance and *shofar* (ram's horn) that stand at the centre of that prayer, as well as the verses used on special fast-days proclaimed in times of drought. More common and more major examples are the *shema*, the Decalogue, the *hallel* ('praise'), the Passover *Haggadah*, the Song at the Sea (Ex 15), the Priestly Benediction (Num 6:24–26) and the trisagion (Isa 6:3). The whole issue of the role of biblical material in the liturgy was a lively and controversial one.

Rabbinic formulations were regarded as preferable to biblical precedents, and biblical verses were to be differentiated from rabbinic prayers. Could, for instance, the verses from Isa 12:6 and Ps 22:4 be employed at any point in the *kedushah* benediction of the *amidah* without valid halakhic objections being raised? The early rabbinic teachers sometimes even made changes in liturgical formulations out of polemical considerations. A good example concerns the use of the Biblical Hebrew word '*olam*' (meaning 'world' as well as 'eternity' in post-biblical Hebrew) in such a way as to ensure that the notion of a future world was not excluded.

Nevertheless, the liturgical pre-existence of such specific items as the *shema*, and others mentioned above, provides positive proof that earlier attitudes had been different.

Perhaps what the talmudic rabbis feared was the potential influence of some groups who were regarded by them as sectarian and who had opted for the inclusion of biblical texts among their prayers. The Jews whose literary remains were found at Qumran, by the Dead Sea, were of such an ilk, and medieval Karaites, whose prayers were exclusively composed of biblical texts, pursued a similar liturgical philosophy. The situation among the Rabbanite Jews changed from the beginning of the Islamic period when, instead of merely a few favourite verses (such as Ps 51:17, 84:5 and 144:15) and complete Psalms (such as Ps 145), substantial blocks of biblical verses, groups of chapters and individual verses, especially from the book of Psalms, came to be incorporated in the traditional daily prayers, and then in the first prayer-books. Either the popular urge to include biblical items was so powerful that the halakhic authorities had to submit to it or it was determined that the most attractive religious practices should not be left exclusively to the theological opposition.

## Jerusalem

Moving further into this more theological use of liturgy, a comparison of the manner in which the theme of Jerusalem is handled in various rabbinic prayers, with careful attention being given to the variants to be found in Genizah fragments, is also instructive. While the Temple was still standing, a realistic picture emerges of that institution and its service, with the priests at their centre and the people of Israel at their edge, all of them the beneficiaries of the special favour expressed by God for Zion, a term that alludes to the whole religious arrangement. During the talmudic period, there is the keen anticipation of a recovery from the disasters that befell these institutions and the expectation of an almost imminent restoration of the city of Jerusalem, the Temple and its service, and the special relationship with God that they represent. God's compassion and mercy will bless Israel with security, and the people's prayers, as well as their offerings, will attract divine favour.

As the passing of the centuries puts paid to even the vaguest folk memories of actual Jerusalem institutions, so the prayers chosen most commonly to relate to them become less embedded in reality and convey a more futuristic and messianic message. God's infinite power will bring unexpected joy and recompense to those suffering the pain of exile and persecution. A detailed picture is painted of an idealized future, with Jerusalem functioning with more than its former glory. The Temple and the Davidic kingdom are presupposed and each group of Jews is seen to be playing a part in the scene. Economy of expression and simplicity of language, particularly as championed by the Babylonian formulations, give way to the kind of generous augmentation and colourful vocabulary that are more characteristic of Palestinian prayer texts.

## RESTORATION

If one examines the theme of restoration in the rabbinic liturgy in a similar manner, one encounters three themes: 1) that God will rectify the situation; 2) the restoration to Israel of Divine favour and warm relations to Israel; and 3) prophetic and messianic visions. Here it is more difficult to separate the themes chronologically and thematically but possible to reach some important broader conclusions. There are undoubtedly instances in which the same words have been interpreted in significantly different ways by various generations. References to Davidic rule, to the holy city and to divine worship did not necessarily convey the same concepts to the Jews of every centre and in each century. Nevertheless, it may confidently be concluded that the standard rabbinic prayers in their totality include all three themes and that the widespread textual, linguistic and theological variations testify to a dynamic process of development, though not one that displays one consistent tendency. It seems likely that this process was affected by the history of the Jewish people as it evolved from epoch to epoch and from centre to centre. Social, political and religious ideas undoubtedly left their mark on the texts of the prayers and, while the nature of such marks are identifiable, the details of their arrival and departure remain obscure in the early centuries of the first Christian millennium. What may be suggested for at least some periods is that, as the idea of restoration became less confidently and expeditiously expected, so it tended to be expressed progressively more in the language of the utopian visionary.

## Sacrifices

If we now move on to the subject of the cultic service, there was clearly substantial talmudic discussion about the future of and/or the replacement of sacrifice and its relative theological importance in rabbinic Judaism. Although there was from the outset a strong body of opinion contending that there was no connection or continuation, there was also a tendency to seek ways of incorporating details of sacrifices into the prayers, and not simply opting for the view that prayers had wholly replaced sacrifices. This tendency subsequently strengthened in the post-talmudic period and is evidenced in the earliest prayer-books. There was also a major move on the part of the liturgical poets to restore the cult to a central role, especially by way of poetic versions of the *avodah* ritual for Yom Kippur, while a belief in the mystical, even magical use of language encouraged the recitation of the relevant passages concerning the cult.

The tenth century saw an enthusiastic interest on the parts of both Karaites and Rabbanites in special circumambulations of Jerusalem and in the recitation of connected prayers but, it must be admitted, without any central concern for details of the sacrificial cult. The Jewish liturgy ultimately incorporated, in conflated format, and not always in a fully logical presentation, two independent trends towards either Torah study or cultic restoration. The kabbalists of the late medieval and early modern periods, for their part, saw a prophylactic value in the recitation of passages concerning the sacrifices and this gave such texts an increased status in the regular prayers. To propose, therefore, that sacrifice was replaced by prayer is undoubtedly a gross over-simplification of a long and complicated liturgical process.

## Physical Medium

Studies of the physical medium used for the transmission of the liturgical texts, as reflected in the Genizah material, also reveal an interesting course of development. It would appear that some fragments represent early attempts on the part of individuals rather than communities to commit oral traditions to writing. As with other areas of rabbinic literature, the adoption of the codex gave the texts a greater degree of canonicity, leading to a growing concern for precise formulation. The

single leaf evolved into the more lengthy codex, the private individual
became the professional scribe, and the texts that had once been brief
and provisional notes gradually turned into formal prayer-books. This
ultimately led later generations to append to such prayer-books their
own notes, instructions, commentaries and decorations, thus enhancing
both their religious status and their physical attractiveness.

## MAIMONIDES AND SON

Maimonides's liturgical work reveals a number of tensions about theological priorities and preferences, especially as they relate to religious
idealism versus social reality. He was capable of innovation where the
circumstances demanded it, particularly where the public reputation
of Judaism was at stake. He was, however, broadly committed to the
continued application of talmudic principles on the one side, and to
the promotion of the religiosity of prayer on the other, while remaining aware of the distinction between legal requirement and customary
practice. What is uncovered in his comments is a contentment with basic
Hebrew liturgy and a desire never to lose sight of the main theme of
a prayer or set of prayers. He demonstrates a preference for intense
preparation over unnecessary expansion, especially of the mystical or
superstitious variety. His preferred liturgy appears to be Egyptian/North
African and to stand between the centralized Babylonian rite emanating
from the geonic authorities and the variegated traditions that flowed
from it. On the other hand, there is evidence that in some respects
he adhered to a Sefardi (Andalusian) liturgical tradition at home. His
preferred liturgy made a major impact only on the Yemenite (*baladi*
not *shami*) rite and appears to have lost much of its influence in the
increasingly powerful centres of Europe. The substantial inroads later
made by the mystics into the liturgical field were at least to some
degree initiated by his son, Abraham, and do not reflect his overall
approach, while the father's discomfort with the Palestinian liturgical
rites led to a powerful and ultimately successful campaign by the son
for their elimination.

As Mordechai Friedman has meticulously demonstrated, Genizah
documents reveal that the war of words between Abraham Maimuni,
the new communal leader, and his opponents continued from the time
of his father's demise in 1204 virtually until his own death in 1237.
Initially, the practice of referring to the leader of the Jewish community

in parts of the synagogal liturgy (*reshut*), as well as in official documents, as an expression of allegiance, had to be abandoned by the leadership because of objections to Abraham's authority and ideology and it took almost a decade before he was able to re-assert this right for himself. Only by taking such action could the leadership forestall the creation of additional synagogues that would regard themselves as independent of the communal leadership. His opponents saw Abraham's pietistic campaign not as a defence of tradition but as a radically novel religiosity bent on mimicking Sufi practice and his rejection of Palestinian practice as an attempt to destroy well-established and authentic rituals. So incensed and desperate were they that on more than one occasion they appealed to the Muslim authorities to rule that his modes of worship were unconscionably innovative. He, for his part, was so convinced of the rectitude of his arguments that he found support for them in tannaitic sources. According to his interpretation, there was already then an established custom uniformly to kneel in rows facing the ark where the scrolls were kept and to conduct all the prayers in the direction of Jerusalem.

## In Truth

The Genizah texts also shed light on the original sense of the first sentence of the post-*shema* paragraph in the evening prayers: אמת ואמונה כל זאת קים עלינו. Taking the Yemenite vocalization קִים in the *piel* perfect and the absence of the words כי הוא in many Genizah texts as the starting points, there are various possible interpretations. A convincing sense could be 'has fulfilled all this for us', i.e. God has kept his promise just recited in the third paragraph of the *shema*, to be our God, 'and we are Israel His people'. The first two words could also be made to yield a better sense if it is recalled that the first of them is often used in the liturgy in the sense of באמת and both are given this sense here. Additional support for such a meaning is available in the variant reading באמת ובאמונה instead of אמת ואמונה which occurs in the morning *ge'ulah* benediction. The translation would then be 'In truth and faith, God has fulfilled all this for us'. Alternatively, אמת is only the introductory 'Truly' and not part of the remainder of the sentence, and just as in the third part of the sentence a claim is made about the fulfilment of God's promise so in the second part is the trustworthiness of what has been recited acknowledged in the words אֱמוּנָה כֹּל זֹאת.

Such a sense and vocalization would admirably fit Ginzberg's theory about the origins of the prayer as an אמן to what has gone before. It would also be linguistically significant. The translation would then be 'Truly, all this is acknowledged'.

This novel treatment of the passage does not, however, provide any reference to the future redemption, apparently presupposed by Rashi and the *Tosafot* in their commentaries on Ber 12a. It may, of course, be the case that they are reading the idea into קים עלינו but, if not, the possibility that קים was here originally קָיַם as it appears in so many other cases, or יְקַיֵּם, should be considered. Perhaps mention should also be made of the possibility that there is here a remnant of some form of קים אמונה, 'keeping a promise'. Changes in other such petitions for the future redemption are well-known and the last phrase ואנחנו ישראל עמו, which would not fit well as the concluding portion of such a petition, would therefore have to be a later addition.

There is the remote possibility that there is here some long-forgotten allusion to a popular text or its interpretation, a text such as Neh 10:1 in which the expression כל זאת occurs in the context of 'making a covenant'. It may be added that the words ברית and אמנה are governed by none other a verb than קום in the *piel* in one of the Zadokite Documents (ed. Rabin 1958, 39).

## Genizah Texts of Al Ha-Nissim

Neither the recitation nor the definitive wording of this prayer were talmudically ordained. The prayer was introduced by the geonic authorities and given expression in historical, poetic and supplicatory styles, perhaps each of them originally separate, but ultimately combined. Although the general structure of the text is agreed in all the versions, there are interesting textual variants. On the linguistic side, one can detect in a number of fragments tendencies towards the replacement of mishnaic philology, vocabulary and orthography with their biblical Hebrew counterparts, sometimes because the transmitters were ill-at-ease with the meanings they attached to mishnaic forms, and towards the use of biblical verses as prototypes. There was a clear tension between those who stressed the historical miracle and those who wished not only to offer thanks for the past but also to make entreaty for the future. Also controversial was the degree to which strong elements of eschatology, the supernatural and lyricism should be included in standard *amidah* benedictions. There are also political considerations (such as in the use of the term מלכות הרשעה), theological concerns about associating Israel with destruction and God with *lèse majesté*, and ambivalence about whether phrases are to be understood politically, theologically or intellectually (as with זדים ביד עוסקי תורתך).

## Aramaic Poem

A close examination of an Aramaic poem in T-S NS 160.11 (ואי פומנא) raises broader issues that are worthy of further discussion. Its style parallels and echoes those of Targum Onqelos and the fixed prayers of the early medieval period. Its vocabulary, grammatical forms and modes of expression closely match the language of the halakhic authorities who held spiritual and cultural sway over much of the Mediterranean area at the end of the geonic period. At the same time, it has to be acknowledged that, although there are no clear indications of the kind of Galilean Aramaic that is characteristic of so many targumic versions to be found in the Genizah collections, there are some linguistic elements that appear to have originated among the communities of the land of Israel. Given the incontrovertible existence of trilingualism on the part of the Jews in the post-geonic period, it hardly seems surprising to encounter texts in which there are switches between languages. It is not unlikely that one of the aspects of this linguistic and literary process was the development whereby Aramaic dialects came to be used that did not represent particular geographical areas. The scholarly authors of the later period chose to write Aramaic in order to expand the range of their literature and made use of a variety of earlier styles and characteristics that were borrowed from a number of different sources.

The manner in which our author re-works the material before him is basically similar to that employed by the Aramaic targumists when they added to the scriptural source but remained thoroughly loyal to its basic content. Recently published research work on such targumim have demonstrated the existence of many types of translation and supplement. In addition to the well-known Targum Onqelos, Pseudo-Jonathan and Yerushalmi renderings, there were also targumic collections that followed the sabbath and festival lectionaries or treated particular chapters or verses of scripture, as well as more general types of *tosefta* (additamenta) versions. In a number of respects, our Aramaic poem, though connected to the fixed liturgy rather than to the biblical text, is similar to such targumim and makes use of words and expressions that are linguistically typical of targumic Aramaic.

What we may therefore have here is a composition that is similar in aim and usage to those Aramaic liturgical poems of post-talmudic Byzantium and later Franco-Germany but certainly does not employ a language and style that is wholly comparable with theirs. It seems reasonable to suppose that it is an example of a literary genre that belongs to the history of Hebrew poetry at the end of the geonic period and that is linked to the emergence of the new centres of Jewish life that replaced those of Babylon and the Palestinian Jewish homeland. As long, however, as no similar such poems have been found and identified, it will not be possible to be more precise about its historical and literary milieu.

A few sentences should now deal with the context in which our previously unknown Aramaic poem was recited. Such a recitation was obviously attached to the *nishmat* prayer. Since the ritual practices of Babylon and Palestine differed as to when that prayer was recited, there are two possibilities that immediately come to mind. Our poem was recited either in the sabbath morning service or as part of the weekday prayers. But there is also a third historical option. Perhaps our author's intention was to include his composition among the special prayers recited on Passover. In that case, it could have been attached to the morning service of the festival, or of its intermediate sabbath, like the other poems that appear on the remaining folios of the fragment, or it might have been recited as part of the *hallel* section of the Passover Haggadah of the first evening. Since the Genizah has revealed fragments that contain novel Aramaic versions of parts of the Haggadah that are generally familiar to us in Hebrew, such a phenomenon need not be regarded as rare or exceptional. The references in lines 5 and 12 to 'youngest speakers' and a gathering of 'young and old' (Aramaic originals: זעטוטין ודעדקין and במיכנש סבין ודרדקין) may certainly allude to the Jewish communal gathering in the synagogue but one cannot rule out the important possibility that the author has in mind the domestic Passover seder. If so, what emerges is that the community in which he operated apparently had the custom of extending the range of the *hallel* beyond what is to be found in the prayer-book of R. Sa'adya Gaon and in many Genizah fragments.

## Genizah Grace

A number of more general conclusions, that are important for an accurate understanding of Jewish liturgical history, may also be derived from the data provided by a Genizah fragment of the grace after meals and from its relationship with other versions. The twelfth-century rabbinic liturgies clearly still displayed a considerable variety of textual detail that remained in flux even if the major factors had become more solidified. The crystallization of the definitively recognizable rites of Europe and the orient was only in its early stages. There were still tensions between traditional transmission and novelty, between inconsistency and standardization, and between the biblical and rabbinic varieties of Hebrew language. The image of God, the nature of his relationship with the worshipper, and the notion of the messianic era were all concepts that were, in their smaller detail if not in their major configuration, open to liturgical adjustment. Historians should be ready to find among the manuscript sources numerous examples of texts that are not purely Babylonian or Palestinian and should place *Seder Rav Amram*, as it has come down to us, among the *formae mixtae* of the post-geonic period and not within the purer Babylonian versions of the ninth century. Our manuscript appears to belong to a genre that is in or close to North Africa and still retains mixed Babylonian and Palestinian elements as well as similarities to the modified version of *Seder Rav Amram* and the prayer-book of Maimonides. The prayer-book of Solomon ben Nathan is simply another example of the variety of 'western' and 'oriental' liturgical elements that still existed in North Africa in the twelfth century.

## Conclusions

Ben Sira, Qumran and the Rabbis share some of the liturgical genres and a number of the dominant themes. Ben Sira moves beyond the biblical definition of worship but does not testify to the regular recitation of prayers at stipulated times or on specific occasions such as is found at Qumran. The Rabbis are inspired by various such earlier traditions but create their own formulation and usage.

Beginning its Jewish liturgical life as some form of amulet, the *shema* comes to be seen as the summary of a central religious message and then as a declaration of faith in the divine kingdom and in the importance of the religious commandments (מצות). Once established in such a role, it is then regarded as the banner of other major aspects of rabbinic theology.

Some biblical verses and passages are used as tannaitic liturgical compositions but there is some apprehension among the talmudic rabbis about opting for biblical rather than rabbinic formulations. After the rise of Islam, and the success of early medieval Karaism, more substantial liturgical use is made by the rabbinic tradition of biblical texts, albeit never with the authoritative liturgical status of the *amidah*.

In the period immediately following the destruction of the Judean state, there is a confidence that Jerusalem, the Temple and the cult, which had been of critical significance to many of the Jewish people, will be restored and God's favour again attracted. As the memory of the reality fades, so the nature of the prayers about these institutions becomes more idealistic and includes more colourful, futuristic and messianic elements.

The topic of restoration includes three themes in rabbinic liturgy: physical improvement, divine favour and messianic ideology. The specific manifestations of such themes are viewed differently by changing generations and in varied locations, often as a result of historical developments.

Although some of the early talmudic rabbis were of the opinion that there was little or no connection or continuation between the sacrificial system and the daily prayers, others felt not only that the latter were the direct replacement of the former but also that ways should be sought of incorporating details of the sacrifices into the prayers. This view found further expression among the liturgical poets of the post-talmudic period and among those who saw such an incorporation either as part of Torah-study or an entreaty for the future.

It seems likely that most prayers were originally transmitted in an oral form and that the commitment to the written folio increased as the codex was more widely adopted by the Jews. Once that form became more standard, and indeed more lengthy, so did it attract to itself more content and a greater degree of authority. This process also laid the foundations for the addition of notes, commentaries and decorations by subsequent generations.

The liturgical preferences of Maimonides in the twelfth century are for talmudic principles, mishnaic Hebrew, personal religiosity and intense preparation but he is capable of innovation when public circumstances demand it and aware of the distinction between legal requirement and customary practice. In a liturgical situation that was obviously still somewhat fluid, his preferred public liturgy seems to have been Egyptian/North African but he sometimes adhered to Sefardi (Andalusian) tradition in his personal behavior. His reservations about following the rites of Eretz Israel and about the place of mysticism were not shared by his son, Abraham, who was willing to involve himself in considerable communal controversy in order to eliminate the Palestinian customs and to implement Sufi-like changes in the local prayer customs.

In the first of four detailed textual studies, it becomes clear that in the opening paragraph of the *ge'ulah* benediction following the *shema* in the evening office, and beginning אמת ואמונה, the semantic range, the syntax and the vocalization of the first five words are all controversial. We may here be dealing with an original meaning that has been lost, some objection to one sense that has lead to the substitution of another, or a misunderstanding that has crept into the text as a result of a false analogy with another phrase. The impetus for change may be theological, linguistic or grammatical.

Our second case concerns the recitation and formulation of the *al ha-nissim* prayer in the *amidah* during the festival of Hanukkah which were products of the post-talmudic period. Although much of the text is fairly standard, the variations documented in the Genizah manuscripts offer some interesting testimony. In addition to some intriguing political, theological and intellectual considerations, there were clearly tensions about whether the prayers should be in biblical or mishnaic Hebrew, whether the stress should be on past events or future hopes, and whether the atmosphere of the prayer should be poetic or prosaic.

The third text is that of an Aramaic poem that appears to be part of the Passover liturgy, either synagogal or domestic, and that treats the biblical source much as the Targumim did. Although it is similar in aim and usage to the poetry of post-talmudic Byzantium and later Franco-Germany, its language and style are different from theirs. It consequently testifies to the insertion into the standard prayers of poetic Aramaic expansions that have links with earlier and later genres but are by no means identical with them.

A Genizah manuscript containing the whole text of the grace after meals constitutes our fourth example. Although this version is unlikely to be earlier than the twelfth century, and few of its elements are totally innovative, it is impossible to identify it in its totality (only in specific parts of its content) with any one liturgical rite known from that period or the centuries immediately before or after it, or indeed to see its source in any purely Babylonian or Palestinian form. It is perhaps closest to a North African rite that still has both 'western' and 'oriental' aspects to it.

What therefore emerges from all these studies and the associated conclusions? There were undoubtedly forms of communal Jewish prayer before Rabban Gamliel and most Qumran scholars currently subscribe to the view that this was not a practice limited to only one small sect. It is possible to detect a process of liturgical evolution from the Second Temple period to the tannaitic, amoraic and geonic eras. Attitudes to the use of biblical verses is not uniform through these periods but appears to be dependent on external factors, revealing both negative and positive responses to the customs of other groups. Rabbinic liturgy is affected by changing political circumstances and by adjustments in theology. Liturgical poets do not necessarily have a revolutionary impact on the prayers but sometimes continue and expand earlier talmudic traditions. The physical medium left a major mark on the liturgical content, style and status. Although there are efforts to establish the basic Babylonian forms, there remains even as late as the twelfth century a considerable degree of fluidity and the clearly definable rites do not emerge wholly and successfully until the thirteenth and fourteenth centuries. Close textual analysis testifies to alterations, misunderstandings and controversies, behind which lie theological, political, intellectual and linguistic considerations.

## LITERATURE

*Earlier findings*

Reif, S.C., *Judaism and Hebrew Prayer; New Perspectives on Jewish Liturgical History*, Cambridge 1993.
———, *Problems with Prayers: Studies in the Textual History of Early Rabbinic Liturgy*, Berlin—New York 2006.

*Scholarly controversy*

Fleischer, E., 'On the Beginnings of Obligatory Jewish Prayer', *Tarb.* 59 (1990) 397–441 [Hebrew].
Reif, S.C., 'On the Earliest Development of Jewish Prayer', *Tarb.* 60 (1991) 677–81 [Hebrew].
Fleischer E., 'Rejoinder to Dr Reif's remarks', *Tarb.* 60 (1991) 683–88 [Hebrew].
Reif, S.C., 'Jewish Liturgy in the Second Temple Period: Some Methodological Considerations', in: *PWCJS* 11 (1994) 1–8.

Greenberg, M., *Biblical Prose Prayer as a Window to the Popular Religion of Ancient Israel*, Berkeley 1983.
Levine, L.I., *The Ancient Synagogue; The First Thousand Years*, New Haven 1999.

## Qumran and Ben Sira

Chazon, E. & A. Pinnick (eds), *Liturgical Perspectives; Prayer and Poetry in Light of the Dead Sea Scrolls* (StTDJ 48), Leiden 2003.
Reif, S.C., 'The Second Temple Period, Qumran Research and Rabbinic Liturgy; Some Contextual and Linguistic Comparisons', in: *Liturgical Perspectives* 133–149.
———, 'Prayer in Ben Sira, Qumran and Second Temple Judaism', in: R. Egger-Wenzel (ed.), *Proceedings of the International Ben Sira Conference, Durham, Ushaw College, 2001*, Berlin—New York 2002, 321–41.

## Shema

See chapter 7 of *Problems with Prayers*.

Kimelman, R., 'The Shema Liturgy: from Covenant Ceremony to Coronation', in: J. Tabory (ed.), *Kenishta: Studies of the Synagogue World*, Ramat Gan 2001, 9–105.

## Biblical texts

Reif, S.C., 'The Bible in Jewish Liturgy' in: A. Berlin & M.Z. Brettler (eds), *The Jewish Study Bible*, Oxford—New York 2004, 1937–1948.
Wiesenberg, E.J., 'Gleanings of the Liturgical Term *Melekh Ha-'Olam*', *JJS* 17 (1966), 47–72.

## Jerusalem

Reif, S.C., 'Jerusalem in Jewish Liturgy', in: L.I. Levine (ed.), *Jerusalem; Its Sanctity and Centrality in Judaism, Christianity and Islam*, New York 1998, 424–37.

## Restoration

Reif, S.C., 'Some Notions of Restoration in Early Rabbinic Prayer', in: J.M. Scott (ed.), *Restoration; Old Testament, Jewish and Christian Perspectives*, Leiden 2001, 281–304.

## Sacrifices

Reif, S.C., 'Approaches to Sacrifice in Early Jewish Prayer' in: R. Hayward & B. Embry (eds), *Studies in Jewish Prayer*, Oxford 2005, 135–50.
———, 'Some Recent Developments in the Study of Medieval Jewish Liturgy', in: N. de Lange (ed.), *Hebrew Scholarship and the Medieval World*, Cambridge 2001, 60–73.

## Physical medium

Reif, S.C., 'Codicological Aspects of Jewish Liturgical History', *BJRL* 75 (1993) 117–31.
———, 'Written Prayers from the Genizah; Their Physical Aspect and its Relationship to their Content', in: J. Tabory (ed.), *From Qumran to Cairo; Studies in the History of Prayer*, Jerusalem 1999, 121–130 [Hebrew].
———, 'From Manuscript Codex to Printed Volume: a Jewish Liturgical Transition?', in: R. Langer and S. Fine (eds), *Liturgy in the Life of the Synagogue*, Winona Lake, Indiana 2005, 95–108.

### Maimonides and son

Reif, S.C., 'Some Recent Developments in the Study of Medieval Jewish Liturgy' in: N. de Lange (ed.), *Hebrew Scholarship and the Medieval World*, Cambridge 2001, 60–73.

See chapter 12 of *Problems with Prayers*.

### In truth

Rabin, C. (ed.), *The Zadokite Documents*, Oxford 1958.

Reif, S.C., 'Liturgical Difficulties and Genizah Manuscripts' in: S. Morag, I. Ben-Ami & N.A. Stillman (eds), *Studies in Judaism and Islam Presented to Shelomo Dov Goitein*, Jerusalem 1981, 99–122.

### Genizah texts of Al Ha-Nissim

See chapter 16 of *Problems with Prayers*.

### Aramaic poem

Reif, S.C., '*We-'ilu Finu*. A Poetic Aramaic Version', in S. Elizur, M.D. Herr, G. Shaked, & A. Shinan (eds), *Knesset 'Ezra; Literature and Life in the Synagogue; Studies Presented to Ezra Fleischer*, Jerusalem 1994, 269–83 [Hebrew].

### Genizah grace

Reif, S.C., 'Ein Genisa-Fragment des Tischdank', in: W. Homolka (ed.), *Liturgie als Theologie; Das Gebet als Zentrum im jüdischen Denken*, Berlin 2005, 11–29.

# BIBLICAL TEXTS IN JEWISH PRAYERS:
## THEIR HISTORY AND FUNCTION

*Ruth Langer*
Boston College, USA

Biblical[1] texts appear in rabbinic liturgy in four primary modes: as the citation of complete biblical pericopes as prayers or study passages; as the explicit citation of verses as midrashic-style proof texts to buttress the theological statement of a prayer; as reused biblical language, often adjusted in grammar or meaning to its new context; and in prayers that consist virtually entirely of concatenated unadapted verses. In these last two, rabbinic Jews use biblical language to construct coherent new compositions, using mechanisms that Judith Newman (1999, 11f) terms 'scripturalizing' and 'biblicizing'.[2] The liturgical reuse of adapted biblical language is a well-recognized but under-discussed phenomenon that characterizes both the statutory prayers that lie at the core of the *siddur* and most of the liturgical poetry written to adorn it. A fuller understanding of this phenomenon is a necessary background for comprehending the final mode's exclusive usage of direct biblical material, a liturgical form that is hardly discussed, little appreciated and even less understood.

## Prayer in Hebrew

All four of these modes contribute to the emergence of a rabbinic liturgy that, by the end of the first millennium, was composed almost entirely in Hebrew[3] and not in anyone's vernacular. The liturgical texts among

---

[1] My gratitude to Clemens Leonhard, not only for his generous help with the research on the Christian parallels to the phenomena discussed here, but also for suggesting that this context would be the right one in which to bring this discussion to a fuller formulation.

[2] Note that she also includes obvious references to biblical figures and events within these categories. I will not discuss this here.

[3] Seth Schwartz (1995, 25–35) suggests that we translate the rabbinic term for Hebrew, *leshon hakodesh*, as 'the language of the Jerusalem Temple,' rather than simply the 'holy tongue.' This suggests that Hebrew was the ritual language of the Temple

the Dead Sea Scrolls already testify to the exclusive use of Hebrew for prayer, a Hebrew that is deeply informed by biblical models and language but not restricted by them. The exclusion of vernacular prayer in Greek or Aramaic in favor of these biblical models was deliberate, perhaps even, for the rabbis, a way of distinguishing Jewish from Christian prayer.[4] It is very possible that vernacular prayer did exist in the Jewish world, particularly though not necessarily exclusively in the diaspora where evidence suggests that non-Jews found the synagogue attractive and hence, we can presume, culturally accessible.[5] Sot 7.1, in its list of ritual texts that may be recited in any language, includes all three central elements of rabbinic liturgy: the recitation of *shema*, the *tefillah*, and the grace after meals. This would suggest that the rabbis recognized that requiring exclusively Hebrew prayer limited their ability to implement their liturgical system. Hence they permitted Jews to continue to pray in their vernaculars.[6] However, over the course of the amoraic era, the rabbis themselves largely ignored the Mishnah's permission for vernacular prayer, even teaching that most petitionary prayer is ineffective unless voiced in the Hebrew that ministering angels understand.[7] There is no evidence that the rabbis themselves performed their major statutory prayers in anything but Hebrew, and the geonic texts all presume Hebrew prayer. By giving rabbinic prayer symbolic and supposedly historical ties to the biblical modes of worship, the use of Hebrew elevated its authority and claims for efficacy.

---

and its use carried overtones of this holy place. The *targumim* call Hebrew 'language of the House of the Holy' but there are differing opinions as to whether this is actually a specific designation of the ritual language of the Temple or whether it applies to other situations also, especially the synagogue (Shinan 1993: 113–115).

[4] Carr (2005, 259) suggests that by 2 Macc 7 and 12:37, Hebrew has emerged as a marker of indigenous, anti-Hellenistic culture.

[5] The evidence is vast. See the articles collected in Fine 1999.

[6] Sot 7.2 continues with a list of ritual texts that may be recited only in Hebrew. Of these biblical and Temple-period rituals, only the priestly benediction had a continued life, in altered form, in the rabbinic liturgical system.

[7] Shab 12b continues to exclude prayers for the sick because the *Shekhinah* is with the sick, making angelic intercession unnecessary. Another exception is Rabbi's requirement in t.Sot 7.7 that *shema* be recited in Hebrew because Deut 6:6 specifies 'these words', i.e., the words of the biblical text as received. See the discussion of these texts in Hauptman (2005, 201–207), who suggests that the Tosefta is chronologically prior to our received Mishnah and that the Mishnah has thus excluded this opinion. See the discussion (Ber 40b) of whether a grace after meals in Aramaic, and hence deviating from the rabbinic formulation, is still adequate. See also my discussion of this in Langer (1998, 22–23). The preservation of the Mishnah's permissive stance has important implications for women's prayers in later times.

## Rabbinic Statutory Prayers

This is not to suggest that Hebrew and biblically influenced prayer was an innovation of the rabbis. Rather, they inherited the mode of scripturalized prayer language and elevated it above other received modes.[8] However, there is significant debate among scholars of Jewish liturgy as to when the texts of the statutory prayers reached their mature forms. Much of this debate centers around the degree of historical weight one gives to the narratives of talmudic and midrashic literature and how one reads these in conversation with extra-rabbinic evidence. Because I am increasingly of the opinion that the expansion of rabbinic prayer to non-rabbinic Jews was the catalyst that led to the fixing of rabbinic prayer texts and (most likely) the elimination of other alternative forms,[9] I push this date well into the amoraic period, perhaps as late as the fourth century. (See Langer 1999, 179–194 and the subsequent correspondence, Fleischer and Langer 2000, 380–387; and Langer 2004, 423–439. See also Sarason 2003, 165ff.)

Significant discussions about fixing prayer language indeed appear mostly in texts attributed to third-century Amoraim and later, suggesting that many then, even among the rabbis themselves, still understood there to be significant flexibility in the prayer texts. In this period we find not only the decisions about the precise formulation of a statutory *berakhah* (Ber 40b and parallels. See Langer 1998, 25–26), but also, and more importantly for our topic here, discussions of proper and improper ways to formulate elements of these prayers. That several of these discussions record the embedding of biblical language in these prayers suggests that the rabbis consciously understood this to be their liturgical ideal.

Hence, Ber 11b (compare p.Ber 2.4 4d) records that Rabbi Oshaiah (early 3rd cent. C.E.) began the first blessing before *Shema* in the morning, as became customary, by citing Isa 45:7a, יוצר אור ובורא חושך

---

[8] A fuller discussion of rabbinic liturgical language should also consider their less biblically derived more ecstatic linguistic modes, shared with Jewish mystical traditions.

[9] Current discussions about the liturgies found at Qumran suggest that they represent a variety of forms common among Second Temple-period Judaisms, and that these included various types but no universal system of communal prayer. There is no reason to believe that this variety disappeared with the destruction of the Temple. See Reif (2003, especially 148–148) and Sarason (2003, 151–172).

(forming light and creating darkness).[10] Although not a letter changes, this is not a verbatim citation. Thanks to the ambiguity of Hebrew participial forms, God's self-description in Isaiah is now a human third-person listing of divine powers. The *stam* (anonymous) gemara, perhaps several centuries later and presuming a freedom to adapt the language, then asks why not make the language more appropriate to this setting and read יוצר אור ובורא נוגה (forming light and creating brilliance)? The response is: we use the language of the verse. The logical question follows: why not continue to use the language of the verse? However, the liturgical language accepted by the time of the later layers of the gemara reads עושה שלום ובורא את הכל (who makes peace and creates everything) instead of Isaiah's ובורא רע (creates evil). So the gemara rather lamely answers: this is the more elevated language. Should this logic not apply to the first part of the verse too? No, for one needs to mention night in the daytime. The brief discussion of the next blessing that follows in the Babylonian Talmud also debates between biblical language, אהבת עולם (eternal love) as in Jer 31:3b, or a semantic but non-biblical equivalent, אהבה רבה (great love). Freedom to adapt verses thus exists, but by the late amoraic period is limited by received customs for specific prayers.

A similar dynamic lies behind an incident recorded in Ber 33b (comp. Meg 25a). We read:

> An anecdote about a person who went down [to lead the *amidah*] in the presence of Rabbi Ḥanina and prayed: The great, mighty and awesome and majestic and powerful, awful, strong, fearless, sure and honored God.
>
> [Rabbi Ḥanina] waited until he had finished, and when he had finished, he said to him: Have you completed *all* the praises of your Master? What is the purpose of all of these? These three that we recite, if Moses our teacher had not said them in the Torah, and had the Men of the Great Assembly not come and established them in the *Tefillah* (*amidah*), we would not even be able to recite these, but you recited all of them and still went on! This can be compared to a human king who had thousands of thousands of gold dinars but they praised him for his silver. Is this not an insult to him?

This student elaborated on the language of the *avot*, listing many attributes of God. Rabbi Ḥanina rebuked him, suggesting that the proper

---

[10] English translations of biblical verses are from or based upon those of the New Jewish Publication Society version.

language of the prayer was determined by Moses' own description of God in Deut 10:17 and established by received tradition. Any other list is theologically unsound. Thus, apparently by the early amoraic period, the rabbis voiced a real preference for Hebrew prayer language that explicitly pointed to biblical precedents.

This literary mode was not an invention of the rabbis, but rather continues a common form of Second Temple-period Hebrew prayer. Moshe Greenberg (1983, 45) insists that biblical people prayed, and they prayed in three modes as appropriate: with the prepared texts of the temple-poets; with spontaneous outpourings that conformed to conventional patterns for confession, petition, etc.; and with "unconventional and artless" prayers. Greenberg's second category is relevant here, suggesting that in addition to conventional patterns to which these spontaneous prayers cohered, biblical worshipers also at times employed received prayer language culled from existing Scriptures. Subsequent research refines this picture. Judith Newman (1999, 103–106; compare Boda 1999) demonstrates that this is precisely the mode by which Ezra's prayer in Neh 9 is constructed. In his synopsis of Israelite history, Ezra not only cites scriptural texts explicitly, both as references to their original contexts and also with transformed purposes, but he also knits together biblical language into new contexts, a phenomenon Newman labels as 'biblicizing' as opposed to the larger category of 'scripturalizing'. She also suggests (101–102, 107) that some of this language has become part of a liturgical idiom, no longer used with reference to its original context. Her example is precisely the language found in our last rabbinic example, Ezra's citation of God's attributes from Deut 10:17. While the rabbis explicitly refer back to the biblical precedent to insist on Moses' language, she suggests that Ezra is just using known prayer language. If Newman is correct, then, the apparent rabbinic insistence on a biblically driven precision may represent a discontinuity with the reality Newman describes and a critique of the Second-Temple period models that lie behind the precentor's formulation.

We can also point to the occurrence of this literary mode in many Qumran prayer texts, both sectarian and non-sectarian. Adele Berlin (2003, 2–3) describes a Qumran lament text (4Q179), saying:

> The style is overtly biblicizing, as are many poems and prayers in Qumran and beyond. Despite the fact that the poem is laced with biblical allusions, to such an extent that it is composed largely of a pastiche of biblical phrases, no biblical verse is quoted in its entirety. Moreover the biblical allusions are obvious but are not exact quotations.

Such prayers and hymns, she continues, 'use scriptural citations for many purposes: to embellish their literary art, to invoke the authority of tradition, and through subtle exegetical techniques, to drive home their message'. Studies of some other Qumran liturgical texts, the Hodayot hymns (Kittel 1981, esp. 48–55), Non-Canonical Psalms (Schuller 1986, esp. 32–34), and Words of the Luminaries (Chazon 1991, esp. 59–66) analyze this use of biblical language and propose schemes for categorizing it more precisely, distinguishing between quotations, allusions, and free use of accepted biblical idiom.[11] Brown (1993; 357–365, 384–392) demonstrates that these same modes appear in the Lucan Magnificat and Benedictus, two of the oldest hymns of the New Testament. Similar analysis of rabbinic prayer language is a desideratum, even in the absence of early prayer texts. Studies of methods of education in this world suggest that the emphasis on memorizing texts combined with the inherent difficulties involved in checking citations in scrolls contributed to a world where biblical language, especially biblical prayer language, created the cultural backdrop against which new liturgy was constructed without deep concern about precise citation (Carr 2005, 230f ).

Thus, even though the rabbis do not cite extra-biblical precedents for their liturgical literary mode, they clearly built on accepted norms. The central prayers of rabbinic liturgy all allude to biblical language while avoiding direct citations of complete verses, perhaps in accordance with the obscure prohibition only recorded in the Jerusalem Talmud (p.Ber 1.8 3d) אין אומרים ברכה פסוק, that one may not recite a biblical verse as a *berakhah*.[12] Table A demonstrates this method in the opening blessing of the *amidah*, the *avot*, where the prayer combines obvious partial citations, like in the opening lines, with more obscure allusions. Hardly a word of the prayer lacks a biblical echo. (Levi 1993 makes note of many but by no means all of the biblical allusions in the prayers.) Notice particularly how this explains the unusual opening of this prayer. At the burning bush in Exod 3, God specifically commands the Israelites to call upon Him by the name 'God of Abraham, God of Isaac, God of Jacob'. That this is indeed effective was proven when Moses calls God to

---

[11] Some Qumran liturgical texts rework extended biblical passages (Chazon 2003). This piece of the spectrum of possible uses of biblical materials does not characterize known rabbinic prayers.

[12] Note that the parallel in p.Taan 2.3 65c reads 'one should not recite a verse after the *berakhah*'. However, the ensuing discussion parallels that in Berakhot and both are sources of great confusion. See, for instance, Ginzberg (1941, 200–202) on the Berakhot text.

covenantal responsibility in the name of the patriarchs at the time of the Golden Calf (Exod 32:13). Rather than wonder, then, why this central prayer lacks the statutory blessing formula, one can instead explain this positive choice as a powerful covenantal move, highly appropriate for the invocation of relationship necessary to precede petitionary prayer (according to Greenberg's categories, 1983).

This sort of allusion to the Bible is of course also characteristic of much piyyut, where the allusion is often to the midrashic interpretation of the verse as well. Both genres fairly freely adjust the biblical language as needed to fit the grammar or the theological statement of the new composition. Hence, as we saw, the liturgy substitutes *hakol* (everything) for *ra* (evil) in the *yotzer* blessing's citation of Isaiah. Several explanations have been offered for this change. Jakob J. Petuchowski taught, following the Talmud, that this was simply the more appropriate language for prayer.[13] Others prefer the explanation that in a world where dualist claims were common, as among the Gnostics or Zoroastrians, it was problematic to identify God as creating evil without a parallel reference to God's creation of good (for instance, Hertz 1948, 109). Thus, the opening of this prayer maintains its biblical allusion to God as the powerful creator but does not slavishly adhere to the language of the rest of the verse, language that in the rabbinic context has become problematic.

## PRAYERS CONCATENATING BIBLICAL VERSES

Not all Jewish liturgical compositions based on the Bible retain this freedom. In a later set of texts, one complete, unaltered biblical verse follows immediately after another, ordered according to the message of the new composition. This may be related to, but is literarily distinct from, the concatenation of complete biblical pericopes, each of which retains its biblical compositional logic. It is also distinct from a cluster of prooftexts supporting a prior element of the composition, especially where these are introduced with citation formulae like 'as it is written'. It is certainly distinct from a lectionary where passages, however brief and interrelated, are recited as biblically authoritative texts.

---

[13] Liturgy I at Hebrew Union College—Jewish Institute of Religion, Cincinnati, October 20, 1983.

There has been almost no scholarly discussion of this genre, and what exists is dismissive. Elbogen (1993, 213–214) explains the adoption of this form as part of a failure of liturgical creativity in the late Amoraic or early Saboraic periods and a turn to develop prayers 'by the simplest possible methods', in this case 'by the use of biblical materials'. Elbogen and others have failed to perceive the beauty and complexity of this admittedly somewhat problematic form. In working towards an appreciation of this genre, several tasks await us: identification of its literary mode; a discussion of its history; and a detailed description of its characteristics.

Shelomo Tal, in his *Siddur Rinat Yisrael* (1976; 45, 47, 90 etc.), labels this form a *leket pesukim*, literally 'a gleaning of verses'. While this term well reflects these prayers' concatenation of verses from throughout the Bible, it fails to indicate anything about their compositional logic. The appropriate non-Hebrew label for this literary form is even less obvious. As we shall see, while the form best corresponds to the Latin *cento*, some expressions of it also have characteristics more like a *florilegium*.

*Cento* is the Latin word for 'patchwork,' and as a literary form, it refers to 'a composition formed by joining scraps from other authors'.[14] These patchwork compositions were common in the Latin-speaking world of Late Antiquity, where verses of Virgil's poetry were similarly concatenated into new compositions, sometimes of philosophical but also sometimes of pornographic content. Christians created religious versions beginning in the late fourth century to retell biblical narratives with Virgil's verses.[15] Whether Christians constructed such new compositions from biblical source materials deserves more study.[16] These ancient forms were indeed full compositions, constructing new meanings from the ancient verses.

*Florilegium*, the Latin for 'gathering together flowers', is a literal translation of the Greek word from which we receive the English 'anthology' (OED online). *Florilegia* anthologize important passages from literary works, often collecting passages that relate to a particular

---

[14] OED online, definition 2. From the Latin for 'a garment of patchwork'.

[15] The most comprehensive discussion of the cento in English is Verweyen and Witting (1991, 165–178). For the early Christian use of the form, see Margoni-Kögler (2001, 140–152). See also Schelkle (1934, 972–973); and Harrison (1996, 309).

[16] Manchester, John Rylands Library Gr. P. 8 and 9, both fifth-century Greek papyri from Egypt, are catalogued as containing biblical centos. However, these texts contain substantial intervening material between their biblical citations and imprecise citations, perhaps from memory (Hunt 1911, 15–18; Leclercq 1937, 1401–1402). Thanks to Daniel Stökl Ben-Ezra for the reference.

theme for didactic or polemical purposes (Chadwick 1969, 1131–1160; Mühlenberg & Brunhölzl 1983, 215–221). This form was common in the ancient world; many rabbinic collections, freestanding like the *Perek Hashalom* or embedded, fit this model. It was continued by the Church, but not necessarily in liturgical contexts. Qumran scholars have used this term rather than *cento* to describe our phenomenon when it appears within larger compositions (Chazon 62, 152f).

Although our liturgical texts concatenate verses, the literary form called a *catena*, Latin for a chain or connected series (OED on line, general definition), does not apply. This form is first documented in Christian literature only in the sixth century and particularly in the Byzantine world, but flourishes first in the High Middle Ages among the Scholastics (Mühlenberg 1989, 14–21). It consists of juxtaposed independent commentaries on individual biblical verses and not of collections of these verses themselves.

Our 'gleaning of verses' thus covers a range of literary structures, ranging from that of a biblical *cento* to that of a *florilegium* anthologizing verses containing a similar theme, or more frequently, similar language. For the most part, the *cento* is the primary form, and embedded within it and serving it, we find subsections consisting of *florilegia*. For the sake of simplicity, we will refer to these prayers as *centos*.

The Rabbanite *centos* appear exclusively in the elements of the liturgy that crystallized after the rabbinic statutory prayers and that are recited before and after them. We find them especially in the daily *pesukei d'zimra* (preliminary 'verses of song') and *tahanun* (supplicatory) prayers, in the penitential liturgies for the High Holy Day period (*selihot*), as the characteristic mode of the prayers accompanying the movements of the Torah scroll before and after its reading, as well as in parts of the *kedushah d'sidra* and the geonic *birkat hapesukim*, and as elaborations on shorter rituals, like the introduction to *havdalah* or the conclusion of the *birkat ha-mazon*. This list is not exhaustive. However, *centos* do not appear in any of the blessings of the *amidah*, the blessings surrounding the recitation of *shema* and the blessings of the *birkat ha-mazon*. Some have suggested that the geonic name *pesukei d'zimra* refers to this sort of composition rather than to the complete Psalms that the *centos* surround.[17]

---

[17] Reuven Kimelman, in a paper delivered at the 2004 conference of the Association for Jewish Studies and Joseph Yahalom in a discussion in 2001.

These locations suggest that, even if this compositional form was occasionally employed at Qumran, the heyday of such compositions began sometime around the late Amoraic period but before the emergence of Karaism as a force demanding rabbinic response. Karaite prayers, at least as we have received them, present *only* this compositional model (and taken to an extreme, at that) for non-biblical prayers. Given the strong opposition to Karaite practices voiced by liturgical authorities like Saadia Gaon (see the numerous discussions throughout Hoffman 1979, esp. 165ff), it is highly unlikely that the geonim would have accepted the borrowing of a Karaite liturgical form. *Centos* can be documented among geonic prayers, both in halakhic discussions and in geniza manuscripts from at least the ninth century (when our evidence begins).[18]

This is not to suggest that all *centos* are products of this period. Some are later compositions, and many expanded (or contracted) over time. Thus, the *centos* accompanying the movements of Torah in the Ashkenazi synagogue expand dramatically from the medieval into the modern periods (Langer 2005); other rites were apparently more stable, but their elaborations on this liturgy probably predate the manuscript evidence. The *cento* concluding *birkat ha-mazon* is present in the geniza texts only in the most inchoate form (According to Avi Shmidman. More study is needed.), and *yehi khavod* appears there in much shorter versions than those known later (Fleischer 1988; 189, 191, 238). *Shefokh hamatekha* varies greatly in its length, as does *mah tovu*. Other *centos* are apparently fully of kabbalistic (and hence later) origin, like the verses before sounding the *shofar* on Rosh Hashanah.[19]

The characteristics of this genre are best understood through reference to specific examples. Selected texts of these genres, generally the briefer exemplars, appear in Tables B through E, the first three representing Rabbanite forms, the last a comparatively brief Karaite

---

[18] *Pesukei d'zimra* as a liturgical unit can be documented only from the ninth century. Moshe Gaon (Sura, 829–839, according to Brody 1998, 344) is the author of the earliest attributed geonic discussion of responsibility to recite this liturgical element, and he shows greater flexibility still than Natronai and Amram half a century later, who present it as mandatory. See Emanuel, *Teshuvot Hageonim Hahadashot*, #137; Brody, *Teshuvot Rav Natronai Gaon* OH 11–12; *Seder Rav Amram Gaon* on this liturgical element (Bar Ilan CDROM). The *cento* beginning *yehi khavod* is mentioned in Massekhet Soferim 18:1 and 3 (Higger edition) and in the geniza (Fleischer 1988, 189 etc.), but the dating of *Soferim* is subject to much debate.

[19] Specific documentation of these impressions gleaned from leafing through liturgical manuscripts is a desideratum but beyond the scope of this paper.

prayer. *Yehi khavod* (Table B) is a psalm-like composition that precedes the daily recitation of Psalms 145–150 in the introductory section of the morning service (*pesukei d'zimra*); *va'anahnu lo neda* (Table C) comes from the supplicatory prayers (*tahanun*) following the weekday *amidah*. Both of these are tightly constructed *centos*. Table D presents a relatively free-standing *florilegium* that introduces Psalm 145. Table E, our Karaite exemplar, is a *cento* built from a series of interwoven *florilegia*. These examples will enable us to distinguish the characteristics of this mode of prayer composition.

The smallest linguistic unit of this genre is the complete biblical verse. We see this not only through the analysis of individual compositions, as shown in the tables, but also in the regular reappearance of the same verses in different compositions (not evident in our examples). Although clusters of verses from the same source occasionally appear within a composition (*yehi khavod*, line 2), such clusters also frequently appear in rearranged or disrupted order (*yehi khavod*, lines 8, 10, 11).[20] The exceptions to these generalizations prove the rule. Rarely, only part of a verse appears. In *va'anahnu lo neda*, which includes two half verses, the extreme brevity of this composition means that full citations would give overmuch weight to extraneous material. In our Karaite prayer, line 4, the omitted section is overly specific to the original setting of the verse, but this conclusion of the verse is a key text for this composition. In most other cases in our examples, only the superscription of a Psalm has been dropped.

These prayers also include a few recurring bible-like but non-biblical elements. A prime example of this is, 'The Eternal reigns, the Eternal reigned, the Eternal will reign for ever and ever' (*yehi khavod*, line 6). While the appearance of all individual phrases of this line in the Bible places this firmly in the world of biblical language, the phrases appear in the Bible neither together nor in unique locations. What distinguishes this from other biblicizing language is that it recurs only in *cento*-style prayers as if it were a verse (Langer 2003, 102); it is part of the standard vocabulary of this genre. This line appears as early as Ele'azar Ha-Qallir, around the time of the Arab conquest of Palestine, who uses it as the verse-like refrain structuring the first *rahit* of his *kedushta* for

---

[20] Compare the consistent ordering of Prov 3:18, 'She is a tree of life to those who grasp her...' before 3:17, 'Her ways are ways of pleasantness...' in the Ashkenazi and Sefardi Torah liturgies.

the first day of Rosh Hashanah (Davidson א 1132–1133). While Qallir does not always use a verse in this position, his predecessors seem to have.[21] While it is possible that his refrain led to the emergence of this 'pseudo-verse' as an independent entity, it seems more logical that the process was the reverse.

Communication through this concatenation of full verses is quite a challenge. But viewed within the context of classical piyyut, a contemporary genre, this becomes a positive intellectual challenge rather than a loss of creativity. Piyyut increasingly accumulated norms of stanza type, rhyme, meter, acrostic and biblical frameworks of various sorts within which the payyetan expressed his creativity. The heralded poet was one who created a work of beauty, demonstrating his cleverness through these constraints. Similarly, construction of a prayer from verbatim biblical materials demonstrated deep knowledge of Bible and a virtuoso ability to manipulate its texts. That gentiles also constructed *centos* of their revered texts certainly helped elevate the genre.

These biblical *centos* communicate in three different ways. The first is through the obvious meaning of the verse, now placed in this new composition. It is relatively rare for this method to be the only explanation for the liturgist's choice of a verse, though this is the best explanation of the concluding lines of our three Rabbanite exemplars.

The second method is characteristic of these *centos* in their most sophisticated forms. As in *yehi khavod* and *va'anahnu lo neda*, the verses generally relate one to the next by interlinking identical words or similar concepts from one verse to the next (underlined in the tables). It is the resulting chain of concepts that communicates the meaning of the composition. This technique has apparent precedent in the biblical period. Reuven Kimelman (1994) demonstrates that Psalm 145 also uses such chaining to communicate its message while organizing the verses according to its alphabetical acrostic. However, nothing suggests that Psalm 145 consists of verses culled verbatim from other compositions. In our prayers, this interlinking of concepts makes it impossible

---

[21] On the nature of the classical *rahit*, see: Fleischer 1975, 148–150, compare 170–171. My thanks also to Michael Rand for clarifying my understanding of this piyyut. As he points out, the lack of acrostic in this poem and the tendency to reuse older materials, substitute new ones, or expand on existing ones means that we cannot know for certain that Qallir is the author of this section of the *kedushta*, but its style suggests a Palestinian provenance. That Simeon bar Isaac (10th cent., Mainz) imitated this form in his *kedushta* (recited on the second day of Rosh Hashanah) suggests that he understood it to be part of the canon.

to construct an adequate narrative paraphrase of the *cento's* message. However, the underlined words suggest that *yehi khavod* begins with a praise of God's constant exaltation not only by the physical world, especially the heavens themselves, but also by all its inhabitants, over whom God reigns eternally. But because of God's special redemptive relationship with Israel, this divine sovereignty over the nations results in God's frustrating their plans, in favor of Israel's protection.[22] *Va'anahnu lo neda* in contrast, simply interlinks the words 'remember' and 'mercy', calling on God to remember to be merciful and compassionate because we humans are incapable by nature of overcoming those aspects of our natures that enrage God.

The third method of communication is characteristic of *florilegia*. These compositions simply collect verses that all begin with or contain a single word, thus constituting a meditation on a particular term. These compositions frequently appear embedded in or appended to *centos* and represent more an elaboration on the *centos'* compositional logic than something fully discrete. However, some are more or less freestanding. Our example here (Table D) is a composition that forms the introduction to Psalm 145, as found in the late 13th century rite of London. Here, the composition collects thirteen Psalms verses (of twenty five found in Pss and forty five in the entire Bible) beginning with or including *ashrei* (happy is...) as applied to Israel.[23] While the dominant Ashkenazi and Sefardi rites include only two verses at this point (lines 12–13), the Italian rite includes three (line 1; Luzzato 1856, 11a), often including them as the end of *yehi khavod* or not providing a visual break between *yehi khavod* and Psalm 145.[24] A geniza text of a Palestinian rite lists eight, not corresponding entirely to our list, but

---

[22] This has not been generally perceived. Rabinowitz (1997) suggests that *yehi khavod*'s organization is driven by a selection of verses from each of the books of the Psalter (except the second). Elbogen (1993; 75, 214) states that the 'tetragrammaton is the unifying principle'. If they are at all correct, they have at best identified secondary principles of composition.

[23] It is difficult to explain the inclusion of lines 10–11 here. They do not appear in other versions, and the theme of vengeance that they embody does not fit well in this context. Compare the text of *Mahzor Vitry*, from the closely related French rite. Goldschmidt's edition (2004, I: 106) lists fourteen or fifteen verses (the manuscripts disagree), including six verses not found in the London rite, all ordered differently except for the first two and concluding verses.

[24] In many manuscripts. See also the facsimile version of a Persian rite (Tal 1980, 38), which begins a paragraph with lines 15 and 16 of *yehi khavod* followed by our *ashrei* text's line 12, Ps 140:14, then line 13 and Psalm 145.

here purely as an introduction to Psalm 145 and in the context of a manuscript providing *cento*-like (but not *florilegia*) introductions to Pss 135 on, probably originally through the end of the Psalter (Fleischer 1988, 283). The European texts apparently reflect a tradition of elaborating on the final verse of Ps 144 (line 13) as a paean of praise beginning the daily recitation of Psalms. Other freestanding examples of *florilegia* are common in the *seliḥot*, like the prayer that begins *zekhor raḥamekha*, in today's Ashkenazi rite containing eight verses, all but one beginning 'remember!'.

These texts direct our attention to places where such *florilegia* are embedded in *centos*. In the rituals surrounding the reading of Torah, various rites collect verses beginning with קומה ה' (Arise, O Eternal!). The most expansive version of this, nine verses, appears in the *shevaḥot* of the Italian rite for the eighth day of Passover, the second day of Shavuot, and Shemini Aẓeret.[25] Such a pattern also appears in Karaite liturgy. In our example, Table E, note the appearance of *barekhu* (bless!) or *barukh* (blessed), sometimes multiple times, in lines 1–4, 7–8 (with some other variants of the verbs in additional lines); or of variants on the Hebrew roots for listening in lines 14, 17–25, 27–31, 41–45. This prayer is the equivalent of the rabbinic call to prayer (*barekhu*) preceding the recitation of at least the first verse of *shema*, line 45. Thus, this *cento* (and much of Karaite liturgy) reinforces its meaning by multiplication, sometimes to the extreme, of verses employing the same word, i.e., of *florilegia*. Here, the interlinking native to the *cento* loses its subtlety.

The consequence of this reliance on verse-length linguistic units is that these prayers often include words and phrases that are probably not part of the prayer's message. The rabbinic prayers in the tables are actually very tightly composed and successful examples that do not necessarily represent the norm. Our Karaite example, Table E, line 7, contains an excellent demonstration of this problem. This morning prayer, in its cluster of verses calling on Israel to bless God, includes a verse that refers to those gathered at night! A similar phenomenon appears in rabbinic liturgies for taking the Torah out of the ark. Both the Ashkenazi and Sefardi rites include Num 10:35, 'When the ark journeyed, Moses said: Arise, O Eternal, may those who hate you be

---

[25] Luzzato (1856, 126b ff) included this elaborate ritual, though without any special title for it. It does appear regularly (though not universally) in manuscripts and editions to that point, but no contemporary printings of Italian-rite prayer books preserve it.

scattered, and may Your enemies flee before You.' The Ashkenazi rite introduced this verse in the medieval period to accompany the actual removal of the Torah from the ark, thus constructing an analogy between the biblical Torah's movements away from Sinai with the people and liturgical moment in the synagogue. In this context, this situational analogy matters, but Moses' actual word's addressed to God add nothing. However, in the Sefardi and Italian rites, this verse appears before another that also calls on God to rise up and deliver Israel; there, the opening of the verse is essentially irrelevant (Langer 2005, 136–141). Thus, understanding these prayers sometimes requires excluding parts of verses as extraneous to the composition's message. Clues to this arise from discerning the compositional logic of the interlinked meanings of the *cento*, sometimes as elaborated upon in the more anthological *florilegium* structure.

If this form emerged in the liturgy of the late-amoraic or early geonic periods, as we posited above, where might it have come from and why did it develop? My answers to these questions are speculative at best. As far as I have been able to determine, there is no real precedent for this literary form in earlier Jewish liturgies. The *florilegia* that have been named as such at Qumran fall more into the category of exegetical literature than liturgy and contain much non-biblical text. The few *centos* appearing in liturgies are not free-standing compositions and are brief. The verses that constitute the core of the Rosh Hashanah *musaf* additions, the *malkhiyot, zikhronot, and shofarot,* are loose lists of proof texts more than a composition, as indicated by the tannaitic requirement that they be presented clustered according to their biblical source rather than by meaning (RH 4.6 and t.RH 2.12), by the freedom to choose alternative texts, and by the citation formulae preceding the verses in actual practice. The same can be said of the clusters of verses concluding the first three poems of the classical *kedushta*. The comparatively extended biblical passages of the *shema* constitute study texts in their own right, though they do indeed have the sorts of thematic connections one to the other that we see in the individual verses of the liturgical *cento*. It is possible that these various sorts of precedents merge in this genre, but fundamentally, we see here the appearance of something apparently new to Hebrew prayer.[26]

---

[26] Of course, the possibility exists that the precedents lie in a perhaps non-rabbinic liturgical form not preserved for us.

Are there outside influences? The parallels to the Latin *cento* and *florilegium* suggest some possible Hellenistic cultural influence. However, if my dating is correct, this prayer form may emerge among Jews in the period of early Islam. Islamic prayer relies entirely on the language of the Quran, not through an equivalent to the scripturalizing discussed here, but through precise recitation of complete suras, more a reuse of received prayers. The Quranic suras range widely in length. Might Jews have perceived their literary equivalent to be the biblical verse? If so, some of the motivation in turning to this form would also be a sense that one must use properly formulated revealed language in turning to God, as Muslims do, and the best, most authoritative source of this is the Bible itself.

I leave the search for parallels of significance in the Christian liturgical world to historians of Christian liturgy. Consultations with experts on various early rites have not yielded rich results but rather isolated examples or examples from areas unlikely to have influenced rabbinic prayer. Jewish and Christian prayer do share a reliance on Scripture, but mostly expressed via the earlier mode of adapting of biblical language and not in this later strict concatenation of verse-length units. Robert Taft suggests that Christian liturgy similarly moves from this free use of Scriptures to the introduction of strict citations. He and other colleagues[27] suggested a list of individual prayers worth consideration ranging geographically from the Roman to the East Syrian rites, but they could not point to a systematic appearance of this literary mode, at least not from a community sharing a cultural sphere with rabbinic Judaism.

To mention one example, the East Syrian Epiphany rites contain a single *cento*, called that by the modern editor, that collects, in the order of their appearance in the Psalter, all the verses that refer to water in one way or another, followed by a few verses from elsewhere in the Bible. However, this is more a collection of verses organized by its source than a new liturgical composition trying to communicate its own meaning (MacLean in Conybeare 1905, 369–373).[28] As it is plausible that this form arose among Babylonian Jews, though, some shared

---

[27] At the Aachen conference where this paper was first presented and in the North American Academy of Liturgy's seminar on 'Problems in the Early History of the Liturgy,' San Diego, January 2006.

[28] My thanks to Clemens Leonhard for locating this text.

cultural realm is possible. However, it would be erroneous to look for parallels only in the Jewish Babylonian context.

Thus, the emergence of this genre seems to reflect an intensification of that which led the rabbis to turn to Hebrew rather than vernacular prayer, and to pray in biblically informed language rather than in free composition. We can understand it to be a product of a confluence of factors: an elevation of Scripture like the Muslim elevation of Quran; the employment of the Hellenistic *cento* and *florilegium* literary forms; perhaps some similar move among eastern Christians; and perhaps some degree of insecurity about the efficacy of humanly-produced prayers in an era when the texts of the rabbinic statutory prayers were themselves increasingly authoritative and sanctified. The result is a new mode of biblically influenced prayers, one that shapes the medieval Jewish prayer book profoundly.

## LITERATURE

Berlin, A., 'Qumran Laments and the Study of Lament Literature', in: E. Chazon (ed.), *Liturgical Perspectives; Prayer and Poetry in Light of the Dead Sea Scrolls* (StTDJ 48), Leiden—Boston 2003.

Boda, M.J., *Praying the Tradition; The Origin and Use of Tradition in Nehemiah 9*, Berlin—New York 1999.

Brody, I. (ed.), *Rabbi Jacob ben Jehuda Hazan of London; The Etz Hayyim*, Jerusalem 1962.

Brody, R., *The Geonim of Babylonia and the Shaping of Medieval Jewish Culture*, New Haven—London 1998.

Brown, R.E., *The Birth of the Messiah; A Commentary on the Infancy Narratives in the Gospels of Matthew and Luke*, New York, etc. updated ed. 1993.

Carr, D.M., *Writing on the Tablet of the Heart; Origins of Scripture and Literature*, New York 2005.

Chadwick, H., 'Florilegium', in: *RAC* 7 (1969).

Chazon, E.G., *A Liturgical Document from Qumran and its Implications; 'Words of the Luminaries' (4QDibHam)*, Ph.D. dissertation, Hebrew University, Jerusalem 1991 [Hebrew].

———, 'The Use of the Bible as a Key to Meaning in Psalms from Qumran' in: Sh.M. Paul, R.A. Kraft, L.H. Schiffman, & W.W. Fields (eds), *Emanuel; Studies in Hebrew Bible, Septuagint, and Dead Sea Scrolls in Honor of Emanuel Tov*, Leiden—Boston 2003.

Conybeare, F.C. (ed.) & A.J. MacLean (trans.), *Rituale Armenorum... together with the Greek Rites of Baptism and Epiphany... and the East Syrian Epiphany Rites*, Oxford 1905.

Davidson, I., *Thesaurus of Medieval Hebrew Poetry*, New York [reprint] 1970.

Elbogen, I. & R.P. Scheindlin (transl.), *Jewish Liturgy; A Comprehensive History*, Philadelphia—Jerusalem—New York 1993.

Fine, St. (ed.), *Jews, Christians, and Polytheists in the Ancient Synagogue; Cultural Interaction during the Greco-Roman Period*, London—New York 1999.

Fleischer, E. & R. Langer, 'Controversy', *Prooftexts* 20.3 (2000).

Fleischer, E., *Eretz-Israel Prayer and Prayer Rituals as Portrayed in the Geniza Documents*, Jerusalem 1988 [Hebrew].

———, *Hebrew Liturgical Poetry in the Middle Ages*, Jerusalem 1975 [Hebrew].

Ginzberg, L., *A Commentary on the Palestinian Talmud* [vol. 1], New York 1941 [Hebrew].

Goldschmidt, A., *Maḥzor Vitry*, Jerusalem 2004 [Hebrew].

Greenberg, M., *Biblical Prose Prayer as a Window to the Popular Religion of Ancient Israel*, Berkeley—Los Angeles—London 1983.

Harrison, St.J., 'cento', in: S. Hornblower & A. Spawforth (eds), *Oxford Classical Dictionary*, Oxford—New York, 3rd edition 1996.

Hauptman, J., *Rereading the Mishnah: A New Approach to Ancient Jewish Texts*, Tübingen 2005.

Hertz, J.H., *The Authorised Daily Prayer Book*, New York revised edition 1948 [reprint 1982].

Hoffman, L.A., *The Canonization of the Synagogue Service*, Notre Dame—London 1979.

Hunt, A.S. (ed), *Catalogue of the Greek Papyri in the John Rylands Library Manchester* [vol. I], Manchester, 1911.

Kimelman, R., 'Psalm 145: Theme, Structure, and Impact', *JBL* 113 (1994).

Kittel, B.P., *The Hymns of Qumran; Translation and Commentary*, SBL.DS 50, Chico 1981.

Langer, R., 'Early Medieval Celebrations of Torah in the Synagogue: A Study of the Rituals of the Seder Rav Amram Gaon and Massekhet Soferim', *Kenishta: Studies of the Synagogue World* 2 (2003) [Hebrew].

———, 'Early Rabbinic Liturgy in Its Palestinian Milieu: Did Non-Rabbis Know the 'Amidah?' in: D. Harrington, A.J. Avery-Peck, & J. Neusner (eds), *When Judaism and Christianity Began; Essays in Memory of Anthony J. Saldarini* [vol. II]; *Judaism and Christianity in the Beginning*, Leiden—Boston 2004.

———, 'Revisiting Early Rabbinic Liturgy: The Recent Contributions of Ezra Fleischer', *Prooftexts* 19 (1999).

———, 'Sinai, God and Zion in the Synagogue: Celebrating Torah in Ashkenaz', in: R. Langer & S. Fine (eds), *Liturgy and the Life of the Synagogue*, Winona Lake, IN 2005.

———, *To Worship God Properly; Tensions Between Liturgical Custom and Halakhah in Judaism*, Cincinnati 1998.

Leclercq, H., 'Papyrus', in *DACL* 13 (1937).

Levi, E., *Torat Hatefillah; Tokhnah Umahutah, Dineiha Umizvoteha, Minhageihah Umeqoroteihah*, Jerusalem 1993 [Hebrew].

Luzzato, Sh.D., *Mahzor Kol Hashanah kefi Minhag Q"Q Italiani*, Livorno 1856.

Margoni-Kögler, M., 'Typologie in den christlichen Vergilcentonen', *StPatr* 36 (2001).

Mühlenberg, E., 'Katenen', *TRE* 18 (1989).

——— & F. Brunhölzl, 'Florilegien', in: *TRE* 11 (1983).

Newman, J.H., *Praying by the Book; The Scripturalization of Prayer in Second Temple Judaism*, Atlanta 1999.

Rabinowitz, L., 'Psalms: In the Liturgy, Statutory Prayers', *EJ* (CD-ROM 1.0, 1997).

Reif, St.C., 'The Second Temple Period, Qumran Research, and Rabbinic Liturgy: Some Contextual and Linguistic Comparisons', in: see A. Berlin 2003.

Sarason, R.S., 'Communal Prayer at Qumran and Among the Rabbis: Certainties and Uncertainties', in: see A. Berlin 2003.

Schelkle, K.H., 'Cento', *RAC* 2 (1934).

Schuller, E.M., *Non-Canonical Psalms from Qumran; A Pseudepigraphic Collection* (HSS), Atlanta 1986.

Schwartz, S., 'Language, Power and Identity in Ancient Palestine', *PaP* 148 (1995).

*Seder Hatefillot Keminhag Hayehudim Haqaraim* [Part I], Ramle 1989.

Shinan, A., *The Embroidered Targum; The Aggadah in Targum Pseudo-Jonathan of the Pentateuch*, Jerusalem 1993 [Hebrew].

Tal, Sh., *The Persian Jewish Prayer Book; A Facsimile Edition of MS ADLER ENA 23...*, Jerusalem 1980 [Hebrew].

———, *Siddur Rinat Yisrael, Nusah Ashkenaz* [Hebrew], Jerusalem 1976.

Verweyen, Th. & G. Witting, 'The Cento: A Form of Intertextuality from Montage to Parody', in: H.F. Plett (ed.), *Intertextuality*, Berlin—New York 1991.

Table A. *Avot*

| | |
|---|---|
| שמות ג, טו: ויאמר עוד א-להים אל משה כה תאמר אל בני ישראל ה' א-להי אבותיכם א-להי אברהם א-להי יצחק וא-להי יעקב שלחני אליכם, זה שמי לעלם וזה זכרי לדר דר. | וא-להי אבותינו א-להי אברהם א-להי יצחק וא-להי יעקב |
| Exod 3:15 And God said further to Moses, 'Thus shall you speak to the Israelites: The Eternal, *the God of your fathers, the God of Abraham, the God of Isaac, and the God of Jacob*, has sent me to you: This shall be my name forever, this my appellation for all eternity'. | and God of our ancestors, the God of Abraham, the God of Isaac, and the God of Jacob |
| מלכים א יח, לו: ויהי בעלות המנחה ויגש אליהו הנביא ויאמר ה' א-להי אברהם יצחק וישראל... | |
| 1 Kgs 18:36 When it was time to present the meal offering, the prophet Elijah came forward and said, 'O Eternal, God of Abraham, Isaac, and Israel!... | (= citation with syntactic adjustment to liturgical context) |
| דברים י, יז: כי ה' א-להיכם הוא א-להי הא-להים ואדני האדונים הא-ל הגדול הגבר והנורא אשר לא ישא פנים ולא יקח שוחד. | הא-ל הגדול הגבור והנורא |
| Deut 10:17 For the Eternal your God is God supreme and Lord Supreme, *the great, the mighty, and the awesome God*, who shows no favor and takes no bribe... | the great, the mighty, and the awesome God<br><br>(= citation) |
| בראשית יד, יט: ויברכהו ויאמר ברוך אברם לא-ל עליון קנה שמים וארץ. | א-ל עליון |
| Gen 14:19 He (King Melchizedek) blessed him, saying, 'Blessed be Abram of *God Most High*, Creator of Heaven and Earth.' | God Most High<br><br>(= citation) |
| ישעיה סג, ז: <u>חסדי</u> ה' אזכיר תהלות ה' כעל כל אשר <u>גמלנו</u> ה' ורב <u>טוב</u> לבית ישראל אשר <u>גמלם</u> כרחמיו וכרוב <u>חסדיו</u>. | גומל חסדים טובים |
| Isa 63:7 I will recount the *kind acts* of the Eternal, the praises of the Eternal—for all that the Eternal *has wrought* for us, the vast *bounty* to the House of Israel that He *bestowed* upon them according to his mercy and His great *kindness*. | who performs acts of tender goodness<br><br>(= allusion) |

Table A (*cont.*)

| | |
|---|---|
| בראשית יד, יט: ויברכהו ויאמר ברוך אברם לא-ל עליון קונה שמים וארץ.<br><br>Gen 14:19 He (King Melchizedek) blessed him, saying, 'Blessed be Abram of God Most High, *Creator of Heaven and Earth*'. | וקונה הכל<br><br>and is Master/Creator of all<br><br>(= allusion/ citation when combined with reference above. Palestinian rite was a precise citation.) |
| ירמיה ב, ב: זכרתי לך חסד נעוריך אהבת כלולותיך לכתך אחרי במדבר בארץ לא זרועה.<br><br>Jer 2:2 I *accounted to your favor the devotion* of your youth, your love as a bride, how you followed Me in the wilderness in a land not sown.<br><br>ויקרא כו, מה: וזכרתי להם ברית ראשונים אשר הוצאתי אותם מארץ מצרים לעיני הגוים להיות להם לא-להים אני ה'.<br><br>Lev 26:45 I *will remember in their favor* the covenant with the ancients, whom I freed from the land of Egypt in the sight of the nations to be their God: I, the Eternal. | וזוכר חסדי אבות<br><br>who is mindful of the loving piety of our ancestors<br><br><br><br>(= allusion) |
| ישעיה נט, כ: ובא לציון גואל ולשבי פשע ביעקב נאום ה'.<br>Isa 59:20 *A redeemer shall come* to Zion, to those in Jacob who turn back from sin, declares the Eternal.<br><br>תהילים קג, יז-יח: וחסד ה' מעולם ועד עולם על יראיו וצדקתו לבני בנים לשומרי בריתו...<br><br>Ps 103:17–18 But the Eternal's *kindness* is for all eternity to those who revere Him, and His beneficence is for the *children's children* of those who keep His *covenant*...<br><br>תהילים עט, ט: עזרנו אלהי ישענו על דבר כבוד שמך והצילנו וכפר על חטאתינו למען שמך.<br><br>Ps 79:9 Help us, O God, our deliverer, for the sake of the glory of your name. Save us and forgive our sin, *for the sake of Your name*. | ומביא גואל לבני בניהם למען שמו באהבה<br><br><br><br>and for His name's sake, He will lovingly bring a redeemer to their children's children<br><br><br><br>(= free use of biblical language, vaguely allusive) |
| תהילים יח, לו: ותתן לי מגן ישעך וימינך תסעדני וענותך תרבני (השוה ש"ב כב, לו)<br><br>Ps 18:36 You have given me the *shield of your salvation*, Your right hand has sustained me, Your care has made me great. (comp. 2 Sam 22:36) | מלך עוזר ומושיע ומגן<br><br>King who helps, saves, and shields |

Table A *(cont.)*

| | |
|---|---|
| תהילים עט, ט: עזרנו אלהי ישענו על דבר כבוד שמך<br>והצילנו וכפר על חטאתינו למען שמך<br><br>Ps 79:9 *Help* us, O God, our *savior*, for the sake of the glory of your name. Save us and forgive our sin, for the sake of Your name. | (= free use of biblical language, vaguely allusive) |
| בראשית טו, א: ...אל תירא אברם אנכי מגן לך שכרך<br>הרבה מאד<br><br>Gen 15:1 ...Fear not, *Abram, I am a shield to you*; your reward shall be very great. | בא"י מגן אברהם<br><br>Blessed are You, Eternal, shield of Abraham.<br>(= allusion) |

## Table B. *Yehi Khavod*

| | | |
|---|---|---|
| יהי כבוד ה' לעולם ישמח<br>ה' במעשיו. | 1.<br>Ps 104:31 | Let the glory of the Eternal be forever, may the Eternal rejoice in His works. |
| יהי שם ה' מברך מעתה<br>ועד עולם. | 2.<br>Ps 113:2–4 | Let the name of the Eternal be blessed, from now evermore. |
| ממזרח שמש עד מבואו<br>מהלל שם ה'. | | From the rising of the sun to its going down, praised be the name of the Eternal. |
| רם על כל גוים ה' על<br>השמים כבודו. | | Supreme above all nations is the Eternal, His glory is above the heavens. |
| ה' שמך לעולם ה' זכרך<br>לדר ודר. | 3.<br>Ps 135:13 | 'Eternal' is Your name forever, 'Eternal' is Your appellation for all generations. |
| ה' בשמים הכין כסאו<br>ומלכותו בכל משלה. | 4.<br>Ps 103:19 | The Eternal has established His throne in the heavens and His reign has sway over all. |
| ישמחו השמים ותגל<br>הארץ ויאמרו בגוים ה'<br>מלך. | 5.<br>1 Chr 16:31 | Let the heavens rejoice and the earth be glad, and among the nations be it declared, "The Eternal reigned." |
| ה' מלך ה' מלך ה' ימלוך<br>לעולם ועד. | 6. | The Eternal reigns, the Eternal reigned, the Eternal will reign forever and ever. |
| ה' מלך עולם ועד, אבדו<br>גוים מארצו. | 7.<br>Ps 10:16 | The Eternal reigns forever and ever; the nations shall have then vanished from His earth. |
| ה' הפיר עצת גוים, הניא<br>מחשבות עמים. | 8.<br>Ps 33:10 | The Eternal frustrates the counsel of nations, He voids the thoughts of peoples. |
| רבות מחשבות בלב איש<br>ועצת ה' היא תקום. | 9.<br>Prov 19:21 | Many are the thoughts in the heart of man, but the counsel of the Eternal, that shall stand. |

Table B (*cont.*)

| | | |
|---|---|---|
| עֵצַת ה' לעולם תעמוד, מחשבות לבו לדור ודור. | 10. Ps 33:11 | The counsel of the Eternal stands forever, the thoughts of His heart to all generations. |
| כִּי הוא אמר ויהי, הוא צוה ויעמוד. | 11. Ps 33:9 | For it was He who spoke and it was, He who commanded and it stood forth. |
| כִּי בחר ה' בציון, אוה למושב לו. | 12. Ps 132:13 | For the Eternal has chosen Zion, He desired it for His habitation. |
| כִּי יעקב בחר לו י-ה, ישראל לסגלתו. | 13. Ps. 135:4 | For the Eternal has chosen Jacob for Himself, Israel for His own possession. |
| כִּי לא יטש ה' עמו, ובנחלתו לא יעזב. | 14. Ps 44:14 | For the Eternal will not cast off His people, nor forsake His heritage. |
| והוא רחום יכפר עון ולא ישחית, והרבה להשיב אפו, ולא יעור כל חמתו. | 15. Ps 78:38 | He, being merciful, forgives iniquity and destroys not, yea many times He turns away His anger and awakens His wrath not at all. |
| ה' הושיעה, המלך יעננו ביום קראנו. | 16. Ps 20:10 | Eternal, save us; may the Sovereign answer us on the day we call. |

### Table C.  *Va'anaḥnu Lo Neda (Taḥanun)*

| | | |
|---|---|---|
| ואנחנו לא נדע מה נעשה כי עליך עינינו. | 1. 2 Chr 20:12b | We do not know what to do, but our eyes are on You. (Jehoshaphat's prayer for help during war) |
| זכור רחמיך ה' וחסדיך כי מעולם המה. | 2. Ps 25:6 | O Eternal, remember Your compassion and Your faithful care; they are from eternity. |
| יהי חסדך ה' עלינו כאשר יחלנו לך. | 3. Ps 33:22 | May we enjoy, O Eternal, Your faithful care, as we have put our hope in You. |
| אל תזכר לנו עונות ראשונים מהר יקדמונו רחמיך כי דלונו מאד. | 4. Ps 79:8 | Do not remember our former iniquities against us; let Your compassion come swiftly toward us, for we have sunk very low. |
| חננו ה' חננו כי רב שבענו בוז. | 5. Ps 123:3 | Show us favor, O Eternal, show us favor! We have had more than enough of contempt. |
| ברוגז רחם תזכור. | 6. Hab 3:2d | Though angry, may You remember compassion. |
| כי הוא ידע יצרנו זכור כי עפר אנחנו. | 7. Ps 103:14 | For He knows how we are formed; He remembers that we are dust. |
| עזרנו א-להי ישענו על דבר כבוד שמך והצילנו וכפר על חטאתינו למען שמך. | 8. Ps 79:9 | Help us, O God, our deliverer, for the sake of the glory of Your name. Save us and forgive our sin, for the sake of your name. |

## Table D. An *Ashrei* Florilegium[29]

|  |  |  |
|---|---|---|
| אשרי תמימי דרך ההולכים<br>בתורת ה'. | 1.<br>Ps 119:1 | Happy are those whose way is blameless, who follow the teaching of the Eternal. |
| אשרי נוצרי עדותיו בכל לב<br>ידרשוהו. | 2.<br>Ps 119:2 | Happy are those who observe His decrees, who turn to Him wholeheartedly. |
| אשרי אדם עוז לו בך<br>מסילות בלבבם. | 3.<br>Ps 84:6 | Happy is the one who finds refuge in You, whose mind is on the [pilgrim] highways. |
| אשרי העם יודעי תרועה ה'<br>באור פניך יהלכון. | 4.<br>Ps 89:16 | Happy is the people who know the joyful shout; O Eternal, they walk in the light of Your presence. |
| אשרי תבחר ותקרב ישכן<br>חצריך נשבעה בטוב ביתיך<br>קדוש היכליך. | 5.<br>Ps 65:5 | Happy is the one You choose and bring near to dwell in Your courts; may we be sated with the blessings of Your house. |
| אשרי אדם לא יחשוב ה' לו<br>עון ואין ברוחו רמיה. | 6.<br>Ps 32:2 | Happy is the one who the Eternal does not hold guilty, and in whose spirit there is no deceit. |
| אשרי נשוי פשע כסוי<br>חטאה. | 7.<br>Ps 32:1b | Happy is the one whose transgression is forgiven, whose sin is covered over. |
| אשרי האיש אשר לא<br>הלך בעצת רשעים ובדרך<br>חטאים לא עמד ובמושב<br>לצים לא ישב. | 8.<br>Ps 1:1 | Happy is the one who has not followed the counsel of the wicked, or taken the path of sinners, or joined the company of the insolent. |
| אשרי שומרי משפט עושה<br>צדקה בכל עת. | 9.<br>Ps 106:3 | Happy are those who act justly, who do right at all times. |
| בת בבל השדודה אשרי<br>שישלם לך את גמולך<br>שגמלת לנו | 10.<br>Ps 137:8 | Fair Babylon, you predator, happy is the one who repays you in kind what you have inflicted on us; |
| אשרי שיאחז ונפץ את<br>עולליך אל הסלע. | 11.<br>Ps 137:9 | Happy is the one who seizes your babies and dashes them against the rocks! |
| אשרי יושבי ביתך עוד<br>יהללוך סלה. | 12.<br>Ps 84:5 | Happy are those who dwell in Your house; they forever praise you. Selah. |
| אשרי העם שככה לו אשרי<br>העם שה' א-להיו. | 13.<br>Ps 144:15 | Happy is the people who have it so; Happy the people whose God is the Eternal. |

---

[29] Brody 1962; I 76.

## Table E.  A Karaite Prayer from the Sabbath Morning Liturgy[30]

|  |  |  |
|---|---|---|
| :ותקום ותאמר היחוד במורא ופחד | | *Stand and recite the 'Unification' in awe and fear:* |
| ממלכות הארץ שירו לא-להים זמרו א-דני סלה. | 1. Ps 68:33–36 | O **kingdoms** of the earth, sing to God, chant hymns to the Eternal, selah |
| לרוכב בשמי שמי קדם הן יתן בקולו קול עו. | | To Him who rides the ancient highest heavens, who thunders forth with His mighty voice. |
| תנו עוז לא-להים על ישראל גאותו ועוזו בשחקים. | | Ascribe might to God, whose majesty is over Israel, whose might is in the skies. |
| נורא א-להים ממקדשך א-ל ישראל הוא נותן עוז ותעצמות לעם ברוך א-להים | | You are awesome, O God, in Your holy places; it is the God of Israel who gives might and power to the people. Blessed is God. |
| קומו ברכו את ה' א-להיכם | 2. Neh 9:5b | Rise, bless the Eternal your God |
| *או תאמר זה:* | | *Or recite this:* |
| בית ישראל ברכו את ה' בית אהרן ברכו את ה'. בית הלוי ברכו את ה' יראי ה' ברכו את ה'. | 3. Ps 135:19–20 | O **house** of Israel, bless the Eternal; O house of Aaron, bless the Eternal; O house of Levi, bless the Eternal, you who fear the Eternal, bless the Eternal. |
| קומו ברכו את ה' א-להיכם מן העולם עד העולם ויברכו שם כבודך ומרומם על כל ברכה ותהלה. | 4. Neh 9:5b,c | **Rise**, bless the Eternal your God who is from eternity to eternity, "May Your glorious Name be blessed, exalted though it is above every blessing and praise. |
| כן בקודש חזיתיך לראות עוזך וכבודך. | 5. Ps 63:3–5 | I shall behold You in the Holy [place] and see Your might and glory. |
| כי טוב חסדך מחיים שפתי ישבחונך. | | Truly Your faithfulness is better than life; my lips declare Your praise. |
| בן אברכך בחיי בשמך אשא כפי. | | **So too**, I bless You during my life, I lift up my hands, invoking Your name. |

[30] *Seder Hatefillot* 1989, 172–176.

Table E (*cont.*)

| | | |
|---|---|---|
| נחפשה דרכינו ונחקורה ונשובה עד ה'. | 6.<br>Lam 3:40–41 | **Let us search** and examine our ways, and turn back to the Eternal. |
| נשא לבבנו אל כפים אל א-ל בשמים. | | Let us lift up our hearts with our hands to God in heaven |
| הנה ברכו את ה' כל עבדי ה' העומדים בבית ה' בלילות. | 7.<br>Ps 134:1–2 | Now bless the Eternal, all you servants of the Eternal, who stand nightly in the house of the Eternal. |
| שאו ידיכם קודש וברכו את ה'. | | Lift your hands toward the sanctuary and bless the Eternal. |
| ברכו עמים א-להינו והשמיעו קול תהלתו.<br>השם נפשנו בחיים ולא נתן למוט רגלנו. | 8.<br>Ps 66:8–9 | O peoples, bless our God, celebrate His praises who has granted us life and has not let our feet slip. |
| עיני תמיד אל ה' כי הוא יוציא מרשת רגלי. | 9.<br>Ps 25:15 | My eyes are ever toward the Eternal, for He will loose my feet from the net. |
| רגלי עמדה במישור במקהלים אברך ה'. | 10.<br>Ps 26:12 | My feet are on level ground. In assemblies I will bless the Eternal. |
| במקהלות ברכו א-להים א-דני ממקור ישראל. | 11.<br>Ps 68:27 | In assemblies bless God, the Eternal, O you who are from the fountain of Israel. |
| פנו אלי והושעו כל אפסי ארץ כי אני א-ל ואין עוד. | 12.<br>Isa 45:22–25 | Turn to Me and be redeemed, all the ends of the earth! For I am God and there is none else. |
| בי נשבעתי יצא מפי צדקה דבר ולא ישוב כי לי תכרע כל ברך תשבע כל לשון. | | By Myself have I sworn, from my mouth has issued truth, a word that shall not turn back: to Me every knee shall bend, every tongue swear loyalty. |
| אך בה' לי אמר צדקות ועוז עדיו יבוא ויבשו כל הנחרים בו. | | They shall say, "Only through the Eternal can I find victory and might. When people trust in Him all their adversaries are put to shame. |
| בה' יצדקו ויתהללו כל זרע ישראל. | | It is through the Eternal that all the offspring of Israel have vindication and glory. |

Table E (*cont.*)

|  |  |  |
|---|---|---|
| יראי ה' הללוהו כל זרע יעקב כבדוהו וגורו ממנו כל זרע ישראל. | 13. Ps 22:24 | You who fear the Eternal, praise Him! All you offspring of Jacob, honor Him! Be in dread of Him, all you offspring of Israel! |
| שומע תפלה עדיך כל בשר יבואו. | 14. Ps 65:3 | You who hears prayer, all humanity comes to You. |
| כי שומע אל אביונים ה' ואת אסיריו לא בזה. | 15. Ps 69:34 | For the Eternal listens to the needy and does not spurn His captives. |
| פנה אל תפלת הערער ולא בזה את תפלתם. | 16. Ps 102:18 | He has turned to the prayer of the destitute and has not spurned their prayer. |
| כי לא בזה ולא שקץ ענות עני ולא הסתיר פניו ממנו ובשועו אליו שומע. | 17. Ps 22:25 | For He did not scorn, He did not spurn the plea of the lowly; He did not hide His face from him; when he cried out to Him, He listened. |
| שמע ה' קולי אקרא וחנני וענני. | 18. Ps 27:7 | Hear, O Eternal, when I cry aloud; have mercy on me, answer me. |
| שמע ה' וחנני ה' היה עזר לי. | 19. Ps 30:11 | Hear, O Eternal, and have mercy on me; O Eternal, be my help! |
| שמע א-להים קולי בשיחי מפחד אויב תצור חיי. | 20. Ps 64:2 | Hear my voice, O God, when I plead; guard my life from the enemy's terror. |
| אמרתי לה' אלי אתה האזינה ה' קול תחנוני. | 21. Ps 140:7 | I said to the Eternal: You are my God; give ear, O Eternal, to my pleas for mercy. |
| אהבתי כי ישמע ה' את קולי תחנוני. | 22. Ps 116:1 | I would that the Lord hear my voice, my pleas. |
| שמע קול תחנוני בשועי אליך בנשאי ידי אל דביר קדשך. | 23. Ps 28:2 | Listen to my plea for mercy when I cry out to You, when I lift my hands toward Your inner sanctuary. |
| שמע ה' תחנתי ה' תפלתי יקח. | 24. Ps 6:10 | The Eternal hears my plea, the Eternal accepts my prayer. |
| שמעה ה' צדק הקשיבה רנתי האצינה תפלתי בלא שפתי מרמה. | 25. Ps 17:1 | Hear, O Eternal, what is just; heed my cry, give ear to my prayer, uttered without guile. |

Table E (*cont.*)

| | | |
|---|---|---|
| א-להים להצילני ה' לעזרתי חושה. | 26.<br>Ps 70:2 | Hasten O God to save me; O Eternal, to aid me! |
| א-להים בשמך הושעני ובגבורתך תדיני.<br>א-להים שמע תפלתי האזינה לאמרי פי. | 27.<br>Ps 54:3–4 | O God, deliver me by Your name; by Your power vindicate me. O God, hear my prayer; give ear to the words of my mouth. |
| האזינה א-להים תפלתי אל תתעלם מתחנתי. | 28.<br>Ps 55:2 | Give ear, O God, to my prayer; do not ignore my plea. |
| אמרי האזינה ה' בינה הגיגי.<br>הקשיבה לקול שועי מלכי וא-להי כי אליך אתפלל. | 29.<br>Ps 5:2–3 | Give ear to my speech, O Eternal, consider my utterance. Heed the sound of my cry, my King and God, for I pray to You. |
| הקשיבה אל רנתי כי דלותי מאד הצילני מרודפי כי אמצו ממני. | 30.<br>Ps 142:7 | Heed my cry, for I have been brought very low; save me from my pursuers, for they are too strong for me. |
| הקשיבה לי וענני אריד בשיחי ואהימה. | 31.<br>Ps 55:3 | Heed me and answer me, I am tossed about, complaining and moaning. |
| אשפוך לפניו שיחי צרתי לפניו אגיד. | 32.<br>Ps 142:3 | I pour out my complaint before Him; I relate my trouble before Him. |
| ביום צרתי אקראך כי תענני. | 33.<br>Ps 86:7 | In my time of trouble I call You, for You will answer me. |
| ביום צרתי ה' דרשתי ידי לילה נגרה ולא תפוג מאנה הנחם נפשי. | 34.<br>Ps 77:3 | In my time of distress I turn to the Eternal, with my hand [uplifted];[my eyes] flow all night without respite. |
| בצר לי אקרא ה' ואל א-להי אשוע ישמע מהיכלו קולי ושועתי לפניו תבוא באזניו. | 35.<br>Ps 18:7 | In my distress I called on the Eternal, cried out to my God; in His temple He heard my voice; my cry to Him reached His ears. |
| אל ה' בצרתה לי קראתי ויענני. | 36.<br>Ps 120:1 | In my distress I called to the Eternal and He answered me. |
| קראתי מצרה לי אל ה' ויענני מבטן שאול שועתי שמעת קולי. | 37.<br>Jonah 2:3 | In my trouble I called to the Eternal and He answered me; from the belly of Sheol I cried out, and Your heard my voice. |

Table E (*cont.*)

| | | |
|---|---|---|
| מן המצר קראתי י-ה עני במרחב י-ה. | 38.<br>Ps 118:5 | In distress I called on the Eternal;<br>the Eternal answered me and<br>brought me relief. |
| עני ה' כי טוב חסדך כרוב רחמיך פנה<br>אלי. | 39.<br>Ps 69:17 | Answer me, Eternal, according<br>to Your great steadfastness; in<br>accordance with Your abundant<br>mercy turn to me. |
| פנה אלי וחני כי יחיד ועני אני. | 40.<br>Ps 25:16 | **Turn** to me, have mercy on me,<br>for I am alone and afflicted. |
| אני קראתיך כי תעני א-ל הט אזנך לי<br>שמע אמרתי. | 41.<br>Ps 17:6 | I call You; You will answer me,<br>God; turn Your ear to me, hear<br>what I say. |
| ה' קראתיך חושה לי האזינה קולי<br>בקראי לך. | 42.<br>Ps 141:1 | I call You, Eternal, hasten to me;<br>give ear to my cry when I call You. |
| ודעו כי הפלה ה' חסיד לו ה' ישמע<br>בקראי אליו. | 43.<br>Ps 4:4 | Know that the Eternal singles<br>out the faithful for Himself; the<br>Eternal hears when I call to Him. |
| בקראי עני א-להי צדקי בצר הרחתי לי<br>חני וישמע תפלתי. | 44.<br>Ps 4:2 | Answer me when I call, O God,<br>my vindicator! You freed me from<br>distress; have mercy on me and<br>hear my prayer. |
| שמע ישראל ה' א-להינו ה' אחד | 45.<br>Dt 6:4 | **Hear, Israel, the Eternal is<br>our God, the Eternal is one.** |
| אחד א-להינו גדול א-דוננו קדוש ונורא<br>שמו לעולם ועד. | 46. | One is our God, great is our Lord,<br>holy and awe-inspiring is His<br>Name forever and ever. |
| מקוה ישראל ה' כל עוזביך יבשו<br>וסורי בארץ יכתבו כי עזבו מקום מים<br>חיים את ה'... | 47.<br>Jer 17:13 | **O Hope** of Israel, O Eternal! All<br>who forsake You shall be put to<br>shame, those in the land who turn<br>from You shall be doomed of men,<br>for they have forsaken the Eternal,<br>the fount of living waters... |

# PARASHAT 'ASSER TE'ASSER' IN PIYYUT AND PIYYUT COMMENTARY

*Elisabeth Hollender*
Heinrich-Heine-Universität Düsseldorf, Germany

The Biblical passage *Asser Te'asser* ('You shall surely tithe') covers Deut 14:22–15:18. This passage deals (1) with the tithe which is to be consumed at the Temple, (2) with the tithe for the poor, which is given every third year (according to rabbinic interpretations instead of the first mentioned tithe), (3) with the remission of debts every seventh year, and (4) with the freeing of the Hebrew slave. The tithe described there usually is referred to as *ma'aser sheni*, 'second tithe', since the rulings in Lev 27:30–33 and Num 18:21–32, while differing from each other, do agree that a (first) tithe is to be given to the Sanctuary or its personnel, the priests and Levites. According to rabbinic teaching, the *ma'aser rishon*, the 'first tithe' is to be given to the Levites who in turn give a tithe from it to the kohanim (the priests)—in the time of the Second Temple it was given to the kohanim, since the number of Levites who returned from Babylonian exile was too low in relation to the number of kohanim who returned. The 'second tithe' is to be consumed during pilgrimages to Jerusalem every first, second, fourth, and fifth year, while it is distributed as *ma'asar-oni*, the tithe of the poor, every third and sixth year. There is no tithe in the seventh year (shemitta), during which the land is not tilled, but left fallow instead.

The tithe is closely connected to the teruma, the obligatory donation of a small part of the harvest (1/48 to 1/60) to a kohen. Teruma and tithe are, according to the Biblical commandments, laws that apply in the land of Israel, when 'all of Israel' is residing there, and they are closely connected to the Temple. Since nobody who is not a kohen in the state of ritual purity is allowed to partake of the teruma, the practice to give teruma to kohanim could not be continued after the destruction of the Temple, for without the ritual involving the ashes of the red heifer, no kohen could achieve ritual purity, e.g. after contact with a dead body. Nevertheless, teruma and tithes were probably separated and handed over to its recipients for some time even after the destruction of the

Second Temple, as quotes from early rabbinic texts and from the Bar Kokhba period indicate. Agricultural tithes were redeemed with money and this money was then put out of use, e.g. by disposing of it into the Dead Sea. But later, and especially in exile, neither teruma nor tithe were practiced according to Biblical and Mishnaic law.

Since both the giving of the tithe and the later memorial act of speaking a blessing and burning a piece of dough before baking did and do take place outside of any liturgical framework, liturgical texts that deal with the tithe are not to be expected. The only framework in which the second tithe is mentioned in the synagogue service is the reading of the portion re'e according to the annual Babylonian cycle of Torah readings, the fifth part of which is Asser Te'asser, the Biblical passage regarding the laws of the second tithe, starting with Deut 14:22. None of the reconstructions of the triennial cycle of Torah reading does include a *seder* that begins with Deut 14:22. Since liturgical poetry usually deals with the beginning of the weekly portion only, there would be no necessity to write poetry on this topic that could bring it to the attention of the community.

But there is evidence that already in late antiquity Asser Te'asser was—contrary to the lists of Torah readings fixed in Mishna and Talmud—read as the beginning of the Torah reading on the Sabbath during Sukkot and the Sabbath during Pesaḥ (Fleischer 1967, 116–155 esp. 153). This assumption is also supported by the position of piska 10 in Pesikta de Rav Kahana, namely in the middle of the piska'ot on Pesaḥ. The homily on Asser Te'asser in Pesikta de Rav Kahana is transmitted almost identically in Tan re'e 10–18 and TanB re'e 4–17. The reading was not accepted unanimously and was replaced by Exod 33:12–34:26 later. But Asser Te'asser was not completely erased from the Torah reading on Sukkot. In the Middle Ages it was customary in some communities to read Asser Te'asser on Shemini Aẓeret, the last day of Sukkot when it happened to fall on a Sabbath. This practice was ostensibly justified because the regular reading for that day, כל הבכור (Deut 15:19–16:17), is not long enough to provide enough text for the seven readings that are halakhically required for a Torah service on the Sabbath. Thus Asser Te'asser, the passage before the required reading, was added. The best known evidence for this Torah reading dates rather late, namely from the 12th century, when Maḥzor Vitry, a compilation of halakhic rulings from the school of Salomo b. Isaac (Rashi) and other sources edited by Simḥa of Vitry, was compiled in Northern France (on this text cf. Lehnardt (2007, 65–99). It contains liturgical rulings, many of which can be traced to Rashi. Rashi wished for Asser Te'asser to be read on Shemini Azeret both on the Sabbath and on weekdays, because he considered this passage to be of great importance. The explanation for the choice of the reading of Asser Te'asser on Shemini Azeret in Mahzor Vitry does not contain the practical argument of how long a pericope has to be when being divided into seven units. Instead it argues on the basis of social responsibility. Rashi points to the laws in this passage that relate to the poor, especially in the time of harvest, when they need to collect their food. In order to strengthen his argument, he refers to the love for the tithes displayed by the ancients, proven in a kedushta (a piece of poetic embellishment of the Amidah) written in the times of Elazar birabbi Qallir, a kedushta that begins with the words אמצה עשירייה ('Strong be the Tenth'; 'the Tenth' denoting Israel), and that is based on the liturgical reading of Asser Te'asser. Mahzor Vitry continues to explain that this piyyut contains a collection of items that occur ten times or tenfold in the Torah. A further reason for the reading of Asser Te'asser is provided by the silluk (the last part) of this kedushta that begins with a quotation from Deut 26:15, namely with the words השקיפה ממעון קדשך מן־השמים ('Look down from your holy abode, from heaven'). Mahzor Vitry understands the second line of the silluk וברך משנני עשר פעמים ('and do bless those who repeat Asser Te'asser twice') to mean that the passage is being read twice a year.

ובפרשת היום עשר תעשר היא. בין שחל להיות בשבת בין בימי השבוע. שכך שנינו בשמיני עצרת. מצות וחוקים ובכור. ומחמת מצות העונקה. דכי קאי בפסח ביום טוב האחרון קרי ליה תנא כל הבכור בהדיא. ש"ם דחג דזמן אסיפא היא. ורישא דשתא לחינוך שמיטין ויובלות. הזקיקו רבותי' להוסיף על כל הבכור עשר תעשר. להכריז על המעשרות. וחוקי שמיטות. ולצוות הענקת עבד ופתיחת יד לאביונים. היינו דקת' מצות וחוקים ובכור. ומחמת חידוש הפרשה וחיבת המעשר ייסדו לו פייטנו קרובה מיוחדת. היא [איום] אמצה עשירייה. ושוררו עליו קיבוץ עשרונות ועשיריות המצויינין בתורה על פי הלכות ואגדות. ורמז המייסד בסילוק פרשה זו נקראת שתי פעמים בשנה. אחת של ראה אנכי. ואחת בשמיני עצרת. וכך התחיל. השקיפה ממעון קדשך מן השמים. וברך משנני עשר פעמים: ובדורו של קלירי עמד המשורר ואחז בידו שער יסודו לפיוט: (Hurwitz 1905, § 384)

And the Torah reading of the day is Asser Te'asser, whether it occurs on a Sabbath or on a weekday, because this is what we learned [in Meg 31a]: On Shemini Azeret: rules and laws and the firstborn. And due to the force of the rule of setting free [the Hebrew slave], which happens on Pesah, one reads it on the final day [of Pesah]. It is taught: 'And each firstborn' (Deut 15:19) on this one. On Shemini Azeret, because it is the festival at the time of the harvest. And on the New Year to educate

regarding the shemitta and yovel years. Our teachers were obliged to aug-
ment 'and each firstborn' (Deut 15:19) with 'you shall surely tithe' (Deut
14:22). To proclaim the tithes and the laws for shemitta years, and to
order the freeing of enslaved [Hebrews] and generosity toward the poor.
That is what has been taught: rules and laws and the firstborn. Because
of (the significance of this) innovative teaching on this passage and the
esteem for the tithe, poets composed a special kerova for it, namely [ ]
אמצה עשירייה (Strong be the Tenth, with 'the Tenth' denoting Israel),
and in their writing, they expand the theme of 'ten' by including items
that occur in tenth or tenfold in the Torah, according to halakhot and
aggada. And the silluk contains a hint that this passage is read twice a
year, once in the Torah reading for ראה אנכי (re'e; Deut 11:26–16:17)
and once on Shemini Aẓeret. And thus it begins: 'Look down from your
holy abode, from heaven, and bless those who recite "You shall tithe"
twice.' The poet belonged to the generation of Qallir and he held in his
hand the measure of composition in order to write poetry.

It is obvious that Maḥzor Vitry considered the two readings to be that
on Shemini Aẓeret and this to be in the context of the reading of re'e
(Deut 11:26–16:17)—six or seven weeks before Shemini Aẓeret. This
is not the only liturgical change that Rashi wished to introduce, and
it shares the fate of almost all of the liturgical changes he advocated:
it was not generally adopted. According to most Minhagim Asser
Te'asser is still being read only when Shemini Aẓeret happens to fall
on a Sabbath, with the exception of Minhag Polin where it is read
on Shemini Aẓeret even on weekdays. Shemini Aẓeret can fall on a
Sabbath as often as 6 times in the 19 year cycle, which is the basis of
the Jewish calendar.

Together with the reading of Asser Te'asser the kedushta אמצה
עשירייה disappeared, and another kedushta was used on Shemini
Aẓeret throughout. In Minhag Ashkenaz, Ẓarfat, and Worms this is
אחות אשר לך כספת by Elazar birabbi Qallir (cf. Goldschmidt/Fraenkel
1981, 376–390). Thus אמצה עשירייה is not transmitted in any of the
Ashkenazic and Ẓarfatic Maḥzorim we know today, neither in print
nor in manuscript. When Leopold Zunz prepared the lists of piyyutim
for his *Literaturgeschichte der Synagogalen Poesie*, he mentioned this kedushta
as איום אמצה עשירייה, obviously from the reference in Maḥzor Vitry,
but did not know the text (Zunz 1966, 52). The erroneous addition of
איום to the beginning of the piyyut (a misreading of the word היום that
occurs in several manuscripts of Maḥzor Vitry before the opening words
of the piyyut) has been perpetuated in Davidson's *Thesaurus of Hebrew
Poetry* (Davidson 1924–1933, א 2665) and into the Hurwitz edition of

Maḥzor Vitry (Hurwitz 1905, 445). Obviously everybody copied from Zunz, but nobody ever saw the text of the piyyut.

Before looking at this 'lost' kedushta in more detail it is necessary to briefly discuss this genre of liturgical poetry. A kedushta is a poetic embellishment of the Amidah in the morning prayer on a Sabbath or holiday. Kedushta'ot cover only the first three benedictions of the shortened Amidah on Sabbath, namely the praise for the God of the fathers who loves and redeems Israel (מגן אברהם), the praise for God who resurrects the dead (מחייה המתים), and the praise of God that parallels the praise spoken by the angels and contains the quote from Isa 6:3 'Holy, holy, holy' (קדושה). The last part of the kedushta, the silluk, has—according to the rules of the genre—to lead into the recitation of the text of Isa 6:3. From the Genizah and later Ashkenazic and Zarfatic Maḥzorim, the three-part structure of Qallirian Kedushta'ot has become well known. In the first section, piyyutim I, II, and III form the beginning of an alphabetic acrostic. Each of these piyyutim consists of four-line stanzas, where the concluding line of the final stanza departs from the acrostic pattern. Piyyut III may include additional poetic stanzas interwoven within a chain of Biblical verses that form a bridge between the final alphabetic line of the piyyut and its closing stanza. The middle section contains piyyut IV, which is typically short and monorhymed, and piyyut V, typically a series of three-lined stanzas whose lines form an acrostic that spells the name of its payyetan. The final section contains three piyyutim that employ a combination of poetic devices: piyyut VI typically forms an alphabetic acrostic using three-lined stanzas; piyyut VII is comprised of a series of rehitim (each based on the same poetic structure for this particular piyyut, that the payyetan would select from a common repertoire of options); and, piyyut VIII, the silluk, a long piyyut that consists of monorhymed sections of varying length. The content of the silluk is very often related to the contents of the first piyyutim, but it can also contain eschatological or even apocalyptic visions (cf. Fleischer 1972, 138–182).

The knowledge about אמצה עשירייה, the 'lost' Qallirian kedushta has changed with the systematic analysis of all poetic texts contained in the Cairo Genizah undertaken by the Genizah Research Institute for Hebrew Poetry in Jerusalem. Ezra Fleischer found the beginning of the kedushta in the Genizah and published it from two Genizah fragments back in 1967 (Fleischer 1967). At present, a third fragment containing abbreviated forms of piyyutim III, IV, and V, a shortened version of piyyut VI, namely the stanzas that make up the letters א to ס in the alphabetic acrostic, and two rehitim, has been found (T-S NS 137,22; still unpublished). The silluk, especially referred to in Maḥzor Vitry, has not yet been found among the texts from the Genizah.

During my preparation of the *Clavis Commentariorum of Hebrew Liturgical Poetry in Manuscripts*, which lists all known piyyut commentaries from more than 400 manuscripts, I found a source for this piyyut that is much closer to the version cited in Maḥzor Vitry. A manuscript of piyyut commentaries which was copied during the 13th century in France contains, among other commentaries that can be traced to Rashi's circle of pupils, a commentary on אמצה עשירייה that includes the silluk which is not extant in the Cairo Genizah (Hollender 2005, nos 3306 and 10623). The medieval commentary covers the first three piyyutim, skips piyyut IV and V, comments on almost every line of piyyut VI from א to ת, has a short commentary on part of the rehitim, and a long commentary on the silluk. We may assume that these were the elements of the kedushta known at that time, since Ashkenazic and Zarfatic traditions often skip the second block of kedushta'ot, namely piyyut IV and V. This would account for the medieval statement that the piyyut was written 'in the time of the Qallir', since the name-acrostic in piyyut V was not part of the medieval version of the text.

The commentary also allows a reconstruction of large parts of the lost silluk, the part of the kedushta in which Elazar birabbi Qallir was less restrained by formal requirements and therefore able to express his ideas most freely. This freedom proves to be one of the great obstacles for the reconstruction, since the lack of an acrostic and the changing rhyme make it more difficult to place the lemmata in relation to one another. Nevertheless it was possible to reconstruct almost 100 lines from the silluk which are currently being prepared for publication.

Obviously, Rashi's attempt to change the liturgy of Shemini Aẓeret included the introduction of אמצה עשירייה into the liturgy which he considered to be written for this day, not for the Sabbath during Sukkot. This was another failed liturgical change of this great sage. No medieval Maḥzor manuscript that came down to us contains this piyyut, and even the commentary is transmitted in one manuscript only, without a copy of the piyyut attached. Piyyut commentary has until recently been an almost forgotten genre (the most notable exception being Urbach 1939), and the commentary on אמצה עשירייה had escaped notice until the inventory of the genre. The usage advocated by Rashi for Asser Te'asser and אמצה עשירייה was not successful, but the reasoning behind it can be reconstructed when we reconstruct the medieval interpretation of the Byzantine piyyut.

Classical piyyutim are usually poetic renderings of Biblical exegesis known from midrashim. Most often they do not follow one prose source only, but combine material from different sources into their piyyutim (cf. Grossman 1994, 293–308 esp. 298–299). In the case of the second tithe the poet had a wealth of rabbinic sources to choose from, for Mishna, Tosefta, and PT each devote a special tractate to the second tithe (מעשר שני), in addition to tractates on tithes (מעשרות), the teruma, (halla), and tithing of agricultural products of doubtful provenience (דמאי). Even though the laws of the tithe apply only in the land of Israel, the BT discusses tithes in several contexts. In the case of אמצה עשירייה it seems that the payyetan was hardly interested in the ample halakhic discourse. In the parts of the piyyut that are transmitted in the Genizah fragments or can be reconstructed from the commentary, no discussion can be found of what products have to be tithed, how and when they have to be tithed, or any other halakhic detail. The closest to a halakhic discussion that is extant is the remark in the commentary on the last line of piyyut VI: אם הוציאו מעשר מכל פירות ופירות לפי גזרנו המפריש כאן וכולן מפורשות {בין} בסדר זרעים הק' יברך לכם התבואה בבטן ובפה. ['If they bring out the tithe from every single fruit according to what we were commanded "He who separates (the tithe) here"—and they all are explained in *Seder Zera'im*—then the Holy One will bless their products in the belly and in the mouth.'] But even here, the reader of the commentary is requested to check the halakhic discourse himself. It is not contained in piyyut or piyyut commentary. Instead the homiletic tradition transmitted in Tanḥuma and Pesikta was an important source of the piyyut. A homily on Deut 14:22–29 is transmitted almost identically in both published Tanḥuma versions and in Pesikta deRav Kahana (Tan re'e 10–18, TanB re'e § 4–17, PRK 10). Parts of it are transmitted in Exodus Rabba as well. Another homily on Asser Te'asser is transmitted in Pesikta Rabbati (25, ed. Friedmann f. 126a–128b). The payyetan made ample usage of the homily transmitted in Tanḥuma and PRK, and added allusions to midrashic units found in several other midrashim, among them several tractates of the Mishna, Mekhilta, Genesis Rabba, Leviticus Rabba, Seder Olam, and others. Near the end of the silluk, the allusions point to apocalyptic midrashim composed at the same time as the piyyut.

The prominence of homiletic sources for the piyyut is important insofar as these texts were originally (although not in their edited

written form) performed in the synagogues of Ereẓ Israel in Late
Antiquity. Even though the role of the derashah in the liturgy is not
completely clear, it did address the same mixed audience of learned
and less educated worshippers that classical piyyutim addressed. While
the literary means employed by the two genres were different, many
parallels between homiletic midrashim and piyyutim have been noted.
A comparison of the tithe-related topics in אמצה עשירייה with the
Tanḥuma/Pesikta-homily on Asser Te'asser reveals the following parallels: (a) the patriarchs donating the tithe, cf. TanB re'e 12 (Tan re'e 14,
PRK 10); (b) the topic of tithing in order to gain wealth, cf. TanB re'e
17 (Tan re'e 18); (c) Levi being the tithe of the tribes, cf. TanB re'e 12
(Tan re'e 14); (d) an exegesis of Mal 3:10—cf. additions to TanB re'e
in Buber's edition. The medieval commentary refers to a few more passages from Tan re'e that he considered to be the sources of the piyyut,
namely: (a) Torah can be cherished in the intestines, cf. TanB re'e 12
(Tan re'e 14, PRK 10); (b) tithe so that you will not be needy, cf. TanB
re'e 17 (Tan re'e 18); (c) an exegesis of Isa 24:5, cf. TanB re'e 11 (PRK
10); (d) an exegesis of Deut 12:21, cf. TanB re'e 16 (Tan re'e 17). In
addition to these textual parallels the general gist of the texts seems to
be similar. In a time when the Temple—and hence the reason for both
the first and the second tithe—had not functioned for several hundred
years, narrative and exegetical units reinforced the need to tithe as a
religious obligation. Tithing is rewarded. As Tanḥuma Asser Te'asser
repeats more than once, a person who does not tithe properly will lose
his wealth. In TanB re'e 7 an interpretation of Prov 28:22 is presented
by Rabbi Levi. A father bequeaths a field to his son. He has always
harvested 1000 measures from this field and he advises his son to be
diligent with regard to the tithes. The son rejects his father's advice and
the less tithes he extracts, the lower the yield of the field. In the end he
harvests only as much as his father set aside as tithes. Those wiser than
the son explain to him that formerly he was the owner of the field and
God received the tithe, 'The Holy One was the priest', and now God
has become the owner of the field and 'you are the priest'.

The ideas expressed in the Tanḥuma homily probably served as
first steps toward transforming the tithe concept from a Temple-based
religious tax in Israel to an obligatory contribution without geographic
bounds. Rabbinic texts that advocate transformation usually include as
many aspects and details of the original concepts as possible, along with
changes that give access to a wider audience. The rabbis who directed
this process wished to apply rules that had been valid for religious elite

groups during the time of the Second Temple to all of Israel following the destruction of the Temple. In addition to emphasizing the continuation of long-standing practices and extending their application to all of Israel, rabbinic texts often introduce new concepts, phrased in a way that presents them as if they had existed all along. Tanḥuma features part of this effort to transform Temple-based religious acts into a 'new' Judaism (cf. Bokser 1984).

The Biblical prooftext from Deut 14:22–29 includes the obligation to give the tithes as charity every third year. Tanḥuma assumes that a tithe is being set aside and that the recipient is God, who 'was the priest' (cf. TanB re'e 7). This image turns the reality from Temple times upside-down, since the priests then received the tithe in lieu of God, not God as substitute for the priest. Thus, the homily assumes—without mentioning this explicitly—a situation where the tithe is not paid to the Temple or the priests as officers of the Temple. Instead it is paid to God, without any description of how this would be achieved.

The answer to the question of how the tithe can be paid to God without the Temple is found only at the very end of the Tanḥuma homily, in the so called 'messianic ending'. After a series of texts that focus on the importance of setting aside the tithe throughout the homily, the last verse of the Biblical prooftexts on the tithe, Deut 14:29 is interpreted by Rabbi Judah birabbi Simon: 'Then the Levite, who has no hereditary portion as you have, and the stranger, the fatherless, and the widow in your settlement shall come and eat their fill, so that the Lord your God may bless you in all the enterprises you undertake'. In the Biblical context, this refers to the tithe for the landless every third year. In Tanḥuma, the four groups mentioned in Deut 14:29 are described as בני בית ('children of [his] house' = dependents) of God. Giving the tithe to them will result in God granting joy to the dependents of the giver, the 'children of [his] house'. But since Tanḥuma literature was composed at a time when there was no Temple, the promise made here will necessarily refer to the messianic future, as indicated by the Biblical prooftext chosen, Isa 56:7: 'I will bring them to my sacred mount and will give them joy in my house of prayer'. Giving the tithe to those in God's special care (i.e. giving it as charity to the poor) is—according to this homily—a step on the way to redemption. The tithe which is intended for God is meant to be given to His dependents, the poor, every single year. Tanḥuma was most probably written during the Byzantine period in Israel, its solution to the question of how and to whom to give the tithe mirrors a political situation in which—at least in Galilee—the Jews made up most of the rural population and cities were mainly inhabited by Christians who were closer to the ruling class. If a percentage of the agricultural product was given to the locally needy immediately after the harvest, the tax-collectors, who collected for cities and the army, would not be depriving the poor when they collected agricultural surplus from the landowners.

As for Elazar birabbi Qallir, who lived and worked at the end of Byzantine rule in Israel, the socio-political situation was slightly different. Due to the Persian conquest of Israel, the following recapture by Heraclius, and the subsequent Arab conquest only seven years later, his lifetime was one of political crisis and it is not surprising that apocalyptic literature thrived both in Jewish and in Christian circles during this time. Writing about the tithe, Elazar birabbi Qallir had three options regarding how to deal with his topic and the present political and spiritual situation. He could follow the model first embraced by the Mishna and deny the changes that had been forced onto Judaism by the destruction of the Temple by simply describing the tithe as if the Temple was still operating. The second option was to actively accept the changes and to offer new interpretations for Temple related laws also aimed at a spiritual strengthening of Judaism, like Tanḥuma did. The third option—though mainly discredited after the unsuccessful revolt of Bar Kokhba—was chosen by some of his contemporaries, the authors and compilers of apocalyptic midrashim at the end of the Byzantine rule. Qallir could thus have used the topic of the tithe to express messianic hopes—e.g. by adding a twist to the idea of the messianic ending in the Tanḥuma homily he used as one of the sources for his piyyut. Since Elazar birabbi Qallir knew of the short-lived reinstitution of sacrifices on the Temple mount with official approval of the Persian conquerors in the early years of the Persian rule (Fleischer 1985, 383–427), this third option might have been open to him, but while some of his sillukim contain eschatological ideas, no explicitly messianic texts of his have been transmitted. Yet it is possible that he followed the well established pattern of homilies to express a vague messianic hope that does not tie any expectations to the contemporary situation and does not fix on a *kairos* in the near future. It seems that Elazar birabbi Qallir chose to follow at least the two first mentioned options in his piyyut on the 'second tithe'.

In fact, in אמצה עשירייה, Elazar birabbi Qallir describes the second tithe from Asser Te'asser as if the Temple was operating and pilgrimages to the Temple were an everyday occurrence. He explains that

Asser Te'asser is read at the time of the harvest, since the tithe has to be set aside immediately after the harvest is brought into the barn. He insists that the tithe has to be given from the best of the harvest. He lists all kinds of cereals and fruit and animals that need to be tithed and recounts that it is better to bring the tithe itself to Jerusalem for consumption, but that the money value of the tithe can be used instead if the distance is too far. Qallir encourages his audience to be generous with the teruma, for which no exact measure is named.

On the other hand, he refers to the spiritual meaning of the tithe when describing that the patriarchs kept the laws of the tithe, that Abraham was the 'tithe', namely the tenth generation after Noah, and was thereby sanctified. In the same manner Jacob/Israel was sanctified as 'tithe', because he is the tenth male descendant of Abraham. Israel is the 'tithe' of the nations, since their land was settled by seven people before, and seven is a tenth (= the tithe) of the seventy nations. Elazar birabbi Qallir stresses that the tithe is as important as all other laws of the Torah together, and that it is one of the legs of God's throne.

In addition to this, there are eschatological aspects to the Qallirian piyyut on the tithe. The Haftara, the reading from the prophets for Asser Te'asser begins with Mal 3:10: 'Bring the full tithe into the storehouse, and let there be food in my house, and thus put me to the test—said the Lord of Hosts. I will surely open the floodgates of the sky for you and pour down blessings on you'. Like many other Haftarot, it is possible to interpret this verse as a promise of salvation for Israel. Qallir uses the verse in piyyut III (where the Haftara must be quoted), in piyyut VI, and extensively in the silluk. But he also mentions that Levi is the 'tithe' of Israel, a concept that is of importance only in a society that actively participates or hopes to participate in Temple service. In addition to that, Elazar birabbi Qallir mentions that the disobedience concerning the laws of the tithe and shemitta caused the Babylonian exile and that this was the reason why the generation who returned to Israel and rebuilt the Temple decided to reinstate the laws of the tithe, even though God himself had considered abolishing them:

על בוגדים מלהשמט ומלעשרה
פוזרו בנוכרייה שבועים שבעים להסגורה
צייתם שומן ודגן חסרה

קצבה הכינה עלי גולה.
רצו מאליהן לקיימה בגולה
מגילה [...]

Because [Israel] spurned the rules of shemitta and tithe,
they were dispersed among the strange [nation], closed up for 70 weeks,
their desolation grew fat and grain was scarce.

The assembly of those who returned from exile
wished out of their own to keep it even in exile
[He agreed to their decision] on the same scroll.

According to the midrash that served as the source for these stanzas
(Ruth Rabba IV.5) God himself interacted with those who wished to
sanctify the tithe, he signed the script of their common decision which
was left for His attendance in the Temple. Qallir added to the narrative the concept that Israel should keep the laws of the tithes even
in exile. In his situation this probably referred to the Jews of the land
of Israel in a time when not all of Israel was living in the land, i.e.
in a situation where according to the Biblical precept, the tithe was
not obligatory. The concept was then open for reinterpretation by the
medieval scholars who lived outside of the land of Israel and therefore
related to the question of exile in a different way.

Near the end of the silluk the payyetan provides a detailed description of how the nations will be punished with tenfold destruction when
God will put on ten garments of revenge to bring about the salvation
of His people.

[עשרה...] יום עברה
להבליע בהן כרכים עשרה
להפוך בהן גבולין עשרה
לשרוף בה מקומות עשרה
ונשלים בעשרה שירים עשרה
בעשור שירים עשרה
להעטת לעוזו לבו[שים] עשרה

     ...[ten] days of awe
     to swallow ten towns
     to turn over ten borders
     to burn down ten places
     then we will complete on ten [occasions] ten songs
     on the ten-stringed harp ten songs
     to answer the might of Him who wears ten garments.

The tenth song mentioned here is the song that Israel will sing in the
days of the Messiah. Only the number ten connects this passage to the
tithe, but it expresses hopes of a speedy and violent salvation Israel Yuval
has taught us to expect in Ashkenaz at the end of the 11th century
(Yuval 1993, 33–90). The predilection of the Ashkenazim for liturgical

poetry and habits from Ereẓ Israel may at some point in time have been inspired by the sentiments shared by the two communities, but it may also be that the more 'violent' Qallirian sillukim were omitted from Ashkenazic liturgy because they did not suit a later generation's taste nor meet their need.[1]

Elazar birabbi Qallir, who lived in a time that he hoped to be a time of transition, created in his kedushta אמצה עשירייה multiple images of the tithe as a halakhic reality, as a spiritual reality, and as a symbol of messianic hope. The small number of Genizah fragments that contain this composition shows that the kedushta was not very popular. But somehow it made its way to the Champagne region and was known in Rashi's academy there. The mentioning of אמצה עשירייה in Maḥzor Vitry and the commentary on the kedushta testify to another attempt to give the subject of the 'second tithe' a place in the liturgy. The difference between Elazar birabbi Qallir and Rashi lies in the motive of why Asser Te'asser should be part of the liturgy and how אמצה עשירייה is to be understood.

As mentioned before, Rashi advocated the reading of Asser Te'asser on Shemini Aẓeret due to the fact that the poor need to collect their food in the time of the harvest. Consequently the commentary, which was composed in Rashi's academy, goes out of its way to interpret the tithe Elazar birabbi Qallir mentions in the kedushta as tithe for the poor (*ma'asar-oni*), whenever possible. Where Qallir tells his audience that it is agreeable to God to separate the tithe diligently and take it up to Jerusalem for consumption as soon as possible, the commentary explains that whosoever separates the tithe for the poor diligently and immediately after the harvest will eventually be rewarded by the prospect to see Jerusalem, while those who delay to give the tithe will be punished in their riches until they themselves will depend on what others give

---

[1] The same manuscript that contains the commentary on אמצה עשירייה also contains a commentary on מי לא יראך מלך, the Qallirian silluk for Musaf on Rosh haShana, that was omitted in favor of ונתנה תוקף in all western minhagim. Again, the commentary is the only testimony that the silluk was ever known in Ashkenaz (or at least in Ẓarfat). The commentary on מי לא יראך מלך is very short and contains almost exclusively lexical explanations and a few paraphrases. Stylistically it cannot be attributed to either Josef Kara or Shemaya, the two great early commentators, but its inclusion in this collection points either to an author who was a student in Rashi's academy or to an earlier date for the commentary who then must have been known in Rashi's academy. The latter assumption is less probable. The silluk and its commentary were published by Yahalom & Leffler 2006, 127–158.

to them as tithe for the poor. Apart from adapting the message of the
piyyut to an audience that lived in exile and conceived of Jerusalem
as the visual symbol for redemption, in a bold act of reinterpretation,
the commentary also changes the tithe mentioned in the piyyut from
the Biblical 'second tithe' to be consumed in Jerusalem, to the tithe
for the poor.

The commentary alludes to the aforementioned episode from Tanḥuma
Asser Te'asser, transmitted also in the Tosafot to Taan 9a: 'A man always
harvested 1000 bushels and immediately separated 100 bushels as tithe'.
But his heir was greedy and separated a smaller tithe only, keeping
ten percent of the tithe for himself. He was punished by a harvest ten
percent less than his father's usual harvest, separated less, harvested
less, etc. until he was harvesting just ten percent of the original harvest.
The commentary refers to this episode as common knowledge for the
audience. It does not even retell the end of the narrative, in which the
friends of the heir tell him to celebrate that God took nine parts of
his harvest and gave him one part, giving him the tithe as it were, as
if God was the landowner and he the priest (TanB re'e 7, see above).
This passage in Tanḥuma is probably one of the earliest texts that
assumes that the tithe—after the destruction of the Temple—is to be
given to the poor, and the piyyut commentary agrees with it. The piyyut
commentary combines the allusion to this narrative with a quote from
Pesikta 9.5 and a slightly expanded version of Rashi's commentary on
Num 5:10. Both Tanḥuma and the piyyut commentary agree in that
the tithe was supposed to be given to the poor. The narrative from
Tanḥuma was transmitted also in the Tosafot on Taan 9a, i.e. it was
discussed in the generations following Rashi and his pupils and was
accepted as a way to describe the importance of giving the tithe.

If we take into account that the same passage in Tosafot demands
that this tithe is to be given from all kinds of income—including trade—
ascribing this rule to the tannaitic lawgivers, we find here one of the first
testimonies for what was later called מעשר כספים, the tithe of monies, a
kind of income-tax devoted to charity. The term מעשר כספים, tithe of
monies, is first attested to in early 13th century Hebrew writings from
Germany, but in these texts it describes a firmly established religious
habit. Thus, there is no reason to doubt that the concept of a diaspora
type of a tithe for the poor to be given from all income was discussed
earlier. I would suggest reading the commentary on אמצה עשירייה and
the fact that Rashi wished to include this kedushta into the liturgy for
Shemini Aẓeret as an indication that the question of monetary tithing

was discussed in Rashi's academy. Instead of leaving the laws of the tithes uncommented, like the Babylonian Talmud did, Rashi, his contemporaries, and his pupils decided to reinterpret the Biblical laws for the needs of their own society, and Rashi obviously wanted to use the liturgy to disseminate this interpretation. While he did not succeed in introducing Asser Te'asser into the Torah-reading on Shemini Azeret when it falls on a weekday, the social issue of the tithe for the poor was a success and is practiced by many Jews to this day.

The second level of description of the tithe in Elazar birabbi Qallir's kedushta אמצה עשירייה, the spiritual understanding of the term, is the level that posed little problem to the commentator. He stresses that the tithe is one of the legs of God's throne because the tithe is צדקה, justice (ever since rabbinic times this term was also used to denote charity). But in all other occasions where the tithe is understood spiritually, the commentary simply quotes the appropriate midrashim and explains that, e.g. Jacob is the tenth descendant of Abraham because the sons of Ketura have to be counted in as well.

Yet there is a twist in the commentary's explanation of Israel being the 'tithe' of the nations that points to the third level of tithe description, the messianic level. According to the piyyut commentary, Israel was promised that they would inherit the land of ten people, and did inherit the land of seven people only. But in the days of the Messiah, God's promise to Abraham will become true and Israel will inherit the land of the last three nations mentioned as well. Here, as in the other occasions where it is possible to see messianic expectations in Qallir's piyyut, the commentary does not deny that the days of the Messiah will come, but it expresses no immediate hope. We learn from the piyyut commentary that the harp in the Temple had seven strings and that this harp will have eight strings in the days of the Messiah. The commentary also lists the ten garments of revenge that God will wear when judging and destroying the nations, including the Biblical prooftexts. But none of these explanations give the impression that the commentator does anything else but provide the midrashim that teach about the contents of the Qallirian kedushta without arguing for an actual application. It seems that salvation was not a topic of immediate importance in Rashi's academy.

In the same manner, the stanzas on the Babylonian exile and the reinstitution of the tithe receive a long commentary that explains the time calculations for the Babylonian exile according to Seder Olam Rabba and Rashi's commentary on Dan 9:25, followed by the explanation that the current and long exile is the time mentioned in Dan 9:24: 'until the measure of transgression is filled and that of sin complete, until iniquity is expiated, and eternal righteousness ushered in'. After this passage, it retells the story of how Zerubabel and those who returned with him received God's approbation for their decision to continue paying the tithe. If anything can be inferred from the way the story is told in the commentary, it is that the tithe should be given outside of Israel as well. And since the commentary has impressed on its audience that the tithe is the tithe of the poor, this is in accordance with Rashi's reasoning for the liturgical reading of Asser Te'asser.

There is, however one point which the commentator stresses, even though the piyyut is less explicit on it. That is the narrative that God considered freeing the righteous of the nations from Gehinnom and sending the evil-doers of Israel there instead. But then the Mishna and Moses came to him and pleaded for Israel, with the result that not even the evil-doers in Israel will have to descend to Gehinnom, and not even the righteous of the nations will be spared from Gehinnom. This narrative is repeated twice in the commentary on the silluk, and while it does not relate to the tithe at all, it is a graphic illustration of the ever growing Jewish polemics against the surrounding and oppressing Christian culture in Northern France after 1096 and until the expulsion from France in 1306.

The comparison of אמצה עשיריה and its commentary has shown how the question of the 'second tithe' was dealt with in two crucial periods of Jewish history and liturgy. The comparison has shown that liturgy can and needs to be studied as literature, but that it should also be read within the context of the historical community that it was intended for. Elazar birabbi Qallir wrote piyyutim for his community in late Byzantine Israel, while Rashi and the piyyut commentary utilize Qallir's poetry for their medieval theological and social agenda. Both use the liturgical context to focus on the importance of keeping the Biblical command of the tithe, adapted to the reality their audiences lived in.

## Literature

Bokser, B.M., *The Origin of the Seder*, Berkeley 1984.
Davidson, I., *Thesaurus of Medieval Hebrew Poetry;* אוצר השירה והפיוט, New York [4 vols] 1924–1933.
Fleischer, E., 'לפתרון שאלת זמנו ומקום פעילתו של ר' אלעזר בירבי קיליר', *Tarb.* 54 (1985).

———, 'פרשת "עשר תעשר" וקריאתה בימות חג לפי מנהגות ארץ־ישראל', *Tarb.* 36 (1967).

———, *שירת הקודש העברית בימי הביניים*, Jerusalem 1972.

Goldschmidt, D., *מחזור סוכות, שמיני עצרת ושמחת תורה. לפי מנהגי בני אשכנז לכל ענפיהם*, J. Fraenkel (ed.), Jerusalem 1981.

Grossman, A., 'שבחי ר' אלעזר בירבי קליר בפירוש הפיוטים של ר"י קרא', in: *כנסת עזרא. ספרות וחיים בבית הכנסת*, Jerusalem 1994.

Hollender, E., *Clavis Commentariorum of Medieval Hebrew Piyyut-Commentary* (Clavis Commentariorum Antiquitatis et Medii Aevi 4), Leiden 2005.

Hurwitz (ed.), S., *מחזור ויטרי לרבינו שמחה אחד מתלמידי רש"י ז"ל. עם תוספות הגהות תקונים ובאורים*, Berlin 2nd ed. 1905.

Lehnardt, A., '"Siddur Rashi" und die Halakha-Kompendien aus der Schule Rashis', in: H. Liss, R. Reichmann, & D. Krochmalnik (eds), *Rashi und sein Erbe*. Heidelberg 2007.

Urbach, E.E. (ed.), *ספר ערוגת הבושם; כולל פירושים לפיוטים*, Jerusalem [4 vols] 1939.

Yahalom, J., & B. Leffler, '"מי לא ייראך מלך" סילוק קלירי אבוד לראש־השנה', in: E. Hazan & J. Yahalom (eds), *לאות זיכרון. מחקרים בשירה העברית ובמורשת ישראל*, Ramat Gan 2006.

Yuval, I.Y., 'הנקם והקללה, הדם והעלילה. מעלילות קדושים לעלילות הדם', *Zion 58* (1993).

Zunz, L., *Literaturgeschichte der synagogalen Poesie*, Hildesheim [reprint of the 1865 ed.] 1966.

# DEVELOPMENTS WITHIN THE STATUTORY
# TEXT OF THE *BIRKAT HA-MAZON* IN LIGHT
# OF ITS POETIC COUNTERPARTS

*Avi Shmidman*
Bar-Ilan University, Israel

The *birkat ha-mazon* prayer,[1] recited at the conclusion of every meal,[2] occupies a primary place within Judaism's liturgy for the home. It is therefore unsurprising that the manuscripts of the Cairo Geniza, representing daily Jewish life in the Mediterranean between the 10th and 13th centuries, abound with copies of this prayer. These documents are especially significant in light of the fact that Rabbinic sources, while specifying the prayer's overall structure, do not delineate a specific prayer text.[3] Thus, the Geniza documents afford us an opportunity to examine the *birkat ha-mazon* at a relatively early point in its development.[4]

---

[1] The present study is based upon a corpus of 469 manuscripts from the Cairo Geniza, containing 213 transcriptions of the statutory text of the *birkat ha-mazon*, and 352 transcriptions of the prayer's poetic counterparts (a single manuscript may contain multiple transcriptions). I am currently preparing a critical edition of the full corpus of the poetic transcriptions as part of my doctoral dissertation, under the guidance of Prof. Ephraim Hazan (Bar Ilan University). In addition, the present collection of statutory transcriptions serves as a preliminary basis for a forthcoming critical edition of Geniza texts of the *birkat ha-mazon*, which I am preparing together with Dr. Uri Ehrlich (Ben Gurion University). Regarding the criteria used to differentiate between statutory and poetic transcriptions, see below (section II).

I would like to thank my colleagues Mr. Tzvi Novick, Dr. Michael Rand, and Mr. Pinchas Roth, who each commented on an early version of this paper. Additionally, I would like to express my gratitude to the following institutions for the use of their catalogs and manuscript collections: The Institute of Hebrew Poetry of the National Academy of Sciences, founded by Professor Ezra Fleischer; the Institute of Microfilmed Hebrew Manuscripts of the Jewish National and University Library in Jerusalem; and the Liturgy Project founded by The Israel Academy of Sciences and Humanities, headed by Dr. Uri Ehrlich. Finally, I extend my appreciation to the libraries around the world who house and preserve the Geniza documents which are cited in this study.

[2] Technically speaking, the prayer is confined to meals in which bread is consumed; its relevance at other meals is a matter of Talmudic debate (Ber 44a).

[3] The primary Rabbinic sources specify only the number of benedictions and the general themes which are to be contained within (see t.Ber 3,9; 6,1; p.Ber 1,5 3d; 7,1 11a; Ber 48a–49b).

[4] The extent to which we can extrapolate information from these texts regarding the pre-Geniza state of the prayer will be considered below (section IV).

The Geniza manuscripts reflect two distinct models of *birkat ha-mazon* recitals. Primary among them is the statutory form of the prayer, in which the basic prayer text remains constant, even as the various manuscripts offer a wealth of additional supplications and variations.[5] At the same time, however, the Cairo Geniza also brought to light over 200 distinct poetic versions of the prayer.[6] Although later European prayer books incorporate such compositions within the statutory text (Finkelstein 1929, 236 n. 49; Davidson 1938–39, 345–387 esp. 362–363), the original intent of the poems was not to supplement, but rather to supplant (Fleischer 1970, 42–63 esp. 55–60; Shmidman 2006, 45–102 esp. 61–64). Indeed, according to the normative liturgical practice during the Geniza period, these poetic texts served as complete alternatives to the statutory text; other than a few set phrases which were appended to the end of the 2nd and 3rd benedictions, the poetic recitals almost entirely disregarded the statutory text (Shmidman 2006, 49–59).

Nevertheless, despite their differences, the statutory text and the poetic compositions do share a number of common features. In the present study, I shall examine two such points of interaction, demonstrating the influence of the poetic forms upon the statutory version of the *birkat ha-mazon*.

## I. Categorizing *Birkat ha-Mazon* Texts

Before we embark on a comparison of the poetic forms of the *birkat ha-mazon* with the statutory text, we must first obtain a reliable method to differentiate between the two types of texts. It is not sufficient to contrast the 'poetry' of the poetic texts with the 'prose' of the statutory text; the statutory text may occasionally incorporate poetic phrases,[7] while at

---

[5] For an overview of the development of the statutory text of the *birkat ha-mazon*, see Finkelstein (1929, 211–262). Note, however, that at the early stage during which he authored his study, the availability of Geniza texts was far more limited; thus, Finkelstein's study only takes account of seven such manuscripts. For a recent survey of the components of the *birkat ha-mazon* as they are found in the Geniza manuscripts, see Reif 2005, 11–29.

[6] For a general introduction to the poetic versions of the grace after meals, see Fleischer (1975, 247–251). For published collections of such hymns, see Habermann (1939, 43–105 esp. 50–105), Raẓhabi (1984, 373–385; 1991, 193–231; 1994, 110–133) and Shmidman (2005, 70–147).

[7] For example, within the second benediction, the Geniza transcriptions of the statutory text always include the line: ארץ חמדה / טובה ורחבה / ברית ותורה / חיים ומזון, written according to the tetracolon meter common among the pre-classical Hebrew

the same time there is no single set of poetic features that characterizes all of the various poetic texts.[8] Instead, in the following paragraphs, I will present two alternate criteria to determine the category to which a given text belongs.

First, although the manuscripts of the statutory text abound with textual variants, they all remain loyal to the majority of the core phrases within each of the benedictions.[9] Among the poetic texts, in contrast, we find an almost complete deviation from these basic formulations; each one of the poetic versions presents an entirely new prayer text. Thus, the set of core statutory phrases serves to unite the various renditions of the statutory text, while separating them from the corpus of poetic forms.

Second, a distinguishing feature of the poetic versions is their compositional structure, in which a systematic poetic paradigm presides across all three benedictions.[10] This characteristic, common to all forms of early Hebrew liturgical poetry (Fleischer 1970, 53 n. 36), serves to differentiate the bona fide poetic compositions from the occasional poetic line or stanza which is sometimes found within one or another of the benedictions of the statutory text.

The foregoing criteria serve to effectively divide the Geniza texts used in this study into two distinct groups: 352 poetic transcriptions

---

poets; regarding this metric pattern, see Fleischer (1975, 84–85). Another poetic flourish, occasionally found near the beginning of the second benediction, is the following line, cited here from Ms. Cambridge T-S NS 122.39: נפארך מלכינו / נשבחך יוצרינו / נמליכך קדושינו / מלך יחיד חי העולמים.

[8] Generally speaking, the poetic forms can be characterized by a combination of rhyme, meter, and acrostic. However, not all of the poetic texts include each of these features. For instance, the composition בורא עולם (Fleischer 2000–01, 1–38 esp. 18), although written in classic tetracolon meter, contains neither rhyme nor acrostic. A further example is the acrostic composition אז בפסח גאלת (Habermann 1939, 66–67), which bears no consistent rhyme or meter.

[9] A selection of these core phrases follows. Within the first benediction: הזן את העולם כי הוא זן ומפרנס לכל and כולו בטוב, נותן לחם לכל בשר,; within the second benediction: the tetracolon beginning ארץ חמדה (cited above n. 7), and the subsequent summation phrase, ועל כולם אנחנו מודים לך; and within the third benediction: ,מלכות בית דוד תחזירה למקומה, רחם...על ישראל עמך, and the concluding formula תבנה עיר קדשך בימינו.

[10] Although in practice the grace after meals contains four benedictions (t.Ber 6,1), the fourth benediction is relegated to a secondary status within Rabbinic literature (p.Ber 1,4 3d; Ber 48b; Finkelstein 1929, 221–222). Additionally, its early form was likely comprised of nothing more than a single doxology, without any body text at all. For these reasons, the poetic versions of the grace after meals generally abstain from offering alternatives for the fourth benediction. For a further discussion of the interplay of this benediction with the poetic recitals, see Shmidman 2006, 60f.

and 213 statutory texts. This categorization is further corroborated
by the scribal patterns within the manuscripts. On the one hand, the
manuscripts categorized as statutory texts consistently present the prayer
within its full liturgical context. The initial blessing formula (ברוך אתה
יי אלהינו מלך העולם) is always indicated at the start of the transcription,
and cited verses are almost always written out in full. In contrast, the
overwhelming majority of the poetic versions are recorded in shorthand
form, without the opening blessing formula, and with Biblical citations
abbreviated to no more than two or three words.[11] Thus, we find that
the Geniza scribes themselves treated the two categories as separate
and distinct. Regarding the poetic versions, the scribes' focus rested
upon the preservation of the specific poetic content, in contrast to the
statutory texts, which were fully transcribed for straightforward use by
the common worshipper.

Nevertheless, as each of these genres is represented by a plethora of
Geniza transcriptions, it is apparent that these two categories of texts
were both in frequent use among the Jews of the Geniza communities.
Furthermore, a number of manuscripts present both statutory and
poetic transcriptions, one alongside the other, as two equally viable
options for the *birkat ha-mazon*.[12] Thus, given the concurrent use of these
two genres of prayer texts within the Geniza communities, it is reasonable to expect that they would influence one another over time.

## II. Biblical Prooftexts

The first liturgical feature we will consider is the use of Biblical prooftexts to conclude the three primary benedictions of the *birkat ha-mazon*
prayer. Among the poetic forms of the prayer, the three benedictions
consistently close with citations from Ps 145:16, Deut 8:10, and Ps 147:2,
respectively.[13] To be sure, these verses are not relegated to the poetic

---

[11] Nevertheless, a number of exceptional manuscripts exist in which poetic forms are
presented in their full liturgical context; these will be discussed below in section III.

[12] For example, such is the case in one prayer book comprised of the following three
Geniza manuscripts: Ms. Cambridge T-S 8H11.4 + Ms. London Or. 7943.3 + Ms.
Leningrad, Antonin Collection, 105. Further examples of this phenomenon can be
found in Ms. Cambridge Or. 1080 15.4 and Ms. Cambridge T-S NS 119.63.

[13] Additional verses, corresponding to the specific occasion for which the hymn was
composed, may appear prior to these prooftexts. For instance, in poetic texts which serve
as the *birkat ha-mazon* for betrothal celebrations, the initial prooftexts are often drawn

forms alone; they can often be found among Geniza transcriptions of the statutory text as well. However, despite the apparent similarity, the status of this feature within the two categories of texts should not be equated. Indeed, I would like to argue that whereas the prooftexts occupy an integral position within the structure of the poetic forms, their appearance within the statutory text is secondary and non-essential, and should be considered a later addition. In the following, I attempt to substantiate this assertion.

First, a quantitative tally serves to highlight the differing roles played by the Biblical prooftexts within the two genres of the *birkat ha-mazon*. On the one hand, among the manuscripts of the poetic versions, we find a virtually universal adoption of the three verse paradigm,[14] reflecting its integral position within the poetic form. In contrast, more than a third of the Geniza manuscripts of the statutory text omit these prooftexts altogether.[15] This latter group of manuscripts does not bear the signs of a single textual branch,[16] and therefore the lack of prooftexts should not be characterized as a specifically Palestinian or Babylonian tendency. Rather, it is reasonable to view the absence of the verses as representative of the early state of the statutory text. Corroborating this outlook is the distribution of extra suppplicatory phrases at the end

from Hos 2:21–22, while compositions intended for weddings generally incorporate Is 61:10 (Shmidman 2005, 24–25). However, in contrast to these latter verses, which appear only as contextually appropriate, the three prooftexts delineated above occupy an essentially inviolable position, consistently concluding the chains of Biblical verses.

[14] As Fleischer (1975, 249) has noted, in rare cases a hymnist may choose to skip the verses for the sake of brevity; three such cases can be found in Habermann's collection (1939, 98–99). However, these exceptional cases may simply reflect scribal omissions, as part of the general tendency toward abbreviation in poetic transcriptions (as noted above, section I). This latter possibility can often be substantiated by means of additional examination and evidence. For instance, in the poem אברך [האל] הטוב (Habermann 1939, 98), the first section concludes with a lexical cue to Ps 145:16 (המשביע כל טוב), indicating that the prooftext was indeed intended to follow, despite its omission in the manuscript. Additionally, although the poem אתא יום ענוגה appears *sans* verses in Habermann's transcription (1939, 98–99), based upon Ms. Cambridge H5.2, it also appears in a parallel transcription from Ms. Cambridge, Westminster College, Liturgica II.54, in which all three prooftexts occupy their usual places within the composition.

[15] Within our corpus of statutory texts, there are 72 transcriptions in which all three benedictions are extant; in 27 of these the prooftexts are omitted entirely.

[16] The group includes manuscripts on either side of the coin of the various defining characteristics of the statutory versions, such as the inclusion of the phrase והתקין מזון לכל אשר ברא in the first benediction; the start of the second blessing with על ארצינו; the elaboration ועל בריתך ששמת בבשרנו in the second benediction; the use of the phrase ועל מלכות בית דוד as part of the initial statement of the third benediction; and the appendage of the word בימינו at the end of the third benediction.

of the first two benedictions of the statutory text, whose presence tends to correlate with the inclusion of the prooftexts.[17] These supplicatory sections are clearly later appendages to the statutory text, as reflected by the wide-ranging variations within their composition,[18] and in view of the inherently non-supplicatory nature of the benedictions in which they appear. Therefore, their appearance together with the prooftexts substantiates a view of the latter as a later addition to the statutory text, rather than as an early element which dropped out over time.

Second, an examination of the statutory text *sans* verses reveals a coherent literary work, leading naturally into the doxologies in a direct manner that allows no place for intervening prooftexts. This is evident within each of the first two benedictions of the prayer. With regard to the first benediction, the phrase כי הוא זן ומפרנס לכל, common to virtually all of the statutory texts in our corpus, was clearly coined in order to mirror the doxology, הזן את הכל. Based upon literary considerations, as well as the Talmudic principle of מעין חתימה (p.Ber 1,4 3d; Pes 104a) which mandates that a benediction's text shall conclude with a formulation akin to its doxology, it is reasonable to presume that the statutory text originally concluded with the phrase כי הוא זן ומפרנס לכל, continuing promptly with the recitation of the doxology (Shoval 2004, 46). And indeed, the benediction is formulated thus in many of the statutory versions among the Geniza manuscripts.[19] Therefore,

---

[17] Within the first benediction, the extra supplications occur in 7 of the 36 texts in which the corresponding prooftext is included, while their occurrence is *never* noted among the 51 texts which omit the prooftext. Similarly, within the second benediction, extra supplications appear in 30 of the 44 texts which include the corresponding prooftext, while they occur in only 8 of the 50 texts which omit the verse.

[18] This property is most evident within the supplicatory section of the second benediction, which includes almost every possible permutation of four distinct phrases: (a) a request for vengeance upon our enemies (והנקם לנו מצרינו); (b) a request for satiation with Divine Goodness (ומטובך תשבע נפשינו); (c) a request that God never cease providing us food (ואל תחסרנו מלכינו מזון); and (d) a request that God heed the Covenant (וזכור לנו מהרה את ברית אבותינו). Examples of their various permutations are the following: Ms. Leningrad Antonin 152 includes only (a); Ms. Cambridge T-S NS 229.36 includes only (b); Ms. Oxford 2738 f74 includes only (d); Ms. Cambridge T-S NS 271.72 includes (b) and (d); Ms. Cambridge T-S NS 152.35 includes (a) and (d); Ms. Cambridge T-S NS 151.18 includes (b), (c), and (d); and Ms. Cincinnati 1200 includes (a), (b) and (d). Within the first benediction, the substance of the phrase is generally stable, but the variations within the wording are still noteworthy. Compare for instance: Ms. Cambridge T-S NS 151.18: רצון תשבעינו ורוח תמציאנו ורזון תעביר ממנו; Ms. Cambridge T-S NS 122.39: ורצון תעטרינו ומזון תשבעינו ואסון העביר מקרבינו; and Ms. Paris AIU IV A162: רצון תעטרינו ורזון ואסון תעביר ממנו לחם תשבעינו בגן עדן תרביצנו...

[19] Of the 51 manuscripts in which the first benediction omits the prooftext, 16 (nearly one third) continue straight into the doxology following the phrase כי הוא זן ומפרנס לכל.

any phrases which interrupt the natural connection between these two textual elements should be viewed as later additions, including the prooftext from Ps 145.

Similarly, an analysis of the text of the second benediction underscores the incongruous position occupied by the prooftext from Deut 8:10. The core section of this benediction bears a symmetrical structure of thanksgiving, in which the text opens with an expression of thanksgiving,[20] continues with a list of specific items which God has granted,[21] and concludes with a general statement of thanksgiving to the Divine name.[22] This coherent structure, comprising the entirety of the benediction in many Geniza manuscripts,[23] also corresponds with a Talmudic directive (Ber 49a), according to which the second benediction must both begin and end with expressions of thanksgiving.[24] Phrases appearing subsequent to the thanksgiving framework deviate both from the literary structure of the text as well as from its Talmudic design; therefore, such phrases, which include the prooftext from Deuteronomy, should be considered later expansions of the text. In fact, in a number of the manuscripts which bear expanded forms of the benediction, a *third* expression of general thanksgiving is appended to the end, prior to the doxology.[25] This phenomenon reflects a recognition of the problems

---

[20] The opening statement of the benediction always contains the phrase נודה לך יי אלהינו. In about half the manuscripts of the corpus, this phrase constitutes the initial words of the statement, while among the others it is introduced by the prepositional phrase על ארצינו ועל נחלת אבותינו.

[21] Minimally, this list contains the tetracolon cited above at the beginning of n. 7. However, in a portion of the manuscripts, an elaboration of each of the items follows afterward.

[22] This statement is generally phrased as follows: ועל כולם אנו מודים לך ומברכים את שמך.

[23] Among the 44 manuscripts in which the second benediction appears without a prooftext, 34 (77%) continue directly into the doxology immediately following the close of the thanksgiving structure.

[24] This directive, which explicitly stipulates that the end of the benediction consist of a thanksgiving phrase, would seem to override the mandate to mirror the language of the doxology at the conclusion of the text (מעין חתימה). However, in a limited number of manuscripts, we witness an attempt to merge the two requirements. An example of such can be found in Ms. Cincinnati HUC 1200, in which the second benediction concludes ונודה לשמך סלה על ארצינו ועל מזונותינו, an expression of thanksgiving which also mirrors the doxology, על הארץ ועל המזון. Nevertheless, formulations such as this one are quite rare, occurring in only 12 of the manuscripts in our corpus.

[25] The corpus contains 47 transcriptions in which extra material is included after the thanksgiving framework, and in which the conclusion of the benediction is extant. Among these, 19 contain a third thanksgiving phrase immediately prior to the doxology. For examples of such, see Ms. Cambridge T-S NS 151.18 and Ms. Cambridge Add. 3162 (for a transcription and discussion of the latter manuscript, see Reif 2005, 11–29).

inherent within the addition of extra material outside the closed thanks-giving framework, while at the same time underscoring the fact that the extra phrases were added at a secondary stage.[26]

In contrast, the poetic texts often conclude with phrases that point unmistakably towards the Biblical prooftexts, rather than to the dox-ologies, indicating that the appearance of the verses is not accidental, but rather an integral part of the compositions. For example, within the first benediction, concluding lines such as שבעינו הטוב מפתיחת ידך (Habermann 1939, 98), ומפתיחת ידך תשבעינו (Shmidman 2005, 102), בחסד ובצדקה אותם להשביע (Shmidman 2005, 111), and להשביעי עם כל חי ברצון (Shmidman 2005, 92) all gracefully anticipate the prooftext from Ps 145:16, פותח את ידך ומשביע לכל חי רצון. Similarly, within the second and third benedictions, we find concluding phrases that reflect the themes of the corresponding prooftexts.[27] Thus, as opposed to the statutory text, which stands alone as a coherent composition without the added prooftexts, the concluding formulae of the poetic versions indicate the organic role played within by the Biblical verses.[28]

Finally, the compositional status of the prooftexts as they appear in the poetic versions reflects their authenticity as part of the poetic form. Within the poetic versions of the *birkat ha-mazon*, all three prooftexts serve together as part of a set structural pattern, wherein each one of the benedictions is comprised of a poetic section followed by a Biblical verse.[29] Indeed, this pattern is well known from other forms of early

---

[26] For, if the extra material were part of the original construction of the text, there would be no need for the general expression of thanksgiving in the middle of the benediction.

[27] Examples of phrases which pick up on the second prooftext from Deuteronomy 8:10: ותאכילינו מחלב ארצך (Habermann 1939, 98); ומטוב ארצו יעודדנו (Shmidman 2005, 93); סודרי ברית יצמחו כרבבה / על הארץ הטובה (Shmidman 2005, 113). Examples within the third benediction, anticipating the prooftext from Ps 147:2: ו[בב]נין עירך תכנס פזורינו (Shmidman 2005, 94); נדחי מארבע תכנס (Shmidman 2005, 111).

[28] As noted above (n. 13), additional contextually-appropriate verses often precede the standard prooftexts. As is to be expected, in these cases the concluding formulae of the poetic text generally anticipate the additional verses, rather than the standard prooftexts which appear only at the end of the string of verses. Nevertheless, such cases still uphold the integrity of the Biblical citations within the poetic form.

[29] Manuscripts which include only a partial representation of the three prooftexts are extremely rare; for examples, see Ms. Cambridge T-S H15.14 (in which the first proof-text is omitted) and Ms. Cambridge T-S Glass 20.134 (in which the second prooftext is omitted). In both of these instances, however, the omissions occur following additional Biblical citations. Therefore, these transcriptions do not represent an aberration from the structural pattern in which poetic sections are succeeded by Biblical prooftexts. Indeed, since the overall structure is maintained, and since the other benedictions do include

*piyyut*, such as the *Qedushtaot* and the *Yotzerot*, both of which conclude their poetic sections with Biblical verses prior to the corresponding doxologies.[30] The consistency with which all of these *piyyut* forms employ Biblical prooftexts at the conclusion of the benedictions underscores the integral structural role played by the citations within the poetic genre. By way of contrast, among the statutory versions of the *birkat ha-mazon* it is extremely uncommon to find a manuscript that includes all three prooftexts in their respective positions.[31] On the contrary, even when Biblical prooftexts are included within the statutory texts, the verses generally appear only in one or two of the benedictions.[32] This sporadic distribution of the prooftexts is indicative of the fact that their presence is not inherent to the statutory form.

Based upon the foregoing arguments, we may conclude that the Biblical prooftexts operate differently within the two categories of texts. Within the poetic versions of the *birkat ha-mazon*, the verse citations form an organic component of the prayer, while within the statutory text, the verses are marginal appendages belonging to a later stage. Furthermore, in light of the common and concurrent use of both

---

the usual concluding prooftexts, it is likely that the omissions represent no more than a scribal error. Regarding an additional set of exceptional cases, in which the verses are omitted altogether from the poetic versions, see above (n. 14).

[30] See Fleischer 1975, 141–142; 214–215. It should be noted that within the *Qedushtaot*, an additional poetic stanza intervenes between the verses and the doxology; however, as Fleischer (1972, 291–295 esp. 293) has demonstrated, such concluding stanzas likely represent a later development.

[31] From among the 72 transcriptions in which all three benedictions are extant, three alone integrate the full array of prooftexts: Ms. Oxford 2734 f6–8; Ms. Paris AIU IV A162; and Ms. Cambridge T-S 155.120.

[32] In the most common case, prooftexts are brought in the first two benedictions, but not in the third. However, these two verses do not always accompany each other. In eight manuscripts, the prooftext of the second benediction is included while the prooftext of the first benediction is omitted (Ms. Cambridge T-S NS 145.46; Ms. Cambridge T-S NS 152.35; Ms. Cambridge T-S NS 229.36; Ms. Cambridge T-S NS 271.185; Ms. Cambridge T-S AS 104.3; Ms. Cambridge, Westminster College, Liturgica I.184; Ms. Vienna, Österreichische NB, Rainer coll. H 119; and Ms. JTS ENA NS 52.12). Conversely, in two other manuscripts, the first benediction includes a prooftext while the second does not (Ms. Oxford 2736 f16, Ms. Cambridge T-S NS 150.8). The third prooftext generally (but not exclusively) occurs in transcriptions intended specifically for the Sabbath. In such transcriptions, the third benediction is altered in order to integrate the Sabbath theme, and in about half of these manuscripts, the additional Sabbath material is succeeded by a string of verses regarding the consolation of Jerusalem. Our third prooftext, from Ps 147:2, integrates naturally into this theme. (For further discussion regarding the use of verses to conclude special prayer supplements, see below, n. 46 and 50.)

forms of the prayer within the Geniza period, it is reasonable to view
the partial integration of the verses within the statutory text as a result
of the influence of the poetic versions. The worshippers and the copyists of the period were certainly familiar with, and perhaps also fond
of, the set of prooftexts which preceded the doxologies in the poetic
versions of the prayer; and therefore, as part of the general tendency
at the time to expand the text of the *birkat ha-mazon* with additional
phrases and requests, they began to insert the very same citations, one
at a time, into their statutory recitals.

### III. The Covenant Phrase

Having established that the prooftexts originated in the poetic versions
of *birkat ha-mazon* and later migrated to the statutory text, we can
proceed to understand the rise of an additional phrase which often
appears at the end of the second benediction of the statutory text. The
phrase reads וזכור לנו מהרה ברית אבותינו ('Speedily remember for us
the covenant of our forefathers'); we will refer to it henceforth as the
'Covenant Phrase'. Approximately one third of the statutory versions
in our corpus include the Covenant Phrase.[33] Thus, while not universal,
its inclusion in the statutory text is nevertheless notable.

In the poetic versions, on the other hand, the popularity of the
Covenant Phrase is not immediately apparent. At first glance, its use
is no more than occasional, appearing in less than 15 percent of the
Geniza manuscripts which record poetic versions of the *birkat ha-
mazon*. However, in order to properly evaluate this evidence, it must be
recalled that the scribes of the Geniza period generally recorded poetic
texts in abbreviated form, including little more than the poetic stanzas
and the initial words of the prooftexts. Therefore, such manuscripts
do not constitute reliable evidence regarding the use or non-use of
additional liturgical passages (Fleischer 1970, 55 n. 39). Rather, such
determinations can only be derived from the transcriptions which present the poetic compositions within a complete liturgical context. As
I have shown in a separate study (Shmidman 2006, 49–54) an examination of this latter group of transcriptions reveals that the overwhelming

---

[33] The corpus contains 89 manuscripts in which the relevant part of the prayer is
extant; of these, 26 include the Covenant Phrase.

majority do indeed include the Covenant Phrase at the end of the second benediction. Therefore, we can conclude that the Covenant Phrase did, in fact, form a standard part of the poetic recitals of the *birkat ha-mazon* during the Geniza period. Indeed, I would like to argue that it is specifically within the poetic texts that the phenomenon developed, and that it only later migrated to the statutory text.

First, in considering the motivation for the emergence of this particular phrase in the second benediction, it is instructive to note the Rabbinic dictum which mandates that this benediction include a reference to the covenant. According to Rabbinic sources, this reference is obligatory; if the covenant is not mentioned in the second benediction, the prayer is invalidated (t.Ber 3,9; p.Ber 1,5 3d; Ber 48b). In accordance with this requirement, the statutory versions of the *birkat ha-mazon* from the Geniza always cite the covenant within the initial list of items for which thanksgiving is due.[34] Furthermore, in a portion of the manuscripts, an additional reference appears as part of an elaborated list that follows soon afterwards: ועל בריתך ששמת בבשרינו.[35] By contrast, among the poetic texts, the mention of the covenant is significantly lacking. Although references to the covenant can be found within a portion of the poetic compositions, more than half of them omit the subject altogether.[36] Therefore, as opposed to the statutory text, in which the covenant theme was fully integrated, the poetic recitals were in need of augmentation in order to be considered valid prayer texts. It is likely, then, that the Covenant Phrase arose initially as a supplement to the poetic forms of the *birkat ha-mazon*, in order to satisfy the Rabbinic requirement of the covenant reference.

Moreover, it is illuminating to consider the connection between the Covenant Phrase and the prooftext of the second benediction (Deut 8:10). Within the poetic texts, the Covenant Phrase always appears immediately following this prooftext. To be sure, this positioning is not surprising. As we saw above, the Deuteronomy verse is always used to conclude the poetic section of the second benediction, with

---

[34] The text of this line is cited above (n. 7).

[35] The corpus contains 85 manuscripts in which the relevant portion is extant. Of these, the extra covenant reference is included in 22 manuscripts, including eight in which the Covenant Phrase also appears. Note that occasionally the texts adopt an alternate phraseology, using the verb חתמת ('stamped') instead of שמת ('placed').

[36] The covenant is referenced in only 62 of the 139 poetic compositions for which the second section is fully extant.

which it forms an inseparable whole. Therefore, the Covenant Phrase
is understandably inserted after the conclusion of the verse. Interestingly, though, this same connection is maintained in the statutory texts,
despite the fact that the verse is far less prevalent there. First of all, the
appearance of the Covenant Phrase within statutory texts is exclusively
limited to those in which the Deuteronomy prooftext is also included.[37]
Additionally, in almost all of its appearances, the Covenant Phrase is
placed exactly as it is within the poetic texts, immediately subsequent
to the prooftext.[38]

The consistent coupling of the Covenant Phrase together with the
Deuteronomy prooftext provides a basis upon which we can understand
the migration of the phrase into a statutory text that already included
one, and often two, prior mentions of the covenant. A well-known path
within liturgical development involves the fusion of two juxtaposed
liturgical elements into a single unit which is then transferred as a
whole, regardless of the relevance of the individual elements (Fleischer
1988, 178 n. 98). Such may have been the case with the Covenant
Phrase, which was consistently recited within the poetic recitals of
the *birkat ha-mazon* immediately after the Deuteronomy verse. In the
eyes of many worshippers, these two juxtaposed elements were likely
viewed as a single inseparable unit.[39] Therefore, when the Deuteronomy
verse began to migrate from the poetic texts into the statutory text, it
was often adopted along with the post-posed Covenant Phrase. This
explanation, which emerges from the otherwise puzzling distribution
of the Covenant Phrase within the statutory texts, also underscores the
origin of the phrase as part of the liturgical recitations of the poetic
compositions.

---

[37] To be sure, as we noted above, extra supplications within the second benediction
do tend to correlate with the presence of the prooftext (see statistics above, n. 17).
However, the Covenant Phrase is distinguished from the other supplications in that it
is *fully* reliant upon the prooftext; throughout the corpus, it only occurs in texts which
also include the Deuteronomy verse.

[38] Of the 26 statutory texts which include the Covenant Phrase, 23 place it immediately after the prooftext. In the three remaining transcriptions (Ms. Cambridge T-S
H11.74; Ms. Cambridge T-S NS 153.139; and Ms. Paris AIU IV A162), one additional
supplication intervenes between the prooftext and the Covenant Phrase.

[39] It is worth noting that the Biblical section containing the Deuteronomy prooftext
concludes, eight verses later, with the phrase למען הקים את בריתו אשר נשבע לאבתיך
כיום הזה. This latter verse likely influenced the formulation of the Covenant Phrase,
and reinforced its connection to the prooftext.

## IV. CHRONOLOGICAL PERSPECTIVES

In the foregoing sections, we have demonstrated that both the Biblical prooftexts as well as the Covenant Phrase originated within the context of the poetic forms, and only later migrated into the statutory text over the course of the Geniza period. Nevertheless, it should be emphasized that from a chronological perspective, the first appearances of these two features within the poetic texts may have been hundreds of years apart.

On the one hand, the Covenant Phrase is clearly a later addition to the *birkat ha-mazon*, not only within the statutory text, but also with regard to the poetic forms. Indeed, even within the latter group, the Covenant Phrase does not occupy an integral position; according to their original intent, the poetic forms were to be recited with their poetry and prooftexts alone, without any additional augmentation. Rather, the hypothesis presented in this paper posits the rise of the Covenant Phrase as a later supplement to the poetic forms, in accordance with the Rabbinic requirements for the prayer. Of course, in order for the Covenant Phrase to migrate into the statutory text along with the Biblical prooftexts, it must have first achieved normative status within the poetic forms; however, it is possible that this status had materialized only shortly prior to the Geniza period. Indeed, even among the Geniza transcriptions which present the poetic compositions within a full liturgical context, the Covenant Phrase is occasionally omitted (Shmidman 2006, 53), perhaps indicating that the acceptance of the Covenant Phrase as a liturgical norm had occurred in the not-so-distant past.

Regarding the Biblical prooftexts, by contrast, our conclusions reflect upon a much earlier time period. As we have demonstrated above, this feature occurs within the poetic forms as an organic, integral component. From this we may infer that the inclusion of the verses dates back to the point at which the early piyyut structures were originally crystallized, a stage which precedes the Geniza transcriptions by several centuries. Indeed, among the poetic compositions of the *birkat ha-mazon* from the Geniza we find two which can be dated to the preclassical period of *piyyut*, including one attributed to the 5th century poet Yose ben Yose.[40] Needless to say, even these earlier compositions consistently integrate the Biblical prooftexts.

---

[40] Regarding this composition (בורא עולם) and its attribution, see Fleischer (1970, 45 n. 9; 2000–01, 17–18); regarding the dating of the hymnist Yose ben Yose, see

It should be noted, however, that the statutory texts which we exam-
ined here do not necessarily represent a similarly antique time period.
As stated, within these manuscripts the prooftexts appear as sporadic
supplements and not as integral components. Thus, the migration of
verses into the statutory text during the Geniza period emerges as a
likely conclusion. However, the development of the statutory text *prior*
to this period certainly may have involved alternate trajectories.

Indeed, Fleischer (1998, 301–350 esp. 307) maintains that the statutory text originally included prooftexts prior to each of the doxologies,
and that these verses fell out of use prior to the Geniza period under
Rabbinic pressure.[41] Unfortunately, due to the dearth of documentation from this early time period, Fleischer cannot appeal to any extant
versions of the prayers in order to support his speculation. Rather,
interestingly, the basis for his theory is the very structure which we
have identified within the poetic compositions. Fleischer contends that
the consistent use of Biblical prooftexts within early *piyyut* cannot be
reasonably explained in and of itself; instead, he concludes that these
structures must have been modeled on the corresponding statutory
prayers of the time.[42] Nevertheless, I believe that Fleischer's speculation is likely mistaken.

First of all, although no fully formed versions of the statutory text
are available from the relevant time period,[43] we do have access to two
fairly parallel early texts. The first of these is the Didache, a first-century
Christian tractate,[44] which delineates a full grace after meals text.[45] This
prayer text contains a number of striking parallels to the statutory text

---

Mirsky (1991, 15–16). The other preclassical poetic text of the *birkat ha-mazon* is the
composition אז בפסח גאלת (Habermann 1939, 66–67), whose style and structure place
it firmly within this period.

[41] Fleischer presents his claims and arguments not just with regard to the *birkat ha-
mazon*, but also regarding the *Amidot* and the benedictions of the *Shema*.

[42] This theory presumes, of course, that the statutory prayers preceded the poetic
ones, as was compellingly demonstrated by Fleischer in a separate study (1970, 47–52).

[43] To be sure, a very early grace after meals fragment was found among the remains
of the Dura Europos Synagogue. However, only the beginning of the text is extant,
and therefore the fragment does not bear upon the question of the prooftexts and
doxologies. Furthermore, as Lieberman (1992, 40–41) has conjectured, this text may
well represent a poetic version of the *birkat ha-mazon*, rather than the statutory text.
For the text of the Dura Europos fragment and a recent discussion of its liturgical
implications, see Fine (2005, 41–71 esp. 46–58).

[44] For the dating of the Didache, see Sandt and Flusser (2002, 48–52).

[45] The grace after meals text comprises chapter 10 of the Didache. For an updated
translation, see Sandt and Flusser (2002, 13–14). Their translation is used in citations
from the Didache below.

of the *birkat ha-mazon*, and is widely considered to have been modeled after the corresponding Jewish prayer of the time (Sandt and Flusser 2002, 311–318). Notable, though, is the complete absence of Scriptural citations in the Didache version of the prayer. Therefore, to the extent that the text in the Didache is indicative of the early structure of the *birkat ha-mazon*, it highlights the use of the prayer without prooftexts.

The second relevant early text is the Dead Sea Scroll fragment 4Q434a, which Weinfeld (1992, 427–440 esp. 427–437; cf. also Weinfeld & Seely 1999, 267–286 esp. 280–281) has identified as a grace after meals text. As opposed to the Didache, the overall structure of this text does not at all resemble that of the *birkat ha-mazon*; nevertheless, in his examination of the fragment, Weinfeld locates indications of each of the Rabbinically mandated themes. Significantly, though, our three prooftexts are completely absent from this text.[46] Therefore, if Weinfeld is correct in his identification of the fragment, it may serve to demonstrate that even at this early proto-rabbinic stage, the basic themes of the prayer were elucidated without reference to the corresponding Biblical verses.[47]

Moreover, as we noted above, the statutory text during the Geniza period stands alone, without prooftexts, as a coherently structured

---

[46] To be sure, the upper half of the fragment does contain a citation of Is 66:13, based upon which Weinfeld concludes that the prayer was intended specifically for use in a house of mourning. Nevertheless, the use of a verse to mark a particular circumstance should not be considered surprising. Mirsky (1958, 1–129 esp. 98) and Fleischer (1972, 293) have already noted that as opposed to the standard statutory text, liturgical supplements for special occasions do tend to conclude with prooftexts, in a manner similar to the poetic compositions. Similarly, as we have noted above (n. 32), the Sabbath supplement found within Geniza manuscripts of the grace after meals often concludes with a selection of verses which prophesy consolation for Jerusalem. Interestingly, Is 66:13 sometimes appears within the latter context; such is the case in Ms. Cambridge T-S H 11.74; Ms. JTS ENA 2138 f8; and Ms. Cambridge, Westminster College, Liturgica III.51–55. In light of this use of the Isaiah verse, it is worth considering whether the prayer text found in fragment 4Q434a might have been intended for the Sabbath, rather than for a house of mourning. (Regarding the function of the prooftexts within the liturgical supplements, see below, n. 50.)

[47] Note that Weinfeld (1992, 427–429) has also designated two other fragments (4QDeut^j and 4QDeut^n) as serving the function of the grace after meals. Although both of these fragments do include Deuteronomy 8:10 (the second of the three standard prooftexts), the verse is not brought as a prooftext, but rather as part of a transcription of the corresponding Biblical section. It is certainly possible, as Weinfeld claims, that these Biblical transcriptions served at one time as the grace after meals prayer, presumably representing a stage in which the liturgy was comprised exclusively of Biblical recitals. However, as such, these fragments cannot shed any light on the question of whether or not Biblical verses were employed as a regular structural element in post-Biblical prayer texts.

literary composition. Had the prayer originally contained prooftexts which later fell out of use, we would expect the literary composition of the text to be negatively affected; although not impossible, it is unlikely that the text would have been so thoughtfully restructured after the removal of the verses. Furthermore, the symmetric thanksgiving structure which we identified within the second benediction of the statutory text finds an exact parallel within the first-century grace after meals delineated in the Didache.[48] This comparison upholds the symmetric thanksgiving structure of the Geniza texts as an authentic part of the early form of the prayer; and, as we demonstrated above, this structure leaves no room for additional prooftext citations.

Finally, Fleischer's speculation rests upon the assumption that the consistent use of prooftexts within the poetic forms can only be explained by appealing to the corresponding statutory forms. Yet, Fleischer himself, in an earlier work (1975, 142), suggested two reasonable alternate explanations. According to the first suggestion, the verses served to highlight the termination of the poetic sections.[49] Since the highly stylized poetic texts were often unfamiliar to the congregants, the poetic tradition adopted the use of easily recognizable Biblical verses to signal the approach of the doxology.[50] Additionally, Fleischer suggests, it may have seemed improper to the hymnists to directly introduce the doxologies with their own novel formulations; instead, they appealed to the authenticity of the Biblical prooftexts as they concluded their original poetic compositions.

---

[48] The relevant section in the Didache opens in 10:2 with the phrase 'We thank you, holy father', continuing in verses 2 and 3 with a list of items for which thanksgiving is due, and concluding in verse 4 with the phrase 'For all things we thank you'. The striking parallel to the second benediction of the *birkat ha-mazon*, which also presents a detailed list of items between the phrases נודה לך and ועל כולם אנחנו מודים לך, is highlighted by Sandt and Flusser (2002, 314).

[49] This explanation is primarily relevant in a congregational setting in which the poetry is declaimed by a single cantor, while the rest of the worshippers listen along. Although *a priori* this situation might seem applicable only to the synagogue recitals of the *Yotzerot* and the *Qedushtaot*, it is also relevant to the mealtime recitals of the *birkat ha-mazon*, which were performed as a group ritual (*zimmun*) when three or more were present. Indeed, as Fleischer (1970, 45 n. 9) has shown, such group recitals originally entailed the declamation of the entire text by a single leader.

[50] This theory can also serve to explain the use of Biblical prooftexts to conclude the special supplements added to the statutory prayers on particular occasions (see above, n. 46). Here too, the verses fill a signaling function, alerting the worshippers to the end of the extraordinary text. (I am indebted to my colleague Tzvi Novick for this suggestion.)

In conclusion, then, Fleischer's speculation has very little evidence upon which to stand. The rise of the prooftexts within the poetic forms can be amply explained without positing their existence within the statutory forms. Rather, based on the evidence presented here, it is more reasonable to assume that the early forms of the statutory text did not contain any prooftexts, in consonance with the coherent literary text which we find later in the Geniza manuscripts.

## V. Conclusion

The comparison of the poetic forms of the *birkat ha-mazon* with the corresponding statutory text thus serves to shed light upon the puzzling sporadic appearance of Biblical prooftexts within the statutory text, as well as upon the surprising adoption of the additional Covenant Phrase into a benediction which already included a sufficient number of covenant references. To be sure, it was the statutory form which existed first,[51] setting an example for the poetic forms in terms of the layout of the benedictions and the concluding doxologies. But in the course of its development, it partially adopted additional elements which arose originally in order to serve the needs of the poetic compositions. Thus, although the poetic forms no longer constitute a mainstream option within contemporary liturgical practice, their influence is still apparent in the Biblical prooftexts that continue to grace the statutory text of the *birkat ha-mazon*.[52]

## Literature

Davidson, I., 'Researches in Mediaeval Hebrew Poetry', *JQR* 29 (1938–39).

Fine, S., 'Liturgy and the Art of the Dura Europos Synagogue', in: R. Langer & S. Fine (eds), *Liturgy in the Life of the Synagogue*, Indiana 2005.

Finkelstein, L., 'The Birkat Hamazon', *JQR* 19 (1929).

Fleischer, E., 'Additional Fragments from Palestinian Prayer Books from the Geniza' [Hebrew], *Kobez al Yad* 15 (2000–2001).

———, *Eretz-Israel Prayer and Prayer Rituals*, Jerusalem 1988 [Hebrew].

———, *Hebrew Liturgical Poetry in the Middle Ages*, Jerusalem 1975 [Hebrew].

———, 'Inquiries in the Structure of the Classical Qedushta', in: *The Proceedings of the Fifth World Congress of Jewish Studies*, volume 3, Jerusalem 1972 [Hebrew].

---

[51] See above (n. 42).

[52] Many contemporary rites include the first prooftext, and almost all of them include the second verse. Nevertheless, the Covenant Phrase has largely fallen out of use, along with the rest of the extra supplications of the second benediction.

————, 'The *Qedusha* of the *Amida* (and other *Qedushot*): Historical, Liturgical, and Ideological Aspects', *Tarb.* 67 (1998) [Hebrew].

————, 'Studies in the Problems relating to the Liturgical Function of the Types of Early *Piyyut*', *Tarb.* 40 (1970) [Hebrew].

Habermann, A.M., 'Poetical Blessings after Meals', *Studies of the Research Institute for Hebrew Poetry in Jerusalem* 5 (1939) [Hebrew].

Lieberman, S., *Yemenite Midrashim*, Jerusalem 2nd ed. 1992 [Hebrew].

Mirsky, A., *Yosse ben Yosse Poems*, Jerusalem 2nd ed. 1991 [Hebrew].

————, 'The Origins of the Forms of Liturgical Poetry', *Studies of the Research Institute for Hebrew Poetry in Jerusalem* 7 (1958) [Hebrew].

Razhabi, Y., 'New Poetical "Birkhot Mazon"', *Sinai* 108 (1991) [Hebrew].

————, 'Poetical "Birkhot Mazon"', *Sinai* 113 (1994) [Hebrew].

————, 'Poetical "Birkhot Mazon" for the Tishri Festivals', *Tarb.* 53 (1984) [Hebrew].

Reif, S., 'Ein Genisa-Fragment des Tischdank', in: W. Homolka (ed.), *Liturgie als Theologie: Das Gebet als Zentrum im judischen Denken*, Berlin 2005 [English ed.: id., *Problems with Prayers; Studies in the Textual History of Early Rabbinic Liturgy* (SJ 37), Berlin—New York 2006, 333–348].

Sandt, H. van de and D. Flusser, *The Didache*, Assen 2002.

Shmidman, A., *Epithalamia for the Grace after Meals from the Cairo Geniza*, MA Thesis, Ramat-Gan 2005 [Hebrew].

————, 'The Liturgical Function of Poetic Versions of the Grace after Meals', *Ginzei Qedem* 2 (2006) [Hebrew].

Shoval, K., *The First Benediction within the Grace after Meals; Formulation and Meaning* [MA Thesis, unpubl.], Beer Sheva 2004 [Hebrew].

Weinfeld, M., 'Grace after Meals in Qumran', *JBL* 111 (1992).

————, & D. Seely, '434.4QBarkhi Nafshi', *DJD* 29 (1999).

# OBSERVATIONS ON THE RELATIONSHIP BETWEEN JPA POETRY AND THE HEBREW PIYYUT TRADITION—THE CASE OF THE *KINOT*

*Michael Rand*
The Jewish Theological Seminary, USA

The aim of this essay is to sketch the development of the Hebrew poetic tradition of writing dirges lamenting the destruction of Jerusalem and the Temple, as it developed from the Bible onward.[1] Once I have established the basic outlines of this tradition, I proceed to compare it with another (related) Jewish poetic tradition—that represented by poems written in the Jewish Palestinian Aramaic dialect, during the Late Antique period.[2] For our present purposes, the goal of such a comparison is to enable us to properly situate the JPA material within the Late Antique Palestinian Jewish literary-cultural complex.

## 1. The Bible and its Epigones

The transition from biblical to post-biblical poetry is marked by the relegation of *parallelismus membrorum* from the status of major poetic organizational principle to that of subsidiary compositional device. Parallelism as such never really disappears from Hebrew poetry (in fact, parallelism in the broad sense is rightly thought of as the very heart and soul of poetic thought—cf. Jakobson 1966, 399–429), but beginning with the Late Antique period, i.e., with the advent of piyyut, it is unambiguously replaced by a triad of poetic organizational devices: acrostic, meter, and rhyme. These are complementary, in the sense that they govern the beginning, middle, and end of the poetic line, respectively. They were not all introduced at the same time: acrostic

---

[1] I would like to thank Prof. Raymond Scheindlin and Prof. Seth Schwartz, both of JTSA, for their valuable comments on an earlier draft of this paper.

[2] This poetry is sometimes referred to as 'Targum poetry', on account of the fact that it may be associated with the reading of the Targum. An illuminating discussion of the import of this association may be found in Leonhard 2006, 353–361. The targumic lecture, however, is not the only possible Sitz im Leben for Palestinian Aramaic poems, as will hopefully become clear from this essay. In view of this fact, a more neutral, objectively descriptive term such as 'JPA poetry' is called for here.

and meter, as obligatory devices, are attested before rhyme.[3] And they do not always appear together in one poem, even at the peak of the development of Classical piyyut. However, they collectively yield the possibility of strophic composition, which is almost entirely absent in the poetry of the Hebrew Bible, while being extensively developed, sometimes to degrees of remarkable complexity, in the Classical piyyut tradition.

The most obvious exception to the claim of a lack of strophic organization in the poetry of the biblical period is the Book of Lamentations. And since we are fortunate enough to have hints of the development of the *eikha*-dirge within the Bible itself, Lamentations can be viewed as (typologically) adumbrating, albeit faintly, the formal changes that came to revolutionize Hebrew poetry with the emergence of piyyut. Once each in the books of Isaiah and Jeremiah, we find poetic pericopes beginning with איכה and lamenting the fate of a city. Isa 1:21ff bewails the moral corruption that has befallen Jerusalem (Figure 1). Jer 48:17ff proposes that a dirge be taken up over the Moabite city Dibon (Figure 2). It would appear on the basis of these cases that a pre-exilic poetic tradition existed whereby the tragic fate of a city, Israelite or otherwise, could be described in a lamentation poem beginning with איכה (cf. also Isa 14:4ff and Ezek 26:17–18). Neither Isaiah's nor Jeremiah's lament shows signs of having either a fixed number of lines, or a strophic structure. In the next stage of development,[4] we note that three of the dirges in Lamentations, all of which is devoted to the fall of Jerusalem, open with an איכה-line. In the case of Lamentations 1, 2, and 4, the acrostic principle has been introduced, the *alef* requirement being satisfied (and perhaps originally suggested) by the opening word (Figure 3). Lamentations 1 and 2 employ a straight alphabetic acrostic whereby every fourth line opens with a

---

[3] In scholarship, the piyyut phenomenon in Palestine is usually divided into two phases: the pre-Classical and the Classical. The former is characterized by the anonymity of the poets, as well as by the absence of both rhyme and complex strophic composition. The latter is characterized by the opposite features: the attribution of the compositions to poets known by name (mostly on the basis of name acrostics), as well as the extensive employment of rhyme and a variety of different strophe-types. The two periods are discussed *in extenso* in what is effectively the only handbook on the subject: Fleischer 1975, 7–275.

[4] In the present context, 'stages of development' are defined formally—i.e., as items in a series whose internal relationship is determined by judgments about structural complexity. It is also probably true, however, that in this case the formal judgment reflects actual chronology (regardless of whether or not one accepts the traditional attribution of Lamentations to Jeremiah).

new letter, such that they are both divisible into strophes of three lines each (Lam 1:7 and 2:19 may each contain an extraneous line). Lamentations 4 introduces a new letter in every third line, such that the strophes are composed of two lines each.

The pervasiveness of the acrostic as the new formal poetic constitutive principle is demonstrated by the case of Lamentations 3 and 5. In Lamentations 3, the letter of the acrostic spreads to the beginning of every line. Every strophe contains three lines, all beginning with the same letter. In addition, and perhaps most significantly, the introduction of the mechanical acrostic principle allows the poet to dispense with the tag-word איכה, replacing it in the opening *alef*-slot with אני (Figure 4). In Lamentations 5, on the other hand, the acrostic is entirely lacking, and so is any form of strophic organization. The influence of the acrostic *principle*, on the other hand, is clearly discernible in the fact that the poem consists of 22 lines—i.e., *alef* through *tav* (and the strophe is therefore equivalent to the poetic line; Figure 5). We see, therefore, how the introduction of a mechanical, obligatory organizational principle can lead to the emergence of a new kind of strophic poetry already within the biblical corpus.

There is unambiguous, though frustratingly fragmentary, evidence in the Dead Sea Scrolls for the post-biblical cultivation of the *eikha*-dirge. The Book of Lamentations is attested at Qumran in several manuscripts. The original compositions attested in 4QApocryphal Lamentations A,B (4Q179, 4Q501) show clear thematic and lexical dependence on the biblical model. It is even possible, though far from certain, that 4QApocryphal Lamentations A frg. 2, ll. 4–10 represents the beginning of an expansive re-working of Lamentations 1, which may retain the acrostic structure of the original (Figure 6; the text follows García Martínez 1997, 1.370 [cf. also Horgan 1973, 222–234]; the ad sensum lineation is mine). Despite this literary activity, however, there is no evidence that the epigone(s) whose work is attested at Qumran introduced any significant formal developments into the genre, in any sense other than the apparent abandonment of the strict acrostic-based strophism of the biblical model.

Following the Qumran evidence, there is a significant hiatus in the textual record relating to the further development of the *eikha*-dirge in the Hebrew poetic tradition. The next developmental stage, though it cannot be dated with any precision, belongs not to the world of post-biblical epigones such as Ben Sira and the author of the Hodayot, but rather to the world of Pre-Classical and Classical piyyut. It is therefore to be dated to the Late Antique period—i.e., ca. 350–640, between the Christianization of the Roman Empire and the Muslim conquest of Palestine.[5] The Late Antique tradition of poetic dirges for the Ninth of Av—for this is the day during which the destruction of Jerusalem came to be commemorated—is attested in two related but distinct formats: Hebrew and (Jewish Palestinian) Aramaic. The former, belonging as it does squarely within the broader context of piyyut, has received a great deal of scholarly attention within the past 150 years (see, for example, Zunz 1967, 1.9–58 [originally published in 1855]). The Aramaic poems, on the other hand, belong to a corpus of JPA poetry that has only recently fully come to light in a volume published by Yahalom and Sokoloff (Yahalom 1999). With the exception of a few scattered articles (Heinemann 1983, 148–167; Yahalom 1996, 33–44), the material has not been (systematically) studied, so that very little can be positively asserted of it. Besides the fact that all of the poems are in JPA, to what extent does the material represent the product of a unified poetic tradition? If the existence of such a tradition can indeed be asserted, what relationship does it bear to the Hebrew piyyut tradition? To the Late Antique Palestinian liturgy? To the Late Antique synagogue? To the rabbinic tradition? In the following pages, I would like to take the JPA poems for the Ninth of Av as a test case, and compare them to their Hebrew counterparts, in order to attempt to determine whether or not these two groups are indeed comparable, and if so, what does the comparison indicate to us about the JPA group?[6]

## 2. The Palestinian Liturgy for the Ninth of Av and the Hebrew Piyyut

Little is known of the development of the payyetanic liturgy for the Ninth of Av. The overwhelming majority of the poetic texts that have

---

[5] There exists a scholarly consensus that the apogee of the Classical period is reached with Ele'azar be-rabbi Qillir, who worked in Palestine at around the time of the Muslim conquest—cf. Fleischer 1985, 383–427. The terminus post quem of the Pre-Classical period cannot really be pinned down, but one might tentatively suggest ca. 350—cf. Schirmann 1953–1954, 123–161. The works of Yose ben Yose, the first payyetan known by name, represent the borderline between the two periods.

[6] The choice of the poems for the Ninth of Av is not entirely random. A global examination of the material published by Yahalom and Sokoloff shows that this group is the most fruitful with regard to (potential) points of contact, or at least direct comparison, with the Hebrew piyyut tradition.

come down to us from Byzantine Palestine were composed by the greatest exponent of the Classical piyyut tradition, Ele'azar be-rabbi Qillir, who flourished sometime in the early 7th century (see note 5 and Goldschmidt 2003 יא-ז). Qillir's compositions for the Ninth of Av show all of the characteristic traits of his fully developed style. The genre therefore appears to us already fully formed, and any reconstruction of its pre-history rests on the most meager bits of evidence. One anonymous composition, however, is quite suggestive. The poem אז בחטאינו חרב מקדש (Goldschmidt 2003, לא-כט) is recited on the eve of the Ninth of Av. It is composed as a simple alphabetic acrostic, one line per letter. Its interest for us lies in the fact that it is organized around the theme of a link between the grief of the Jews on earth and that of the heavenly bodies in the sky. In the working out of this theme, a list is given of the 12 signs of the zodiac (Figure 7; for lists in the piyyut, see Fleischer 1975, 110–111). On the one hand, this text lacks some of the basic, characteristic features of the developed Classical piyyut: allusions to rabbinic (mostly aggadic) midrash, poetic epithets, rhyme, and complex strophic structure. For this reason, it is reasonable to date it (typologically) to the pre-Classical phase, a judgment that is further confirmed by its use of the so-called *meruba* meter (also known as 'the meter of Yose ben Yose'), which is typical of pre-Classical compositions (see Mirsky 1991a, 50–62). On the other hand, its use of a list the zodiac signs as a poetic organizational principle links it, first, to the Classical piyyut, where use of this list is well attested, and second, to the physical plant of the Late Antique Palestinian synagogue, where one frequently finds the zodiac circle represented in mosaic floors (see Schwartz 2001, 263–274; Mirsky 1991b, 93–101; Yahalom 1986, 313–322).

The emergence of the Qillirian kina tradition is closely linked to the Palestinian liturgy of the Ninth of Av. The custom of reading Lamentations on the eve of the Ninth of Av is now common to all of the Jewish liturgical rites. It is first attested in Tractate Soferim 18:4, which also mentions the possibility of reciting it in the morning, after the reading of the Torah: יש שקורין ספר קינות בערב ויש שמאחרין עד הבקר לאחר קראית ס"ת. Seder Rav Amram Gaon also refers to the reading of Lamentations on the eve of the Ninth of Av, calling it the custom of the two yeshivot (see Goldschmidt 1971, §צט).[7] In at least some versions of the Palestinian rite, we may speculate that the reading of Lamentations

---

[7] Siddur Rav Saadya Gaon does not mention the reading of Lamentations at all.

was followed by the recitation of kinot. In the Ashkenazic liturgy, the kinot recited on this occasion are all anonymous (e.g., אז בחטאינו), and terminate in a series of scriptural verses whose main theme is consolation (Zech 1:16, 17, Isa 51:3; see Goldschmidt 2003, לא).[8]

According to the Palestinian custom, the Amidah of the morning service of the Ninth of Av was accompanied by a kerova (as on other fast days). This kerova extended up till the 14th benediction, at which point a series of independent poems called kinot were inserted. The old Ashkenazic rite employed the Qillirian kerova אאביך ביום מבך, while the Roman and Romaniot rites still preserve the Qillirian kerova זכור איכה (Goldschmidt 2003, קס-קמז). Three others have been published by Fleischer, bringing the total number up to five (see Fleischer 1974, מ-א and the literature cited therein). In some cases, it was possible to 'complete' the kerova (i.e., those portions of it extending past the 14th benediction) after the recitation of the kinot (see Fleischer 1975, 206). As far as can be established from the textual record, Qillir was the first to establish the custom of reciting kerovot with kinot. In any case, no such compositional complexes are attested before him.[9] This would not be surprising, as he is likely to have been an innovator with regard to several other important areas of the payyetanic liturgy.[10] Note, however, that the Qillirian compositional complexes are situated in the morning service, and it is therefore reasonable to suppose that the liturgy of the evening service was not (directly) affected.

---

[8] As opposed to Ashkenaz, the recitation of kinot after the reading of Lamentations on the eve of the Ninth of Av is not attested in either the Roman or the Romaniot rite (according to the earliest printed sources).

[9] Fleischer 1970, קפ-קעח and 1977, 280–283 has published a kerova for the Ninth of Av together with complementary strophes for the remaining 4 benedictions. In addition, he has shown conclusively that the complementary kina סילה וגם הוגה (Goldschmidt 2003, קמו-קמז) belongs to this kerova (cf. note 11). The complementary strophes contain the acrostic signature יני חזן, so that it is possible, though by no means certain, that this material is to be attributed to the Classical payyetan Yannai, who was Qillir's predecessor. If this attribution is accepted, then it would appear that Qillir's liturgical/poetic tradition for the Ninth of Av is based on an earlier model. However, it should be pointed out that there is no positive evidence that the tradition of יני החזן included any kinot other than the complementary kina סילה וגם הוגה. Because of this, as well as the doubtfulness of the attribution, is seems preferable to regard Qillir as the innovative figure of greatest significance in this regard. In either case, his compositions certainly form the backbone of the Ashkenazic, Roman, and Romaniot liturgical rites for the Ninth of Av.

[10] Cf., for example, Qillir's use of a *seder olam* in his kedushta'ot for Shavuot, noted as a first in Elizur 2000, 15 n. 8. Thus also in the case of the *seder beriyot* that precedes the Qillirian *seder olam*, as noted in ibid., 32, and discussed in Rand, 2005, 667–683.

The fact that five Qillirian kerovot for the Ninth of Av are attested means that the payyetan devoted quite a bit of attention to the liturgy of this day. Originally, each kerova was accompanied by its own series of kinot. For the most part, these kinot do not contain an acrostic signature of the poet's name, which, however, appears in short connecting strophes (called סלסלה in some mss) that link the kinot together into a chain by means of anadiplosis (שרשור). In the mss, the original order and composition of these kinot chains has been disturbed, and the signed connecting strophes moved or simply dispensed with by later copyists, so that not only is it frequently quite difficult to reconstruct the original form of each of the chains, but the Qillirian authorship of certain kinot cannot be established with certainty. However, the number of known Qillirian kerovot and kinot for the Ninth of Av is sufficient to enable us to give a reasonably accurate description of them.

Both the kerovot and kinot show the typical features of Qillirian (i.e., Classical piyyut) language: profusion of poetic epithets, non-standard morphology and syntax, and general avoidance of Greek and Latin loanwords (see Yahalom 1985; Rand 2006). The themes are determined to a large extent by the liturgical occasion, and one finds a wealth of references to historical/aggadic traditions contained in p.Ta'anit and in Lamentations Rabbah. Structurally, the kerovot show a complex strophism that in some cases depends on the text of Lamentations, bits of which are used as fixed words and phrases, as well as on lists. Where these features appear, they conspire to make the Qillirian kerovot for the Ninth of Av some of the most profoundly opaque compositions of the poet's oeuvre. As a sample, we might take the first two strophes of the most difficult of these: אהלי איכה בשלי (Figure 8; Fleischer 1974, יא-ד). This text fragment conveniently highlights a number of important literary features. First, the use of lists as structural devices is quite prominent: the composition in question incorporates lists of (a) the 12 signs of the zodiac, (b) the 12 months of the year, (c) the 24 priestly courses, (d) the 24 levitical courses, and (e) the 12 tribes. We have already seen that the use of the list of the 12 zodiac signs connects the piyyut to the physical reality of the Late Antique Palestinian synagogue (cf. also l. 12 of Qillir's kina אאדה עד חוג Goldschmidt 2003, מא: אומללו מזלות בקרעי מעילי). Thus also with the list of the 24 priestly courses, which is also attested in the synagogues of the period in question (see Schwartz 2001, 273 n. 86; Fleischer 1977, 256–262).

Secondly, we see that the Book of Lamentations plays an important compositional role. Not, as in the case of the Qumran compositions, as a model to be imitated and adapted, but rather as a source of ordered text fragments which are to be incorporated into the new piyyut composition as little colored stones are incorporated into the matrix of a mosaic. The use of fixed words and framing verses is actually rather common in Classical piyyut, so that in this regard the Qillirian kerovot add nothing new to the repertoire of structural poetic devices. However, the present composition is unusual in its demand that two mechanically inserted words be juxtaposed within a syntactic string, with the result that quite frequently awkward or completely nonsensical strings are produced. Take, for example, the first line of the second strophe of the kerova in question. It is clear that the mechanical juxtaposition of שׁוֹדָד (Jer 10:20) and בָּכֹה תִבְכֶּה (Lam 1:2) perforce yields syntactic gibberish. It is important to note, however, that this sort of gibberish is different on principle from the sorts of convoluted and opaque syntactic structures that are usually associated with Classical piyyut. The latter are deliberately (though not always entirely freely) created by the payyetan, so that we may assume the opacity to have been part of the artist's intent, while in the present case, we are faced with a mechanical compositional principle (albeit self-imposed) that automatically generates syntactic strings over which the payyetan has no control.

The kinot show a great variety of structural features and compositional elements: acrostics, fixed words, framing verses, refrains, etc.[11] They can be alphabetic iterations of a single idea (i.e., a *rahit*-type), narratives (based on midrashic or scriptural sources), dialogues, etc. Perhaps their most prominent common feature is the plethora of formal patterns that they represent. One does not, as a rule, find in them the overbearing weight of accumulated poetic strictures that is associated with the kerovot.

## 3. The JPA Poems for the Ninth of Av

It is against this background that I would like to examine the JPA lament poems. Yahalom and Sokoloff have published a corpus of 10 poems

---

[11] This discussion does not extend to the complementary kina (קינת השלמה), whose structural purpose is to complete the alphabetic series begun in the kerova, which is interrupted at the 14th benediction—i.e., at the letter *nun*.

lamenting the destruction of Jerusalem and Beitar (Yahalom 1999, 142–169 [poems 17–25], 344–349 [appendix]; the poems are referred to below to by means of the number assigned to them by the editors). These poems are gathered by the editors under the rubric 'Ninth of Av', a liturgical designation that is amply justified not only by their content, but also by the headings found with some of them, to which we turn presently.

As we have seen above, the Hebrew, Qillirian liturgical tradition consists of the compositional complex 'kerova + kinot,' recited during the morning service. The Aramaic tradition, on the other hand, shows no parallel to the kerova. The Aramaic poems appear to be the functional equivalents of the Hebrew kinot. With regard to these piyyutim, the Hebrew liturgical tradition shows a fairly consistent terminology: the poems are called קינה, while the short connecting strophes are referred to as סלסלה. The Aramaic poems show no such consistency. The headers of the Aramaic piyyutim, where they attested, are as follows: 17 = קינה; 18 = ט' באב; רהט לילי 19,20 = שלשלתא.[12] The header קינה makes an explicit connection between the Hebrew and the Aramaic traditions. The header רהט לילי ט' באב clearly indicates the liturgical locus for which the piyyut is intended. The term רהט is found in Genizah manuscripts in connection with a simple post-Classical type of piyyut that is usually found outside of a particular liturgical context. Fleischer surmises that originally, piyyutim of this type were written as 'independent units designed to expand kerovot for 18 benedictions for special days or fasts' (Fleischer 1975, 301; translation mine). It is reasonable to surmise, therefore, that this term might have been (secondarily) applied to an Aramaic composition that was felt to be the functional equivalent of a Hebrew kina.

Poems 19–23, together with the poem published in the appendix, are all found in one manuscript (TS H14/64), and appear to belong to the same series.[13] The first two poems in the series bear the header שלשלתא,

---

[12] The headers of poems 21 (אנא אזיל ואבכה) and 22 (פז' שירו לנו) are not relevant in this regard, since they constitute an introductory phrase and a refrain, respectively. Neither is the header of poem 25 (בשם רחום), which is generic (and probably related to the *basmala*, which serves as a header in Muslim Arabic mss).

[13] The last poem is published in an appendix presumably on account of its showing non-JPA linguistic features. However, the incidence of at least one of these features—the use of *nun* in the suffix of the 3rd masc. pl. perfect—is not consistent (cf. הוון 'they were' [l. 21], חזון 'they saw' [l. 36] versus חטו 'they sinned' [l. 29]; דקרו 'they pierced' [l. 4], etc. versus גרמן 'they caused' [l. 53]), and for this reason I feel justified in including it in the series represented by poems 19–23.

a term that is reminiscent of the סלסלה, or connecting strophe, of the Hebrew kina tradition (Yahalom 1999, 153). All of the poems in the series, including the poem published in the appendix, show a certain homogeneity in that they all employ some form of mechanically fixed word(s) as a method of simple strophic organization: in poem 19 each 3-line strophe opens with the fixed word היך (cf. the Qillirian kina איכה אצת [Goldschmidt 2003, מ-לח], each of whose strophes begins with the fixed word איכה), and concludes with a refrain (Figure 9),[14] while in poem 20 each 2-line strophe concludes with the refrain אללי לי (cf. the Qillirian kina אם תאכלנה נשים [Goldschmidt 2003, עז-עה], using the same refrain), which is introduced at the end of a 6-line introduc-tory/transitional (non-acrostic) strophe (Figure 10). Poem 21 opens with the words אנא אזיל ואבכה, which head a series of 2-line strophes that open with the fixed word על and conclude with the refrain עיני עיני יורדה מים (Lam 1:16, Figure 11). It is therefore structurally very close to poem 19. Poem 22 is a dialogue, with the Levites and Israel-ites speaking in alternating strophes. The odd strophes end with the refrain שירו לנו משיר ציון (Ps 137:3), while the even strophes end with the refrain איך נשיר את שיר יי' (Ps 137:4, Figure 12). The poem in the appendix is composed of 4-line strophes. The last line in each strophe is occupied by a verse fragment from Lamentations 1, the verses being quoted seriatim (Figure 13). Poem 23 contains 2-line strophes. The first line of each strophe ends in the fixed word ציון, while the second line ends in the fixed word ירושלים (Figure 14). This poem, whose main theme is consolation, is the last of the series, and is followed by two of the same scriptural verses that appear at the end of the series of kinot recited after the reading of Lamentations on the eve of the Ninth of Av according to the Ashkenazic rite: Zech 1:16 (corresponding to Zech 1:16, 17 in Ashkenaz) and Isa 51:3.

On the basis of these structural similarities, it seems reasonable to suggest that these poems were intended (if only by the copyist of TS H14/64) as a liturgical series.[15] This suggestion is further bolstered by

---

[14] The refrain, which is not subject to an acrostic and rhymes with the lines of its strophe, is the same in all but the last strophe. Consequently, all strophes but the last show the same rhyme. In the last strophe, the rhyme changes, and the refrain line begins with *tav*—i.e., it is used to fill out the acrostic series.

[15] It is possible that the composition of the series is not original. This is suggested by the fact that the introductory/transitional strophe at the beginning of poem 20 is not connected by anadiplosis to poem 19—i.e., it does not really function as a connecting

the fact that the series of dirges concludes with a poem of consolation. In this regard, the Aramaic poems show a typological similarity to the Qillirian tradition, in which the kinot are followed by piyyutim of consolation (פיוטי נחמה).[16] In light of these considerations, it would appear that the genre term שלשלתא, instead of referring to a connecting strophe, as with סלסלה in the Hebrew kina tradition, refers either to a poem that is meant to be recited as part of a liturgical series/chain, or to the series itself. Furthermore, on the basis of the analogy to the Ashkenazic rite, it appears that the series was intended to be recited after the reading of Lamentations on the eve of the Ninth of Av. We see, therefore, that where explicit evidence about liturgical genre is available in the mss, the Aramaic poems are not only seen as analogues of the Hebrew kina tradition (poem 17), but also appear to be intended for the eve of the Ninth of Av (poems 18, 19, 20 + verses at the end of 23), rather than for the Amidah of the morning service. This conclusion points in the direction of a likely interpretation of the liturgical function of these poems vis-à-vis the Hebrew, Qillirian kina tradition. The Aramaic poems and the Qillirian tradition were probably not mutually exclusive, in the sense that they did not directly compete for the same liturgical locus. The Aramaic poems are situated in the evening service, after the reading of the Scroll, while the Qillirian 'kerova + kinot' are designed for the Amidah of the morning service. From the point of view of the history of the liturgy, the two poetic traditions are only typologically, rather than organically, related.

## 4. The Hebrew and Aramaic Traditions Compared

Let us now mention the similarities between the Hebrew and Aramaic traditions. First, both cite and refer to historical/aggadic traditions, most prominently drawn from p.Ta'anit and in Lamentations Rabbah. In neither corpus is this feature consistent, for some Hebrew kinot, as well

---

strophe. Because of lack of *comparanda*, we cannot be certain that anadiplosis was a feature of these introductory/transitional strophes. However, the analogy with the Hebrew kina tradition, along with general structural considerations, makes this likely.

[16] The piyyutim of consolation are not in use in Ashkenaz, but are found in the Roman and Romaniot rites—cf. Goldschmidt 2003, ע. For a very informative discussion of the liturgical/poetic realization of the theme of consolation in the Classical tradition of 'kerova + kinot', see Elizur 2003, 125–138.

as most of the Aramaic laments, speak of the destruction in a more-
or-less general way, without referring to the rabbinic sources. However,
the sources do appear prominently in the Aramaic poems 17 and 18.
Nevertheless, the general impression is that the Hebrew kinot are much
more saturated with the rabbinic traditions than the Aramaic poems.
This impression is doubtless partially due to the fact that the corpus
of Aramaic lament poems is so small. On the other hand, where the
Aramaic poems do cite these traditions, they do so in a rather direct
way, which seems crude and naïve when compared with the rich skein
of lexical and thematic allusions that one is used to in the Qillirian
Hebrew kinot in particular, and in Classical piyyut in general.

Second, the two traditions show similarities in terms of poetic
structure. Both employ acrostics, along with a number of other poetic
devices: refrains, fixed verses, fixed words, etc. I have already given a
structural description of poems 19–23, all of which employ straight
alphabetic acrostics. Of the others, poems 18, 24, 25 are composed of
rhymed strophes arranged in a straight acrostic series. Poem 17 also
has rhymed strophes and a simple acrostic. In addition, each of the
strophes is followed by one of two alternating refrains: סחי >ומאוס
תשימנו בקרב העמים >אלי< (Lam 3:45) and <אלי> למה תריבו ( Jer 2:29), as
is the case with the Qillirian kina איכה תפארתי (Goldschmidt 2003,
מז-מג). As with their use of the aggadic sources, so here too the Aramaic poems are rather impoverished in comparison to their Qillirian
Hebrew counterparts with regard to the repertoire and combination of
forms that they employ. Mention should also be made of the fact that
whereas both the Aramaic and the Hebrew poems employ rhyme as
a major structural device, the former use end-rhyme only—i.e., they
show no acquaintance with the discontinuous (so-called 'Qillirian')
rhyme norm that demands the participation of two root consonants
within the rhymeme (cf. Hrushovsky 1971, 738–742).[17]

Third, I have already referred to the extensive use of lists as a structural device both in the Qillirian Hebrew tradition, as well as in the

---

[17] One further difference between the Hebrew and Aramaic rhyme norms is that whereas
the former rarely, if ever, rhymes the vowels /a/ ~ /e/ (cf. Rand forthcoming) the latter seems
to have allowed this poetic license rather more freely: סתיר//אוֹתֵר//אתותר//בית תר
(17:2–5); יוסף//כסיף//איתוסף//כסף (17:10–13); מיתובא//כוזבא//שליוֵה//חביבא
(18:2021).

pre-Classical kina אז בחטאינו. An analogous phenomenon is attested in the Aramaic lament poems. The fragmentary poem 25 is based on the theme of the intercession of the patriarchs and matriarchs with God on behalf of Israel (also attested in the Qillirian kina אז בהלוך ירמיהו [Goldschmidt 2003, קצח-ק]). In it, we find the beginnings of a list: יצחק, סרה, אברהם, י. The list of the zodiac signs is not attested in the extant Aramaic lament poems. However, it does appear in Aramaic poems for the New Moon of Nisan: poems 36, 37, 38, 39.[18]

Together with these points of contact with the Hebrew tradition, there are a number of significant differences, to which I now turn. These differences are primarily of a generic nature—i.e., they are best explained in terms of the obvious fact that the two traditions are different. A brief examination of them does, however, effectively highlight some salient features of the Aramaic poems. As I have already mentioned, the Classical piyyut in general is composed in a form of Hebrew that is marked by numerous morphological and syntactic idiosyncrasies vis-à-vis the Biblical Hebrew (and sometimes Mishnaic Hebrew) standard. On the lexical level, the piyyut is marked by extensive use of allusive epithets, as well as by an almost complete avoidance of the Greek and Latin loanwords so commonly encountered in Mishnaic Hebrew, and the Palestinian rabbinic literature in general. None of these features are present in the Aramaic poems.

The Aramaic poems show no compunction about employing Geek and Latin loanwords. Here is a list of the loanwords attested in our poems: אכלסין, etc. (17:5,18,22,28,42); אננקי (25:2); איפרכין (18:1); ננסא (17:34); פולמיה (18:36); פיליה (22:6); פטרונן (17:30); סופסטין (18:24,27,34); קינטורנין (18:21). The use of poetic epithets קולריא (18:25, 19:20, 21:17); is, indeed, attested in the Aramaic lament poems, but in a manner that is not nearly as rich—both in terms of quantity and syntactic/referential complexity—as the use known from the Hebrew tradition. Here is a list of the most obvious epithets attested in our poems: אריה Titus/ Hadrian (17:1); עם עליזין Rome (17:31); ננסא Nebuchadnezzar (18:24, 27,34); גברא רחימא Abraham (24:14); נורא God (18:43); עליון ונורא (25:6); נורא עלילה (18:27); חיא (18:32, 22:12); רמה (22:30); מלכא רמא (24:2,26, appendix:41); חדא ומיוחדא (22:36); יונה תמה Israel (24:4); ביתא Temple (appendix:36); בית קרבני (19:23); בית מעוני (19:24); בית חדותי

---

[18] Poem 37 is organized around a list of 'months + zodiac signs', while poem 38 gives 'months + tribes + zodiac signs'.

(appendix:59); מעונה the heavens (20:18). To the extent that some of these epithets make reference to the biblical and/or the rabbinic textual tradition, the manner of reference is fairly uncomplicated, as in the case of ננסא (also attested in 13:1), which is derived directly from the midrashic source—cf. חמון מה עבד לי ננסא דבבל (PRK 13:8), itself based on שפל אנשים (Dan 4:14). Worth noting also is the fact that all of the epithets are nouns or noun phrases, so that the syntactic inventory is quite limited, as opposed to the Hebrew tradition. Parallel to its use of epithets, the Hebrew piyyut tradition typically (though not entirely consistently) avoids the use of proper nouns, or even widely used nouns referring to unique entities, generic classes, etc. The Aramaic tradition, on the other hand, shows no compunction whatsoever about the use of such lexemes.

The morphological idiosyncrasies of the Hebrew piyyut are entirely absent from the Aramaic lament poems, as well as from the rest of the corpus assembled by Yahalom and Sokoloff. Strictly speaking, of course, the fact that the two traditions employ two different languages makes a direct comparison illegitimate. However, since the two languages are closely related, many (though not all) of the peculiar morphological types attested in piyyut Hebrew would have been theoretically possible—and equally peculiar vis-à-vis the 'standard' JPA—in the JPA poems. In other words, the outstanding feature of the grammar of piyyut Hebrew is its dissonance with regard to both Biblical and Mishnaic Hebrew, each of which might be viewed (and clearly functioned) as a standard in its own right. No such dissonance is observable in the case of the JPA poems. Related to this lack of dissonance is the fact that certain portions of the poems are hardly more than more-or-less loose translations from Hebrew. Here are some of the outstanding examples of translation from Scripture:

(18:12) → ולא שמע ליה כד אסהד בה//ובביקעת מגידו תקף לביה

(2 Chr 35:22) ולא שמע אל דברי נכו מפי אלהים ויבא להלחם בבקעת מגדו

(18:15) → ובמרכבתה תיניתא ארכבו יתיה//וכד על לירושלים פרחת נשמתיה

(2 Chr 35:24) ויוליכֻהו לו רכב המשנה אשר לו ויוליכֻהו ירושלם וימת

(Lam 1:16) על אלה אני בוכיה → (19:14) על אלין אנא בכיא

(Lam 4:15) סורו טמא קראו למו → (19:17) סורו סאבין צֻוחין לי אומיא

These strictly philological peculiarities of the Aramaic tradition are doubtless related to the differences in status between Hebrew and Aramaic in Late Antique Palestine. Roughly speaking, Hebrew was the dominant language of culture—the sacrosanct vessel of the religious/national tradition whose use and even simply invocation could presumably command ideologically motivated allegiance. This status rested on the fact that Hebrew was the language of Scripture, as well as the language of the destroyed Temple (viz., לשון קודש). But the prominence of Hebrew as an ideological locus was probably also aided by the fact that it was no longer associated with an everyday, spoken dialect, and was therefore free to be functionally specialized—as is so clearly the case with piyyut Hebrew—and ideologically marked. Put simply, Hebrew became self-conscious. Aramaic, on the other hand, was presumably the common spoken idiom of the society that produced both the Hebrew as well as the Aramaic poetic traditions. In addition, it also functioned as the language of Targum—i.e., as the language that helped to mediate between the high culture of rabbinic learning and the more prosaic needs of common synagogue goers (cf. Leonhard 2006, 346, who argues convincingly for 'the early Rabbis' idea of the public reading of the Tora as a popularized study session'). It is thus not surprising that when Aramaic came to be used in poetic composition the resulting poems were much less manneristic than their Hebrew counterparts. To put it simply, they were simpler.

I believe that it is now possible to make certain, albeit preliminary, assertions about the Aramaic lament poems. First, it seems clear that from a qualitative if not from a quantitative perspective, they are as much a product of the rabbinic thought-world as their Hebrew counterparts. Second, it seems equally clear that, generally speaking, their proper Sitz im Leben is the same Late Antique Palestinian liturgy that hosted the Hebrew piyyut. As to differences, it is likely that from the liturgical point of view, the Aramaic lament poems were primarily reserved for recitation after the reading of Lamentations on the eve of the Ninth of Av, and therefore did not interact directly with the Qillirian 'kerova + kinot' tradition. Furthermore, it is clear that from the formal point of view, the Aramaic lament poems are typologically similar to, while being much less well developed than, their Hebrew counterparts.

On the basis of these conclusions, it is tempting to attribute a chronological meaning to typology, and to thereby see the Aramaic materials as pre-dating the Qillirian tradition. It is, furthermore, tempting to suppose that the massive innovations wrought by Qillir in the liturgy of the Ninth of Av were in part responsible for the decline of the Aramaic tradition, to the point where it is only marginally represented in the Genizah, and not at all in the known liturgical rites. Such conclusions are only tentative, and they may turn out to have nothing but heuristic value. To the extent allowed by the data, however, they seem to be likely at this stage of our understanding of the development of post-biblical poetry.

## LITERATURE

Elizur, Sh., רבי אלעזר בירבי קליר—קדושתאות ליום מתן תורה, Jerusalem 2000.

—— 'מאבל לנחמה: על מנהג קדום בתפילת מנחה של תשעה באב', *Tarb.* 73 (2003).

Fleischer, E., 'פיוט ליניי חזן על משמרות הכהנים', *Sinai* 64 (1970).

——, 'קומפוזיציות קליריות לתשעה באב', *HUCA* 45 (1974).

——, שירת-הקודש העברית בימי-הביניים, Jerusalem 1975.

——, 'חדשות בנושא המשמרות בפיוטים', in: Sh. Verses et al. (eds), ספר דב סדן, Jerusalem 1977.

——, 'לפתרון שאלת זמנו ומקום פעילותו של ר' אלעזר בירבי קילירי', *Tarbiz* 54 (1985).

García Martínez, F. & E.J.C. Tigchelaar (eds), *The Dead Sea Scrolls Study Edition*, Leiden—New York—Köln 1997.

Goldschmidt, D. (ed.), סדר רב עמרם גאון, Jerusalem 1971.

——, (ed.), סדר הקינות לתשעה באב, Jerusalem 2003.

Heinemann, J., 'שרידים מיצירתם הפיוטית של המתורגמנים הקדומים', in: idem, עיוני תפילה, Jerusalem 1983.

Horgan, M., 'A Lament over Jerusalem ('4Q179')', *JSS* 18 (1973).

Hrushovsky, B., 'השיטות הראשיות של החרוז העברי מן הפיוט עד ימינו', *Hasifrut* 2 (1971).

Jakobson, R., 'Grammatical Parallelism and Its Russian Facet', *Language* 42 (1966).

Leonhard, C., *The Jewish Pesach and the Origins of the Christian Easter; Open Questions in Current Research* (SJ 35), Berlin—New York 2006.

Mirsky, A., פיוטי יוסי בן יוסי, Jerusalem 1991 [quoted as 1991a].

——, 'גדי ודלי בכתובת עין-גדי ובפיוטי קדמונים', in: idem, הפיוט—התפתחותו בארץ-ישראל ובגולה, Jerusalem 1991 [quoted as 1991b].

Rand, M., 'The *Seder Beriyot* in Byzantine-Era *Piyyuṭ'*, *JQR* 95 (2005).

——, *Introduction to the Grammar of Hebrew Poetry in Byzantine Palestine* (Gorgias Press Dissertations 22, Language and Linguistics 1), New Jersey 2006.

——, 'בשולי שיטת החריזה הקילירית', *Jerusalem Studies in Hebrew Literature*, forthcoming.

Schirmann, J., 'Hebrew Liturgical Poetry and Christian Hymnology', *JQR* 44 (1953–54).

Schwartz, S., *Imperialism and Jewish Society; 200 B.C.E. to 640 C.E.*, Princeton—Oxford 2001.

Yahalom, J., שפת השיר של הפיוט הארץ-ישראלי הקדום, Jerusalem 1985.

——, 'גלגל המזלות בפיוט הארץ ישראלי', *Jerusalem Studies in Hebrew Literature* 9 (1986).

——, 'Angels Do Not Understand Aramaic: On the Literary Use of Jewish Palestinian Aramaic in Late Antiquity', *JJS* 57 (1996).

——, & M. Sokoloff, שירת בני מערבא—שירים ארמיים של יהודי ארץ-ישראל בתקופה הביזנטית, Jerusalem 1999.

Zunz, L., *Die synagogale Poesie des Mittelalters*, Hildesheim 1967.

## Appendix

*Figures*

Acrostic and list items are given in large letters. Biblical material whose citation is incorporated into the structure of a piyyut is highlighted by means of a citation within the poetic text. Words subject to anadiplosis are indicated in italics.

1.   אֵיכָה הָיְתָה לְזוֹנָה//קִרְיָה נֶאֱמָנָה      [ישע' א:כא]

2.   אֵיכָה נִשְׁבַּר מַטֵּה עֹז//מַקֵּל תִּפְאָרָה      [ירמ' מח:יז]

3.
| | |
|---|---|
| הָעִיר רַבָּתִי עָם | אֵיכָה יָשְׁבָה בָדָד |
| רַבָּתִי בַגּוֹיִם | הָיְתָה כְּאַלְמָנָה |
| הָיְתָה לָמַס | שָׂרָתִי בַּמְּדִינוֹת |
| [איכה א:א-ב] | בָּכוֹ תִבְכֶּה... |
| | |
| אֲדֹנָי אֵת בַּת צִיּוֹן | אֵיכָה יָעִיב בְּאַפּוֹ |
| תִּפְאֶרֶת יִשְׂרָאֵל | הִשְׁלִיךְ מִשָּׁמַיִם אֶרֶץ |
| בְּיוֹם אַפּוֹ | וְלֹא זָכַר הֲדֹם רַגְלָיו |
| [איכה ב:א-ב] | בִּלַּע... |
| | |
| יִשְׁנֶא הַכֶּתֶם הַטּוֹב | אֵיכָה יוּעַם זָהָב |
| בְּרֹאשׁ כָּל חוּצוֹת | תִּשְׁתַּפֵּכְנָה אַבְנֵי קֹדֶשׁ |
| [איכה ד:א-ב] | בְּנֵי... |

4.
| | |
|---|---|
| בְּשֵׁבֶט עֶבְרָתוֹ | אֲנִי הַגֶּבֶר רָאָה עֳנִי |
| חֹשֶׁךְ וְלֹא אוֹר | אוֹתִי נָהַג וַיֹּלַךְ |
| יָדוֹ כָּל הַיּוֹם | אַךְ בִּי יָשֻׁב יַהֲפֹךְ |
| [איכה ג:א-ג] | בָלָה... |

5.
| | |
|---|---|
| הַבֵּיט וּרְאֵה אֶת חֶרְפָּתֵנוּ | זְכֹר יי' מֶה הָיָה לָנוּ |
| בָּתֵּינוּ לְנָכְרִים | נַחֲלָתֵנוּ נֶהֶפְכָה לְזָרִים |
| אִמֹּתֵינוּ כְּאַלְמָנוֹת | יְתוֹמִים הָיִינוּ וְאֵין [קר'] אָב |
| [איבה ה:א-ג] | מֵימִינוּ... |

6.
```
[איכה ישבה] בדד העיר [הג]דו[לה ירוש]לים
ר[בתי הע]מים שרתי כל לאום[ים] שוממה כעזובה
וכל [בנ]ותיה עזוב[ות כ]אשה ער[י]ריה כעצובה וכעזובת [אישה]
כל ארמנותיה ורחו[בותיה] כעקרה וכמסככה
כול אורחו[ת]י[נ]ה        ]ה כאשת מרורים
וכל בנותיה כאבלות על בע[ליהן
                                ]יה כמשכלות ליחידיהן
בכו תבכה ירו[שלים דמעות ירד]ו על לחיה
על בניה]                    [
```
            [4Q179 frag. 2, ll. 4–10]

7.
| | |
|---|---|
| וּצְבָא הַשָּׁמַיִם/שַׂק הוּשַׂם כְּסוּתָם | זֶרַע קֹדֶשׁ/לָבְשׁוּ שַׂקִּים |
| וְכוֹכָבִים וּמַזָּלוֹת/אָסְפוּ נָגְהָם | חָשַׁךְ הַשֶּׁמֶשׁ/וְיָרֵחַ קָדָר |
| עַל כִּי כְבָשָׂיו/לַטֶּבַח הוּבָלוּ | טָלֶה רִאשׁוֹן/בָּכָה בְּמַר נֶפֶשׁ |
| כִּי עַל צַוָּארֵנוּ/נִרְדָּפְנוּ כֻּלָּנוּ [אָז בחטאינו, טו' 7-10] | יְלָלָה הִשְׁמִיעַ/שׁוֹר בַּמְּרוֹמִים |

8.
| | |
|---|---|
| אֵיכָה [איכה א:א] בְּשָׁלְיֵ הַזֹּעֲם | אָהֳלִי [ירמ' י:כ] |
| אֵיכָה [איכה ב:א] בּוֹ הִנְבִּיךְ טְלָאַיו רוֹעֵם | |
| אֲנִי [איכה ג:א] יְזַמְתִּי עָדֵי צוּר מְשַׁעְשְׁעָם | |

אוֹתִי [איכה ג:ב] כְּפֶסַח בְּנִיסָן כֵּן יוֹשִׁיעָם
אַךְ [איכה ג:ג] לֹא שָׁעָם
מִמְרוֹן רְשָׁעָם
אֵיכָה [איכה א:א] שׁוֹרֶשׁ גְּזָעָם
אֵיכָה יוֹעַם [איכה ד:א]

אֵיכָה אָסַף נָע כְּשִׁכּוֹר
קִינִים תָּמוֹר שִׁירִים לַעֲכוֹר
כְּנוֹפֵץ בְּרֹאשׁ גּוֹלִים בְּכוֹר
בְּלֹא הוֹן לִמְכוֹר
עַד נָכְרִי בְּלֶחֶךְ וָכוֹר
לְגוֹנְנָם נָא הַיּוֹם זְכוֹר [איכה ה:א] ב' מגן אברהם

שׁוֹדַד [ירמ' י:כ]            בָּכֹה תִבְכֶּה [איכה א:ב] כְּעָשׁ בּוֹ בְּצִיבְיוֹן...
[אהלי איכה בשלי, טו' 1-8]

9.     היך     אתחתם גזר דינא מן שמיא
בכן שלח עלי נורא מן שמיא
געון עלי כאריא כל שניא
עד ידיק ויחמי יי' מן שמיא
[פיוט יט, שירת בני מערבא]

10.     ארעים במר קלי
דאתרע שור מגדלי
ושנאה אגלי ית כל קהלי
ושתק אולפן ממללי
ואתקטיל מלכי מסגיאות מעלי
לכן צוחת אללי לי

אוי מה דהות מחתי קשיא
בתכיף כד איתקטיל מלכא יאשיה
אללי לי
[פיוט כ, שירת בני מערבא]

11.     אנא אזיל ואבכה
על     אומה רחימא
בחירה מכל אומא
עיני עיני יורדה מי
[פיוט כא, שירת בני מערבא]

12.     גליין ומטלטלין יתבינן
דכעס עלן פטרונן
איך נשיר את שיר יי'

הא אתון מערבבין
ובחשוכא יתבין
שירו לנו משיר ציון
[פיוט כב, שירת בני מערבא]

13.     דרכו בי סנאי בחבלות
דקרו עולימין ואסגיאו קטילות
דינא כד אתעביד אשתארו שבילות
דרכי ציון אבלות [איכה א:ד]
[נספח, שירת בני מערבא]

14.     אדיק בבעו על ציון
ברחמין תבני ירושלים
[פיוט כג, שירת בני מערבא]

# WHAT JACOB ACTUALLY WROTE ABOUT EPHRAIM

*Andrew Palmer*
School of Oriental and African Studies, United Kingdom
Institute of Eastern Christian Studies, The Netherlands

## INTRODUCTION

The verse homily (Syriac: *mēmrā/mimro*) on the deacon Ephraim/Ephrem by Jacob, bishop of (Baṭnon da-) Serugh refers to Exod 15:20f as a justification for Ephraim's boldness in setting aside Paul's ban on women speaking in church (1 Cor 14:34f; for a recent article with references to earlier and forthcoming studies, see Ashbrook Harvey 2005). In the passage from the Pentateuch, which was attributed to Moses, we read: 'And Miriam the prophetess, Aaron's sister, took up her tambourine, and all the women followed, dancing to the sound of tambourines; and Miriam sang them this refrain: Sing to the Lord, for he has risen up in triumph; the horse and his rider he has hurled into the sea.' (New English Bible) Jacob assumes that Moses gave the command for this; he says that Ephraim (a mere deacon?) instructed women to join in praising Christ for his redemption of the human race and compares his initiative to that of Moses in instructing the women to celebrate the crossing of the Red Sea.

It ought to go without saying that Jacob should be judged on the basis of what he wrote. The judgment that he is prolix might have to be modified in the light of my findings. If to be prolix is to repeat oneself in a boring manner, interpolations have made Jacob seem prolix; each of his own lines can be savoured for its new turn of phrase. If what is meant is that Jacob uses more words than are necessary, he should not be criticized for falling short of an ideal of laconic expression which had no place in his culture. As we shall see, predetermined numbers and formal constraints determined the structure of the poem he chose to write about Ephraim, just as they do a Shakespearian sonnet. He filled the requisite number of lines elegantly, entertainingly and imaginatively. He may also have used layout to awaken at a delightfully intellectual level the appreciation of his few readers, while not overburdening his many listeners.

The present paper uses Amar's (1995) collation of six of the eleven mss listed by Vööbus (1973–1980) to begin the groundwork for an edition which seeks to establish what Jacob actually wrote. Firstly, I show that there must be nineteen interpolated couplets (thirty-eight interpolated lines) in Amar's base text; this proof begins with the record, preserved by one ms., that the original composition comprised 330 lines. Secondly, I show that eleven of these must be in Section 1 and I go through that section, judging which couplets are at home there and which are intruders. Thirdly, I show that the disproportionate number of interpolated lines in Section 1 can be explained as glosses originally written in the large gaps left by Jacob between the four parts of this section for symbolic reasons. Finally, in footnotes to a new verse translation of the homily, I point out the flaws in the remaining eight spurious couplets and show how Sections 2–15 might have been laid out, leaving two-line spaces between the sections and, in places, wider gaps at the bottom of a page where (in one case) four lines were written by a glossator.

## 1   Proof that Nineteen Couplets have been Interpolated in Amar's Base Text

Three hundred and thirty-one is the sum of the five letters א, ף, ר, י and ם which also do service as the numbers 1, 80, 200, 10 and 40 (see Table 1). This means that the numerical value of the name Ephraim אפרים, which is spelled with these five letters in Aramaic, is 331.

Table 1: Primary numerical values of the Aramaic letters, showing that Ephraim אפרים = 331

| א | ב | ג | ד | ה | ו | ז | ח | ט | י |
|---|---|---|---|---|---|---|---|---|---|
| **1** | 2 | 3 | 4 | 5 | 6 | 7 | 8 | 9 | **10** |
| י | כ | ל | מ | נ | ס | ע | ף | צ | ק |
| 10 | 20 | 30 | **40** | 50 | 60 | 70 | **80** | 90 | 100 |
| ק | ר | ש | ת | א | ף | ר | י | ם | אפרים |
| 100 | **200** | 300 | 400 | **1 +** | **80 +** | **200 +** | **10 +** | **40** | **= 331** |

The oldest extant copy of Jacob of Serugh's homily on Ephraim is the forty-second text in a ms. in the collection of the Syrian Orthodox Patriarchate at the Monastery of Saint Ephraim in Maʿārat Sayyidnāya, near Damascus, namely D[amascus] P[atriarchate] 12/14. DP 12/14, which Vööbus (1973) dates to the early eleventh century, was used by Joseph Amar as the base text for his edition (Amar 1995). In DP 12/14 the homily closes with the following words:

> End of that on Saint Ephraim, three hundred and thirty lines.

No other ms. collated by the editor contains this record of the original number of lines. Its authenticity is guaranteed by the fact that it is at variance with the number of lines in the text as transmitted. Amar prints the 184 couplets (368 lines) of DP 12/14 with the variants from five other mss (including three extra couplets at the end which are found in two of these mss) in the apparatus criticus, five extra couplets which are found in all the mss except DP 12/14 being relegated to three appendices. This information is set out in Table 2.

Table 2: Stages in the transmission of Jacob's homily on Ephraim

| Stage | Witnesses | No. of couplets/lines |
|---|---|---|
| 1 | Record at the end of DP 12/14 | 165/330 |
| 2 | DP 12/14 | 184/368 |
| 3 | Chicago, Oriental Institute, A 12,008 = B (Amar) | |
| | Paris Syriaque 195 and 196 = D and C (Amar) | |
| | (c. 1–35 are now missing in Par. Syr. 196) | 189/378 |
| 4 | DP 12/15 | |
| | Harvard Syriac 100 | 192/384 |

Three hundred and thirty is one short of Ephraim's number, but, considering that Jacob composed in couplets, it is close enough to indicate that Jacob's original text was made on purpose to approximate in the number of its lines to three hundred and thirty-one. The missing number, one, stands for God, who, as 'the ground of all being', can be compared with the surface on which the homily is written. I aim to establish which couplets have been interpolated by subjecting the text of the oldest and least interpolated ms., DP 12/14, to critical scrutiny.

## 2   Proof that Eleven Couplets in Section 1 (c. 7–9, 15–17, 24, 26–29) are Spurious

Symbolic arithmetic can be done with the numerical value of Ephraim, giving it a meaning consonant with Ephraim's Trinitarian Faith. Three (the number of the Divine Persons, Father, Son and Holy Spirit) is multiplied by eleven (composed of two heads: the first of the units and the first of the tens, appropriate symbols for the Father and the Son) and by ten (the numerical value of the initial ' with which the names of both the Father יהוה and the Son ישוע begin) to make three hundred and thirty, to which we add one (God) to get 331. The numbers which emerge from this as keys are one and two and three. Together, whether you add them up or multiply them, they make six. Six is the first and simplest of the perfect numbers. Three hundred and thirty is fifty-five times six. The number six was used by Jacob as the base of his structural arithmetic. This emerges from the way the composition breaks down into sections, parts of sections (in the case of Section 1) and thematic units. (To help the reader analyze the structure I have marked off thematic units from one another within the paragraphs of my translation, below.) To begin with, six is a divisor of eight out of the fifteen sections into which the homily most naturally falls (see Table 3).

Table 3: Total numbers of lines in the sections of the homily as transmitted in DP 12/14

| § | Lines | × 6 | § | Lines | × 6 | § | Lines | × 6 |
|---|---|---|---|---|---|---|---|---|
| 1 | 70 | – | 6 | 22 | – | 11 | 12 | = 2 × 6 |
| 2 | 30 | = 5 × 6 | 7 | 12 | = 2 × 6 | 12 | 8 | – |
| 3 | 48 | = 8 × 6 | 8 | 24 | = 4 × 6 | 13 | 28 | – |
| 4 | 8 | – | 9 | 24 | = 4 × 6 | 14 | 14 | – |
| 5 | 12 | = 2 × 6 | 10 | 26 | – | 15 | 30 | = 5 × 6 |

The total number of lines in the fifteen sections of the homily, as divided in Table 3, is three hundred and sixty-eight, which has to be reduced by thirty-eight to three hundred and thirty. Thirty-eight lines constitute nineteen couplets. If eleven of these nineteen couplets are in section 1, one in section 4, two in section 6, one each in sections 10 and twelve, two in section 13 and one in section 14, then all the totals will be divisible by six (see Table 4).

Table 4: Total lines in the sections of the homily as hypothetically restored.

| § | Lines | × 6 | § | Lines | × 6 | § | Lines | × 6 |
|---|---|---|---|---|---|---|---|---|
| 1 | **70 − 22 = 48** | 8 | 6 | **22 − 4 = 18** | 3 | 11 | 12 | 2 |
| 2 | 30 | 5 | 7 | 12 | 2 | 12 | **8 − 2 = 6** | 1 |
| 3 | 48 | 8 | 8 | 24 | 4 | 13 | **28 − 4 = 24** | 4 |
| 4 | **8 − 2 = 6** | 1 | 9 | 24 | 4 | 14 | **14 − 2 = 12** | 2 |
| 5 | 12 | 2 | 10 | **26 − 2 = 24** | 4 | 15 | 30 | 5 |

I offer here a literal translation of the eighteen couplets of the augmented first half as represented in DP 12/14, with the variant readings
of other mss after a forward slash. Those variants which are underlined
seem to me more likely to be correct, but this judgment is not based
on any study of the relationships between the mss. It will be seen that
c. 10 introduces the subject of painting, which dominates Part Two.
Three interpolated couplets have therefore to be found in Part One and
another three in Part Two. The couplets suspected by me are placed
in curly brackets { } and printed **bold**.

> 1 How shall I come near to your successful exploits, O graceful one, and
> by means of which melodies shall I sing the tradition about you, owner
> of the graces? 2 For while I want to tell the tradition about you/relate
> your graces, I am afraid that your/the great homily will grow small in
> my feeble mouth. 3 Chosen Ephraim, great head/head (Ps 60:7) and
> master of teaching, what speech succeeds in exhausting your matter in
> chants? 4 Astonishing man, who used speech spiritually, how shall I relate
> the whole tradition about you with a tongue of flesh? 5 O hard worker,
> whose talent (Matt 25:14–30) bore interest at ten thousand times its value,
> how/whereby shall a bad and lazy servant speak about you? 6 O athlete,
> who was victorious in the contest of teaching, what crown does my speech
> possess that it might offer you/I might offer one to you? {**7 Stalwart,**
> **who brought down by his combativeness/by combativeness**
> **all the teachings (of heretics), whereby shall a wretch who**
> **accomplishes nothing with empty words exhaust your matter?**
> **8 Competitor who completed his course with justice/faith, it**
> **is an insult for the effort you made to be praised by me. 9 O**
> **merchant, who was not robbed at the crossroads, who would**
> **allow me to proclaim/relate your divine riches?**}
> 10 How shall I, the hateful one (*sanyo*), depict you, the graceful one, for
> the colours of my speech are too ordinary/drab for the task of telling
> about you? 11 A layman cannot paint the portrait of a king; no more
> can I succeed in singing the tradition about you. 12 My own pigments
> are dirty, because of my hatefulness/hateful deeds (*sanyot[y]*), whereas
> your portrait/a portrait of you asks for colours which blaze. 13 I am dry

grass and hateful (*sanyo*) tares (*ya'ro*, compare the thornbush = *sanyo* of Exod 3:2), but the story of your life requires a roaring fire, that a flame may depict your exploits.[1] 14 The colours of my speech are bespattered with mud (*syono*, written with the same four letters as *sanyo* and visually resembling this word) from my crimes and if I touch the panel (prepared for the portrait) of your graces/of the tradition about you, it will be soiled. {15 **These pigments of mine are mixed with contaminated/dirty water and if they are spattered on your narrative it will be made hateful/be harmed. 16 My colours are dirty and resemble a sombre shadow, but your icon/the tradition about you asks for flashes of fire by reason of its beauty/<so that> its beauty may flash. 17 If I, the weak one, approach <that> I may sketch your image/Behold, I think that if I approach that I might depict your image/your grace/your graces, this man is a dolt, because who has depicted you out of his pigments?}** 18 So shall I then be silent (and refrain) from telling about you, knowing as I do that a homily about you is too high and glorious (an enterprise) for my feebleness?[2]

The interpolated couplets in Part One are c. 7–9. No objection can, I think, be raised to the recognition of c. 1–6 as the opening paragraph of the homily. Couplet 7 exaggerates grotesquely in calling the poet 'a wretch who accomplishes nothing with empty words'; Jacob is modest, but he calls his tongue feeble and his colours drab, not totally useless. Couplet 8, likewise, goes too far in calling it 'an insult' for Ephraim to be praised by a lesser poet; Jacob is only afraid that he may diminish Ephraim, not that he will offend him. The imagery of c. 9 bears no relation to the preceding couplets, or indeed to those which follow. Jacob claims to use simple speech (c. 129), a description which may be applied with justice to c. 183, which is also about Ephraim not getting robbed; this couplet is also better integrated with its context. As for Part Two, c. 10–14 form a unit consistent in punning on the word *sanyo*, while c. 18, as we have seen, closes the first half of the section. Couplet 15 repeats ideas from c. 14 without the same clarity of conception, for how does one daub colours on a narrative? Couplet 16 is similarly a poor imitation of c. 12. Couplet 17 is clumsy and weak in all its versions;

---

[1] AE omit the beginning up to the word 'but' and have 'The story of your life asks for a metaphorical (for *nsibo* = *š'ilo* see Awdo's lexicon) fire, the colour of which gives light/which gives light to its colour' instead.

[2] ACD have 'knowing as I do that the tradition about you is too high for my feebleness, that you should be praised by me (i.e. too high for feeble me to be able to praise you)'.

and the use there of the word 'dolt' as an insult surely goes against Matt 5:22. We may now go on to look for the five interpolated couplets in Parts Three and Four, the second half of Section 1.

19 But I am afraid of silence (šetqo), too,/of silence itself, because it causes damage: the tradition about you would be completely lost/would be lost from every point of view. 20 I shall speak, therefore, although I know that I am not worthy of the high/great tradition about you, because the truth (qušto, almost, but not quite, an anagram of šetqo 'silence') bears witness to your heroic exploits. 21 O listeners, listen with limpid/great love to the story about Ephraim the Great, which is full of the exploits of heroism/perfection/faith, 22 that true advocate (snigro = συνήγορος d-qušto) of the Faith, who became its mouth, and the truth revealed (by God) was spoken out by him in a sustained voice. 23 That sweet source made blessed water flow (ardi, phonetically close to arwi, as in c. 25) in our land and the forest of the chosen trees of the Faith (literally: the chosen forest of the Faith) was raised to maturity (etrabbi) by it. {24 That new wine, the colour and the bouquet of which are (derived) from (the soil of) Golgotha, by drinking which men and women became so intoxicated that they gave glory.} 25 That wellspring of melodies which, as you see, (still) comes cascading down into all sorts of mouths and which intoxicates (marwe, phonetically close to marbe = 'raises to maturity', as in c. 23) the land with his anthems, so that it might contemplate him (d-tet-hagge beh, suggesting, though not quite mentioning, a festive party: haggo; in my verse-translation, below, I render this implicit pun by 'cerebrate', which is meant to make the reader think of 'celebrate').
{26 That man whose actions showed him to be a divine philosopher, who first practised and then preached to him who listened to him. (Literally: A divine philosopher ( filosufo = φιλόσοφος) in the things which were done by him, who while/although [sic] he was doing them, afterwards used to teach/used to teach everything to the one who <was> listening to him.) 27 That true labourer, who worked hard to finish what he had begun, and who actually showed in himself <both> deeds and words. 28 He was an architect and he/who built on the bedrock (literally: foundations) of the truth and he/who used gold and precious stones to seal his buildings. 29 That true master, who practised what he preached, as it is written, and gave/painted for his disciples an example to imitate/emulate.}
30 That simple man, who in his deep wisdom ('rimuteh) avoided learned words (hekmoto), so as not to stray from that road of apostolic teaching (hoy urho da-šlihuto, which could also mean 'that road of nakedness', i.e. simplicity). 31 That man of deep wisdom ('rimo), who spoke in simple terms in order to be helpful and succeeded in becoming a dove ( yawno) and a serpent, as he had been commanded (Matt 10:16). 32 That amazing

public speaker (*rhiṭro* = ῥήτωρ), who vanquished the Greeks (*yawnoye*) by his eloquence in that he was capable of <u>catching</u>/imprisoning in a single word ten thousand matters. 33 <u>That bard (*qitorodo* = κιθαρῳδός) in God's house</u>/That divine bard, who <u>imprisoned</u>/thought out his sentences in his measures to project a joyful sound to the great astonishment (of all). 34 That son of the apostles (*da-šliḥe*, which can also mean 'of stripped men'), who with them obtained/<u>built</u> the Word of Truth, which cannot be uprooted by the winds of deceit (blowing) all (together). 35 That ocean of homilies, on which, as you see, all sorts of preachers sail, without having fathomed its depth or the wide space of its vastness.

The interplay of the words *šetqo* 'silence' and *qušto* 'truth' runs through c. 19, 20 and 22, as that of the words *marde* 'irrigates', *marbe* 'raises to maturity' and *marwe* 'intoxicates' does through c. 23 and 25. The image of the 'sweet source' of 'blessed water' in c. 23 develops in c. 25 into that of the 'wellspring of melodies', and as all rivers end in the sea so the second half of Section 1 ends with the image of the 'ocean of homilies' in c. 35. This development is interrupted by c. 24, a couplet on the wine which was produced from the 'vine' which was 'planted' on Golgotha (John 15:1, 19:34; 1 Cor 11:25). This couplet is out of keeping with Jacob's style and reads like a gloss on the word 'intoxicates' in c. 25. By contrast with this learned couplet, c. 26 is barely literate and, like c. 27 and 29, which add nothing new to it, is a poor imitation of the genuine c. 158f, a meditation on the words 'do and teach' in Matt 5:19. Couplet 28 reads like a gloss on c. 34 with the preferable variant 'built': a meditation on Matt 7:24–27.

## 3   Gaps on the Page as an Explanation for the Accumulation of Glosses

How to explain the fact that there are so many interpolations in Section 1? Forty-eight genuine lines, which cannot have occupied more than two pages, were augmented by twenty-two spurious ones. In the rest of the homily two hundred and eighty-two genuine lines were augmented by sixteen spurious ones. In other words, Section 1 has nearly one spurious line for every two genuine ones, as against, very approximately, one for every twenty in the rest of the homily. Such a discrepancy cannot be explained by the mere fact that Section 1 comes at the beginning, since the authors of c. 26, 27 and 29 chose this point at which to insert glosses on c. 158f and the author of the spurious couplet 9 was referring to Jacob's couplet 183.

The most obvious explanation is that Section 1 was laid out generously with plenty of space between Parts One and Two on the right and Parts Three and Four on the left. Some surviving fifth-century mss have the parchment folios scored for fifty lines of writing and this is also the page-length indicated by my researches on the layout of Ephraim's cycles on Paradise and Faith. (See the two articles by Palmer.) The longest single sections in Jacob's homily, Sections 1 and 3, have 48 lines; Section 3 is likely to have occupied a single page, but Section 1 was probably laid out in alternate twelve-line blocks of lines filled with writing and lines left empty. (The title will have been on the top line of the right-hand page, with a line left blank beneath it.) This arrangement will have produced, incidentally, a white cross on the opening, the upright bar being formed of the margins to either side of the valley, while the horizontal bar, twelve scored lines deep from top to bottom, will have stretched across the opening between the upper and the lower blocks of writing (see Figure 1). The alternation of squares filled with speech and squares filled with silence is an icon of the balance which the poet seeks between the two under the pretence of hesitating between them (cf. Ephraim, *Hymni de fide* 38).

This yawning gap, scored for writing, attracted lesser imitators of Jacob's art, who saw the empty lines as an invitation to write glosses on the text in the same poetic form. Couplets 7–9 accumulated in the arm of the cross on the right-hand page, c. 15–17 in the space below Part Two of the writing on that page. The gap between Parts Three and Four on the left-hand page would not have been quite filled by c. 24 and c. 26–29. A later copyist, perceiving that these couplets were not original, nevertheless acted as if they had been added by the author himself as an afterthought, though not always in the right place. This interpolator made his own decisions about the most appropriate place to insert these 'afterthoughts' in Jacob's text. Couplet 18 obviously belonged before c. 19, so he inserted c. 15–17 before c. 18. There may well have been a space of two empty lines after c. 24, which inspired the interpolator to place this couplet in Part Three, moving it back one to allow c. 25 to do what it does best, that is close a paragraph.

## Literature

Amar, J.P., *A metrical homily on holy Mar Ephrem by Mar Jacob of Sarug; Critical edition of the Syriac text, translation and introduction* (PO 47/1, no. 209), Turnhout 1995.

Ashbrook Harvey, S., 'Revisiting the Daughters of the Covenant: Women's choirs and sacred song in ancient Syriac Christianity', *Hugoye: Journal of Syriac Studies* 8/2 (July 2005) [internet].

Palmer, A., 'Nine more stanzas to be banished from Ephraim's *Paradise*', in: J. Tubach (ed.), [*Festschrift for Arafa Mustafa*], Halle [forthcoming].

———, 'Interpolated Stanzas in Ephraim's Madroshe LXVI–LXVIII on Faith', *OrChr* 90 (2006) 1–22.

Vööbus, A., *Handschriftliche Überlieferung der Mēmrē-Dichtung des Ja'qub von Serug* [4 vols. (CSCO 344–345 = CSCO.Sub 39–40, CSCO 421–422 = CSCO.Sub 60–61), Louvain 1973–1980.

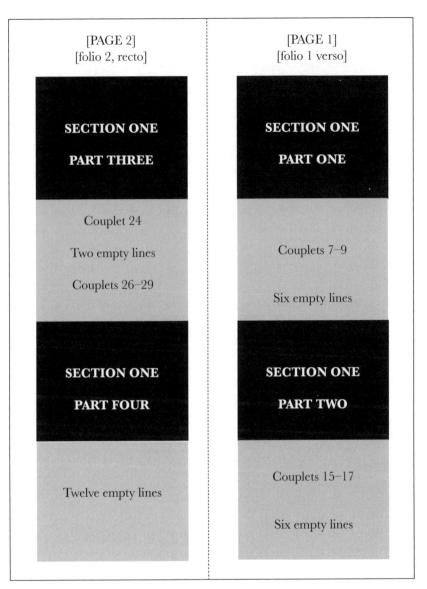

Figure 1
First opening of lost autograph with position of glosses (conjectural).
(Note the division of the area into six columns and six rows!)

## Homily on Saint Ephraim by Jacob the Doctor

Amar/Jacob

| | | |
|---|---|---|
| 1/1 | How should I touch, charmed master, your perfection? How, | §1.1, 12 ll. |
| | To music, sing the tale of him that owns all charm? | |
| 2/2 | Much as I want to tell your tale, its greatness will, | |
| | I greatly fear, be lessened by my puny tongue. | |
| 3/3 | Ephraim, the head and master of the Teaching Art, | |
| | What utterance of poetry can equal yours? | |
| 4/4 | Astounding man, whose utterances were Spirit-filled, | |
| | How can this flesh, this cloddish tongue, encompass you? | |
| 5/5 | Steward, who made his talent grow ten thousand-fold, | |
| | How can this bad and lazy slave extol your zeal? | |
| 6/6 | Athlete, who won the contest of the teaching art, | |
| | What crown does my poor utterance have to offer you? | |

| | | |
|---|---|---|
| 10/7 | How should I paint your beauty with my ugly tongue? | §1.2, 12 ll. |
| | The colours of my utterances are far too pale. | |
| 11/8 | No layman can portray by art the Emperor: | |
| | No more have I the competence to tell of you. | |
| 12/9 | My pigments are all mucky from my ugly ways; | |
| | Your every part requires a brush that paints in flame. | |
| 13/10 | I'm dried-out weeds and hateful thorns; your exploits call | |
| | For roaring fire, a tongue of flame with which to paint. | |
| 14/11 | My colours all are muddied by my greediness: | |
| | My touch would soil the panel primed to paint your grace. | |
| 18/12 | Should I refrain from speaking, then, because I know | |
| | Your tale is far too splendid for my lowly style? | |

| | | |
|---|---|---|
| 19/13 | My silence might result, though, in the total loss<br>Of memory concerning him: this, too, I fear. | §1.3, 12 ll. |
| 20/14 | Unworthy though I know I am, I'll trumpet you:<br>For truthfulness bears witness to your great success. | |
| 21/15 | Attend with love's untroubled ear, dear listeners,<br>To this, the tale of one who lived a hero's life! | |
| 22/16 | Ephraim the Great, true advocate and mouthpiece of<br>The Faith, through whom the truth revealed was spoken loud. | |
| 23/17 | Sweet source, which made blest waters flow throughout our land,<br>And raised the Faith, that forest, to maturity. | |
| 25/18 | His stream of song, cascading down to all our mouths,<br>Inebriates our land and makes us cerebrate. | |

| | | |
|---|---|---|
| 30/19 | Simple, he shunned all cunning in his wisdom, lest<br>He lose the way, the Apostles' road of nakedness. | §1.4, 12 ll. |
| 31/20 | Wise though he was, he helpfully used simple words,<br>Combining dove and serpent, as the Gospel bids. | |
| 32/21 | Astonishingly, he beat the Greeks in rhetoric<br>In that he caught ten thousand thoughts in one short word. | |
| 33/22 | He was the bard in God's high hall, imprisoning<br>In measured bars his sentences, to make them ring. | |
| 34/23 | The Apostles' son, who built with them the Word of Truth,<br>The walls of which deceitful winds can't undermine. | |
| 35/24 | He is the sea of homilies which we preachers sail,<br>A vastness, whose great depth and width are unexplored. | |

| | | |
|---|---|---|
| 36/25 | My tongue's too small to sing your praise, O Man of Truth; | §2, 30 ll. |
| | Your beauty's wealth encloses me on every side. | |
| 37/26 | In David's book, mysteriously, your name occurs: | |
| | 'Strengthener of my head,' he calls you in a psalm. | |
| 38/27 | Ephraim, the son of Joseph, was the man he meant; | |
| | But, secretly, the Spirit that spoke had you in mind. | |
| 39/28 | Doctrina,[3] too, your bride, may call you so, because | |
| | You made her climb the podium of victory. | |
| 40/29 | Our sisters, too, you strengthened and they learned to praise: | |
| | Women were not allowed to speak in church before. | |
| 41/30 | Eve's daughter's mouth was closed until you opened it; | |
| | The Bride of Christ now thunders in response to her. | |
| 42/31 | A novel sight: women that preach the Word of God. | |
| | 'Teachers', they're called among the folk who go to church. | |
| 43/32 | The aim of all your teaching was a world renewed, | |
| | Where women would be like men within God's palaces. | |
| 44/33 | Your efforts framed two lyres for these two regiments | |
| | And women and men began to sing God's praise as one. | |
| 45/34 | You strove to be like Moshé, Head of Israel, | |
| | Who let young girls hold cymbals in the wilderness. | |
| 46/35 | For Hebrew girls made music with their cymbals then, | |
| | As Aram's girls sing praises with madroshê[4] now. | |
| 47/36 | Moses was wise to tell the virgins not to keep | |
| | Inside themselves the praise for which the occasion called. | |
| 48/37 | Ephraim, who was the Moses of the female sex, | |
| | Instructed them in singing hymns melodiously. | |
| 49/38 | The Hebrews saw that they were free and clapped their hands | |
| | In praise of Him that freed them, doing as Moses bade. | |
| 50/39 | The Gentiles, doing as Ephraim bade, make music too | |
| | In thanks for their salvation from the jaws of Death. | |

---

[3] The Teaching Art, personified; both translations represent the Syriac *malfonuto*.

[4] Teaching songs; Jacob exploits the fact that the Syriac word has the same beginning and ending as the name of Moses (*Moshé*).

| | | |
|---|---|---|
| 51/40 | The latter praise is greater than the former one, | §3, 48 ll. |
| | Because our own salvation was the greater one. | |
| 52/41 | Salvation came for Jacob's tribes when waves were split; | |
| | Salvation came for us when graves were cracked in half. | |
| 53/42 | There Pharaoh drowned, because his heart was hardened; here | |
| | Death, swallowed up by Life, was left to rant and rave. | |
| 54/43 | There, in the breach between two seas, a staff made walls; | |
| | Here, in the slabs' smooth surfaces, the Cross made cracks. | |
| 55/44 | Back there a way was opened through the sea for Jews; | |
| | Here Sheol, breached, makes way—and out the Gentiles come! | |
| 56/45 | Their rescue made of living men Egyptian dead; | |
| | Our rescue raised dead parents from their sepulchres. | |
| 57/46 | Back there the floods—so heavy!—fled before the staff; | |
| | Here idols in their thousands crash before the Cross. | |
| 58/47 | Back there God's Bride in all her pride rose from the sea | |
| | And Hebrew girls gave glory with a clash of brass; | |
| 59/48 | Here, though, because the rescued Church has been baptized, | |
| | Our sisters ring with Ephraim's songs to celebrate. | |
| 60/49 | Audience, speak! Which of the two is greater? Say! | |
| | Compare them, in all justice, with intelligence! | |
| 61/50 | The staff that saved the Hebrews did astounding things; | |
| | Performed great signs; exhibited mysterious powers; | |
| 62/51 | Struck Egypt down; left Ham in shreds; disturbed the earth; | |
| | Troubled the air; caused hail to fall; extinguished fire; | |
| 63/52 | Brought up the frogs; shape-shifted; caused catastrophes; | |
| | Made darkness thick; brought down a blade on first-born sons; | |
| 64/53 | Divided seas; made liquid stand, as though in skins; | |
| | Waged war upon the elements, transforming them; | |
| 65/54 | Glared with its power at creatures, till they shook with fear; | |
| | Loomed over seas—those prison-gates—and opened them. | |
| 66/55 | It caught the wild up-rearing waves and bridled them; | |
| | Imposed its yoke on breakers and subjected them; | |
| 67/56 | Took in its grasp the liquid streams and bundled them; | |
| | Beat bullies like a champion and entangled them; | |
| 68/57 | Threw fighters in a dungeon and imprisoned them; | |
| | Drew the proud down between two seas, extinguished them. | |
| 69/58 | Led the twelve tribes by novel ways and rescued them; | |
| | Used currents which swept rebels up and smothered them, | |
| 70/59 | Forcing the swift, riders and all, to bow the knee | |
| | And breaking up the chariots on those watery steppes. | |
| 71/60 | It used a lake to grind that snake, the Egyptian king; | |
| | Battered his brood of vipers with two tidal waves; | |
| 72/61 | Used floods to strike the Egyptian snake that caught that dove, | |
| | The Synagogue, which flew out between its poisoned fangs; | |
| 73/62 | Drowned the bad wolf that took the lambs from Jacob's fold, | |
| | Who fled the flood which filled its den and came back home. | |
| 74/63 | In such dire straits, the Hebrews saw their Saviour's strength | |
| | And clapped their hands to glory in His victory. | |

| | | |
|---|---|---|
| 75/64 | Watching this act of God with his discerning gaze, | §4, 6 ll. |
| | Moses set up, as food for thought, a chant of praise: | |
| 76/65 | 'Tribes one and all, now praise the Lord's Magnificence! | |
| | How gloriously has He drowned the whole Egyptian host!' | |
| 77/66 | The Levite's cry, so powerful, bade the Synagogue, | |
| | Women and men, exult, as one great instrument. | |
| *78* | *He gave a tambourine to the virgins to give praise,* | |
| | *And a new (hymn of) glory was struck up there in a loud voice.*[5] | |
| 79/67 | The following words are more or less what Moshé said | §5, 12 ll. |
| | To stimulate the adult girls to glorify: | |
| 80/68 | 'Even you girls may not repress God's praise to-day: | |
| | Make cymbals for the Saviour who has freed his flock! | |
| 81/69 | Not for the men alone did He divide the sea, | |
| | That they alone should praise the One who rescued them. | |
| 82/70 | Together with your brothers and your fathers you | |
| | Crossed over, so with them be loud in psalmody! | |
| 83/71 | Both you and they saw wonderful catastrophes: | |
| | With them send up hosannas, then, to mighty God! | |
| 84/72 | United as you are with them in being saved, | |
| | Equal shall be the praise your mouths send up to Him!' | |

| | | |
|---|---|---|
| 85/73 | In numbers thus did Moses raise his voice in praise: | §6, 18 ll. |
| | His people heard and, struck with awe, they glorified. | |
| 86/74 | Saint Ephraim thought upon these writings and perceived | |
| | That he should vie with Moses and enrich his praise; | |
| 87/75 | Saw that the Cross was raised against the pagan gods, | |
| | To shake the ranks of Evil with the fear of One; | |
| 88/76 | Parting that lake—the Underworld—and bringing out | |
| | Its denizens, deprived of whom Perdition wailed; | |
| 89/77 | Grinding the Worm that swallowed all our ancestors; | |
| | Defeating Death and Satan through its feebleness; | |
| 90/78 | Bringing down gods in front of all their worshippers; | |
| | And shattering all the graven stones to which men bowed; | |
| 91/79 | Melting them down, the statues cast in gold and bronze; | |
| | Exposing gods; uprooting all their colonnades; | |
| 92/80 | Breaking in half the useless slabs of sacrifice; | |
| | Demolishing walls *Idolatry*[6] had built up high; | |
| 93/81 | Enfolding all the Gentiles, whom *Idolatry*, | |
| | So virulent till overturned, had once dispersed. | |
| *94* | *It summoned the serene one, the church of the nations, that had been driven away and gave* | |
| | *peace to the afflicted (church) which had been persecuted.* | |
| *95* | *(The church) took comfort in (the cross) when it was delivered, for (idolatry) was overturned;* | |
| | *and (she) who had been silenced clapped (her) hands, to give praise.*[7] | |

---

[5] Elsewhere (c. 42, 43, 99 and 102) the word *ḥadto* 'new, unheard-of' is chiefly used of Ephraim's initiatives. Interpolations (quoted from Amar 1995) are italicized.

[6] The Syriac word *ṭuʿyay* means something like 'misguidedness', but it is usually translated 'idolatry'. As a feminine word, it lends itself to personification as a bad woman, a foil to Ephraim's 'bride' *Doctrina*.

[7] C. 95 is the only one in this series which does not have the Cross for subject; also, the Church never was actually silenced. If the authenticity of c. 95 is in doubt, then

| | | |
|---|---|---|
| 96/82 | The women used to take no part in singing psalms, | §7, 12 ll. |
| | But Ephraim, in his wisdom, judged that this was wrong. | |
| 97/83 | With cymbals given by *Moshé* girls made noise to God; | |
| | *Madroshé* [filled with symbols: A. Palmer!] gave a voice to maids. | |
| 98/84 | Fine for Ephraim to stand erect among the chaste, | |
| | Arousing all the sisters with his glory-songs! | |
| 99/85 | It suited him, an eagle perched amongst the doves, | |
| | To teach them praise unheard-of with all innocence! | |
| 100/86 | A humble flock of partridges surrounded him, | |
| | Learning to sing so sweetly with all modesty! | |
| 101/87 | He taught them all the lullabies that swallows sing | |
| | And all the church resounded to their chirruping. | |

| | | |
|---|---|---|
| 102/88 | The following words are more or less what Ephraim said | §8, 24 ll. |
| | In teaching pure women to sing unheard-of praise: | |
| 103/89 | 'You Gentile women, approach and learn to praise the One | |
| | Who saved you from your ancestors' idolatry! | |
| 104/90 | He rescued you from worshipping dead images, | |
| | So glorify the One whose death has set you free! | |
| 105/91 | You rose, just like your brothers, from the water's womb, | |
| | Arrayed in light: aloud, like them, respond with thanks! | |
| 106/92 | One and the same the Body you and they received; | |
| | One and the same the Cup from which you both did drink; | |
| 107/93 | One and the same Salvation's yours and theirs; so why | |
| | Have *you* not learned to glorify, allowed, like them! | |
| 108/94 | Your mouth, the womb from which God's praise is born, was closed | |
| | By Eve, but now it's open, thanks to Miriam [ = Mary; cf. Exod 15:20]. | |
| 109/95 | Eve tied the thread of silence round your tongues, the hag! | |
| | The Virgin's Son has loosed them: they should whoop with joy! | |
| 110/96 | The Mate [Gen 2:18] imposed a muzzle on your docile mouths; | |
| | The Maid produced the key with which to unlock your tongues! | |
| 111/97 | Flat on her back your sex had been, because of Eve, | |
| | But Miriam's lifted you to sing for evermore. | |
| 112/98 | The Judge declared you guilty of your Mother's Sin, | |
| | But now you're free, acquitted by your Sister's Son. | |
| 113/99 | Remove your shame and, bare-faced, sing in praise of Him, | |
| | Gotten to give you boldness at the Court of Heaven!' | |

---

that of c. 94 becomes doubtful as well. These four lines belong together: they pick up the passive construction from the end of c. 93 and make of it a kind of refrain.

114/100   These were the words that wise man used to encourage them   §9, 24 ll.
          To lend their mouths to homage in surprising songs.
115/101   | In time of siege that Moses filled the breaches in;
          | *Doctrina* had been laid out flat: he raised her up.[8]
116/102   | Commander of a regiment of women, he
          | Sallied to fight the Rebel who had sacked the earth.
117/103   There was a war on earth, by which the Devil hoped
          To silence all the teaching that the Apostles gave.
118/104   Doctrines arose: *Idolatry* had brought them up
          As highwaymen, to hollow out the Gospel's Truth.
119/105   Edessa, rid of idols by her saint, Addai,
          Was filled again with faithless men by Satan then.
120/106   | With teachings, as with ambushes, from every side
          | He strove to gag the Church of God by every means.
121/107   | On this side stood the followers of Marcion
          | And, over there, the legions of the Manichees.
122/108   | He formed a gang of Arians and Sabellians,
          | Batallions of insidious Bar Dayṣonians.
123/109   Such companies, and others not worth mentioning,
          That rebel ranged around the Church, besieging Her.
124/110   *Idolatry* had winged the Faith with feathered words,
          Aiming to make the Apostles' Way impassable.
125/111   In all his sects, as diverse as he made their words,
          Satan pursued one object in his evil will.

---

[8] Syriac: *aqim*; cf. c. 111. The Hebrew name מרים Miriam (Mary) spells 'he raises up' in Syriac.

| | | |
|---|---|---|
| 126/112 | 'But,' you may say, 'your story strays from Ephraim's praise! | §10, 24 ll. |
| | Don't list for us such teachings in your homily!' | |
| 127/113 | Dear listeners, *that* is why I said these things: to show | |
| | For what great cause he struggled and how brave he was. | |
| 128/114 | Children, you need formation: don't begrudge the time! | |
| | Love lore, for he who gets it gains great opulence! | |
| 129/115 | Attend to my instruction with unflagging ears | |
| | And let your thoughts not criticize my simple words! | |
| 130/116 | Take refuge in the shadow of the Word of God! | |
| | Escape the World of Hollowness, that parching heat! | |
| 131/117 | Bread, for the soul, is learning: give the soul her due! | |
| | Don't starve the poor companion of your body's wealth! | |
| 132/118 | Why only for the body think of nourishment? | |
| | Why grudge the cost of feeding her? It's small enough! | |
| 133/119 | If you are just, then allocate with rectitude | |
| | To soul and body each its due, discerningly. | |
| 134/120 | Why do you store up wine for years to drink at ease, | |
| | And, when you hear the Word of Life, begin to yawn? | |
| 135/121 | You take great pains in cooking food that turns to turds, | |
| | But the pure gold of lore, to you, is turgid fare. | |
| 136/122 | O Children of the Truth, love lore and think on it! | |
| | Once formed, the soul grows richer by discoveries. | |
| 138/123 | The sun is fine for the clear eye to thrive upon | |
| | And lore is, too, for the sound soul to think upon. | |

*137  With its perceptions, the mind is enlightened to delight; it is living food which has no wastage*
*to the nourishment it gives.*[9]

| | | |
|---|---|---|
| 139/124 | As you love life, do not rebel against your Lore! | §11, 12 ll. |
| | Work for him! Draw his plough! His yoke is sweet to bear. | |
| 140/125 | See that you love your Mother with an untouched heart! | |
| | For Teaching gives Her children life, and hope of more. | |
| 141/126 | Treasures concealed and wealth untold are in Her store: | |
| | Her children are enriched by all Her benefits. | |
| 142/127 | She has something higher than words and eloquence, | |
| | Too great to be detected by the human ear. | |
| 143/128 | She is above the world: this place is not Her home: | |
| | Her children are invited to a better world. | |
| 144/129 | Beauties She has which intellects can never grasp; | |
| | *Doctrina*'s voice can never be heard, unless with love. | |

---

[9] Couplet 137 is a gloss on c. 135, but it did not originally follow either c. 135 or c. 136 (where the interpolator placed it), because, if it had, then the pronouns in c. 137 would be feminine. As it is, they are masculine, referring back to *yulpono* 'learning' in c. 138. Understandably, then, Amar misunderstands this couplet, which should be translated: 'By his desserts (cf. Ephraim, *Hymni de fide* 81:8) the mind becomes all luminous. That living food does not result in excrement.' This translation omits *l-metbassomu* which perhaps is short for 'and therefore we have reason *to enjoy* eating it'. Learning is compared with Christ in c. 139 and by Ephraim in *Sermones de fide* 13f and 215f. The parallel passage in *The Acts of Judas Thomas*, ed. Wright, p. 177 has, like c. 137, both the verb *nhar* and the phrase *apusia layt leh*. This close verbal parallel shows that the author was comparing the process of learning the truth from Scripture with that of receiving Christ in the Eucharist. This is subtle stuff—too learned, surely, for the listeners Jacob had in mind.

| | | |
|---|---|---|
| 145/130 | Why should a tale so full of life grow tedious now? | §12, 6 ll. |
| | Pay heed to me! You'll relish what is coming next. | |
| 146/131 | Outstanding as a teacher, he was tireless: why | |
| | Should you grow tired of listening to his praises, then? | |
| 147/132 | Long was the fight he fought against false teaching, so | |
| | Long let the speech run on that speaks about <u>this man</u>! | |

*148  It is not as though I am qualified to speak; my mind is weak, and I am inadequate for his*
*narrative.*[10]

| | | |
|---|---|---|
| 149/133 | <u>This man</u> who made the Church so rich in excellence | §13, 24 ll. |
| | By teaching Her to magnify the Infinite. | |
| 150/134 | <u>This man</u> who came, like April, to the sleeping earth: | |
| | Like blossoms, his *madroshé* made our churches glad. | |
| 151/135 | <u>This man</u> who forged—outstanding blade!—that sword of faith | |
| | From which our side—simplicity's—derives its strength. | |
| 152/136 | <u>This man</u> who chose prize-teachers from the womenfolk: | |
| | That tenderness might win the war with heresy. | |
| 153/137 | <u>This man</u> whose words were arrows from that bow, his mouth, | |
| | Who forged his chants, like lances, for his armoury. | |
| 154/138 | <u>This man</u> who loosed at wicked men breathtaking songs, | |
| | Dispelling with his airs a mass of obstacles. | |
| 155/139 | <u>This man,</u> the crown of Aram, who, in him, all but | |
| | Drew level with the grace attained by men of Greece. | |
| 156/140 | <u>This man,</u> who was unique among the Syrians | |
| | In rhetoric: our teachers all were formed by him. | |
| 157/141 | <u>This man</u> whose words were measured out and counterpoised, | |
| | Who organized his teaching like a general. | |
| 158/142 | <u>This man</u> whose deeds were just as fine as what he said, | |
| | His way of life the summit of integrity. | |
| 159/143 | <u>This man</u> who taught not only by the work of words, | |
| | But by his own high standards and example, too. | |
| 162/144 | <u>This man</u> has more, however much I say of him: | |
| | I'm overwhelmed: his ocean stops my stream of praise.[11] | |

*160  This man overcame the apostasy of the Marcionites, who rejected the incarnation of the Son*
*of God.*
*161  This man humbled with the straightforwardness of his teaching the logic of the cunning followers*
*of Bardaisan.*[12]

---

[10] This is a scruple dismissed by Jacob in c. 20; besides, 'this man' in c. 147 is the
cue for the series of epigrams beginning with those two words to begin.

[11] It would be appropriate if the homily appeared to end at this point. This could
have been achieved by leaving the rest of this page blank. That this may have been
done is suggested by the accumulation here of two couplets; in most other places where
a gloss was added between sections there seems to have been room for just one couplet.

[12] Jacob himself deals with the Marcionites and the Bardesanites in a more appropriate context: see c. 121f. These added verses must have been intended as glosses on
c. 152. The interpolator, who failed to see this, did realize that c. 162 was intended
to be followed by a silence, after which the homily is resumed in c. 163, so he moved
the glosses back one place to their present position as c. 160 and 161. Compare his
procedure with c. 15–17, 24 and 137.

163/145   Ah! Truth is prodding me again to prod my tongue:     §14, 12ll.
         *I'm* speechless, but the truth booms on, for *he* was true.
164/146   I'll lend my mouth: let his great tale be told through me!
         Left to myself, I have no strength to praise that man.
165/147   That man's own truth is prompting me to celebrate
         A fragment of his virtues in the Church's ears.
166/148   The Truth has blown upon me, as upon a flute,
         And made me sing, with voice sustained, His Spirit's songs.
167/149   The will that claims my singing tongue is not my own:
         Compelled by Truth, I raise my voice to speak of him.
169/150   Lend me your ears serenely, while I tell—at length!—
         How Ephraim stood, a champion, in the ring of sand,

168   *A labourer for the truth I have become today, if I am worthy to weary myself with the story*
     *of the accomplished master among his students.*[13]

170/151   …when, battling with the heresies for his lady-love,     §15, 30 ll.
         *Doctrina*, he showed manliness and stood his ground;
171/152   …when he was stripped, divested of the wicked world,
         which might have tripped him, costing him perfection's prize;
172/153   …when, like those men who risk their lives in theatres,
         he stood there, soaked in sweat, and fought his corner well;
173/154   …when, bathed in blood—the Son of God's—he made himself
         too slippery for his challengers to wrestle with;
174/155   …when, dragged around by heresies and hollowness,
         he shouted threats, high-spirited, despising them;
175/156   …when, breaking off *Idolatry's* sharp arrowheads—
         insidious lies—that lion would not bow the knee;
176/157   …when, sending forth *madroshé*, serried regiments,
         he had Her bound, knees bended, with Her own deceits;
177/158   …when all the winds of darkness blew against him, but
         that shining light, his teaching, proved unquenchable;
178/159   …when, waiting at the entrance of the Word of God
         for something good, he daily stood, erect in pain;
179/160   …when he confirmed his teaching by example, first
         showing the deed, then saying the word which speaks of it;
180/161   …when, like a dog, he barked at wolves which prowled the fold,
         and kept the sheep of God's good house from predators;
181/162   …when he made folds of *mimré* and *madroshé*, where
         the flock might find a refuge from their enemies;
182/163   …when heresies, like animals, surrounded him
         and, shooting barbs with certain aim, he scattered them;
183/164   …when, keeping watch against the thieves who rob by night,
         he prayed and thought in melodies, contemplative;
184/165   …when, chasing off the demons with his prayerful songs,
         he kept them from the flock redeemed by God's Son's Blood.

---

[13] This couplet interrupts the flow of c. 167 and 169 ('I raise my voice to speak… Lend me your ears'); besides, the academic image of an accomplished master among his students is not in keeping with the passage introduced by c. 169, in which Ephraim is compared with a naked fighter in the Roman arena, a lion, a general, a barking dog and a sharp-shooting shepherd.

PART THREE

THEOLOGY AND HISTORY

# REFLECTIONS ON THE EXPLORATION OF JEWISH AND CHRISTIAN LITURGY FROM THE VIEWPOINT OF A SYSTEMATIC THEOLOGY OF LITURGY

*Stephan Wahle*

Albert-Ludwigs-Universität Freiburg, Germany

The focus of Christian liturgical studies that no longer ignore past and present forms of Jewish liturgy, but are instead deliberately aware of these forms and take them into consideration is by nature on the exploration of the historical correlations between particular texts, prayers and songs, sacred areas, feasts, and celebrations in both religions (cf. Gerhards 2003, 183–211 esp. 186–194). Questions regarding the origin, development, influence, and differences between the Christian and Jewish liturgy are the main concern in this regard. However, these reflections shall concern themselves more with the *theological* relevance of Jewish-Christian liturgical research, which must be considered an important supplement to *historical* liturgical studies of the interrelations between Jewish and Christian liturgy.

Before considering the question of the necessity of Christian liturgical studies reflecting in theological terms on past and present forms of Jewish liturgy, there follow some brief remarks on the characteristics of a systematic theological consideration of the Christian liturgy. A concrete example of the hermeneutics of the Eucharistic celebration and the Passover will subsequently illustrate the *theological* location of Christian liturgy in the biblical and Jewish tradition. This will be followed by a short ascertainment based on the Council decree 'Nostra Aetate' and finally some liturgical theological views of Jewish-Christian liturgical research.

## 1  ON THE SCOPE OF SYSTEMATIC LITURGICAL STUDIES

This is not the appropriate place to declare the Christian liturgy to be a pneumatically affected encounter between God and humankind in its relationship to the Holy Scripture and the tradition of the Church as a *locus theologicus* (cf. Grillo 2006). It should, however, be considered that the Christian liturgy is neither a 'prayed dogma' nor an obvious source of revelation. The linguistic and symbolic acts within the liturgy only lead directly to theo-*logy* when other theological, philosophical, and cultural disciplines are included. In this regard, Helmut Hoping and Jan-Heiner Tück outline the task and the self-conception of systematic theology as follows: 'It is determined by the scripture, the apostolic Creed, its teaching and the place of liturgy in which the *Symbolum* originates. Its purpose is the hermeneutic development of the tradition of faith, which depends on the historical reconstruction of respective evidence without restricting itself to this aspect' (Hoping & Tück 2003, 26–32; cf. Haunerland 1989, 5–62; Stuflesser 1998, 17–143). Both professors of systematic theology consider liturgy *and* dogma to be the decisive connection between academic theology and the faith that is associated with and lived within the Church. This therefore precludes an absolutization of the liturgy.

The words of the Council regarding liturgy as 'the summit towards which the activity of the Church is directed; at the same time it is the font from which all her power flows' (Sacrosanctum Concilium [SC] 10) should always be considered in relation to the statement of the Second Vatican Council (SC 9): 'The sacred liturgy does not exhaust the entire activity of the Church. Before men come to the liturgy they must be called to faith and to conversion.' Christian liturgy and prayer are based on related processes and not on non-historical, more or less abstract metaphysical categories, which means that their exploration can never be restricted to texts only.

What is decisive in this regard is the performative and representative quality of the real occurrence within a given period and place. If we add to these reflections the faith of revelation, then we exclude a metaphysical model for the interpretation of reality, to which the phenomenon liturgy belongs and in which history is not considered as a history of salvation. Instead of proceeding from a priori truths, the theological draft derived from the liturgy demonstrates theology's quality as an a posteriori science that accounts for its forms of celebration and statements of faith in terms of reason. In this way, the Christian liturgy is not simply the use or symbolization of the biblical and traditional faith of the Church; it allows humankind to experience a God-human reality, in which theology occurs in the true sense of the word.

What is the situation in Judaism, where the meaning of *Jewish theology* in the context of Halakha and Aggada is already controversial? Depending on the denomination in question, different importance is attached to the relationship between 'celebrating faith' and 'reflecting on faith' in the same way as the changing effect of the old ecclesiastical axiom 'Lex orandi'—'Lex credendi' in Christianity (cf. Petuchowski 1986, 28–32; 1980, 530–533). One should therefore always consider that a theology that does not really qualify as *scientia conclusionem* in Judaism (cf. Kirchberg 1991, 102–105), can only be developed within the intra-disciplinary discourse between the existing written and oral tradition of Judaism, commentaries about the liturgy that have been handed down to us, the history of reception, and other scientific disciplines that would appear to be relevant for the liturgy as a prayer and ritual happening. This is why significant works that claim to contain reflections on Christian liturgy that span all methods have been published in the field of German-language liturgical studies since the 1980s. Nevertheless, the highly developed *theology of liturgy* of the English, French, and Italian-speaking world seems to be less established in Germany.

In Judaism we find liturgical-*theological* reflections on the Jewish liturgy in such highly important works as Franz Rosenzweig's *The Star of Redemption* and in the works of Emmanuel Levinas, Abraham Joshua Heschel, and, to a certain extent, Jakob J. Petuchowski. It is however, impossible for a Christian liturgical scholar to determine the value of such works, which are often of a philosophical nature, in Jewish liturgical studies. As regards the attempt to develop a theology of liturgy on the basis of the quality of liturgy as a concrete prayer or ritual happening, one is faced in every form of liturgical-theological reflection with the dilemma of having to abstract from the concrete form of celebration, make general observations, and arrive at theological principles. Despite the problems inherent in abstracting from a concrete liturgical celebration to basic liturgical-theological models, it is incontestable that one ought to be able to define key theological criteria that determine whether a specific liturgical action qualifies for a Christian, Catholic, or Jewish liturgy. For example, one important question would be whether one can assign a theological *core of meaning*, a comprehensive theological content to various forms of liturgical celebration according to both diachronic and synchronic analysis. My theory here is that without ascertaining the theological *content* of the developed forms of Jewish liturgy, one cannot reach the liturgical-theological goal of understanding the theological core of meaning of the Christian liturgy. This presupposes a theological procedure of reduction and interpretation of liturgy. Agreement would have to be reached about the criteria for this procedure in the field of Jewish-Christian liturgical research (cf. Gerhards 2006, 53–57). This means that Judaism (in its broad diversity) and its liturgies is not relevant to Christian liturgical studies solely from an historical point of view. It would, in fact, be another error of catastrophic proportions if as a result of this Christian theology were to consider Judaism to be nothing more than an historical dimension without perceiving its existence in the present as a *theological* inquiry into the self-image of Christianity. In 1979, Hans Hermann Henrix wrote:

> Wherever Christians are only motivated by an interest in their own roots and past to see and hear with interest that which distinguishes the Jewish liturgy and how it is celebrated, the face of the contemporary Jewish community—the community which comes together in its synagogues to celebrate the liturgy and to pray, to read from and listen to the Hebrew bible, and to profess its faith—is rendered faceless (Henrix 1979, 7–12 here 11).

Even if recent Christian-Jewish research into the history of liturgy ought to question many of the similarities and the reciprocal influences in the period of constitution and differentiation of early Christianity and Rabbinic Judaism as a result of a new evaluation of existing sources, it is essential for a Christian theologian of liturgical studies for liturgical theological reasons to pursue hermeneutics of the Jewish liturgy. Why?

Before addressing this question, let us briefly examine this problem on the basis of a concrete example from the form of the celebration of Christian liturgy.

## 2  THE THEOLOGICAL LOCATION OF CHRISTIAN LITURGY IN THE BIBLICAL AND JEWISH FAITH AS EXEMPLIFIED BY THE EUCHARIST

Christian theologians and, above all, scholars of liturgical studies who concern themselves with the Passover are generally searching for indications that explain mutual influences, dependencies, or divergences in the historical development of Passover and Easter, of the Jewish Passover Seder and the Christian Eucharist. Recent research shows, however, quite a differentiated image of the supposedly successive transition from the Jewish Passover to the Christian Eucharist. Let us recall the words of Günter Stemberger:

> The Pesach-Seder in hand is that of the Mishnah. Comparisons of the Haggadah with the Mishnah and other rabbinic texts never permitted us to get to the bottom of the Mishnah, even though many items regarding the format of the meal are presupposed to be self-evident and well-known.

However, to conclude from this an advanced age is impermissible. (...) If one considers this view to be overly sceptical, it is important to remember that there was no description of the Passover Seder before the text of the Mishnah. (...) A general adoption of the Haggadah for Passover—if such a one existed before 70—can only be assumed to have occurred after the lasting destruction of the Temple (Stemberger 1987, 147–158 here 156–157).

In contrast to this there is the theory, which has been prevalent until now, that the description of the Passover feast in the Mishnah treatise Pesaḥim 10 (2nd century) generally reflects the feast as it was celebrated in Hellenistic times and the time of Jesus. Clemens Leonhard roundly rejects the assumption that the Haggadah for Passover came about before the Mishnah (cf. Leonhard 2003, 11–31 esp. 17). Considering this historical development in the field of research, the focus of the search for parallels and relationships between Jewish and Christian liturgy shifts from the early years of Christianity, for which very few sources exist on either side, to later times, which boast a wealth of such sources so that while the Haggadah for Passover does not play an important role in understanding the Last Supper, i.e. of the *verba testamenti*, it is very important for the gradual development of institutionalized liturgy. At the same time, New Testament reports of the suffering, death, and resurrection of Jesus Christ are so closely and directly linked to the Passover feast that this situation makes it impossible to avoid a theological presentation and interpretation of these decisive events and the theological content of the contemporary Jewish Passover. The synoptic Gospels describe the Last Supper as a Passover meal, whereas in the Gospel according to John, Jesus is said to have died on the day the Passover lambs were slaughtered.

However, in his letter to the Corinthians (1 Cor 11:23–26), the oldest textual evidence of Jesus' Last Supper, Paul does not make any explicit reference to the Passover. In this respect, the evidence provided by the New Testament provides a broader scope for interpretation than a concentration on a Christian form of a meal in the context of the Passover, whatever form that meal may take (cf. Haarmann 2004).

This becomes apparent when exemplified as follows: similarities and differences between the Passover (Seder) and Easter (Eucharist) must not only be sought at textual level or in the actual form of the feast—something which is barely or entirely impossible to verify for the early years of Rabbinic Judaism and early Christianity as a result of the lack of sources—but also at the level of the indicated theological content. A complete understanding of the Christian Eucharist, which recognises its roots in the Jewish Passover, only reveals itself when the main theological sense of the Passover is determined, to which above all the New Testament and early Christian sources refer. Despite all historical uncertainty, it is still imperative to search for places containing tendencies that indicate the *development* of a theological, meaningful motif of the Passover feast, which was considered a decisive theological interpretation of the death and resurrection of Jesus Christ for early Christians. Such a tendency for the mutuality of the theological meaning of Passover and Eucharist lies in the basic principle of the soteriological, liberating meaning of God's acts on his people with the prospect that God will remain faithful to his covenant and protect his people, thus making the future possible (cf. Bradshaw 2003, 21–36 esp. 34). The category of remembrance, the mighty effect of God's remembrance, is an essential common theological concept, which is why the Eucharist is rooted in the theology of the Passover (cf. Kampling 2005, 130–153). The commonalities in the theological interpretation disappear at the point where different eschatological awareness appears. Starting with the evidence contained in the New Testament, the main structure of the glorification of God's remembrance or the basic anamnetic-epicletic state is changed in Christian texts by the element of certainty about the reign of God in Jesus Christ, which has already begun, is anamnetically ascertained, and for which Christians now ask when they pray. In contrast with the Old Testament and early Jewish tradition, the epiclesis or the request is no longer at this point only the reverse of the anamnesis or the thanksgiving/praise, but the expression of the outstanding completion of salvation which, according to the principle of eschatological reserve in the liturgy, happens in an anticipatory way (cf. Ebenbauer 2005, 63–106).

3   Incidental Remark: The Significance of Nostra Aetate 4
for Liturgical Studies

The council's understanding of a 'spiritual bond' and 'common heritage', which brings the Church together with the chosen people of Israel and binds them to each other is of fundamental theological importance. In 'Nostra Aetate', (the declaration on the relation of the Church to non-Christian religions) the 2nd Vatican Council wrote: 'this sacred synod wants to foster and recommend that mutual understanding and respect which is the fruit, above all, of biblical and theological studies as well as of fraternal dialogues' (NA 4; cf. Oesterreicher 1967, 406–478; Siebenrock 2005, 591–693; Kirchberg 1991, 13–44). From the point of view of liturgical studies, the as yet little acknowledged necessity of perceiving and reflecting on the Jewish liturgy its *continuing* history results from the theological reality of the non-rejection of Jews and God's covenant with his people, which was never dissolved (cf. Rom 9–11). In principle, this is primarily a matter of *understanding* and achieving a hermeneutics of this other liturgy with which the Christian liturgy is theologically associated in a unique way (cf. Gerhards 2003, 183–211 here 185; cf. Lurz 1999, 273–290).

Certain criteria, which must be considered criteria of truth for one's own point of view, are needed for such hermeneutics. By pointing out the following, Jürgen Werbick contradicts certain objections to such a procedure expressed in the so-called pluralistic theology of religion:

> If I want to take the other option seriously as *the other* option—take it so seriously as to call my own options into question and possibly even force myself to make corrections or revisions—then I *must* apply criteria of truth that apply to all points of view; criteria which I consider binding for myself and whose binding nature compels me to not only consider the options of others as fascinating phenomena, but also admit them as a challenge' (Werbick 1996, 140–157 here 155).

It is only when I consider the binding nature of criteria from my own tradition and religion in the light of understanding another religion that there can be a discourse about these criteria, my criteria of truth. A neutral approach cannot result in a reconsideration of my criteria of truth, if it becomes necessary as a result of academic argumentation. Here we can identify the outlines of a methodological approach, which must appear absolutely essential in a consistent consideration of Jewish and Christian liturgy in both the past and the present. If the Second Vatican Council taught us to define not only the Eucharist, but also each sacramental act of the Church as a commemoration of the *mysterium paschale* of Jesus Christ, then all comparative Jewish-Christian questions relate to the theological classification of the salvation event in God's act of salvation on Israel and Jesus Christ as well as the theological significance of the continuance of the Jewish people after Jesus Christ. If the exegetical research of recent decades, especially that concerned with the theme of the covenant or the statements of Paul regarding the eschatological salvation of all of Israel, are taken seriously, all forms of thinking based on the substitution theory ought to be prohibited. This is why in addressing the Jewish liturgy, we must also consider systematic questions, which arise as a result of the soteriological significance of the Jewish liturgy and the reproach of 'soteriological "rivalry"' (Fiedler 2002, 68–94 here 94 remark 69). By speaking about the 'soteriological rivalry' or, to put it another way, about the multitude of *ways of salvation* we encounter the currently virulent theology of religions, which does not include to a sufficient degree the liturgy of Judaism and Christianity in the theological dispute. Are we forgetting at this point that for Christians—at least in its Catholic and Orthodox forms, but also increasingly in its Lutheran and Anglican forms—the liturgy is 'the fount and apex of the whole Christian life' (*Lumen Gentium* 11), of faith and of all ecclesiastical solemnities; and does it not also analogously apply that for most devout Jews, the heart of their religion is prayer and worship?

## 4   Theology In and From the Liturgy

One decisive reason why Christian theologians and theologians of liturgical studies concern themselves with neither historical nor contemporary forms of Jewish liturgy despite the aforementioned similarities, dependencies, and differences is—among other things—a specific understanding of mercy and salvation. According to Christian theology, which is heavily influenced by St. Augustine, the relationship between God and humankind was so much corrupted by the fall of man, that humankind cannot by itself celebrate a true adoration of God. Only redemption from the power of sin through the cross and the resurrection of Jesus Christ re-establishes the paradisiacal tie between heaven and earth and enables the believer to enter into a relationship with God. According to this concept, which is heavily influenced by the notion of original sin and a sin-based theological reason of why God sent Jesus, the idea of redemption would appear to be a purely Christian phenomenon. Jewish forms of liturgy can therefore be a remembrance of God the Creator, who revealed himself to humankind on several occasions—as illustrated in Exodus and the offering of the Tora linked to God's promise of a covenant with Israel. However, according to this theological concept, they do not provide an eschatological 'redemption' or 'salvation'.

This stance raises the widely discussed question as to the 'ways of salvation' in the different religions, which is currently being discussed within the confines of a theology of religions or alternatively the so-called pluralistic theology of religion, which has already been mentioned (cf. Hick 1996; Knitter 1988; Smith 1981; Schmidt-Leukel 2005). The celebration of the liturgy assumes a strangely disregarded role in these theological approaches. The situation only differs in a few Church documents and among a few Christian theologians who include the liturgy as the basis for argumentation within the Jewish-Christian dialogue (cf. Kranemann 2001, 92–98). However, these documents and theological treatises are generally isolated liturgical texts (e.g. the intercession for the Jews on Good Friday), and concern themselves less with the liturgical act as a whole. Moreover, there can be no question of a widespread reception of the renewed intercession on Good Friday within the research and teaching of theology and the theology of religion.

The only significant exception is the question of the entitlement of the forms of interreligious prayer, for example in connection with the prayer for peace in Assisi 1986 and again in 2002, to which Pope John Paul II invited representatives of all religions (cf. Henrix 2004, 12–26). Nevertheless it is unquestionable that the significance of *non-verbal forms of expressions* of piety is increasing as a result of the focus on other traditional religions beyond occidental culture. In the context of non-scriptural religions, Hans Waldenfels refers to 'the sacred signs, the internal and external images, the ritual behaviour, the feasts and celebrations, non-argumentative forms of literature but also the methods of non-verbal communication, methods of treatment, the role of media, gestures, facial expressions, types of donations, the embodiment as a place of communication, dance, the masque' (Waldenfels 1994, 64).

Naturally, the aforementioned religious forms cannot be reduced to the non-written religions alone. In fact, they create a greater awareness of one's own tradition. We must ask ourselves at this point the extent to which such ritual or religious acts have a deep significance that transmit something like *salvation, blessing* or even *the experience of God*. John Hick, the most prominent representative of the so-called pluralistic theology of religion, assesses a religion not on the basis of dogma or celebration of faith, but according to its 'soteriological effectiveness' (Hoping 2003, 117–159 here 126). This is why reflected dogmas as well as cultic and symbolic-ritual acts of expression in a religion (cult/liturgy) loose significance in comparison with the practice of faith (ethos), which is rooted in religion. However, is it possible to comprehend a religion sufficiently if—at least from a Christian perspective—the inner connection between *reflected* faith, *lived* faith and *celebrated* faith is no longer taken account of? On the condition that one can only say something appropriate about religion and theology by *also* taking ritual or liturgical speech and symbolic acts into consideration, the search for the aforementioned *theological content* of liturgy is now our main focus.

In terms of the Jewish liturgy, Jakob J. Petuchowski points out that the three-step 'creation, revelation, redemption' is not Franz Rosenzweig's invention, but according to his interpretation of the Jewish liturgy, is the basis of the Jewish liturgy as theological content. He refers, for example, to daily morning prayer and above all to the theological structure of Shema Yisra'el with its benedictions (cf. Petuchowski 1994, 407–462 here 424f), the Shabbat prayers, the form of the Musaf prayer on Rosh ha-Shana with the theme of the remembrance of God (ibid. 423f) or Ps 19 (Petuchowski 1981, 59–82). In Rosenzweig's work, the claim as to which liturgy rightly celebrates a commemoration of redemption or fulfilment, even turns in favour of Judaism. According to Rosenzweig, Christianity as a 'religion of the way' is still waiting for the completed redemption, while Judaism as a 'religion of the beginning' realises salvation in the present. Josef Wohlmuth has repeatedly criticized this determination of the relationship and pointed to the presential dimension of Christian eschatology, according to which 'the intrusion of eternity into the present' substantially influences Christian liturgy (cf. Wohlmuth 1992, 79–89; Gerhards 1999, 21–26).

It remains a very urgent liturgical-theological wish to correctly classify through dialogue with Jewish theologians of liturgical studies such important Jewish traditions as, for example, the celebration of the Kabbalat Shabbat each Friday evening, which—in the Kabbala tradition—celebrates in an impressionable way an eschatological or messianic entrance of God into time (Wahle 2006, esp. 243–252). The extent to which this theory is accurate must be clarified, the theory according to which we can link the theological content of the Jewish liturgy with the three-step 'creation, revelation, salvation'. The aforementioned Jewish philosopher of religion Abraham Joshua Heschel—and also Rabbinic Judaism—speaks in the context of the feast of Shabbat about a 'spiritual presence' (Heschel 1990, 4). The metaphor of the Shabbat as a 'bride' which features in the Shabbat hymn 'lekha dodi' does not stand for a mystic personification of this day with God's presence. It is an expression of God's 'loving relationship' with his people, his hidden nearness in time, which is often ignored in everyday life. The metaphor of the 'bride Shabbat' is not intended to provide an image of God's being or a heavenly reality, but instead to illustrate God's presence in his relationship to humankind. Heschel's interpretation of Shabbat contains a definite notion of a qualified perception of God's nearness in the hidden structure of a sacred day, which can be set in a presential understanding of God's Kingdom.

How does the consideration of being able to encounter God in the Jewish liturgy (according to the Christian faith the same God whom the Christians call the Father of Jesus Christ) relate to the principle of a Christian liturgy that is shaped by the idea of the universal significance of the saving work of Jesus Christ? Does the main content of Christian liturgy as effective commemoration of the *mysterium paschale* of Jesus Christ not exclude other forms of 'encounter with God'?

At this point, we must take the eschatological thread of the Christian faith into account, the thread which runs through the celebration of the Christian liturgy. In his letter to the Romans, Paul says that all those who have received God's spirit are saved. But in what way? For Paul, salvation is realized above all in the gift of *hope*, a legitimate hope of a new creation without any sighs and complaints that is well founded in the death and resurrection of Jesus Christ. 'But if we see what we hope for, then it is not really hope. For who hopes for something he sees?' (Rom 8:24). The principle of the *eschatological reservation* is linked to this statement, under which the time of the world has stood since Jesus Christ.

The 'fullness of time' is set in the event of Christ (cf. Mark 1:14f), but is not fulfilled within it. The expectation of the fulfilment of God's Kingdom within the eschatological return of Jesus Christ points to an outstanding element which gives the Christian liturgy a *temporary* character. Such statements prevent an exclusivist interpretation of Christian liturgy as the only form of worshiping the one God, the only source of salvation and encounter with God. A new canonical reading of the entire Holy Bible, which is convinced of the lasting 'very good' (Gen 1:30) of creation and of God's upheld covenant with Israel and which does not consider the people of God in the Old Testament exclusively by focussing on the fall of man, distinguishes a one-sided understanding of Christ's mission through God by the theory of satisfaction. Facing such significant liturgical traditions as some Eucharistic prayers of Eastern Churches, which draw a wide positive image of history from creation to its completion, and remembering the eschatological thread that runs

through the Christian liturgy, Christian worship itself is pointing the
way towards a differentiated understanding of 'ways of salvation' in
other religions, especially in the Jewish religion. In his essay, 'Liturgical
Studies "coram Israel"', Peter Ebenbauer investigates a 'common level
of communication, which allows us to speak theologically about and
from within liturgy in such a way that it is possible to have a Jewish-
Christian discussion about the concept, sense, and aim of the liturgical practice of faith' (Ebenbauer 2004, 306–321 here 317). To this
end, the development of an 'aesthetics of realized liturgical religious
appearances' (ibid. 319), that brings the aesthetic forms of expression
of Jewish and Christian liturgy (symbol, metaphor, poetry, music) into
a hermeneutical and comparative dialogue is therefore necessary. As a
possible aid to understanding, Ebenbauer suggests the aforementioned
common theological basis of Jewish and Christian liturgy as a eulogical-
anamnetic act of remembrance, which has unfortunately been lost in
practice and liturgical education. In this context, Ebenbauer refers to
'Franz Rosenzweig's impulse for confrontation and his theory of the at
least partial complementarity of the Jewish and Christian liturgy' (ibid.
315f). To understand Jewish and Christian liturgy as a celebration to
counteract cultural amnesia is by no means an abuse of liturgy, but a
decisive statement about the essence of the matter, which is ultimately
supported by the faith in God's 'remembrance' wherein God's whole
sacred history is preserved and which both in Jewish and Christian
liturgy will be realised in the remembrance of human beings (cf. Wahle
2006). This leads to the hope for future Jewish and Christian liturgical
studies that further comparative study of the theological content of Jewish and Christian liturgy as an anamnetic-epicletical form of worship
within which an 'encounter' with the God of Israel and the Father of
Jesus Christ is requested, remembering God's grand acts of salvation
as well as the expectation of an eschatological fulfilment.


## 5   OUTLOOK

One significant piece of evidence of the dialogue between Jews and
Christians is the renewed intercession on Good Friday for the Jews.
Even before the Council Declaration 'Nostra Aetate', Popes Pius XII
and John XXIII made changes to the Rite (the re-introduction of
the genuflection in 1956) and the prayer-text ('pro perfidis Iudaeis').
Pope John XXIII's revised version of the prayer from 1959 with the

deletion of the disputed words 'perfidi Iudaei' and 'iudaica perfidia' must be interpreted as the spark that triggered the subsequent reform of the liturgy. At a theological level, the renewed intercession can also be considered a 'decisive impulse for the renewed reflection in the 'declaration about Jews' regarding the Christian-Jewish relationship' (Kirchberg 1991, 41; cf. more generally with comprehensive literature Kranemann 2001, 79–84). In the present context, reference must be made to the expressed conviction in the liturgical text that at the end of time *fullness of salvation* (ad redemptionis plenitudinem) will be granted to the chosen people, the Jews. The liturgical text makes no explanation of how this salvation will take place. It is left to God's unfathomable decree, thereby following Paul's concept of the eschatological salvation of Israel in Rom 11:33. The text avoids all reference to a Christological intermediation of salvation, nor is it explicitly rejected. The first new draft of the intercession from 1965 still contained an explicit reference to Christ's universal intermediation of salvation (cf. the comparison of the individual drafts from 1965, 1969 and finally the qualified one from 1970/1975 in Kranemann 2001, 234f).

It is important here to consider the form of speech. It is the place of the epiclesis, of the request to God's acts and actions with regard to Israel, not of the reflected clarification of the link between covenant and salvation. However, it makes no sense to ask God to keep his covenant with Israel, if this adherence to God's promise did not contain any implications of the theological message of salvation.

According to Albert Gerhards, a glance at the intercessions of Good Friday (and the intercessions of the Eucharistic Prayer) shows a change from 'the Church's traditional salvation universality (...to) the universality of the intercession' (Gerhards 1989, 111–126 here 117). The intercessions bear witness to the Christian conviction of God's ultimate eschatological self-communication for all nations in Jesus Christ and at the same time they express tolerance towards non-Christian religions and ideologies—a tolerance that has its warranty in the intercessional attitude of the church for the complete knowledge of God, which awaits us at the end of time. At the end of time, Christ will also submit himself to the will of the Father and thus 'God may be all in all' (1 Cor 15:28).

Liturgy can be considered as the expression of faith, which cannot be translated into a doctrine, but which carries out the faith. Only a liturgy that is lived has the ability to hand down the truth of faith, thereby playing a fundamental role in the transmission of faith. In other words, each theology remains abstract and theoretical if it is not founded in the lived experience of God within the liturgy. And it is exactly at this point that we find the natural limits of commonality in the dialogue between Christians and Jews (cf. Gerhards 1996, 245–258 esp. 254–248). A systematic theology that is based on the liturgy leads to a theology of promise in the language of the glorification of God's remembrance, which replaces an outwardly orthopractical effectiveness and an ethical idealization and functioning of religion in terms of the *conditio humana*.

## Bibliography

Bradshaw, P.F., 'Parallels between Early Jewish and Christian Prayers; Some Methodological Issues', in: A. Gerhards, A. Doeker, & P. Ebenbauer (eds), *Identität durch Gebet; Zur gemeinschaftsbildenden Funktion institutionalisierten Betens in Judentum und Christentum* (Studien zu Judentum und Christentum), Paderborn 2003.

Ebenbauer, P., 'Eingekehrt in Gottes Zeit; Gebetstheologische Beobachtungen zu Lobpreis und Danksagung in biblischen und nachbiblischen Kontexten', in: A. Gerhards & S. Wahle (eds), *Kontinuität und Unterbrechung; Gottesdienst und Gebet in Judentum und Christentum* (Studien zu Judentum und Christentum), Paderborn 2005.

———, 'Liturgiewissenschaft "coram Israel"; Einige Perspektiven zukünftiger Forschung', in: A. Gerhards & H.H. Henrix (eds), *Dialog oder Monolog? Zur liturgischen Beziehung zwischen Judentum und Christentum* (QD 208), Freiburg i. Br. 2004.

Fiedler, P., 'Kultkritik im Neuen Testament?', in: M. Klöckener & B. Kranemann (eds), *Liturgiereformen; Historische Studien zu einem bleibenden Grundzug des christlichen Gottesdienstes 1. Biblische Modelle und Liturgiereformen von der Frühzeit bis zur Aufklärung* (LQF 88), Münster 2002.

Gerhards, A., 'Die großen Fürbitten am Karfreitag und die Interzessionen des Eucharistischen Hochgebets als Spiegel des Selbstverständnisses der Kirche', in: N. Klimek (ed.), *Universalität und Toleranz; Der Anspruch des christlichen Glaubens*, Essen 1989.

———, 'Absolutheitsanspruch der Christen? Liturgiewissenschaftliche Anmerkungen zur gegenwärtigen Verhältnisbestimmung von Judentum und Christentum', in: G. Risse, H. Sonnemans, & B. Theß (eds), *Wege der Theologie; an der Schwelle zum dritten Jahrtausend*, Paderborn 1996.

———, 'Liturgie in Judentum und Christentum; Ein Rekurs auf Franz Rosenzweig', in: G. Höver (ed.), *In Verantwortung vor der Geschichte; Besinnung auf die jüdischen Wurzeln des Christentums* (Kleine Bonner theologische Reihe 2), Bonn 1999.

———, 'Impulse des christlich-jüdischen Dialogs für die Liturgiewissenschaft', in: P. Hünermann & T. Söding (eds), *Methodische Erneuerung der Theologie; Konsequenzen der wiederentdeckten jüdisch-christlichen Gemeinsamkeiten* (QD 200), Freiburg i. Br. 2003.

———, & Kranemann, B., *Einführung in die Liturgiewissenschaft* (Einführung; Theologie), Darmstadt 2006.

Grillo, A., *Einführung in die liturgische Theologie; Zur Theorie des Gottesdienstes und der christlichen Sakramente* (APTh 49); [translated by M. Meyer-Blanck], Göttingen 2006 [= *Introduzione alla teologia liturgica; Approccio teorico alla liturgia e ai sacramenti cristiani*, Padova 1999].

Haarmann, M., *'Dies tut zu meinem Gedenken!'; Gedenken beim Passa- und Abendmahl; Ein Beitrag zur Theologie des Abendmahls im Rahmen des jüdisch-christlichen Dialogs*, Neukirchen-Vluyn 2004.

Haunerland, W., *Die Eucharistie und ihre Wirkungen im Spiegel der Euchologie des Missale Romanum* (LQF 71), Münster 1989.

Henrix, H.H., 'Einführung', in: idem (ed.), *Jüdische Liturgie; Geschichte—Struktur—Wesen* (QD 86), Freiburg i.Br. 1979.

———, Jüdische und christliche Liturgie im Kontext des christlich-jüdischen Dialogs, in: A. Gerhards & H.H. Henrix (eds), *Dialog oder Monolog?; Zur liturgischen Beziehung zwischen Judentum und Christentum* (QD 208), Freiburg i.Br. 2004.

Heschel, A.J., *Sabbat; Seine Bedeutung für den heutigen Menschen* (Information Judentum 10), Neukirchen-Vluyn 1990 [= German translation of *The Sabbath; Its Meaning for Modern Man*, New York 7th ed. 1981].

Hick, J., *Religion; Die menschlichen Antworten auf die Frage nach Leben und Tod* (Theologische Berichte 26) [translation by C. Wilhelm], München 1996.

Hoping, H., 'Die Pluralität der Religionen und der Wahrheitsanspruch des Christentums', in: H.J. Münk & M. Durst (eds), *Christliche Theologie und Weltreligionen; Grundlagen, Chancen und Schwierigkeiten des Dialogs heute*, Freiburg/Schweiz 2003.

——— & H.-J. Tück, 'Thesen zur inhaltlichen Bestimmtheit des Glaubens und zur Aufgabe der Dogmatik', in: *SaThZ* 7 (2003).

Kampling, R., '"Groß erzeigt sich ER über die Mark Israels"; Zur Gegenwart und Vergegenwärtigung Israels in der christlichen Liturgie', in: W. Homolka (ed.), *Liturgie als Theologie*, Leipzig 2005.

Kirchberg, J., *Theo-logie in der Anrede als Verständigung zwischen Juden und Christen* (IThS 31), Innsbruck 1991.

Knitter, P.F., *Ein Gott—viele Religionen; Gegen den Absolutheitsanspruch des Christentums*, München 1988.

Kranemann, D., *Israelitica dignitas?; Studien zur Israeltheologie Eucharistischer Hochgebet* (MThA 66), Altenberge 2001.

Leonhard, C., 'Das alttestamentliche und das jüdische Pesachfest', in: H.J. Auf der Maur [posth.; ed. by R. Meßner & W.G. Schöpf], *Die Osterfeier in der alten Kirche* (Liturgica Oenipontana 2), Münster 2003.

Lurz, F., 'Für eine ökumenische Liturgiewissenschaft', in: *TThZ* 108 (1999).

Oesterreicher, J.M., 'Erklärung über das Verhältnis der Kirche zu den nichtchristlichen Religionen; Kommentierende Einleitung', in: *LThK* 2nd ed. (1967).

Petuchowski, J.J., 'Den Menschen mit Weisheit, geformt. Zur Theologie des jüdischen Gebetbuchs', *LuthMon* 19 (1980).

———, *Gottesdienst des Herzens; Eine Auswahl aus dem Gebetsschatz des Judentums*, Freiburg i.Br. 1981.

———, 'Die Liturgie als Thema der jüdischen Theologie', in: K. Richter (ed.), *Liturgie—ein vergessenes Thema der Theologie* (QD 107), Freiburg i.Br. 1986.

———, 'Die Geschichte des synagogalen Gottesdienstes', in: G. Mayer (ed.), *Das Judentum* (Die Religionen der Menschheit 27), Stuttgart 1994.

Schmidt-Leukel, P., *Gott ohne Grenzen; Eine christliche und pluralistische Theologie der Religionen*, Gütersloh 2005.

Siebenrock, R.A., 'Theologischer Kommentar zur Erklärung über die Haltung der Kirche zu den nichtchristlichen Religionen; Nostra Aetate', in: *Herders Theologischer Kommentar zum Zweiten Vatikanischen Konzil* 3 (2005).

Smith, W.C., *Toward a History of Religion; Faith and Comparative History of Religion*, Philadelphia 1981.

Stemberger, G., 'Pesachhaggada und Abendmahlsberichte des Neuen Testaments', *Kairos* 29 (1987) [= idem, *Studien zum rabbinischen Judentum* (SBAB 10). Stuttgart 1990, 357–374].

Stuflesser, M., *Memoria Passionis; Das Verhältnis von lex orandi und lex credendi am Beispiel des Opferbegriffs in den Eucharistischen Hochgebeten nach dem II. Vatikanischen Konzil* (MThA 51), Altenberge 1998.

Wahle, S., *Gottes-Gedenken; Untersuchungen zum anamnetischen Gehalt christlicher und jüdischer Liturgie* (IThS 73), Innsbruck 2006.

Waldenfels, H., *Phänomen Christentum; Eine Weltreligion in der Welt der Religionen*, Freiburg i.Br. 1994.

Werbick, J., 'Der Pluralismus der pluralistischen Religionstheologie; Eine Anfrage', in: R. Schwager (ed.), *Christus allein?; Der Streit um die pluralistische Religionstheologie* (QD 160), Freiburg i.Br. 1996.

Wohlmuth, J., *Jesu Weg—unser Weg; Kleine mystagogische Christologie*, Würzburg 1992.

# ETHIOPIAN ANAPHORAS
## STATUS AND TASKS IN CURRENT RESEARCH
## VIA AN EDITION OF THE ETHIOPIAN ANAPHORA
## OF THE APOSTLES

*Reinhard Meßner and Martin Lang*
Universität Innsbruck, Austria

The present paper is an interim report of our projected edition of the Ethiopian Anaphora of the Apostles. In the first part we will treat more general questions, the second part is dedicated to the disclosure of the sources of the anaphora and dating it.

Just as is the case regarding the origins of Christianity in Ethiopia in general, the same also applies to research of the position and history of the Anaphora of the Apostles concerning aspects of the history of tradition and theology. There remains a cluster of unanswered questions. And it is advisable to formulate the various aspects of the *status quaestionis* as questions.

## I. SOME ASPECTS REGARDING THE STATUS OF CURRENT KNOWLEDGE

### 1. *What is known about the Ethiopian anaphoras?*

There are about twenty Ethiopian anaphoras. In a recent overview (Habtemichael Kidane 2003, 251–253) the prayers are classified according to their tradition: Fourteen anaphoras (respectively, in the edition of 1996/97, fifteen) are found in Ethiopian orthodox missals, three additional ones are printed in the Ethiopian Catholic *Mäṣḥafä qəddase* (Rome 1945), and another two are only to be found in manuscripts or scholarly editions.

Ethiopian anaphoras can be divided into

a) translations, e.g. Basil (Euringer 1934), James, the Lord's Brother (Euringer 1915, 1–23) and Mark, which was lost for a long time (Semharay Selim 1928, 507–531), in each case derived from Arabic most probably,

b) original Ethiopian compositions, e.g. the two versions of the Anaphora of St. Cyril (Löfgren & Euringer 1932, 210–234; 1933/34, 44–86), Epiphanius (Euringer 1927, 98–142), the Anaphora of our Lady Mary by Cyriacus of Behnesa (Euringer 1937, 63–102, 248–262), etc.,

c) eucharistic prayers from ancient church orders. The Anaphora of the Apostles is a reworking of the eucharistic prayer in the so-called Apostolic Tradition of Hippolytus. There are evident influences from the Egyptian-Coptic liturgy, namely from the Mark/Cyril-tradition and undeniable interference with its sister, the Anaphora of our Lord Jesus Christ, which also stems from an ancient church order, the Testamentum Domini. These facts should be kept of the back of our minds, until we begin to handle more specialized questions—especially in the second part of our paper.

Most of the Ethiopian anaphoras were edited by Sebastian Euringer and Oskar Löfgren in the first decades of the twentieth century (for a bibliography, cf. Hammerschmidt 1956, 285–290). Since this time, there has not been a new edition of any anaphora, until the recently published edition of the Anaphora of St. John Chrysostom (Priess 2006). The *status quaestionis* is still well documented in the irreplaceable work done in 1957 by Ernst Hammerschmidt (the ed. of 1987 is practically a reprint). The basic desideratum concerning Ethiopic anaphoras is expressed straightforwardly: all previously edited Ethiopian anaphoras are to be re-edited. The editions of Löfgren and Euringer are based on a more or less accidental selection of relatively recent manuscripts, and—as they state themselves—these editions are to be viewed as a basis for further, more exact editions and research. The Anaphora of the Apostles and the Anaphora of our Lord are still unedited, whereas these two prayers were printed at a very early time: in the Ethiopic New Testament published by *Täsfa Ṣǝyon*, also called Petrus Aethiops, in 1548. An early print of the Anaphora of our Lord was presented by Hiob Ludolf in 1691. Our oldest manuscripts are from the 15th century.

In the meantime some things have changed. The extant manuscripts are rather well documented. One of our next projects will be the recording of all Ethiopic anaphoras from the manuscript catalogues in order to publish these lists of manuscripts separately in compact form. One of the main reasons for our call for re-editions is that there are manuscriptal traditions which reflect theological controversies in the

14th and 15th centuries, especially in Trinitarian theology (Getatchew Haile 1981, 102–136). The knowledge of these traditions would contribute new aspects to the history of theological thought of the Ethiopian church, especially with regard to the very formative era of Ethiopian literature during the 14th and 15th centuries. Hammerschmidt argues for a comparison of biblical quotations with the Ethiopic versions of the Bible in order to define the age of the Ethiopic anaphoras more precisely. The crucial problem is that there are only a few parts of the Ethiopic Bible critically edited (Hammerschmidt 1987, 165). These new views could sharpen and correct the picture of the facts we already know and be placed within a new research context.

## 2. Open questions concerning the origin of the Anaphora of the Apostles and actual questions in our work

When did the Anaphora of the Apostles, originally being part of an ancient church order, begin to play its role in the Ethiopian liturgy, or, expressed in a more sophisticated way: when and how did the anaphora, along with the Anaphora of our Lord, get its eminent position (Every 1963, 156–160 esp. 157; Winkler 2002, 86) in the Ethiopian liturgy? 'Eminent position' does not simply mean 'normal liturgy of the Ethiopian church' as often stated. The anaphora is celebrated on the memorial day of any apostle (Daoud 1954, 56). 'Eminent position' means the consistent tradition and its nearly immutable position at the beginning of the *Ordo communis*, followed by the Anaphora of our Lord. This state of affairs is already attested to in the earliest extant manuscripts which can be traced back to the 15th century. It remains the tradition in the printed copies of the *Mäṣḥafä qəddase*. There is one remarkable exception known to us: the manuscript Florence, Bibliotheca Medicea Laurenziana, San Marco 741 (15th century), which begins with the Anaphora of St. Basil followed by the Anaphora of the Apostles (Marrassini 1987, 81–116; 1988, 69–110; esp. 1987, 103–104).

There are two main theories concerning the origins of the Anaphora of the Apostles:

First, the use of the Anaphora of the Apostles was introduced at a very early time (Hammerschmidt 1987, 42; Bandrés 1984, 6–13). As a logical consequence, the Anaphora of the Apostles would derive directly from a Greek text of the so-called Apostolic Tradition. The hitherto known Ethiopic version of the so-called Apostolic Tradition has been demonstrated by its editor Hugo Duensing to be a translation of an Arabic Vorlage (Duensing 1946, 9–13).

Whether this can be said about the eucharistic prayer is, however, not clear because it is not contained in the extant Arabic and Coptic manuscripts. But some years ago, a manuscript was found in Northern Ethiopia seemingly containing a version of the Apostolic Tradition translated from the Greek in Axumite times (Bausi 2002, 146–151; Bausi 2003, 13–55 esp. 32–33). This highly significant document, as yet unpublished, will give new insights into the reception history of the Apostolic Tradition in Ethiopia. It seems to demonstrate the existence of the Vorlage of the Anaphora of the Apostles in the period of the Axumite empire, but it does not in any way prove its reworking for liturgical use.

Second, there is a contrary position to this early dating, i.e. that the Anaphora of the Apostles got its place in the Ethiopian liturgy in the medieval period (Every 1963, 159; Dalmais 1980, 109–117 esp. 110; Brakmann 1994, 160–161). This position is based on the fact that the Ethiopic version of the Apostolic Tradition is a part of the Senodos. The Senodos, translated from Arabic (Duensing 1946, 9–12) in the 13th and 14th centuries (Bausi 1990, 5–73), was the main basis of *Zär'a Ya'əqob's* (1434–1468) reform of the church. The most ancient manuscript of the Senodos can be dated to the beginning of the 15th century (Bausi 2003, 28). Moreover the Senodos is explicitly mentioned in sources datable considerably earlier, indicating that the Senodos was well known and e.g. quoted in the argumentation for the observance of the Sabbath during the great struggles in the Ethiopian church in the 14th and 15th centuries (Bausi 1990, 37–41).

One historical date is to be mentioned here, because it sheds light not only on the liturgical development and the historical-theological questions connected to it, but also on the historico-political background of the reign of *Zär'a Ya'əqob*. In the *Mäṣḥafä bərhan* the emperor claimed the use of the two anaphoras based on ancient church orders, that is the Anaphora of the Apostles and the Anaphora of our Lord (Conti Rossini & Ricci 1965, 41; Dillmann 1884, 66; Getatchew Haile 1981, 102–136 esp. 127–128). This is to be seen only as one aspect of the measures of the religiously well educated *Zär'a Ya'əqob* to establish an increasingly stronger and more centralized church closely attached to the state and obviously as a response to formerly disintegrated religious structures (Wendt 1960, 137–146; Piovanelli 1995, 189–228). During his reign there is a period of a rich literary production—translation works and genuine Ethiopic literature as well (Taddesse Tamrat 1972, 243–244; Beylot 1993, 219–260 esp. 243–248).

However, this well recorded point in the history of the anaphora cannot be a sufficient reason for dating the introduction of the anaphora to this period. It could mean either that the emperor inculcates a eucharistic prayer from ancient times to be used exclusively, or that the anaphora is introduced for the first time and exclusively with a striking strategy of legitimation: it is of apostolic origin. In the second part of this paper we will try to demonstrate that the second alternative is the correct one.

We are convinced that no serious claim can be made about the Ethiopian liturgy in the Axumite period. Brakmann's proposal (1994, 160–161) that from the beginning of the Christianization of the Axumitic empire the eucharistic prayer was an anaphora according to the Alexandrian type cannot be verified; that the Anaphora of St. Mark was the first anaphora used in Ethiopia, as supposed by Semharay Selim (1937, 7–10), is mere speculation.

It is obvious that the anaphora in the form handed down to us is enveloped in an already established framework, namely a rather late version of the Coptic Liturgy of St. Basil. In all manuscripts, the Anaphora of the Apostles is integrated in this liturgy as part of the *Ordo communis*. There is only one exception: In Codex Florence Bibliotheca Medicea Laurenziana, San Marco 741 the Anaphora of St. Basil precedes the Anaphora of the Apostles. This manuscript from Florence will serve as the most important source for our edition. Its text of the Anaphora of the Apostles contains peculiarities not found in the other manuscripts. The Florence manuscript seems to have a less developed, more original state. Some passages are more rudimentary and show a different word order or entirely different words or phrases. For this reason we would venture to speak of a Recension I and a Recension II. The translation offered in the following part of the paper is from the Florence manuscript if not stated otherwise.

## II. The Ethiopic Anaphora of the Apostles and Its Sources

In the second part of this paper we would like to show the construction technique of the Anaphora of the Apostles by means of some textual examples. As has already been said, the Anaphora of the Apostles is an enlarged and enriched version of the eucharistic prayer in the so called Apostolic Tradition, the main sources for the enlargement being the Coptic liturgy, especially the Anaphora of St. Cyril (Coptic text: ⲧϢⲟⲙⲧ ̀ⲚⲀⲚⲀⲪⲟⲣⲀ 1993, 468–542; ⲧϢⲟⲙⲧ ̀ⲚⲀⲚⲀⲪⲟⲣⲀ 2001, 294–347; English translation: Brightman 1896, 164–180), and the Testamentum Domini (anaphora: Beylot 1984, 35–40 [Ethiopic text], 167–171 [French translation]), a late antique church order that was possibly translated into Ethiopic from the Greek in Axumite times (Beylot 1984, VIII). From the Testamentum stems the Anaphora of our Lord Jesus Christ (no critical edition; printed text: Ludolf 1691, 341–345; *Mäṣḥafä qəddase* 1996/97, 81–87), which in most parts is identical with its Vorlage, except for the Sanctus and the epiclesis. This latter exception will shortly be shown to be a clear indication that the Anaphora of our Lord is not to be considered earlier than the Anaphora of the Apostles; as a consequence, the Testamentum, not the Anaphora of our Lord, is the direct source of the respective parts of the Anaphora of the Apostles. This conclusion was already drawn in 1911 by E. Bishop on the basis of a detailed comparison of the eucharistic prayer in the so-called Apostolic Tradition, the Anaphora of the Apostles, the Ethiopic Testamentum Domini and the Anaphora of our Lord Jesus Christ (Bishop 1911, 396–400 esp. 399).

## 1. *Enlargement and modification of the source text: the case of the epiclesis*

The epiclesis of the Anaphora of the Apostles is a modification and an enlargement of the epiclesis in the so called Apostolic Tradition:

| **Ethiopic 'Apostolic Tradition'** | **Anaphora of the Apostles** |
|---|---|
| We beseech you, | We ask and beseech you, |
| that you will send your holy spirit | that you will send the holy spirit and power |
| upon the oblation of the church, | upon this bread and upon this cup and (that) you will make it the body and blood of our Lord and our Saviour Jesus Christ. |
| joining together, | Joining together, |
| give all them, | give all them, |
| who take | who take of it, |
| holiness (*i.e. the holy mysteries*) | that it be to them for holiness |
| and (!) for fullness of the holy spirit | and for fullness of the holy spirit |
| and for confirmation of faith in | and for confirmation of faith in |
| truth... | truth ... |
| (Duensing 1946, 22) | |

The epiclesis of the so called Apostolic Tradition is very simple and not explicitly consecratory (though, without doubt, it is meant as a petition for filling the oblation with the Holy Spirit and to that extent is implicitly consecratory); it does not have an explicit petition for transforming the bread and the cup into the body and blood of Christ. This deficiency is remedied, in the Anaphora of the Apostles, by the sentence: 'that you will make it the body and blood of [...] Jesus Christ'; moreover, the Holy Spirit is to be sent precisely upon 'this bread and this cup'.

In the Alexandrian and Coptic tradition, the explicit request for making bread and wine the body and blood of Christ is, as a rule, bipartite: God respectively the Holy Spirit is to make—firstly—the bread the body of Christ and—secondly—the cup his blood:

> *Coptic Cyril*: And send down [...] the paraclete, your Holy Spirit [...] upon us [...] and upon these your precious gifts, which before have been set forth before you, upon this bread and upon this cup, that they be purified and changed, and that he makes this bread the holy body of Christ and this cup, again, the precious blood of his new covenant (ϯϣⲟⲙϯ ⲛ̄ⲁⲛⲁⲫⲟⲣⲁ 1993, 537–539; ϯϣⲟⲙϯ ⲛ̄ⲁⲛⲁⲫⲟⲣⲁ 2001, 344–346; Brightman 1896, 179).
>
> *Bohairic Basil*: May your Holy Spirit come down upon us and upon these gifts set forth, and may he purify them and change them and manifest them as the holy of your holy (things), and that he makes this bread the holy body of our Lord and our God and our Saviour Jesus Christ [...], this cup, again, the precious blood of the new covenant of our Lord and our God and our Saviour Jesus Christ [...] (Budde 2004, 161–163).

Both anaphoras have a short petition for purifying (which means sanctifying; ⲧⲟⲩⲃⲟ˙ is the translation for ἁγιάσαι) and transforming bread and cup. In the Anaphora of St. Cyril this petition is an enlargement, as can be seen by comparison with manuscriptal evidence of the first millennium (PVindob. G 26134 [5th/6th cent.]: Hammerstaedt 1999, 97 [Greek]; PRyl. gr. 465 [6th cent.]: Hammerstaedt 1999, 79–80 [Greek]; Sahidic Mark [7th/8th cent.?]: Quecke 1971, 40–54 esp. 44); in the Anaphora of St. Basil it is originally the whole epiclesis (including the characteristic petition for 'manifesting' [ἀναδεῖξαι resp. ⲟⲩⲱⲛϩ ⲉⲃⲟⲗ] bread and cup as the holiest of holy), the double petition for making the bread the body and the cup the blood of Christ being a secondary enlargement (Sahidic Basil: Doresse 1960, 20, does not have the double petition; short discussion: Budde 2004, 407–408). But the general petitions of both anaphoras do not have any particular similarity to the epiclesis of the Anaphora of the Apostles.

A closer parallel to the epiclesis of the Anaphora of the Apostles can be found in the Coptic Anaphora of St. Gregory, which, in this section, obviously has the more ancient wording than the Greek version (Gerhards 1984, 36 [Greek text], 89 [commentary]):

Do you (i.e. Christ) send down upon us the grace of your Holy Spirit,
that he purifies and changes these gifts set forth before you to the body
and the blood of our redemption, and that he makes this bread your holy
body [...] and this cup, again, the precious blood of your new covenant
(Hammerschmidt 1957, 40–42).

As in St. Basil, the double petition for turning the bread into the body
and the cup into the blood of Christ, is, with some probability, secondary (Botte 1954, 48–72 esp. 56; Gerhards 1984, 90), but there is no
manuscriptal evidence for its lacking in the epiclesis of the Anaphora of
St. Gregory. There is certainly a parallel between this epiclesis (without
the double petition) and the epiclesis of the Anaphora of the Apostles
concerning their structure, but there are hardly any correspondences
in the specific wording of the two texts.

The source of the enlargement of the epiclesis in the Anaphora of
the Apostles is, therefore, not one of the three main anaphoras of the
Coptic liturgy (St. Cyril, St. Basil, St. Gregory). The closest parallel we
could find is the Sahidic Anaphora of St. Matthew in the Euchologium
Z 100 of the White Monastery:

| Anaphora of the Apostles | Coptic Matthew | Coptic Gregory |
|---|---|---|
| **We ask and beseech you,** | **We ask and beseech you**, [...] | |
| **that you will send** the **Holy spirit** | **that** [...] **you will send** us your **Holy spirit**, the paraclete, the spirit of truth, | Do you (i.e. Christ) **send** down upon us the grace of your **Holy Spirit**, |
| and power | | |
| **upon this bread and** upon **this cup and (that) you** will make it **the body and blood of our Lord** and our Saviour **Jesus Christ**. | **upon this bread and this cup and that you** will change them (ⲛⲅⲡⲟⲟⲛⲟⲩ) to the **body and blood of our Lord Jesus Christ** [...], | that he purifies and changes (ⲛⲧⲉϥⲟⲩⲱⲧⲉⲃ) these gifts set forth before you to **the body and the blood** of our redemption, |
| Joining (it) together, | so that the bread becomes the body of Christ | and that he makes this bread your holy body [...] |
| [...] | and the cup becomes the blood of Christ of the new covenant (Lanne 1958, 356–358) | and this cup, again, the precious blood of your new covenant [...] (Hammerschmidt 1957, 40–42) |

Here we find not only a formal agreement, as in the anaphora of St.
Gregory, but, contrary to the epiclesis in the anaphora of St. Gregory

(cf. the words in bold type), also extensive correspondence in the wording:

> that [...] you will send [...] holy spirit [...] upon this bread and [...] this cup and that you will [*anaphora of the Apostles:* make / *anaphora of St. Matthew:* change] them (to) the body and blood of our Lord [...] Jesus Christ

To be sure, it seems very improbable that the anaphora of St. Matthew is the direct source of the epiclesis in the anaphora of the Apostles, but it could well mirror a local tradition of Southern Egypt that was adopted in Ethiopia. As is well known, a considerable number of Ethiopian monks lived in Egypt, not only in the Scetis, but also in Upper Egypt, e.g. in the famous monastery of Dayr al-Muḥarraq (Meinardus 2005, 243–245; Störk 2005, 116–117). It is possible that these monks brought liturgical traditions from Upper Egypt to Ethiopia.

A last item to be mentioned is the identity of the epiclesis in the Anaphora of the Apostles and in the Anaphora of our Lord Jesus Christ. The epiclesis in the vorlage of the Anaphora of our Lord, the Ethiopic version of the Testamentum Domini, is hardly understandable and was replaced, in the process of adapting the anaphora for liturgical use, by the epiclesis of the Anaphora of the Apostles:

| *Anaphora of the Apostles* | *Anaphora of our Lord* | *Ethiopic Testamentum Domini* |
|---|---|---|
| We ask and beseech you, | We ask you, o Lord, and beseech you, | Furthermore we offer to you this |
| that you will send the Holy spirit | that you will send the Holy spirit | thanksgiving, eternal trinity, o Lord, father |
| and power | and power | of Jesus Christ, |
| upon this bread and upon this cup | upon this bread and over this cup, | before whom every creature and (every) |
| and (that) you will make it the body and blood of our Lord and our Saviour Jesus Christ. | (that) he will make it the body and blood of our Lord and our Saviour Jesus Christ, for ever and ever [...] | soul is trembling; and be poured out in it [??] by you [??] this gift, not food and drink, that we have offered to you, |
| Joining together, give all them, | O Lord, give conjunction to us all, | make them for us your holy (things) |
| who take of it | who receive | [???]. Not be it for us |
| that it be to them for holiness | your holiness (*i.e. holy things*) | in judgement [...][1] |
| and for fullness of the Holy spirit | so that we will be filled with Holy Spirit | (Beylot 1884, 38) |

---

[1] This is a very tentative translation, interpreting the syntax of the text in a rather different way than the printed translations of Ludolf, Harden and Beylot. In fact, the text is hardly understandable. Harden translated: 'Again we offer to Thee this Thanksgiving,

and for confirmation    and confirmation of faith,
of faith in truth ...    that is in truth ...
                         (Ludolf 1691, 344)

As the epiclesis in the Anaphora of the Apostles is an enlargement of its Vorlage, the so called Apostolic Tradition, whereas there is no connection at all between the epiclesis in the Anaphora of our Lord Jesus Christ and the text in the Testamentum Domini, the identity of the two epicleses is an indication, that (1) either the Anaphora of our Lord Jesus Christ was redacted later than the Anaphora of the Apostles (and got its epiclesis from the latter one) or (2) that the two anaphoras, both stemming from ancient church orders, were redacted simultaneously by the same person(s). The latter alternative seems more probable (Bishop 1911, 399 opted for the first alternative). The actual use of liturgical elements of the Testamentum Domini in Ethiopia since Axumite times, as proposed by some authors (Beylot 1993, 239; more cautiously: Dalmais 1980; 110, 116), cannot be substantiated, at least concerning the anaphora. Both the Anaphora of the Apostles and the Anaphora of our Lord Jesus Christ are to be considered late redactions of ancient literary, not of liturgically used texts.

## 2. *An insertion of Coptic origin: the diptychs and intercessions*

| Anaphora of the Apostles, Rec. I | Anaphora of the Apostles, Rec. II | Sources |
|---|---|---|
| | | Eth. 'Apostolic Tradition' |
| this word, that is from you, by whom you made all things according to your will, | this word, that is from you, by whom you made all things by your will, | this word, that is from you, by whom you made all things, as is your will, |

Eternal Trinity, O Lord, the Father of Jesus Christ (before) whom every creature and (every) soul trembleth and returneth into itself. Thine is this gift; not food and drink is it that we offer to Thy holiness. Make that it be not unto us for condemnation [...]' (Harden 1922, 44–49 esp. 47). In his critical edition of the Testamentum, Beylot gives the following translation, without saying a word about the difficulties of the text: 'Encore: nous t'offrons cette action de grâces, Trinité éternelle, Seigneur, Père de Jésus-Christ (par) qui toute créature et (toute) âme tremble, qu'il se répande en elle, ce don pour toi (qui n'est) plus la nourriture et la boisson que nous t'avons offertes, à ta sainteté, fais que pour nous (cela) ne soit pas pour la condamnation [...]' (Beylot 1984, 169). Ludolf renounced a complete translation and justly wrote: 'Mutilus hic videtur locus & sensus imperfectus' (Ludolf 1691, 344). The Syriac version of the epiclesis (Rahmani 1899, 42) diverges considerably and it, too, is difficult in some points (some interesting discussion is to be found in Botte 1947, 241–251; Richardson 1948, 357–359).

*Diptychs*:
Here the deacons
remember the
names (*remembering
of the dead*)

*Egyptian style diptychs,
consisting of the naming
of the patriarch and
the metropolitan; a list
of names of saints
beginning with Sts
Stephen, Zechariah
and John the Baptist
Prayer of benediction
of S. Basil (incipit:
'O holy trinity')
including a long list
of names*

**cf. Egyptian diptychs**
(*for the characteristics of the
Egyptian diptychs cf. Taft
1991, 76–94*)

**Dismissal prayer of
the Coptic liturgy**
(ϯϣⲟⲙϯ ⲛ̅ⲁⲛⲁⲫⲟⲣⲁ
1993, 343 l. 7–348 l. 4,
including 115 l. 1–119
l. 16)

[*concluding formula of
the diptychs:*] And bring
to rest their souls and
(the souls of) all and
have mercy on them.

[*concluding formula of
the diptychs:*] And bring
to rest their souls and
(the souls of) all and
have mercy on them.

**Eth. 'Apostolic
Tradition'**

whom you sent from
heaven, your son, into
the bosom of the
virgin

whom you sent from
heaven, your son,
into the bosom of
the virgin

and you sent him from
heaven into the bosom
of the virgin
(Duensing 1946, 20)

The textus receptus of the Anaphora of the Apostles (Recension II) has a diptych formula and an extensive intercessional prayer (incipit: 'O holy trinity'), inserted into a sentence of the vorlage, the eucharistic prayer of the so-called Apostolic Tradition, which is awkwardly broken into two segments by this insertion. This state of affairs is in evidence in almost all of the manuscripts we have collated to date. In the Florence manuscript (Recension I) it is only said that the deacons are to 'remember the names', that is to say, to speak the diptychs as lists of names. This could be done silently without interrupting the Eucharistic prayer uttered by the priest. The concluding formula of the diptychs ('bring to rest their souls etc.') possibly was likewise said silently by an assistant priest. Cod. Vat. Eth. 66 has the diptychal formula but not the intercessions which are part of all the other manuscripts of the 15th and 16th centuries.

The source of these intercessions is to be found in the Coptic liturgy, although they are not a citation from any extant Coptic anaphora. Instead, the intercession of the Anaphora of the Apostles is a Coptic dismissal prayer, which got a new function in the middle of the Eucharistic prayer. Cod. Vat. Eth. 66 (lacking the intercession in the Eucharistic prayer) has this prayer in the precommunion rites, after the prayer of absolution; Cod. Vat. Eth. 34 which has the intercession in the Eucharistic prayer, additionally notes the prayer in its original position as a dismissal prayer.

### 3. *Influence of the Coptic Anaphora of St. Cyril: the Ante-Sanctus*

The Ante-Sanctus is directly taken over from the Coptic anaphora of St. Cyril. The Eucharistic prayer in the Apostolic Tradition is lacking the Sanctus as is well known. The redactors of the Anaphora of the Apostles felt the urgent need to insert it in the prayer and borrowed the introduction to the Sanctus from the anaphora of St. Cyril:

| **Anaphora of the Apostles** | **Coptic Anaphora of St. Cyril** |
|---|---|
| To you whom sanctify [*Florence ms.; all other mss*: before whom are standing] | You are he, before whom are standing |
| thousands of thousands and myriads of myriads of holy angels and the archangels | thousands of thousands and myriads of myriads of holy angels and the archangels *serving you.* |
| | *You are he, before whom are standing* |
| and your honourable living beings, those with six wings, | your *two* honourable living beings, those with six wings *and with many eyes,* |
| the cherubs and the seraphs; with two wings they cover their face, | the seraphs and the cherubs; with two wings they cover their faces *because of your godhead that cannot be contemplated and conceived,* |
| and with two wings they cover their feet and with two wings they fly. | with two wings they cover their feet, while they are flying with the other two. |
| And always all are sanctifying you. | Always all things are sanctifying you. |
| But with them all, who sanctify you, likewise receive our sanctification, | But with all, who sanctify you, likewise receive our sanctification, *Lord,* |

| who are saying: | who are *praising you with them and* saying: |
| --- | --- |
| Holy. | Holy. |
| | (ϮϢⲟⲘϮ ⲚⲀⲚⲀⲪⲟⲣⲀ 1993, 521– 522; ϮϢⲟⲘϮ ⲚⲀⲚⲀⲪⲟⲣⲀ 2001, 333–334) |

As is evident, each word of the Ethiopian Ante-Sanctus can be found in its Coptic counterpart. On the other hand, the Coptic text has some words and phrases that are not part of the Ethiopic text. That the 'living beings' (ζῷα) standing before God—a motive from the vision of the divine throne chariot by Ezekiel (Ezek 1) respectively from the vision of the heavenly throne room in the Revelation of St. John (Rev 4:6–8)—are two in number, according to the two living beings of Hab 3:2 LXX, and not four as in Ezek 1 and Rev 4, is typical for the Alexandrian tradition. In the Alexandrian and Egyptian Ante-Sanctus, the number two is interpreted as the heavenly vision of the seraphs by Isaiah (Isa 6) to Christ and the Holy Spirit glorifying God, as referred to by Origen (Peri archōn 1,3,4; 4,3,14; cf. Kretschmar 1956, 62–94 [with references to a number of other sources], 152–165 [to the Egyptian Sanctus]; Williams 1997, 350–363). The number two was not transmitted to Ethiopia, probably because the special trinitarian interpretation it represented was no longer known.

The interesting reason given for the covering of the seraphs' faces ('because of your godhead that cannot be contemplated and conceived') stems, in the last analysis, from the Targumic reading of Isa 6:2 ('with two [wings] he is covering his face for not to see'). It occurs in the Coptic, but not in the Ethiopic Ante-Sanctus and could well be a later stratum in the development of the Coptic text. It is lacking in the Greek text of the Anaphora of St. Mark (Cuming 1990, 37; in the Greek Mark, the phrase 'serving you' is not there either), the Vorlage of Coptic Cyril, but is contained in the Greek text of the Anaphora of St. Cyril by the Kacmarcik codex of the 14th century, a copy from a manuscript of the late 13th century (Macomber 1979, 75–98 esp. 93; the Ante-Sanctus is principally more similar to the Greek Mark than to the Coptic Cyril). In any case, it was obviously not contained in the Vorlage of the Ante-Sanctus of the Anaphora of the Apostles. Unfortunately, there is no edition of the manuscripts of the Anaphora of St. Cyril to date.

### 4. *Conflation of two sources: the doxology*

The case of the doxology is very interesting:

| ***Ethiopic 'Apostolic Tradition'*** | ***Anaphora of the Apostles*** | ***Ethiopic Testamentum Domini*** |
|---|---|---|
| so that we glorify and praise you by your son Jesus Christ, by whom to you be glory in the holy church, now and ever and unto the ages of ages. Amen. *[short blessing of the oil]* As it was, it is and will be from generation to generation and for ever and ever. Amen. (Duensing 1946, 22–24) | so that we glorify and praise you and your son, our Saviour Jesus Christ, with the Holy spirit. <br><br> As it was, it is and will be from generation to generation and for ever and ever. Amen. <br><br> With all the heart let us beseech the Lord to bestow on us the unity of the Holy spirit. <br><br> Give us to be one by your Holy spirit. And heal us by this prosphora so that we live in you, for ever and ever and world without end. Amen. Give us [...] Blessed the name of the Lord — Amen <br><br> Blessed who comes in the name of the Lord, and be blessed the name of his holy glory. Be it, be it. | With all (our) heart let us beseech the Lord, our God, to bestow on us the unity of the Holy spirit. <br><br> Give us to be one by your Holy spirit. And heal us by this prosphora so that we live in you, for ever and ever and world without end. <br><br> Be blessed the name of the Lord for ever and ever—Amen. <br><br> Blessed who comes in the name of the Lord, and blessed the name of his glory. Be it, be it. (Beylot 1984, 40) |

The doxology of the vorlage ('by whom to you be glory in the holy church etc.') has been cancelled. Instead, in the Anaphora of the Apostles we have, firstly, the formula of eternity ('Ewigkeitsformel') adopted from the Ethiopic version of the Apostolic Tradition (not contained in the Latin version and certainly not part of the original Greek text). This formula ('as it was, it is and will be etc.') is not exclusively Coptic (cf., e.g., Syriac James: Heiming 1953, 105–179 esp. 170), but very characteristic for Coptic liturgies (Greek Mark: Cuming 1990, 48; Coptic Cyril: ϯϣⲟⲙϯ ⲛ̀ⲁⲛⲁⲫⲟⲣⲁ 1993, 541; ϯϣⲟⲙϯ ⲛ̀ⲁⲛⲁⲫⲟⲣⲁ 2001, 347; Coptic Basil: Budde 2004, 203; Coptic Gregory: Hammerschmidt 1957, 62). Secondly, the actual doxology comes from a very interesting passage of the Testamentum Domini. It has the form of a tripartite berakha:

> Be blessed the name of the Lord for ever and ever. Blessed who comes in the name of the Lord, and be blessed the name of his glory.

The main word is the 'name' of God which is the object of the blessing/doxology, not directly God himself. The second sentence ('blessed who comes in the name of the Lord'), a quotation from Ps 118:26, but directly taken over from the New Testament (Matt 21:9), where it is related to Christ entering Jerusalem, gives a Christological interpretation to the doxology. The reference point of this sentence is Christ's coming in the Eucharistic communion. The last member of this berakha/doxology ('be blessed the name of his glory') is called in the Testamentum Domini 'the seal of the Eucharist' and therefore obviously of the highest importance. It is certainly to be linked—though, of course, not genetically—with the famous berakha used in the temple worship after the uttering of God's name: ברוך שם כבוד מלכותו לעולם ועד ('Blessed the name of the glory of his kingdom for ever and ever', Yoma 3.8; cf. the remarks of Heinemann 1977, 134–137). This is one of many examples for the reception of temple motives in Christian worship. The source of the berakha/doxology in the Anaphora of the Apostles is, as clearly shown by the above synopsis, the Testamentum Domini, not, as claimed by Gabriele Winkler, the Ethiopic Book of Henoch (Winkler 2002, 94–96; Winkler 2004, 117–128 esp. 123–127). The barukh formula in the Anaphora of the Apostles resp. in the Testamentum Domini as well as the formulae in 1 Henoch, adduced by G. Winkler, are both part of the reception history of Jewish berakhot, more precisely: of temple berakhot.

### 5. *External influences on the manuscript tradition of the Anaphora of the Apostles*

Up to now, we have illustrated the use of written sources by the redactors of the Anaphora of the Apostles. Our last two examples concern the textual history of the anaphora, once redacted and used in the Ethiopian liturgy in the course of its manuscript tradition. Ongoing influences from the Coptic liturgy and from the Testamentum Domini (respectively the Anaphora of our Lord Jesus Christ) can be observed here and there. One representative example for this trend is the institution account:

| *Anaphora of the Apostles, Rec. I* | *Anaphora of the Apostles, Rec. II* | **Test. Domini/** *Coptic Cyril* |
|---|---|---|
| In the night, in which they betrayed him, | In the night, in which they betrayed him, | |
| he took bread | he took bread | he took bread |
| in his holy hands, | in his holy **and blessed, spotless** hands, | in his holy **and blessed, spotless** hands, |
| he looked up | he looked up *to heaven,* | *[Cyril:] to heaven* |
| to you, his father, | to you, his father, | |
| he gave thanks, | he gave thanks, | |
| blessed | blessed | |
| and sanctified | | |
| and broke | and broke | broke |
| and gave | and gave | and presented |
| to his disciples | to his disciples | to his disciples, |
| and said to them: | and said to them: | speaking, while he said: |
| Take, eat, | Take, eat *of it,* | Take, eat *[Cyril:] of it,* |
| all of you, | all of you, | |
| this bread is my body, | this bread is my body, | this is my body, |
| which will be given for you, | which will be **broken** for you | which will be **broken** for you |
| by which sin is forgiven. | **for the remission of sin.** | **for the remission of sin**. |
| And likewise the cup, | And likewise the cup, *(Cod. Vat. Eth. 66; EMML 2064: after they had eaten, he mixed water and/ with wine)* | (Beylot 1984, 37) cf. *Coptic Cyril = Coptic Basil = Eth. Basil: after the supper, he mixed it from wine and water* |
| after having given thanks [...] | after having given thanks, [...] | (Cyril: ⲧⲱⲟⲙϯ ⲛ̄ⲁⲛⲁⲫⲟⲣⲁ 1993, 529; ⲧⲱⲟⲙϯ ⲛ̄ⲁⲛⲁⲫⲟⲣⲁ 2001, 338; Copt. Basil: Budde 2004, 155; Eth. Basil: Euringer 1934, 156) |

The text of the codex of Florence (recension I) is already an enlargement of the original source, the Eucharistic prayer in the Apostolic
Tradition. Recension II (i.e. the text of all other manuscripts) has some
further enlargements taken over from the Testamentum Domini (the
words in bold type) and from the Coptic tradition (in italics). These
enlargements, with the exception of the sentence in the cup word ('after
they had eaten, he mixed water and wine'), which is peculiar to two
manuscripts, are to be found in the textus receptus up to the printed
missals of the 20th century.

Finally, some manuscripts provide interesting evidence for the process
of the primarily oral tradition of the anaphora:

| Anaphora of the Apostles (Florence ms.) | Variants from Vatican mss | Ethiopic Testamentum Domini |
|---|---|---|
| to loose the sufferers, | to **redeem** the sufferers (*mss 9, 18, 34*), | to **redeem** the sufferers |
| those who trust in you, | those who trust in you, | |
| [...] | [...] | [...] |
| | **to bring up the infants** (*ms. 66*) | **and bring up the infants** |
| and to make known resurrection | and **proclaim** (*ms. 66*) **his** (*7 mss*) resurrection | and **proclaim his** resurrection (Beylot 1984, 37) |

For example, Cod. Vat. Eth. 66 has inserted a phrase from the Testamentum Domini ('to bring up the infants') into the anamnetic section
of the prayer which is otherwise not a part of the Anaphora of the
Apostles. The scribe had not only the passage of the Anaphora of the
Apostles in mind that he was writing down, but also the similar passage
of the Testamentum Domini respectively of the Anaphora of our Lord
and amalgamated the two texts.

A much more extensive amalgam of these two passages was made
by the scribe of the manuscript 2064 of the Ethiopian Manuscript
Microfilm Library (EMML) in St. John's University, Collegeville. In
this case, a person in the 15th century filled up some blank space in
a manuscript of the 14th century with the text of the Anaphora of
the Apostles, obviously without written Vorlage, but writing down
the text from memory. In the following passage he totally departs from

the Anaphora of the Apostles towards the parallel passage in the Testamentum Domini resp. the Anaphora of our Lord:

| Anaphora of the Apostles | EMML 2064 | Eth. TestDom |
|---|---|---|
| to loose the sufferers, | to **redeem** the sufferers | to **redeem** the sufferers |
| | **and to strengthen** | **and to strengthen** |
| those who trust in you, | **those who were** | **those who were** |
| who was delivered | **disheartened,** | **disheartened,** |
| by his own will to the passion | **to find the lost** | **to find the lost** |
| | **and restore to life the dead** | **and restore to life the dead** |
| to destroy death | and destroy death | and *loose* death |
| and break the bonds of Satan | and break the bonds of Satan | and break Satan's bonds |
| | | *and fulfil the will of his father* |
| and trample down sheol, | and trample down sheol, | and trample down sheol |
| | | *and open the doors of life* |
| to lead the saints, | **to enlighten the just**, | and **enlighten the just** |
| to plant a limit | to plant a limit, | and plant a limit |
| | **to take away darkness** | **and take away darkness** |
| | **and bring up the infants** | **and bring up the infants** |
| and to make known resurrection | and **proclaim his** resurrection | and **proclaim his** resurrection |
| | | (Beylot 1984, 37) |

This is a good example how a primarily oral tradition of texts actually transpires.

### III. Conclusion: Literality Precedes Orality

What conclusion can be drawn from all this? We hope to have shown by means of a few textual examples that the Anaphora of the Apostles did not develop organically from early times on, but that it is a conscious redaction and actualisation of a written text that was considered to be of the highest authority because it was part of the Senodos, i.e. a text of apostolic authority. The redactors used other written sources for their updating purposes. The Anaphora of the Apostles is therefore an artificial product of a rather late date, redacted possibly during the reign of *Zär'a Ya'əqob* or some decades before, certainly not earlier than the 14th century. With regard to the Anaphora of the Apostles, there never was the usual transition from orality to literality, rather it was vice versa: Once artificially redacted from literary sources, the anaphora has been in use in the Ethiopian liturgy and from then on undergone a process of primarily oral tradition, ranging up to the printed missals of the 20th century.

## LITERATURE

Bandrés, J.L., 'The Ethiopian Anaphora of the Apostles: Historical Considerations', *POC* 36 (1984).

Bausi, A., 'Alcune considerazioni sul "Sēnodos" etiopico', *RSEt* 34 (1990).

———, 'New Egyptian texts in Ethiopia', *Adamantius* 8 (2002).

———, 'San Clemente e le tradizioni clementine nella letteratura etiopica canonico-liturgica', in: Ph. Luisier (ed.), *Studi su Clemente romano; Atti degli Incontri di Roma, 29 marzo e 22 novembre 2001* (OCA 268), Roma 2003.

Beylot, R., *Testamentum Domini éthiopien; Édition et traduction*, Louvain 1984.

———, 'Langue et littérature éthiopiennes', in: A. Guillaumont (ed.), *Christianismes orientaux; Introduction à l'étude des langues et des littératures* (ICA), Paris 1993.

Bishop, E., 'Liturgical Comments and Memoranda VI', *JThS* 12 (1911).

Botte, B., 'L'épiclèse de l'anaphore d'Hippolyte', *RThAM* 14 (1947).

———, 'L'épiclèse dans les liturgies syriennes orientales', *SE* 6 (1954).

Brakmann, H.-G., Τὸ παρὰ τοῖς βαρβάροις ἔργον θεῖον; *Die Einwurzelung der Kirche im spätantiken Reich von Aksum*, Bonn 1994.

Brightman, F.E., *Liturgies Eastern and Western; I: Eastern Liturgies*, Oxford 1896 [reprint Piscataway 2002].

Budde, A., *Die ägyptische Basilios-Anaphora; Text—Kommentar—Geschichte* (Jerusalemer Theologisches Forum 7), Münster 2004.

Conti, Rossini, K. & L. Ricci, *Il libro della luce del negus Zar'a Yā'qob (Mash'afa berhān) II* (CSCO.Ae 51), Louvain 1965.

Cuming, G.J., *The Liturgy of St Mark edited from the manuscripts with a commentary* (OCA 234), Roma 1990.

Dalmais, I.H., 'La tradition apostolique et ses dérivés dans les prières eucharistiques éthiopiennes (Anaphore des Apôtres et Anaphore de Notre-Seigneur Jésus-Christ)', *Aug.* 20 (1980).

Daoud, M., *The Liturgy of the Ethiopian Church*, London 1954 [reprint 2005].

Dillmann, A., *Über die Regierung, insbesondere die Kirchenordnung des Königs Zar'a-Jacob* (AAWB 1884, 6), Berlin 1884.

Doresse, J. & E. Lanne, *Un témoin archaïque de la liturgie copte de S. Basile; En annexe: Les liturgies 'basiliennes' et saint Basile par B. Capelle* (BMus 47), Louvain 1960.

Duensing, H., *Der aethiopische Text der Kirchenordnung des Hippolyt; Nach 8 Handschriften herausgegeben und übersetzt* (AAWG.PH 3. F. 32), Göttingen 1946.

Euringer, S., 'Die Anaphora des hl. Jakobus, des Bruders des Herrn; Nach dem *Ms. Aeth. 74* der Bibliothèque nationale zu Paris ediert und übersetzt', *OrChr* NS 4 (1915).

———, 'Die äthiopische Anaphora des hl. Epiphanius Bischofs der Insel Cypern; Nach zwei Berliner Handschriften herausgegeben und übersetzt', *OrChr* 23 (1927).

————, 'Die aethiopische Anaphora des heiligen Basilius; Nach vier Handschriften herausgegeben, übersetzt und mit Bemerkungen versehen', *OrChr(R)* 36 (n. 98). Roma 1934.

————, 'Die äthiopische Anaphora unserer Herrin Maria; Herausgegeben, übersetzt und mit Bemerkungen versehen', *OrChr* 34 (1937).

Every, G., 'Ethiopian anaphoras', *StLi* 2 (1963).

Gerhards, A., *Die griechische Gregoriosanaphora; Ein Beitrag zur Geschichte des Eucharistischen Hochgebets* (LQF 65), Münster 1984.

Getatchew Haile, 'Religious Controversies and the Growth of Ethiopic Literature in the Fourteenth and Fifteenth Centuries', *OrChr* 65 (1981).

Habtemichael Kidane, 'Anaphoras', in: S. Uhlig (ed.), *Encyclopaedia Aethiopica*, vol. 1 [A–C], Wiesbaden 2003.

Hammerschmidt, E., 'Zur Bibliographie äthiopischer Anaphoren', *OS* 5 (1956).

————, *Die koptische Gregoriosanaphora; Syrische und griechische Einflüsse auf eine ägyptische Liturgie* (BBA 8), Berlin 1957.

————, *Studies in the Ethiopic Anaphoras*, Second revised edition (ÄthF 25), Wiesbaden 1987 [1st ed. Berlin 1957].

Hammerstaedt, J., *Griechische Anaphorenfragmente aus Ägypten und Nubien; Text und Kommentar* (Abhandlungen der Nordrhein-Westfälischen Akademie der Wissenschaften; PapyCol 28), Opladen 1999.

Harden, J.M., 'The Anaphora of the Ethiopic Testament of our Lord', *JThS* 23 (1922).

Heiming, O., *Anaphora syriaca sancti Iacobi fratris Domini* (ASy 2.2), Roma 1953.

Heinemann, J., *Prayer in the Talmud; Forms and Patterns* (SJ 9), Berlin 1977.

Kaplan, St., 'Seeing is Believing: The Importance of Visual Culture in the Religious World of Aşe Zar'a Ya'eqob of Ethiopia (1434–1468)', *JRA* 32 (2002).

Kretschmar, G., *Studien zur frühchristlichen Trinitätstheologie* (BHTh 21), Tübingen 1956.

Lanne, E., *Le Grand Euchologe du Monastère Blanc; Texte copte édité avec traduction française* (PO 28.2), Paris 1958.

Löfgren, O. & S. Euringer, 'Die beiden äthiopischen Anaphoren des "heiligen Cyrillus, Patriarchen von Alexandrien"', *ZS* 8 (1932), 9 (1933/34).

Ludolf, J., *Ad suam historiam Aethiopicam antehac editam commentarius*, Frankfurt/Main 1691.

Macomber, W.F., 'The Anaphora of Saint Mark according to the Kacmarcik Codex', *OCP* 45 (1979).

Marrassini, P., 'I manoscritti etiopici della Bibliotheca Medicea Laurenziana di Firenze', *RSEt* 30 (1987) 81–116; 31 (1988) 69–110.

*Mäṣḥafä qǝddase*, Addis Abäba 1996/97.

Meinardus, O., 'Ethiopian monks in Egypt', in: S. Uhlig (ed.), *Encyclopaedia Aethiopica* vol. 2 [D–Ha], Wiesbaden 2005.

*Novum Testamentum translatum per Petrum Tesfa Zion Malhazor* […], Rom 1548/49.

Piovanelli, P., 'Les controverses théologiques sous le roi Zar'a Yā'qob (1434–1468) et la mise en place du monophysisme éthiopien', in: A. Le Boulluec (ed.), *La controverse religieuse et ses formes* (Patrimoines), Paris 1995.

Priess, M., *Die äthiopische Chrysostomos-Anaphora* (ÄthF 68), Wiesbaden 2006.

Quecke, H., 'Ein saïdischer Zeuge der Markusliturgie (Brit. Mus. Nr. 54 036)', *OCP* 37 (1971).

Rahmani, I.E., *Testamentum Domini nostri Jesu Christi; Nunc primum edidit, latine reddidit et illustravit I.E. R.*, Mainz 1899 [reprint Hildesheim 1968].

Richardson, C.C., 'A Note on the Epicleses in Hippolytus and the Testamentum Domini', *RThAM* 15 (1948).

Semharay Selim, T.M., 'Textus aethiopicus anaphorae sancti Marci', *EL* 42 (1928)

————, *La messe éthiopienne*, Rom 1937.

Störk, L., 'Dayr al-Muḥarraq', in: S. Uhlig (ed.), *Encyclopaedia Aethiopica* vol. 2 [D–Ha], Wiesbaden 2005.

Taddesse Tamrat, *Church and State in Ethiopia 1270–1527* (Oxford Studies in African Affairs), Oxford 1972.

Taft, R.F., *A History of the Liturgy of St. John Chrysostom* (OCA 238); *Vol. 4: The Diptychs*, Roma 1991.

ϯϣⲟⲙϯ ⲛ̀ⲁⲛⲁⲫⲟⲣⲁ ⲛ̀ⲧⲉ ⲛⲓⲁⲅⲓⲟⲥ ⲃⲁⲥⲓⲗⲓⲟⲥ, ⲅⲣⲏⲅⲟⲣⲓⲟⲥ ⲛⲉⲙ ⲕⲩⲣⲓⲗⲗⲟⲥ, no place of publication 1993.

ϯϣⲟⲙϯ ⲛ̀ⲁⲛⲁⲫⲟⲣⲁ ⲛ̀ⲧⲉ ⲛⲓⲁⲅⲓⲟⲥ ⲃⲁⲥⲓⲗⲓⲟⲥ ⲛⲉⲙ ⲅⲣⲏⲅⲟⲣⲓⲟⲥ ⲛⲉⲙ ⲕⲩⲣⲓⲗⲗⲟⲥ, *The Divine Liturgies Of Saints Basil, Gregory, and Cyril*, no place of publication 2001.

Wendt, K., 'Die theologischen Auseinandersetzungen in der äthiopischen Kirche zur Zeit der Reformen des XV. Jahrhunderts', in: *Atti del Convegno Internazionale di Studi Etiopici (Roma, 2–4 Aprile 1959)*, (Accademia Nazionale dei Lincei), Roma 1960.

Williams, R.D., 'Angels Unawares: Heavenly Liturgy and Earthly Theology in Alexandria', *StPatr* 30 (1997).

Winkler, G., *Das Sanctus; Über den Ursprung und die Anfänge des Sanctus und sein Fortwirken* (OCA 267), Roma 2002.

———, 'A New Witness to the Missing Institution Narrative', in: M. Johnson & L.E. Phillips (eds), *Studia liturgica diversa; Essays in honor of Paul F. Bradshaw* (Studies in Church Music and Liturgy), Portland 2004.

# EARLY EUCHARIST IN TRANSITION?
## A FRESH LOOK AT ORIGEN

*Harald Buchinger*
Universität Wien, Austria

### 1 INTRODUCTION

#### 1.1 *Methodological problems*

Liturgiological investigations into the Eucharist in Origen[1] are confronted with a number of methodological problems:

First one has to distinguish between testimonies of Alexandrian and Palestinian provenance; almost all relevant statements of Origen come from the time after his final move to Caesarea, and are therefore only of very limited advantage, if any at all, to the Alexandrian Liturgy of the early period (Schermann 1912, 33–96). Secondly, the majority of his writings is preserved only in translations of the late fourth century; from time to time is caution advisable in concrete formulations.

The principal obstacle regarding content lies, however, in the method of Origen himself: The spiritualizing principal trait of his hermeneutic makes it frequently difficult to distinguish Eucharistic-theological statements from more general theological reflections; 'the few scholars who have plunged into the wealth of allegory and philosophical speculation...have sometimes seen eucharistic allusions in places where others might hesitate to suggest them' (Bradshaw 2004, 107). The question of what is to be identified as Eucharistic, leads, to be sure, to circular reasoning with the preconception of what is assumed as theory and as praxis about the Eucharist in the third century. Since this preconception has significantly changed as of late, a liturgiological rereading of Origen's texts seems appropriate.

---

[1] The material which in this article has to be presented with very limited documentation for editorial reasons will be discussed in much greater detail and with comprehensive references as well as ample quotations from the sources in my forthcoming book *Wortgottesdienst und Eucharistiefeier bei Origenes*, Münster (Liturgica Oenipontana), which will also contain some investigations into the Eucharistic theology of Origen. For the English translation of this paper my warmest thanks go to Dom Daniel Nash of Stift Klosterneuburg.

## 1.2   *The changed state of research*

The theological understanding of the Eucharist in Origen has, admittedly, been thoroughly reviewed in a number of smaller contributions (Camelot 1957, 129–145 esp. 130–139; Crouzel 1962b, 81–104 esp. 92–103; Jacquemont 1976, 177–186; De Lorenzi 1987, 189–204; Laporte 1995, 11–48; Fernández 1998, 179–188; Gramaglia 2000, 150–154) and, above all, in the dissertation of Lothar Lies (Lies 1982); the last and until now only strictly liturgiological monograph on the Eucharistic celebration according to the works of Origen comes, however, from the year 1942 (Grimmelt). Since then, the picture has been added to through some valuable investigations (Daniélou 1948, 74–79; Crehan 1950, 368–373; Capelle 1952, 163–171; Hanson 1961, 173–176; Nautin 1961, 221–232; Schütz 1984, 156–172; Bouley 1981, 138–142, Ledegang 2004, 96–99); at the same time, the state of research into the Eucharist in the Early Church has changed considerably (Kretschmar 1977, 229–278). The more recent research, represented in the work of Paul F. Bradshaw (1999, 1–17; 2002; 2004), Albert Gerhards (1982, 219–230; 1992, 75–96), Andrew McGowan (1999), Reinhard Meßner (2003, 340–441 esp. 418–439; 2005, 3–41; 2006), Gerard Rouwhorst (1993, 89–112), Robert F. Taft (1978; 1988, 47–77; 1991; 1991–1992; 1992, 489–502; 2000; 2003a, 1–25; 2003b, 482–509; 2004, 129–149) and others, takes seriously on the one hand the indications of a large ritual and theological diversity in the literature of the first three Christian centuries—inclusive of the Apocrypha, which are no longer assessed as mere, possibly heterodox-regarded deviations from the alleged mainstream (Prieur 2004, 253–269; Meßner 2005, 40f); on the other hand, the renewed discussion about the not-unproblematicly so-named 'Traditio Apostolica' (Bradshaw, Johnson, & Phillips 2002) has brought into question this presumed fixed star of the only supposedly pre-Nicene Eucharistic prayer which stands in unambiguous formal continuity to anaphoras of the later mainstream churches (Smyth 2007, 95–118).

It is therefore no longer taken for granted as a starting point that already by the time of Justin, the 'Mass-schema' of the Eucharistic celebration had become a general standard; even after the separation from the actual meal, the rites of bread and cup must not everywhere similarly have coincided (Bradshaw 2004, 75f), and both their ordering and also the content of the chalice might have been prone to considerable variation well into the third century (McGowan 1999; Bradshaw 2004, 51–59). As a result, a common Eucharistic prayer over both elements from the outset is also not to be assumed (Bradshaw 2004; 75f, 104f, 121–123). The few preserved testimonies as to the form, structure, and content of Eucharistic praying make it clear that conventions gained acceptance only slowly (Vogel 1980, 401–410; Gerhards 1992; Bradshaw 2004, 116–138; Meßner 2005): That God the Father was the addressee of the Eucharistic prayers in the early period is not universal, but it is striking that also Christ and the Holy Spirit were frequently addressed (Gerhards 1982). The integration of the Institution narrative at a time before the fourth century is increasingly put into question (Taft 2003; Bradshaw 2004; 11–23, 135, 140); exclusively epicletic prayers are as well attested as simple acts of thanksgiving, even if the inception, the form, the addressee and the object of the epiclesis are to be evaluated with discrimination (Taft 1992; Bradshaw 2004, 124–128; Meßner 2005, 26–35). Explicit statements of offering and sacrificial metaphors (Hanson 1976, 75–95; Frank 1978, 70–78; Stevenson 1986, 10–37; Bradshaw 2004, 78–83) did not belong from the beginning to the fundamental elements of Eucharistic prayers; the rise of the sacerdotal interpretation of the ordained presider goes along with the development of the sacrificial understanding (Bradshaw 2004, 85–87). Furthermore, even after the becoming independent of the Eucharistic liturgy, the question must be asked about its connection with a liturgy of the word as well as about its form (Bradshaw 2004; 69–75, 146f; Meßner 2006, 60–85 esp. 75–84). Finally, Paul F. Bradshaw has recently turned attention to the phenomenon of non-communicating attendance as well as to the opposite phenomenon of communion outside of the Eucharistic celebration (Bradshaw 2004, 157 etc.; cf. Taft 2003, 2f).

Following on this shifting of supposedly fixed grounds, and in the face of a growing sensibility for the variety of the liturgical development before the fourth century, the question is therefore newly posed as to how Origen should be classified in this altered system of liturgical and historical coordinates.

## 2 ORIGEN AND THE EUCHARISTIC PRACTICE OF HIS TIME

### 2.1 *Origen's restraint in explicit statements about the liturgical performance*

Even if one must not necessarily see Origen's restrained statements in light of the disputed concept of an arcane discipline (Powell 1979; 1–6, 5f; Jacob 1990), it is not a matter of doubt for him that the Mysteries of the church become accessible only to the initiated:

> Whoever is initiated into the mysteries knows the flesh and the blood of
> the Word of God. For that reason we do not want to linger over that
> which to the initiated is known and which, to the uninitiated, can not be
> accessible (HomLev 9, 10).

Even in the homilies directed to catechumens he is able to recall the
*ecclesiastica mysteria*: 'one need not discuss in detail that which is, through
mere recalling, adequately understood' (HomLev 13, 3). The actual
meaning of the rite, however, requires exposition: As with the mysteries
of the Scripture, the reception and the carrying out of the Eucharist
belong to those not easily explained 'ecclesiastic customs, which while
it is necessary for them to be carried out by all, their meaning/sense
(*ratio*), however, is not clear to all' (HomNum 5, 1; cf. Bornert 1966,
60f). One looks to Origen, admittedly almost in vain, for concrete
references to this 'rite, according to which it (the Eucharist) is to be
carried out'; his extensive remarks about the prayer of Christians in
general (Perrone 2000, 364–371; Buchinger 2003, 307–334) help us
only a little further. Where Origen alludes to unambiguous liturgical
material, or hands down rules for the internal structure or the external
carrying out of prayer, he is not necessarily referring to the context of
a Eucharistic celebration.

### 2.2   *The shape of the celebration of the Eucharist assumed by Origen*

*Occasion*

About the occasion of the Eucharistic celebrations, Origen does not
express his views explicitly. That the Lord's Day is marked by the celebration of the Lord's Supper may certainly be assumed (cf. HomExod
7, 5); it is clear on the basis of HomIsa 5, 2 that Sunday was dedicated
to the memory of the passion and the resurrection (Rordorf 1962,
213–233; Cabié 1992, 47–60 esp. 49–51; Buchinger 2005a, 2, 784
with n. 2134) and that a greater number of people came together on
it than did so on the other days of the week:

> And because a crowd of people is present now because of Friday, and
> above all on the Lord's Day, which is dedicated to the memory of Christ's
> Passion—the resurrection of the Lord is celebrated namely not (only) once
> a year and not (also) every eight days—, beg the almighty God that his
> Word should come to us.

Even if it is in no way proven, it seems probable, in the face of this
parallel citation, that Friday was also set apart by a celebration of the

Eucharist; unfortunately, Origen does not describe in a detailed way, even in *Contra Celsum* 8, 22, 'what with us on the preparation days (= Fridays) and on the Lord's days...occurs (τὰ περὶ τῶν παρ' ἡμῖν κυριακῶν ἢ παρασκευῶν...γινόμενα)'. There is absolutely no evidence in Origen's works for the existence of a Eucharistic service on Wednesdays, the second weekday dedicated to fasting in the ancient church.

*Towards a linking of the celebration of the Eucharist with a Liturgy of the Word*

Paradoxically, Origen, the first and the most prominent witness for the institutionalizing of a regular independent liturgy of the word in the Early Church (Salzmann 1994, 430–438; Grappone 2001b, 329–362; Buchinger [forthcoming]), gives no unambiguous testimony for the connection of the celebration of the Eucharist with a liturgy of the word (Schermann 1912, 35). The preserved homilies come principally from non-eucharistic, catechetically oriented assemblies during the week; none of them can be demonstrated to have been given on a Sunday, and for Friday (on which Origen preached, according to the testimony of HomIsa 5, 2) the celebration of the Eucharist—as presented—is not proven but only presumed.

There are, however, several bits of circumstantial evidence which point to a linking of the celebration of the Eucharist with a liturgy of the word: In the first place, the mention in HomLuke 7, that 'you come in a festal mood/on the feast day to the house of the Lord (*ut festivi veniatis ad domum Dei*), and give ear to the reading of the word of God', refers possibly to the imminent Sunday church attendance of his listeners; in this case, one would be further able to assume that in the corresponding assembly a Gospel pericope would be read out and interpreted. From other homilies in the same cycle, it emerges that a non-Gospel reading preceded, at least occasionally, the interpreted Gospel reading (HomLuke 12; HomLuke 14; HomLuke 31bis; cf. Buchinger [forthcoming]). It is, however, neither proven that a reading from the Gospel was always read on Sunday, nor is it, on the other hand, to be excluded that New Testament, as well as Old Testament scriptures, were read and interpreted as a *lectio continua* during the workday services. Every further reconstruction remains simply a projection of later conditions (Grappone 2001a, 27–58; Buchinger [forthcoming]; pace Nautin 1977, 389–409).

If the Homilies on Luke would in fact derive from Sunday Eucharistic liturgies, one would be tempted to see in the final passage of HomLuke

39 an allusion to the following offertory: 'Hence, let us rise up and pray to God to be worthy of offering him gifts that he can restore to us, and in place of earthly things bestow heavenly things on us' (English translation J.T. Lienhard, FaCh 94, 162). However, since already the preceding homily develops the theme of offering and restoring of gifts in a merely exegetical way, Origen probably follows a custom which can be observed in many other places, namely to draw on a central theme of a homily in the latter's final prayer (Rossi 2003). In any way, the liturgical and the homiletical aspect of the passage need not necessarily exclude one another.

Thirdly, Origen speaks of the kiss of peace, which, 'at the time of the mysteries in the church' would be exchanged (CoCant 1); further on, he locates its place 'after the prayers' (CoRom 10, 33; Thraede 1968/69, 124–180 esp. 152f; Taft 1978, 375–377; Phillips 1996, 21). Since the kiss of peace following the Eucharistic prayer is attested to only in Rome and North Africa (Jungmann 1962, 2, 399–401), it would be completely implausible not to see in these prayers the Common Prayer of the Faithful, which regularly concluded the liturgy of the word; the mentioning of the kiss of peace in the Eucharistic celebration is, therefore, to be interpreted as indirect reference to its connection with a liturgy of the word.

Thus it can be assumed that in Origen's community the Eucharist was linked to a liturgy of the word, which would have consisted—as on days without Eucharist—of a reading, a homily, prayer and the kiss of peace. In consequence, the 'Mass-schema' of the Eucharist seems to have been established in Caesarea well before the middle of the third century.

*The shape of the Eucharistic celebration and its elements*
There is admittedly no single text which expressly proves the *emerging as independent of the sacramental action* out of the context of a meal-celebration; the entire architectonic, ritual and theological framework allows, however, no doubt that the Eucharistic mysteries (on the terminology, perhaps only by Rufinus applied to the Eucharist, cf. Crouzel 1961, 30f with n. 10; 1962, 81–83) in Origen's community were understood and celebrated as liturgy in the strict sense of the word, which clearly was separated from other, non-liturgical actions. Even if some individual formulations might have come only from the quill of the translator, the church building in Origen appears, in various places, as a separate, spacious building (above all, see HomExod 12, 1; furthermore cf. Hom-

Josh 2, 1; HomExod 2, 2; on the lost CoPhlm cf. Harnack 1919, 144f)
with a raised Presbyterium in which the (bishop and) priests could sit
around the altar (HomJudg 3, 2; for further evidence, see Buchinger
[forthcoming]), whereas the deacons stood (CoCant 2; HomJer 12, 3).
Even though the Christian altar is obviously not to be confused with
the pagan altar (Ledegang 2001, 331f; cf. Contra Celsum 8, 17–20), it
was decorated not only with the gifts of the faithful (HomJosh 10, 3),
but 'hallowed by the precious blood of Christ' (HomJosh 2, 1).

Origen does not express himself about how the *offering of the Gifts*
concretely occurred; he alludes only once to the bread, 'which is laid
on the table' (CoMatt Ser. 85) although he makes it known that the
offering/presentation (προσάγειν) is a fundamental act of the Eucharistic
celebration (Contra Celsum 8, 33). Occasionally Origen speaks in the
plural of 'breads' (Contra Celsum 8, 33; cf. FragmCor 34). It does not
become clear if the Eucharistic chalice was mixed or unmixed (HomJer
12, 2; CoMatt Ser. 127; cf. Grimmelt 1942, 74). Origen gives no hint
that, in a clearly Eucharistic context, elements other than bread and
wine were offered; it must remain an open question whether one may
conclude from the mentioning of the altar in the invitation to offer the
first fruits for the support of the clergy by Christians (HomNum 11,
2), that this custom might have been ritualized (Schermann 1912, 51f;
Grimmelt 1942, 7).

In Origen there is no clue that more than *one single Eucharistic Prayer for
both Gifts* would have been spoken, even if the opposite supposition cannot positively be ruled out. He speaks in the singular of the προσφορά
(Dial. 4, 24. 27) and also of the 'prayer (εὐχή), which over' the matter
of the Eucharist 'is accomplished', and of the 'word, which over it (the
matter of the Bread) is spoken' (CoMatt 11, 14). If Contra Celsum 8, 33
says that we 'who with thanksgiving and prayer... eat the bread offered',
this double expression is to be regarded as a hendiadyoin, particularly
as both expressions stand in the singular, and immediately beforehand
Origen speaks only of the 'thanksgiving'. Origen does not express an
opinion about the direction in which the presider prays; however it is
to be presumed that the community faced towards the East:

> ...'and he will take from the blood of the calf and will sprinkle it with
> his finger upon the mercy seat to the east' (Lev 16:13f). Indeed, how the
> rite of atonement for men, which was done to God, should be celebrated
> was taught among the ancients. But you who came to Christ, the true
> high priest, who made atonement for you to God by his blood (cf. Rom
> 3:25?) and reconciled you to the Father (cf. Rom 5:10f?), do not hold fast

to the blood of the flesh. Learn rather the blood of the Word and hear
him saying to you, 'This is my blood which will be poured out for you
for the forgiveness of sins' (composite quotation; cf. Matt 26:28par). He
who is inspired by the mysteries knows both the flesh and the blood of
the Word of God. Therefore, let us not remain in these which are known
to the wise and cannot be laid open to the ignorant. But do not take the
statement that 'he sprinkles to the east' (Lev 16:14) as superfluous. From
the east came atonement for you; for from there is the 'man whose name
is east' (Zech 6:12), who became 'a mediator between God and man' (cf.
1 Tim 2:5). Therefore, you are invited by this 'to look' always 'to the east'
(cf. Bar 4:36) whence 'the Sun of Righteousness' (Mal 3:20) arises for
you... (HomLev 9, 10; English translation G.W. Barkley, FaCh 83, 199.
On the orientation of prayer in Origen, cf. HomNum 5, 1; On Prayer
32. More generally, see Wallraff 2000, 169–184.)

There exists no reason to doubt that the presidency of the Eucharist
had been reserved to the higher clergy (Minnerath 2004, 271–298
esp. 283f; more generally on the presidency in church according to
Origen, see Buchinger [forthcoming]), even if Origen never explicitly
speaks about this (in Eucharistic context, cf. only FragmJer 50, where
no concrete rank is mentioned; on FragmLev 10, 9; HomLev 7, 1, see
Vogt 1974, 41–43). The development of the three-tiered offices of deacon, priest, and bishop was concluded without any doubt (Vogt 1974,
3–6), and the sacerdotal understanding of the Christian priest was in
its full development (HomJer 12, 3; Vilela 1971; 83–91, 110–112). In
addition there were obviously various ministries which were also open
to the laity (HomJosh 10, 3 generally mentions *officia*; HomNum 15,
1 and HomJudg 1, 1 speak about the lector; on non-liturgical offices,
see Vilela 1971, 59f).

Beyond the commentary on the pericope of the Last Supper (CoMatt
Ser. 85), Origen does not speak about the *breaking of the Eucharistic
bread*; he makes it clear, however, that the Church's celebration of the
Eucharist stands, in this respect, in continuity to the actions of Jesus
(CoMatt Ser. 86).

*Communion* is a rite characterized by the greatest reverence:

> You, who are accustomed to take part in the divine mysteries know, when
> you receive the body of the Lord, how you protect it with all caution and
> veneration lest any small part fall from it, lest anything of the consecrated
> gift be lost. For you believe, and correctly, that you are answerable if
> anything falls from there by neglect (HomExod 13, 3; English translation
> R.E. Heine, FaCh 71, 380f).

It is worthy of note that, through other texts, frequent, presumably regular communion within the Eucharistic celebration is attested as a matter of course (CoMatt Ser. 82; CoJohn 28, 4 § 30), whereas communion at home is not proven in Origen. Homily 2, 6 on Psalm 37 (38) 19, translated by Rufinus, describes the 'participation in the body of Christ' as—and this is entirely to be understood in a spatial manner—'approaching the Eucharist' (*Communicare...corpus Christi accedens ad eucharistiam*; on On Pascha 1, 76 [P 25, −8—−4], see Buchinger 2005a, 2, 881f; Buchinger 2005b, 12–31); this is a clear indication for a progressing ritual development of the Eucharistic celebration.

The participation in the Eucharist requires not only the spiritual and ethical *preparation* (CoMatt 10, 25) which Origen describes in various biblical images (ascent to the upper room, in which Jesus, according to Mark 14:15par, celebrated the Last Supper: HomJer 19, 13; FragmEzek 18, 31; CoCant 2; CoMatt Ser. 79; CoMatt Ser. 86; Buchinger 2005a, 2, 644f; show bread of Lev 24:6–9 and 1 Sam 21:5–7: FragmCor 34; HomLev 13, 5; HomEzek 9, 5; preparation for the theophany of Exod 19:10f: HomExod 11, 7; girding of one's loins at the Passover meal Exod. 12:11: On Pascha 1, 105–109 [P 35, 29–37, 14]; see Buchinger 2005a, 2, 881f) and, with the support of 1 Cor 11:27–34, drastically accentuates (Hom 2, 6 in Ps 37 [38] 19; FragmJer 50; FragmCor 34; CoMatt 10, 24f; CoMatt 11, 14; CoJohn 32, 24 § 309; CoJohn 28, 24 § 27; HomLev 13, 5), it also demands preceding sexual abstention (Crouzel 1962a, 55f):

> It is therefore necessary, that one be pure 'from a woman' in order to take the show bread (cf. 1 Sam 21:5–7); is it not far more necessary that one be purer for receiving the greater Show Bread over which the name of God, of Christ, and of the Holy Spirit has been invoked, so that he might receive the breads truly to his salvation and not 'to his judgment/ condemnation' (1 Cor 11:34)? (FragmCor 34)
>
> All the more is it required from the minister, who, 'after the (sexual) uniting behaves indifferently to the impurity to be found in himself as he prepares to pray over the bread of the Eucharist: thus one desecrates the Holy and commits a pollution' (FragmEzek 7, 22; on the metaphor of pollution, but without explicit reference to sexuality, cf. also FragmJer 50).

### 2.3    *Origen and the Eucharistic Prayer*

*'Conventions' about the addressee of the Eucharistic prayer*

In his discussion with Heracleides and his episcopal colleagues, Origen permits a valuable insight into his fundamental conception about the Eucharistic prayer: for him it is clear that God the Father is the addressee of the προσφορά and Christ is the mediator, and that this convention is to be observed:

> Oblation is constantly made to God the all-powerful through Jesus Christ by reason of his communication in divinity with the Father. Nor is it made twice but (once) to God through God. I will seem to speak daringly: in prayer it is necessary to respect the conventions... (Dial. 4, 24–28; English translation R.J. Daly, ACW 54, 60f; cf. Crehan 1950; Capelle 1952; Nautin 1961).

The reference to conventions (συνθῆκαι) in Eucharistic praying must not necessarily mean a verbally fixed text; it documents, however, on the one hand a causal connection between the *lex supplicandi* and the *lex credendi* (Hanson 1961, 174; Bouley 1981, 140f; Driscoll 2002, 85–100; see also CoMatt 11, 14), and on the other hand the obviously still to be found in flux building up of recognized conventions and, thereby, the not too long previously occurring changing of differing practices (Klinghardt 1996, 461).

> In other places as well, Origen documents the wrestling about the in no way obvious position of God as the addressee of prayer, in regard to whom Christ is only assigned the role of the (high priestly) mediator of prayer (Laporte 1995, 28–42; Hermans 1996, 8–10): 'One may pray to no created being, not even to Christ himself, but only to the God and Father of all, to whom even our redeemer had prayed...it remains therefore only to pray to God, the Father of all, but not without the high priest, who, "with an oath" (cf. Hebr 7:21) was appointed by the Father...' (On Prayer 15, 1; cf. On Prayer 15, 4; 16, 1). The apology against Celsus distinguishes in fact: 'We worship (θεραπεύομεν) but one God, the Father and the Son' (Contra Celsum 8, 12; English translation H. Chadwick 460); 'That is why we worship (σέβομεν) the one God and his one Son (!)..., bringing our prayers to the God of the universe through the mediation of His only-begotten son. We bring them to him first, asking him who is a 'propitiation for our sins' (cf. 1 John 2:2; 4:10), to act as a high-priest (cf. Hebr 2:17) and to bear our prayers and sacrifices and intercessions to the supreme God' (Contra Celsum 8, 13; English translation H. Chadwick 461; cf. also Contra Celsum 8, 26; 8, 34; 8, 37. For examples of such prayers, see HomIsa 1, 5; HomNum 11, 9). But Origen also admits to exceptions to this rule, 'if we are capable of a clear understanding of the absolute and the relative sense of prayer' (Contra Celsum 5, 4; cf. also Contra Celsum 5, 11; 8, 69 and CoRom 8, 4, the latter possibly being influenced by Rufinus). He defends not only the 'faith of the common folk', of which God approves as well as 'the rational piety towards him of more intelligent people who send up their prayers to the creator of the universe with thanksgiving, an offering of

prayer which they make as by the mediation of a high priest who has shown to men the pure way to worship God' (Contra Celsum 7, 46; English translation H. Chadwick 434). Even Origen himself gives not a few examples of praying to Christ (Bigg 1913, 226–231; Crouzel 1956, 117–119): In his work are found numerous more or less spontaneous invocations of Christ (invocations of Christ alone: HomExod 13, 3; HomLev 5, 5; HomNum 26, 3; HomJer 19, 14; HomEzek 3, 4; HomLuke 6; invocations of Christ and the Father: HomEzek 12, 5; HomLuke 15; invocations of Christ and the Holy Spirit: HomLev 1, 1; invocations of Christ, the Father and the Holy Spirit: HomNum 13, 5. On the prayer of HomIsa 5, 2 to Jesus the footwasher, see Russell Christman 1997, 304–308). Finally, the marked limitation found in his discourse On Prayer that one may not even pray to Christ Himself, applies only for the prayer (προσευχή) in the narrowest terminological sense: the remaining three types of prayer, mentioned by 1 Tim 2:1—petition, intercession, and thanksgiving—'it is not inappropriate, even to offer to men..., if however, to these holy men it is to be offered, all the more is Christ to be thanked...and intercessions to be directed to him' (On Prayer 14, 6; cf. Riggi 1974, 370–378. This is all the more true of other genres, as for example 'hymns of praise'; cf. Contra Celsum 8, 67.). From this, however, a Eucharistic prayer directed to Christ in the terminological sense cannot yet be derived.

The orientation of the community at prayer gives this a pronounced Christological perspective; the turning is directed towards 'him, whose name is Rising' (Zech 6:12), but, following Origen, at the same time to him 'who has become mediator between God and men' (1 Tim 2:5; HomLev 9, 10 as quoted above, p. 214).

*Genre, form and content of the Eucharistic prayer*
It is more difficult to identify the genre, form and content of the προσφορά familiar to Origen (CoMatt 11, 14, as quoted above, mentions a 'prayer' and the 'word' said over the matter of the Eucharist). From the general reasoning of Origen about prayer—even about thanksgiving (cf. for example CoJohn 28, 6 § 39–42)—one may not, especially not automatically, infer about the praxis of Eucharistic praying of his time; neither the differentiation of the four types of prayer, which at the beginning of his discourse 'On Prayer' was derived from an exegesis of 1 Tim 2:1 (On Prayer 14, 2–6), nor the prayer structure developed at the end of the same document (On Prayer 33, 1–6) necessarily reflects concrete liturgical texts.

What is clear, on the one hand, is the *essential Eucharistic feature* of the prayer spoken over the gifts; it arises not only from the terminology (FragmJer 50; FragmEzek 7, 22; Hom 2, 6 in Ps 37 [38] 19; CoMatt

Ser. 86; CoJohn 32, 24 § 310) and from the direct application of the Institution narrative to the liturgy of the Church (CoMatt Ser. 86; HomJer 19, 13; FragmEzek 19, 31), but is also expressly testified to by Origen:

> We give thanks to the Creator of the universe and eat the loaves that are presented with thanksgiving and prayer over the gifts, so that by the prayer they become a certain holy body which sanctifies those who partake of it with a pure intention (Contra Celsum 8, 33; English translation H. Chadwick 476).

About the precise content of the thanksgiving only suppositions can be employed. In defence against the accusation of ingratitude Origen defends the Christians with the indication of the fundamental Eucharistic attitude of the Christians and its sacramental expression; it is admittedly not clear, whether, and in what form, the enumerated motives for gratitude—the mighty deeds of God, his creation and his providence as well as the eschatological hope—were also explicit subjects of the Eucharistic prayer:

> We avoid being guilty of ingratitude to God who loads us with His benefits. We are His creatures and are cared for by His providence. Our condition is subject to His judgement, and we entertain hopes of Him beyond this life. Moreover, we have a symbol of our thanksgiving to God in the bread which is called 'Eucharist' (Contra Celsum 8, 57; English translation Henry Chadwick 496).

On the other hand, an *epicletic element* is clearly identifiable. About the addressee and the form of the epiclesis Origen expresses himself in a contradictory manner: on the one hand, he speaks of the 'bread, over which the name of God and of Christ and the Holy Ghost was called upon' (FragmCor 34), thus of a trinitarian epiclesis (or an epicletic text in a broader sense, yet in some way invoking the Trinity). On the other hand, one wants to see an allusion to a Logos-epiclesis in Origen's position that the Eucharist is hallowed, according to 1 Tim 4:5, 'through the Word of God and a supplication' (CoMatt 11, 14ter; cf. the report on research in Bouley 1981, 139 with n. 212).

Several arguments can be brought into play for a Logos-epiclesis: First, it would fit well into the general view of the early history of liturgy (Taft 1992; Johnson 1995, 233–253). Secondly, the prayer for the coming and the appearance of Jesus belongs absolutely to Origen's repertoire of praying (see above); admittedly, it remains unclear whether one may hear the echo of a Logos-epiclesis when Origen is primarily speaking of the understanding of Scripture (HomIsa 5, 2; HomJer 19, 10f. 14; CoMatt Ser. 79; HomLuke 22). Thirdly, the accusation of Theophilus of Alexandria, cited by Jerome, would also fit in, according to which Origen would have denied that the hallowing of the Eucharist comes about 'through the calling upon and the arrival of the Holy Spirit' (*per inuocationem et aduentum sancti spiritus*; ep. 98, 13).

There are, however, several reasons to be critical about a Logos-epiclesis: First, the historical credibility of this accusation suffers from the fact that it was raised one and a half centuries later, and out of a profoundly changed theological and liturgico-historical situation, and with polemic intention (Johnson 1995, 242f); furthermore, it is obviously false in its context, where Jerome raises the same accusation with regard to the baptismal water: an invocation (ἐπίκλησις) of the Trinity over the baptismal water is repeatedly attested to by Origen (Auf der Maur & Waldram 1981, 41–95 esp. 79–83). Why should the accusation concerning the Eucharist contain a sting, when it proves to be untenable regarding baptism? Secondly it is to be held that Origen gives the above-quoted clear indication of a trinitarian epiclesis in unambiguous Eucharistic context, and in a fragment preserved in Greek, whereas the grounds for a Logos-epiclesis are indirect, vague, and ambiguous. Thirdly, Origen indeed attributes to the Spirit a crucial role in the Eucharistic action: 'We grasp the holy mysteries through the grace of the Holy Spirit, from whom everything that is holy, has been made holy' (HomLev 13, 6). Whether and when this conviction shaped a liturgical text is not apparent; at least a pure Logos-epiclesis appears not very plausible for the reasons mentioned above.

The indication of the Eucharistic prayer as προσφορά suggests, presumably, the existence of an explicit *statement of offering* (Dial. 4, 24. 27 as quoted above, p. 216). The term belongs not to Origen's Eucharistic-theological vocabulary but was taken over from the tradition (Lies 1982, 158f; Hermans 1996, 84–89; Buchinger 2005a, 1, 200); it is to be assumed that an element in the obviously already established literary form (Lies 1982, 151f) corresponds to the genre-identification. Further details are not, to be sure, to be recognized.

Further structural elements of the Eucharistic prayer are left to speculation, even if it is, particularly in Origen, not methodologically permissible to conclude their non-existence from the failure to mention liturgical customs. No trace of an introductory *dialogue* is found in Origen (but cf. Taft 1988, 67; 77). It is no longer assumed that Origen knew the

*Sanctus* as part of the Eucharistic Prayer, although his influence can
clearly be identified in later Alexandrian anaphoras (Spinks 1991, 2–4;
Taft 1991–1992, 89–95; Johnson 1996, 671–702 esp. 673–680; 2000,
405–442); 'Indeed, Sarapion's sanctus-unit appears to be nothing other
than the theological interpretation of Origen expressed in a liturgical
form' (Johnson 1996, 680).

The anamnetic character of the Eucharistic celebration is, however,
quite familiar to Origen (Schütz 1984, 161f; Lies 1982 passim, above all
162–165, 299–304, 313–318); he interprets the show bread 'presented
before the Lord as a memorial' (according to Lev 24:7) in view of the
liturgy of the Church (*ecclesiastica mysteria*) and in an express looking
back to the iteration command of 1 Cor 11:24/Lk 22:19 (on the latter,
see De Margerie 1984, 43–69 esp. 53–56):

> But if these things (i.e. Lev 24:5–9) are referred to the greatness of the
> mystery, you will find this 'remembrance' (Lev 24:7) to have the effect of a
> great propitiation. If you return to that 'loaf which descends from heaven
> and gives life to this world' (John 6:33), that shew bread 'whom God set
> forth as a propitiation through faith in his blood' (Rom 3:25) and if you
> turn your attention to that 'remembrance' about which the Lord says,
> 'Do this in remembrance of me' (1 Cor 11:24f/Lk 22:19), you will find
> that this is the only 'remembrance' which makes God gracious to men.
> Therefore, if you recall more intently the ecclesiastical mysteries, you will
> find the image of the future truth anticipated (cf. Hebr 10:1?) in these
> things which the Law writes. But there is not much more to discuss about
> these things because it is enough to be understood by a single recollection
> (HomLev 13, 3; English translation G.W. Barkley, FaCh 83, 237).

Whether an explicit *Anamnesis* was, therefore, already a fixed element
of the Eucharistic prayer does not become clear, and about its possible
content one can only make suppositions.

Origen cites the *Institution Narrative* of the Last Supper in such differing versions that he, on the one hand, lets the frequent use of the
text be recognized but, on the other hand however, no fixed liturgical
formulation.

| Words over the bread: | *accipite et manducate* (CoMatt Ser. 86; HomLev 5, 8) |
| | λάβετε, φάγετε (CoJohn 32, 24 § 305. 309) |
| Words over the cup: | *accipite, et bibite ex hoc* (HomLev 7, 1) |
| | *bibite, quia hic est sanguis meus novi testamenti* (CoMatt Ser. 86) |
| | *hic sanguis meus est, qui pro vobis effundetur in remissionem peccatorum* (HomLev 9, 10) |

λάβετε, πίετε, τοῦτό μου ἐστι τὸ αἷμα, τὸ
ὑπὲρ ὑμῶν ἐκχυόμενον εἰς ἄφεσιν ἁμαρτιῶν·
τοῦτο ποιεῖτε, ὁσάκις ἐὰν πίνητε, εἰς τὴν
ἐμὴν ἀνάμνησιν (HomJer 12, 2).
*hoc facite in meam commemorationem* (HomLev
13, 3)

It is remarkable that Origen speaks often of the 'cup of the New Covenant' (FragmEzek 18, 31; HomJer 12, 2; HomJer 19, 13; CoCant 2;
CoMatt 17, 33; CoMatt Ser. 79; CoMatt Ser. 114; CoRom 5, 1); this is
a significant simplification of 1 Cor 11:25/Luke 22:20.

The text-critical instability is most likely to be understood against the
background of a catechetical—but hardly liturgical—tradition still in
flux.

Origen testifies to the institutionalising of *Intercessions*, which will
be found again in later liturgies; the closer liturgical context does not,
unfortunately, thereby become clear. Firstly, he cites a portion of a
regularly used prayer, which asks that God would grant to the faithful
a share along with the prophets and the apostles:

> Often in prayer we say, 'Almighty God, give us the lot of the Prophets,
> give us the lot of the Apostles of Christ so that we may be found also
> with Christ himself.' But when we say this, we do not realize what we
> pray. For in effect we are saying this: 'Let us suffer what the Prophets
> have suffered, let us be hated as the Prophets were hated, let befall us the
> kind of misfortunes which befell the Apostles.' For to say, 'Give me a lot
> with the Prophets,' yet not suffer the pains of the Prophets nor want to
> suffer, is unjust. To say: 'Give me a lot with the Apostles,' yet, truthfully
> speaking, not wanting to say, using Paul's expression, 'far greater labors,
> with countless beatings, far more imprisonments, and often near death'
> (cf. 2 Cor 11:23), and so on, is the most unjust thing of all (HomJer 14,
> 14; English translation J.C. Smith, FaCh 97, 149f).

It is worthy of note that Origen speaks of an at least content-wise
rather established matter of prayer, if he does not even testify to a
marked formulation (cf. the repeated introduction of the prayer as a
quotation as well as its repetition in the following HomJer 15, 1); is it
furthermore to be regarded as a sensational earlier bit of evidence for
the intercessions of the anaphora—the text is widely seen in continuity
to the Egyptian liturgy of St. Mark (to be precise, the papyrus Strasbourg gr. 254; Cuming 1990, 114)—or a quote from a formulary for
the general intercessions at the end of the liturgy of the word?

Secondly, Origen mentions that the Christians (in compliance with
the command of 1 Tim 2:1f) offer prayers for the emperor and for the

authorities (Contra Celsum 8, 73); when and how that exactly occurred, is not, however, to be seen (Schermann 1912, 45f, thinks about the Common Prayer of the Faithful, as he does in the case of HomJer 14, 14). Furthermore, it remains obscure if and how Origen's frequently represented conviction of a communion of prayer (and meal; cf. Contra Celsum 8, 32) between the faithful and the angels (among other texts, cf. Contra Celsum 8, 34; 8, 36; HomNum 5, 3; 11, 9) might have found a liturgical expression in the Eucharistic celebration, particularly since no relevant bits of evidence are found in an unambiguous Eucharistic context (Monaci Castagno 2000, 6–13 esp. 11). Lastly, Origen is convinced that not only Christ and the angels, but also the souls of the departed saints unite themselves with the prayer of the Christians (On Prayer 11, 1; 31, 5); if this may be understood as an allusion to the diptychs of the dead in such an early period, has to remain open (pace Schermann 1912, 48; Grimmelt 1942, 53), because in Origen this conviction is never connected with the Eucharist.

It must likewise remain an open question whether from the prominent role of the trinitarian *doxology* in Origen's rule of prayer (On Prayer 33, 1. 6) one may conclude a corresponding structural element of Eucharistic praying.

### 3    Conclusion: Origen and the Transition to the Liturgy of the Imperial Era

Looking through the citations from Origen about the Eucharistic celebration brings forth, as expected, no new data; it is not so much the picture which has changed, but its frame. If, however, one takes it as a starting point that documents of the pre-Nicene period are not from the outset to be interpreted in continuity to the unfolding of the liturgy in the imperial Christian period, Origen's testimony gains new weight: and even if many questions of detail must remain open, it becomes clear that he testifies to developments which were later generally to be implemented, but for which there is little, if any, evidence at his time.

Thus can the connection of the liturgy of the word and the Eucharistic celebration probably be assumed, which has still not been unambiguously testified to among the North African contemporaries of Origen (Salzmann 1994, 386–429, esp. 395, 399f, 404 on Tertullian, 438–440 on Cyprian), who thereby, and even with his admittedly sparse evidence about the Eucharistic praxis, becomes a valuable witness to the consolidating of the 'Mass-schema' of the Eucharistic celebration. A Eucharistic prayer, which contains, aside from the thanksgiving, an *epiclesis* as well, and perhaps also an explicit statement of offering, is anything but obvious in the first half of the third century, though it was to become standard in the following century (cf. Bradshaw 2004, 136f: 'The structural similarities between the Strasbourg Papyrus and seemingly earlier forms of the Eucharistic prayers of Sarapion and of the *Apostolic Tradition* imply that one particularly prevalent form, at least from early in the fourth century onwards if not before, was the combination of praise and petitionary units by means of an "offering" or "thanksgiving/offering" formula linking them together'); and wherever the intercessions cited by Origen had their exact placement—it is quite possible that he is the first witness of intercessions being an integral part of the Eucharistic prayer—, they are a valuable detail of early liturgical praxis of prayer.

Both Origen's formal recourse to fixed 'conventions' about Eucharistic praying, as well as the rule tied to these conventions regarding their content—that the προσφορά is to be directed to the Father—confirm the picture gained from other sources, that both, at that time, were not yet taken for granted. The precious insight, which Origen furthered with his intervention in conversation with Heracleides, lets it be recognized as well that Origen was not only a witness but also a protagonist of a Eucharistic praxis of prayer in a unity from rule of faith and rule of prayer. His influence, however, goes far beyond this well-known theological-liturgical engagement: on the one hand Origen embodies in his person the transfer of views and conceptions—not necessarily practices—between Alexandria and Palestine; on the other hand, his direct or indirect subsequent influence in motifs and formulations of later Eucharistic and Eucharistic-theological texts and in liturgical ordering is to be recognized, although these are, admittedly, not the object of this investigation.

## LITERATURE

Auf der Maur, H.J. & J. Waldram, 'Illuminatio verbi divini—confessio fidei—gratia baptismi. Wort, Glaube und Sakrament in Katechumenat und Taufliturgie bei Origenes', in: H.J. auf der Maur et al. (eds), *Fides Sacramenti; Sacramentum Fidei* (FS Pieter Smulders), Assen 1981.

Bigg, C., *The Christian Platonists of Alexandria*, Oxford 2nd ed. 1913.

Bornert, R., *Les commentaires byzantins de la divine liturgie du VII^e au XV^e siècle* (AOC 9), Paris 1966.

Bouley, A., *From Freedom to Formula; The Evolution of the Eucharistic Prayer from Oral Impro-visation to Written Texts* (SCA 21), Washington 1981.

Bradshaw, P.F., 'Continuity and Change in Early Eucharistic Practice: Shifting Schol-arly Perspectives', in: R.N. Swanson (ed.), *Continuity and Change in Christian Worship; Papers Read at the 1997 Summer Meeting and the 1998 Winter Meeting of the Ecclesiastical History Society* (SCH[L] 35), London 1999.

———, *The Search for the Origins of Christian Worship; Sources and Methods for the Study of Early Liturgy*, London 2nd ed. 2002 [1st ed. 1992].

———, *Eucharistic Origins* (ACC 80), London 2004.

———, M.E. Johnson, & L.E. Phillips, *The Apostolic Tradition; A Commentary* (Herme-neia), Minneapolis 2002.

Buchinger, H., 'Gebet und Identität bei Origenes: Das Vaterunser im Horizont der Auseinandersetzung um Liturgie und Exegese', in: A. Gerhards, A. Doeker, & P. Ebenbauer (eds), *Identität durch Gebet; Zur gemeinschaftsbildenden Funktion institution-alisierten Betens in Judentum und Christentum* (Studien zu Judentum und Christentum), Paderborn 2003.

———, *Pascha bei Origenes* (IThS 64/1–2), Innsbruck 2005 [quoted as 2005a].

———, 'Towards the Origins of Paschal Baptism: The Contribution of Origen', *StLi* 35 (2005) [quoted as 2005b].

———, *Wortgottesdienst und Eucharistiefeier bei Origenes; Mit einem Anhang: Perikopenverzeichnis zu den erhaltenen Homilien* (Liturgica Oenipontana), Münster [forthcoming].

Cabié, R., 'Le dimanche et le Temps pascal au temps d'Origène', in: A. Dupleix (ed.), *Recherches et Tradition* (FS Henri Crouzel; ThH 88), Paris 1992.

Camelot, T., 'L'eucaristia nella scuola alessandrina', in: A. Piolanti (ed.), *Eucaristia; Il mistero dell'altare nel pensiero e nella vita della Chiesa*, Roma 1957.

Capelle, B., 'Origène et l'oblation à faire au Père par le Fils, d'après le papyrus de Toura', *RHE* 47 (1952).

Crehan, J., 'The *Dialektos* of Origen and John 20:17', *TS* 11 (1950).

Crouzel, H., *Théologie de l'image de Dieu chez Origène* (Theol[P] 34), Paris 1956.

———, *Origène et la 'connaissance mystique'* (ML.T 56), Paris 1961.

———, *Virginité et mariage selon Origène* (ML.T 58), Paris 1962 [quoted as 1962a].

———, 'Origène et la structure du sacrement', *BLE* 63 (1962) [quoted as 1962b].

Cuming, G.J., *The Liturgy of St Mark edited from the manuscripts with a commentary* (OCA 234), Roma 1990.

Daniélou, J., *Origène* (GenChr), Paris 1948.

De Lorenzi, L., 'L'eucaristia in Origene', in: *La Cena del Signore* (PSV 7), Bologna 1987.

De Margerie, B., '"Hoc facite in meam commemorationem" (Lc. 22,19ᵇ). Les exégèses des Pères préchalcédoniens (150–451)', *Div.* 28 (1984).

Driscoll, J., 'Uncovering the Dynamic *Lex orandi-Lex credendi* in the Trinitarian Theology of Origen', *EO* 19 (2002) [= id., *Theology at the Eucharistic Table; Master Themes in the Theological Tradition* (StAns 138), Roma—Leominster, UK 2003, 83–98].

Fernández, S.E., 'La dottrina sull'Eucaristia in Origene', in: *Dizionario di spiritualità biblico-patristica; 20: L'Eucaristia nei Padri della Chiesa*, Roma 1998.

Frank, K.S., 'Maleachi 1,10ff. in der frühen Väterdeutung. Ein Beitrag zu Opfertermi-nologie und Opferverständnis in der alten Kirche', *ThPh* 53 (1978).

Gerhards, A., 'Zu wem beten? Die These Josef Andreas Jungmanns († 1975) über den Adressaten des Eucharistischen Hochgebets im Licht der neueren Forschung', *LJ* 32 (1982).

———, 'Entstehung und Entwicklung des Eucharistischen Hochgebets im Spiegel der neueren Forschung. Der Beitrag der Liturgiewissenschaft zur liturgischen Erneuer-ung', in: A. Heinz & H. Rennings (eds), *Gratias agamus; Studien zum eucharistischen Hochgebet* (FS Balthasar Fischer; Pastoralliturgische Reihe in Verbindung mit der Zeitschrift 'Gottesdienst'), Freiburg 1992.

Gramaglia, P.A., 'Eucarestia', in: A. Monaci Castagno (ed.), *Origene; Dizionario; La cultura, il pensiero, le opere*, Roma 2000.

Grappone, G., 'Annotazioni sulla cronologia delle omelie di Origene', *Aug.* 41 (2001) [quoted as Grappone 2001a].

———, 'Annotazioni sul contesto liturgico delle omelie di Origene', *Aug.* 41 (2001) [quoted as Grappone 2001b].

Grimmelt, L., *Die Eucharistiefeier nach den Werken des Origenes; Eine liturgiegeschichtliche Untersuchung* [Diss., unpubl.], Münster 1942.

Hanson, R.P.C., 'The Liberty of the Bishop to Improvise Prayer in the Eucharist', *VigChr* 15 (1961).

———, 'Eucharistic offering in the Pre-Nicene Fathers', *PIA.C* 4 (1976).

Harnack, A. v., *Der kirchengeschichtliche Ertrag der exegetischen Arbeiten des Origenes; II. Teil: Die beiden Testamente mit Ausschluß des Hexateuchs und des Richterbuchs; Anhang: Origenistisches Gut von kirchengeschichtlicher Bedeutung in den Kommentaren des Hieronymus zum Philemon-, Galater-, Epheser- und Titusbrief* (TU 3/12, 4 = 42, 4), Berlin 1919.

Hermans, T., *Origène; Théologie sacrificielle du sacerdoce des Chrétiens* (ThH 102), Paris 1996.

Jacob, C., *'Arkandisziplin', Allegorese, Mystagogie; Ein neuer Zugang zur Theologie des Ambrosius von Mailand* (Theoph. 32), Frankfurt 1990.

Jacquemont, P., 'Origène', in: *L'Eucharistie des premiers chrétiens* (PoTh 17), Paris 1976.

Johnson, M.E., *The Prayers of Sarapion of Thmuis; A literary, liturgical, and theological analysis* (OCA 249), Roma 1995.

———, 'The Archaic Nature of the Sanctus, Institution Narrative, and Epiclesis of the Logos in the Anaphora Ascribed to Sarapion of Thmuis', in: R.F. Taft (ed.), *The Christian East: Its Institutions & Its Thought; A Critical Reflection; Papers of the International Scholarly Congress for the 75th Anniversary of the Pontifical Oriental Institute, Rome, 30 May–5 June 1993* (OCA 251), Roma 1996.

———, 'The Origins of the Anaphoral Sanctus and Epiclesis Revisited. The Contribution of Gabriele Winkler and Its Implications', in: H.-J. Feulner et al. (eds), *Crossroad of Cultures; Studies in Liturgy and Patristics* (FS Gabriele Winkler; OCA 260), Roma 2000.

Jungmann, J.A., *Missarum Sollemnia; Eine genetische Erklärung der römischen Messe*, Wien 5th ed. 1962 [1st ed. 1948].

Klinghardt, M., *Gemeinschaftsmahl und Mahlgemeinschaft; Soziologie und Liturgie frühchristlicher Mahlfeiern* (TANZ 13), Tübingen 1996.

Kretschmar, G., 'Abendmahlsfeier I. Alte Kirche', *TRE* 1 (1977).

Laporte, J., 'Modèles eucharistiques philoniens dans l'Eucharistie d'Origène', in: idem, *Théologie liturgique de Philon d'Alexandrie et d'Origène* (Liturgie 6), Paris 1995 [= 'Philonic Models of Eucharistia in the Eucharist of Origen', *LTP* 42 (1986) 71–91].

Ledegang, F., *Mysterium Ecclesiae; Images of the Church and its Members in Origen* (BEThL 156), Leuven 2001.

———, 'Eucharist', in: J.A. McGuckin (ed.), *The Westminster Handbook to Origen* (Westminster Handbooks to Christian Theology), Louisville 2004.

Lies, L., *Wort und Eucharistie bei Origenes; Zur Spiritualisierungstendenz des Eucharistieverständnisses* (IThS 1), Innsbruck 2nd ed. 1982 [1st ed. 1978].

McGowan, A., *Ascetic Eucharists; Food and Drink in Early Christian Ritual Meals* (Oxford Early Christian Studies), Oxford 1999.

Meßner, R., 'Der Gottesdienst in der vornizänischen Kirche', in: L. Petri (ed.), *Die Geschichte des Christentums; Religion—Politik—Kultur; Band 1: Die Zeit des Anfangs (bis 250)*, Freiburg 2003.

———, 'Grundlinien der Entwicklung des eucharistischen Gebets in der frühen Kirche', in: A. Gerhards, H. Brakmann, & M. Klöckener (eds), *Prex Eucharistica; Volumen III: Studia. Pars prima: Ecclesia antiqua et occidentalis* (SpicFri 42), Fribourg 2005.

——, 'Die Synode von Seleukeia-Ktesiphon 410 und die Geschichte der ostsyrischen Messe', in: R. Meßner & R. Pranzl (eds), *Haec sacrosancta synodus. Konzils- und kirchengeschichtliche Beiträge* (FS B. Kriegbaum), Regensburg 2006.

Minnerath, R., 'La présidence de l'eucharistie chez Tertullien et dans l'Église des trois premiers siècles', in: C. Grappe (ed.), *Le Repas de Dieu/Das Mahl Gottes; 4. Symposium Strasbourg, Tübingen, Upsal; Strasbourg, 11–15 septembre 2002* (WUNT 169), Tübingen 2004.

Monaci Castagno, A., 'Angelo', in: see Gramaglia 2000.

Nautin, P., 'Origène et l'anaphore eucharistique', in: idem, *Lettres et écrivains chrétiens des II<sup>e</sup> et III<sup>e</sup> siècles* (Patr. 2), Paris 1961.

——, *Origène; Sa vie et son œuvre* (CAnt 1), Paris 1977.

Perrone, L., 'Preghiera', in: see Gramaglia 2000.

Phillips, L.E., *The Ritual Kiss in Early Christian Worship* (Alcuin Club/GROW 36), Bramcote 1996.

Powell, D., 'Arkandisziplin', *TRE* 4 (1979).

Prieur, J.-M., 'L'eucharistie dans les Actes apocryphes des apôtres', in: see Minnerath 2004.

Riggi, C., 'Tipi di preci liturgiche e struttura eucologica nel trattatello origeniano "Sulla Preghiera"', *EL* 88 (1974).

Rordorf, W., *Der Sonntag; Geschichte des Ruhe- und Gottesdiensttages im ältesten Christentum* (AThANT 43), Zürich 1962.

Rossi, G.E.P., *Bibel und Gebet in den Predigtepilogen bei Origenes* [Diss., unpubl.], Jena 2003 [nondum vidi].

Rouwhorst, G.A.M., 'La célébration de l'eucharistie dans l'église primitive', *QuLi* 74 (1993).

Russell Christman, A., 'Origen's Prayer to Jesus the Footwasher', in: M. Kiley et al. (eds), *Prayer from Alexander to Constantine; A critical anthology*, London 1997.

Salzmann, J.C., *Lehren und Ermahnen; Zur Geschichte des christlichen Wortgottesdienstes in den ersten drei Jahrhunderten* (WUNT 2/59), Tübingen 1994.

Schermann, T., *Ägyptische Abendmahlsliturgien des ersten Jahrtausends in ihrer Überlieferung* (SGKA 6/1–2), Paderborn 1912.

Schütz, W., *Der christliche Gottesdienst bei Origenes* (CThM.B 8), Stuttgart 1984.

Smyth, M., 'L'anaphore de la prétendue "Tradition apostolique" et la prière eucharistique romaine', *RevSR* 81 (2007).

Spinks, B.D., *The Sanctus in the Eucharistic Prayer*, Cambridge 1991.

Stevenson, K., *Eucharist and Offering*, New York 1986.

Taft, R.F., *A History of the Liturgy of St. John Chrysostom; Volume II: The Great Entrance; A History of the Transfer of Gifts and other Pre-anaphoral Rites* (OCA 200), Roma 1978.

——, 'The Dialogue before the Anaphora in the Byzantine Eucharistic Liturgy. II: The *Sursum corda*', *OCP* 54 (1988).

——, *A History of the Liturgy of St. John Chrysostom; Volume IV: The Diptychs* (OCA 238), Roma 1991.

——, 'The Interpolation of the Sanctus into the Anaphora: When and Where? A Review of the Dossier', *OCP* 57 (1991) [281–308]; 58 (1992) [83–121] [quoted as 1991–1992].

——, 'From logos to spirit. On the early history of the epiclesis', in: see Gerhards 1992.

——, *A History of the Liturgy of St. John Chrysostom; Volume V: The Precommunion Rites* (OCA 261), Roma 2000.

——, 'Home Communion in the Late Antique East', in: C.V. Johnson (ed.), *Ars Liturgiae; Worship, Aesthetics and Praxis* (FS Nathan D. Mitchell), Chicago 2003 [quoted as 2003a].

————, 'Mass Without the Consecration? The Historic Agreement on the Eucharist between the Catholic Church and the Assyrian Church of the East Promulgated 26 October 2001', *Worship* 77 (2003) [quoted as 2003b].

————, 'The Order and Place of Lay Communion in the Late-Antique and Byzantine East', in: M.E. Johnson & L.E. Phillips (eds), *Studia liturgica diversa* (FS Paul F. Bradshaw; Studies in Church Music and Liturgy), Portland, OR 2004.

Thraede, K., 'Ursprünge und Formen des "Heiligen Kusses" im frühen Christentum', *JAC* 11/12 (1968/69).

Vilela, A., *La condition collégiale des prêtres au III$^e$ siècle* (ThH 14), Paris 1971.

Vogel, C., 'Anaphores eucharistiques préconstantiniennes. Formes non traditionnelles', *Aug.* 20 (1980) [= Saxer, V. (ed.), *Ecclesia Orans* (FS Adalbert G. Hamman)].

Vogt, H.J., *Das Kirchenverständnis des Origenes* (BoBKG 4), Köln 1974.

Wallraff, M., 'Die Ursprünge der christlichen Gebetsostung', *ZKG* 111 (2000).

# THE CREED IN THE LITURGY:
## PRAYER OR HYMN?

*Wolfram Kinzig*
Rheinische Friedrich-Wilhelms-Universität Bonn, Germany

Creeds are an integral part of the Christian identity.[1] Even though Christians today would certainly have no trouble confirming this assertion, it is by no means a foregone conclusion; after all, other religions get by without creeds of the kind with which Christians are familiar. We have no knowledge of creeds in ancient cults. In the two other major non-Christian monotheistic religions, Judaism and Islam, the existence of creeds is, at least, controversial. In Judaism, for example, the *Shema Israel* (Deut 6:4–9), which is recited together with Deut 11:13–21 and Num 15:37–41 in the synagogue service before the Amidah, bears close resemblance to a creed. Here, however, the emphasis is on the oneness of God ('Hear, O Israel: The LORD is our God, the LORD alone.'). There is no mention of *faith*, the oneness of God is stated as a fact.[2] The same can be said of the *Tashahhud*, which must be recited by every devout Muslim five times a day during the *Salah* (obligatory prayer). In its shortest form, the *Tashahhud* reads as follows: 'There is no God but Allah, Muhammad is Allah's messenger.' Obviously, this is primarily a statement of fact, which applies regardless of the person professing faith. In contrast to Christianity, the faith of the individual does not play a role here (cf. Lanczkowski 1984, esp. 385. This view is, however, also controversial; cf., for example, Heine 1999, 305f; Gimaret 1997, 201, and for a more detailed examination of the subject Gardet 1971, 1170–1174).

In view of this fact, it is not surprising that patristic research on Christian confessions of faith has over the past two hundred years been extensive (for a fundamental treatment of this subject, see Vinzent 2006). Nevertheless, their emergence and history continue to raise

---

[1] Translation by Aingeal Flanagan.
[2] Cf. Finkel 1984, 391. At the conference, a debate as to whether creeds that are comparable with Christian creeds exist in Judaism arose during the subsequent discussion among Jewish participants.

questions that have not been satisfactorily answered to this day. Some of the most frequently addressed problems in recent decades include, among others:

- the emergence and form of questions relating to trinitarian faith at baptism;
- the emergence of the declaratory creed in the 4th century;
- the origin of the Nicene (N) and the Niceno-Constantinopolitan Creeds (C);
- and the origins of the Old Roman Creed (R) and the transition from the Roman to the Apostles' Creed (T).

The relationship between the creed and the liturgy in the early Church, on the other hand, has not been a primary focus of late. This is astonishing considering the fact that the creed is part of Sunday liturgy in all major Christian denominations.

However, closer examination of this area of research into the creed is necessary, not only as a result of the plain fact that the creed is part of the liturgy. From a Protestant point of view, the relationship between the creed and the liturgy must be re-examined for two reasons. Firstly, because recent liturgical handbooks, regardless of the denomination in question, claim that the creed is a prayer or a hymn, or even both,[3] and

---

[3] In an influential paper dating from 1952 ['Das Wesen des kirchlichen Gottesdienstes' ('The nature of the liturgy')], the Lutheran systematic theologian Peter Brunner wrote: 'The creed complements the prayer [...]. The creed is a confession of sins. Sinners who confess receive grace. This encounter raises us up and places the creed on our lips. The creed is the congregation's Amen to the message of God. The creed becomes a testimony to faith [...]. The creed becomes a sacrifice of thanksgiving and praise. The creed is the public acclamation of God's saving work, the work of Christ, the new creation of the spirit. It is the jubilation of redemption. It is almost a hymn' (cited in Meyer-Blanck 2001, 223; this is taken up in Brodde 1961, 401). The liturgist Christhard Mahrenholz was of the opinion that the creed in the sunday liturgy is more than just a 'profession of faith' in the sense of the repetition of the baptismal creed: a 'hymn of adoration' (1963, 69). Karl Ferdinand Müller noted that: 'In terms of its content and its liturgical performance, the creed is considered to be first a hymn of praise and a prayer' (1955, 35). With regard to the use of the creed in the liturgy, Friedrich Kalb recommends 'alternating between saying and singing it together, to make it clear that this is not a doctrinal formula, but a "hymn of adoration"' (1982, 138f). From the reformed tradition, one could mention Theophil Müller at this point. However, his statements deviate from the others cited here. He made it clear that the abolition of the creed recited by the congregation in church in reformed Switzerland was a consequence of the aversion of Pietism and Enlightenment to reciting creeds and not a consequence of the Swiss reformation. He appears to share this 18th century stance without actually expressly saying so. While he does mention the function of the

secondly because worshippers in many Protestant parishes in Germany consider the creed to be a prayer as can be seen from the fact that the congregation stands—hands joined in prayer and heads bowed—for the recitation of the Apostles' Creed, while it often remains seated for the remainder of the liturgy (with the exception, perhaps, of the prayers of intercession and the Our Father).

This interpretation can be traced right back to St. Augustine, who is known to have used the term *confessio* in three different ways (cf. most recently Fuhrer 2004, 106 and, for a fundamental treatment of the subject, Mayer 1986–1994). It can mean a 'confession of sins' (*confessio peccatorum*)—this could imply a close link to the prayer genus. It can also mean a 'confession of praise' (*confessio laudis*), in which case the *confessio* shows an affinity with the hymn. As a matter of fact, some passages in the *Confessions* do demonstrate such literary traits. Finally, St. Augustine uses the term *confessio* to mean 'confession of faith' (*confessio fidei*).

The particular focus of this conference is on the phenomenon of 'transitions'. In my paper I would like to examine this phenomenon in the context of the creed in two ways in particular. I shall begin by examining how the creed passed into Christian liturgy. I shall then show how the liturgical status and functions of the creed have changed within the liturgy. This will enable us, finally, to describe both the theological and liturgical character of the creed vis-à-vis the prayer and the hymn.

---

creed as a 'hymn or prayer' (1993, 181), he chose not to apply it. He advocates the use of the term 'anamnesis', but it must be accompanied an aid to comprehension. He also proposes a new creed, formulated by himself, which is meant to be instantly comprehensible. The *Evangelische Gottesdienstbuch* (a German service book uniting both Lutheran and Reformed traditions) considers the creed in liturgical terms to be an anamnesis and/or doxology: 'Different aspects come to the fore depending on the manner in which the creed is recited (spoken or sung): the spoken creed reminds us of our personal commitment to our faith as a result of the baptismal creed, while the sung creed is of a more doxological nature...' (2001, 27). This is also the essential position adopted by Rainer Volp who said (after Herder): 'The confession of faith as an exemplary *symbolum* is not only the result of a process, but also a proposition for analogous liturgical actions. By establishing the creed as a doxological activity in church worship, we are indicating freedom for further *symbola*, which create a link with the origin' (Volp 1994, 792).—The perception of the creed as a prayer can be traced back to Luther, especially as Luther himself occasionally referred to 'faith' as a 'creed or prayer' (for example in a homily dating from the year 1535: WA 41.276.20; cf. also ibid. 275.29). Cf., however, the reference to Luther later on in this paper. I am indebted to my assistant, Dr. Ulrich Volp, for this overview.

# I

The liturgical use of the creed can be divided into *three phases*:

## 1   *The interrogative creed as an element of baptism*

The origins of the liturgical use of the creed or its preceding forms are lost in the mists of time. We do know (for what follows, cf. Kinzig 1999, 87ff and Kinzig & Vinzent 1999, 542–550), however, that starting in the middle of the 3rd century, it was customary in Rome to question catechumens about their faith when they were being baptised. In this context (letter 69.7.1f), Cyprian speaks of *symbolum* (symbol), in other words he already uses the term, which was probably taken from the terminology of the mystery cults (Plutarchus, *Consolatio ad uxorem* 10 [611D]; Clement of Alexandria, *Protrepticus* 15.2; 16.2: 18.1; 22.5; Firmicius Maternus, De errore profanarum religionum 18. For additional evidence, see Riedweg 1987, 83f), for the interrogative creed, which subsequently became the standard designation for the creed in the West (for a history of the term, see Merkt 2001). The same probably applies to Firmilian in a letter to Cyprian (letter 75.10f). The original meaning of *symbolum* was 'watchword' or (secret) 'password', and it will be shown that this understanding of the term corresponded to the liturgical use of the creed for a long time afterwards. It is possible that the *Sacramentarium Gelasianum Vetus* contains a complete version of the old Roman baptismal questions (for evidence, see Kinzig 1999).

It is not clear how the baptismal questions came about. They were probably based on the trinitarian baptismal formula (Matt 28:19; Did 7.1.3). It is also possible that they were formulated as questions in order to emphasise the binding nature of the baptismal act and to highlight its theological significance (cf. Kinzig 1999, 95 with note 337).

The Church got by with these relatively short baptismal questions until well into the 4th century. Today, there is widespread agreement that while there were no declaratory creeds as such in the first three centuries, there were indeed preceding forms thereof, namely the so-called *regulae fidei*, which were flexible summaries of the central doctrines of the Christian faith and served primarily as arguments to counter heterodox teachings without becoming part of the liturgy.

## 2   *The declaratory creed in the preparation for baptism*

This situation changed radically during the course of the 'Constantinian Era' as a result of the massive influx of candidates for baptism. It now became necessary to adapt the baptismal instruction to suit the large number of candidates and to formalise it. The aim was to ensure that candidates for baptism had a minimum level of knowledge about the Christian faith. This minimum level of knowledge was contained in the creed. At the same time, in order to safeguard doctrinal orthodoxy within the Empire, the Church had to make sure that no heterodox beliefs spread throughout the congregations of the imperial Church. (cf. Ritter 1984, 408).

In the West at least, the emerging double rite of *traditio* and *redditio symboli* assumed a central role in this regard. The initiation rite was celebrated as an initiation into the mysteries of the Christian faith.[4] This was done when the symbol was solemnly 'handed over' to the candidate by the bishop on a Sunday before the Baptism (*traditio*). During this ceremony, the bishop explained the individual elements of the creed;[5] the candidates now had to memorise the creed and recite it on the following Sunday (before the baptism) or during the baptismal service itself (so-called *redditio*). The same probably applied to the Our Father as the fundamental Christian prayer. In view of the fact that it did not contain the difficult dogmatic formulae of C and was, therefore, more suitable for the spread of Christianity in a missionary context, the central creed for the catechumenate in the West was the Apostles' Creed. An exception here would appear to be the liturgies influenced by Rome, where preference was actually given to C (cf. Kelly 1972, 346f). It was only at some stage before the tenth century that T was adopted here as the baptismal creed, too—probably as a result of Frankish-German influences (cf. the discussion in Kelly 1972, 426–434; Vokes 1978, 544f). Be that as it may, the introduction of the *traditio* and *redditio symboli* did not lead to the abolition of the old baptismal questions. In fact, these questions were retained—sometimes in very antiquated

---

[4] For what follows, cf. Kretschmar 1970, 238–240; Kelly 1972, 30–40; Kleinheyer 1989, 69f. I am not certain what role was played by the so-called 'arcane discipline' in this regard. For this matter, see Kretschmar 1970, 154–159; Powell 1979; Ritter 1984, 407f; Jacob 1990 (with the critique by Ritter 1994). For the broader context, see also Kippenberg & Stroumsa 1995.

[5] A large number of such *explanationes symboli* dating from Late Antiquity and the Middle Ages have survived.

forms (for more details on these forms, see Kinzig 1999)—which to a
certain extent resulted in a very strange duplication.

Scholars are divided on the question as to whether this liturgical
duplication also existed in the East (Ritter 1984, 407 claims that this
duplication existed in Jerusalem, a fact that is disputed by Kretschmar
1970, 157. Cf. also Kelly 1972, 30–40). There the interrogatory or
declaratory creed remained directly linked to the actual act of baptism
(for what follows, cf. Kleinheyer 1989, 89f). However, as is clearly
illustrated by the appropriate catecheses of Cyril of Jerusalem, John
Chrysostom, Theodore of Mopsuestia, and others, here, too, candidates
received detailed instruction about the content of the creed during the
preparation for Baptism.

During the baptismal ceremony itself, the creed became part of the
new liturgical ritual of the *syntaxis* (for detailed analysis, see Kirsten
1960), which followed the *apotaxis*; at this stage, the creed often took
the form of a declaration rather than that of an interrogation, as
had previously been the case. The (Western) Apostles' Creed did not
succeed in establishing itself here. In fact, a large number of creeds
existed in the second half of the 4th century; starting in the 5th century, these were gradually supplanted by C (for more details, see Kelly
1972, 344–348).

### 3    The creed in the Liturgy of the Eucharist

No less complicated is the situation with regard to the introduction of
the creed in the Liturgy of the Eucharist. The creed is not mentioned
in our oldest liturgical sources. The earliest liturgical evidence[6] is to be
found in Syriac sources. Both in Narsai's *Homily* 17 (Narsai, d. 502; cf.
Connolly 1909, 5f) and in the *Codex Syriacus* 303 from the Bibliotheca
Rahmani, the creed is part of the preanaphoral rites. While the *Codex*
dates from the 8th or 9th century, the liturgy itself is now considered to
date from the 6th century (cf. Taft 1975, 40–42). Our oldest Byzantine
source, Maximus the Confessor's *Mystagogy* (628–630), in which the creed
appears as an element of the preanaphoral rites of Constantinople, is

---

[6] For a possible reference to the creed see *De ecclesiastica hierarchia* 3 (PG 3.425C,
436C–D) of Ps.-Denys the Areopagite, cf. Capelle 1951/1967, 60 note 2; Taft 1975,
49f. See also Heil 1986, 117 with note 40. The description of the rite in Ps.-Denys
does not, however, really fit in with the recitation of a creed, but more to a prayer
covering God's saving works.

not much more recent (*Mystagogia* 18; PG 91.696A–B; cf. Taft 1975, 43–45).

Even though it is a well known fact that great care must be taken regarding *argumenta e silentio* in historic documents, the sources are such that it stands to reason to assume that the symbol was introduced into the Liturgy of the Eucharist at some stage in the 6th century.

Liturgical rites are known to be generally equivocal. Nevertheless, the position of the creed in the Byzantine liturgy is so prominent that at least *one* of its functions can be determined more clearly. In both the Liturgy of St. Basil and the Liturgy of St. John Chrysostom (and virtually throughout the entire Eastern liturgical tradition), it immediately follows the order to close the doors (for detailed treatment, see Jungmann 1962 I, 606–614; Taft 1975, 405–416), thereby marking the beginning of the Liturgy of the Eucharist, from which both unbaptised and the catechumens were excluded. This can only mean that the recitation of the creed (by the entire congregation) was meant to ensure that only baptised people—i.e. full members of the congregation—took part in the Eucharist, thereby preventing the profanisation of the sacred liturgy by the non-initiated. In this case, therefore, the symbol fulfilled the old function of a 'password' or 'watchword' or 'distinctive mark' that was known only to the initiated (in this regard, cf. the overview in Merkt 2001 and above p. 232). Expositors of the creed in Late Antiquity were certainly familiar with this meaning of the creed (cf., for example, Augustine, *Sermo* 214.12; PL 38.1072. Cf. also Rufinus, *Expositio symboli* 2; Isidorus, *De ecclesiasticis officiis* 2,23f PL 83,815–820). It is, incidentally, only at this point and in the declaration of belief in the trinity—which may originally have concluded the Mass of the Catechumens—that there is a clear reference to the trinitarian decrees of the Council of Constantinople in 381.

There is also external evidence of this process (for what follows, cf., among others, Jungmann 1962 I, 598–606; Kelly 1972, 348–357, Taft 1975, 396–425). Theodorus Lector makes reference to it on two occasions. The first reference is taken from an unknown source and reports that the Monophysite Peter the Dyer (Petrus Fullo, *d*.488) introduced the creed into all forms of divine worship (συνάξεις) for the first time at an unidentified point in time (Theodorus Lector, *Historia ecclesiastica*, epit. frag. 429 ed. Hansen 118.27f). If this is indeed the case, he must have done so between his election as Patriarch of Antioch in 471 and his death. Nothing is known about the circumstances surrounding these liturgical changes which, in view of the many amendments to the liturgy made by Peter the Dyer, are not necessarily *a priori* implausible. It is, however, not very likely that this was the origin of the subsequent Byzantine custom (cf. in this regard, among others, Capelle 1951/1967, 61–63).

It is much more probable that the origin lies in a liturgical amendment that Theodorus Lector ascribes to the Monophysite patriarch Timothy I of Constantinople (511–518). According to Theodorus Lector, Timothy decreed that the Creed of the 318 Fathers be recited during every divine worship (σύναξις) in order to defame his Chalcedonian predecessor Macedonius II and to create the impression that Macedonius II had never accepted this creed. Theodore says that before, this creed was only recited once a year, namely during the catechism of the bishop on Good Friday (ibid. fragment 501 ed. Hansen 143.16–19).

According to this source, therefore, Timothy integrated the symbol into the Liturgy of the Mass for denominational reasons or—to be more precise—to draw a distinct line between Monophysitism and the Chalcedonian beliefs of Patriarch Macedonius II. Earlier scholars have sometimes suggested that the creed in question was in fact N because the Monophysites referred to N as the 'unadulterated' faith (for example, Dix 1945, 486). This has, however, since been refuted (cf. the arguments of Kelly 1972, 350f; Taft 1975, 400f).

In the year 518 at any rate, recitation of the creed during Mass was already customary in Constantinople. On 16 July, after the deaths of Patriarch Timothy and Emperor Anastasius I (who was succeeded by the orthodox Christian Justin I), the population of Constantinople succeeded in wresting a proclamation of the canons of Chalcedon from Patriarch John II during a mass in the Great Church. This proclamation took place after the Liturgy of the Word as part of the Liturgy of the Eucharist; 'after the doors had been closed and the holy doctrine (ἅγιον μάθημα = 'the creed', cf. Lampe 1961, s.v. 5, with further references) had been said as usual', the canons of the four Ecumenical Councils were read out (ACO III, 76.18–25 ed. Schwartz). The point at which C is included in the liturgy therefore corresponds to the Liturgy of St. Basil and the Liturgy of St. John Chrysostom, i.e. after the doors had been closed.

However, there is a confusing reference made by John of Biclaro (*c.* 540–*c.* 621) who claims in his continuation of the chronicle of Victor of Tunnuna for the year 567 to 590 (written in 590/91) that Emperor Justin II (565–578) decreed—after the destruction of all anti-Chalcedonian documents—that C be recited as the Chalcedonian symbol by the congregation in all churches prior to the Our Father (MGH.

AA, XI: Chronica minora II, ed. Mommsen 211.13–17. Cf. Capelle 1951/1967, 63: 'La notice est passablement fantaisiste'). In view of the fact that C was already part of the mass at this point in time, this cannot be the case. The identity of the anti-Chalcedonian texts that Justin II had destroyed is also unclear. The only remaining possibility is that John of Biclaro was mistaken in asserting that Justin *introduced* the symbol into the liturgy.

Another conspicuous aspect is the fact that John of Biclaro claims that C was recited before the Our Father (i.e. apparently after the canon), which does not correspond to Eastern practice at all and would instead appear to reflect a Western practice. There is evidence that proves that it was the Visigoth king Reccared who introduced C 'in accordance with the version of the Eastern Churches' into the Sunday liturgy at the Third Council of Toledo in 589 'so that before the Our Father is said, (the creed) is sung by the congregation in a loud voice to ensure that the true faith is openly proclaimed and the people can step forward with a heart cleansed by faith to partake of Christ's flesh and blood' (Council of Toledo 589, can. 2, ed. Vives 1963, 125). This should be seen from an anti-Arian or, better still, from an anti-Homoian point of view, especially because Reccared renounced the Homoian ('Arian') faith at the very same council (for details of the differences between the Homoian and Arian faiths of the Visigoths see the relevant essays in Schäferdiek 1996). What is conspicuous is that here, too, the recitation of the creed and the Our Father immediately precede the Eucharist in that order. The Eastern version is decisive for the wording of C.[7] The purpose of reciting C is to avow the *vera fides*, i.e. the doctrine of the Trinity of the Council of Constantinople in 381. In conjunction with the Our Father, it is used in direct preparation for the receipt of the Eucharist. It must, therefore have followed the canon, and thus come at a different point than in the Eastern liturgies. The information provided by John of Biclaro, who is generally not reliable, is, therefore, directly linked to the decree of the Third Council of Toledo and does not correspond to the Eastern custom, but instead to the Western or—to be more precise—Visigoth practice (cf. Taft 1975, 402f. This position of the creed is also confirmed by manuscripts of the old Spanish/Mozarabic

---

[7] This is probably how the phrase 'secundum formam orientalium ecclesiarum' must be understood. The translation given in Kelly 1972, 351 'according to the use of the Eastern churches' is not accurate. For this version see Gemeinhardt 2002, 51 and 560.

Liturgy of the Mass; cf. Capelle 1951/1967, 64 and, for general treatment, Meyer 1989, 157–159; Gemeinhardt 2002, 52).

The object of moving the creed to a different part of the liturgy in this way is not difficult to comprehend. Once it was no longer necessary to determine whether a member of the congregation had been baptised or not, the primary purpose of the creed was—in view of the controversy over the doctrine of the Trinity in the Visigoth Empire—to verify and confirm the orthodoxy of the faithful by joint recitation. This was particularly effective in those cases where the creed was positioned at an especially central and, as it were, particularly 'sacred' part of the Eucharistic celebration, namely before the Our Father, which was obviously the case in Toledo. Nevertheless, this change in the Mozarabic liturgy was not generally adopted in the Western development of the Mass.

In the Celtic liturgy, on the other hand, the creed was situated—as illustrated by the Stowe Missal (which dates from the late 8th century)—between the reading of the Gospel and the Offertory (cf. Capelle 1951/1967, 66f; for more general treatment, Meyer 1989, 160f). It then appeared at this point of the liturgy on the continent (possibly via England; cf. Capelle 1951/1967, 67–75; Kelly 1972, 353). The first testimony of this comes to us from Walafried Strabo, abbot of Reichenau (*d.* 848). Walafried noted the following:

1. In the celebration of mass, the confession of faith (*symbolum fidei*) followed the Gospel, because the Gospel awakens faith in man's heart, thus leading to justification, whereas the creed proclaims the faith, thus leading to salvation (cf. Rom 10:10).
2. The inclusion of the creed in the liturgy was modelled on the Greek custom.
3. The fact that the Greeks sang the Creed of Constantinople instead of the Nicene Creed during the liturgy, even though N was the older of the two creeds, apparently posed a problem for Walafried. He explained this on the one hand by the fact that C was more suited to being sung than N and on the other by C's greater anti-heretical effect; C had, after all, been composed in the city where the emperors resided and we must add that it had, therefore, greater authority.
4. From Byzantium the custom travelled to Rome.
5. In Gaul and Germania the recitation of the creed only entered into widespread use after the deposition of the heretic Felix of

Urgel (condemned 798, *d.* 818), the major theologian of Spanish adoptionism.

6. Finally, Walafried quotes the already cited provision from the documents of the Third Council of Toledo, albeit altered in such a way 'that the symbol is recited every Sunday (!) in accordance with the use (!) of the Eastern Church' (*De exordiis* 23; MGH Capit. vol. II/1, ed. Krause 499.32–500.6).

These statements must also be treated with a degree of circumspection. The custom did not, for example, travel to Rome where, as it is known, the creed was *not* introduced into the Eucharistic liturgy. There are, however, good reasons to assume that the liturgical use of C really did catch on as a reaction to the condemnation of Felix of Urgel in the Frankish Empire, which is in line with the fundamentally anti-heretical function of the creed (for detailed treatment cf. Capelle 1951/1967, 66–75; Kelly 1972, 355f; Gemeinhardt 2002, 90–107).

This corresponds to the situation described in the minutes of an interview between negotiators of Charlemagne and Pope Leo III in the year 810 (for detailed treatment cf. Gemeinhardt 2002, 160–163 and also Kelly 1972, 354f). This colloquium took place at the behest of the Synod of Aachen (809), which had remitted the problem of the inclusion of the *filioque* to the pope. The minutes show that while Leo III (795–816) had in principle approved the liturgical use of the creed in the Frankish Empire in accordance with the Roman model (for further evidence from the ninth century, see Capelle 1951/1967, 77f and Jungmann 1962 I, 603), it was only read in Rome (by the bishop) for catechetical purposes and not—as was the case with the Franks—sung (by the congregation during Mass). In order to reduce the normative nature of the creed and to find a diplomatic solution to the problem of removing the *filioque* from liturgical use, Leo III now demanded that Charlemagne's palace chapel also conform to the Roman rite (cf. *Ratio Romana de symbolo fidei* 25f MGH.Conc. II/Suppl., vol. II, ed. Willjung 293.30–294.11).

However, Walafried's testimony is more important for another reason: the creed was now no longer considered to be the opening of the Liturgy of the Eucharist, but the conclusion of the Liturgy of the Word. In terms of the theology of liturgy, its position *after the Gospel* instead of *before the preparations of the offerings* is decisive. Here, too, the change in the Church's situation is evident: in the Middle Ages when it was the

Church of the masses, there was no need to verify whether members of the congregation belonged to the Church or not. This 'freed up' the creed for other liturgical functions.

Eventually, the Order of the Mass of the Rhineland (*Rheinischer Messordo*), which originated in St. Gallen, replaced all its predecessors at the turn of the millennium, thereby becoming the 'original form of the order of the Mass, which then remained in force until the reforms of Vatican II for the ordinary parts of the mass.' It was 'adopted not only in the countries to the north of the Alps, but also in Italy and Rome', which 'led to a further harmonisation of the occidental liturgy of the Mass, which was promoted by the Benedictine monks (Cluny), but also particularly by the (Ottonian) Roman-German emperors' (Meyer 1989, 204).

Originally, this ordo of the Mass did not contain a creed! In fact, it was apparently at the request of the last Saxon dynasty emperor, Henry II, who travelled to Rome in 1014 for his coronation, that the creed was integrated into the Mass of the Church of Rome. Berno, abbot of Reichenau (*d.*1048), witnessed the event and reported that when asked why the recitation of the creed was not customary in Rome, the Romans replied that the Roman Church had never sullied itself with the dregs of heresy, but had instead remained stalwart in the purity of the Catholic faith according to Peter's doctrine. This is why, they continued, those who had allowed themselves to become besmirched by heresy needed to sing the creed more often (Berno, *Libellus de quibusdam rebus ad missae officium pertinentibus* 2; PL 142.1060D–1061A paraphrased by Kelly 1972, 357; cf. Capelle 1951/1967, 78; Gemeinhardt 2002, 313–316). Here too, in other words, the symbol was considered primarily a test of orthodoxy.

In the Ordo of the Rhineland, too, however, the creed was now (as it was in the days of Charlemagne) situated after the Gospel or after the homily (which had since been inserted after the Gospel) and before the preparation of the offerings. Here, too, we see the close connection with the Gospel, which explains how the Prayers of Intercession, public confession, and other elements could be inserted into the liturgy after the creed and before the preparation of the offerings (for more details, see Jungmann 1962 I, 614–633. For information on the various different uses of the creed in the Middle Ages see ibid.: 601–606).

Even though the exact details of the introduction of C into the Liturgy of the Eucharist are only partially known, the overall picture is relatively consistent. The evidence suggests that

1) the creed used for instruction of the catechumens and the preparation for baptism 'immigrated' into the Liturgy of the Eucharist in
   the early 6th century, perhaps initially in Constantinople;
2) the recitation of the creed originally preceded the Eucharist and
   constituted the opening of the Liturgy of the Eucharist;
3) the creed fulfilled the function of verifying that the person attend-
   ing the Eucharist had been baptised and was orthodox in his/her
   faith;
4) the creed was later considered the (orthodox) answer of the congregation to the Gospel and its confirmation of the same and, therefore,
   the conclusion of the Liturgy of the Word of God.

This meant that after Constantine, the significance of the creed in the
liturgy changed appreciably: it no longer served to verify the Christian
beliefs of candidates for baptism—as had most frequently been the
case in the first to the third centuries; rather, it was increasingly used
to demonstrate the orthodoxy of the faithful during the celebration of
the liturgy in the context of the conflicts surrounding the doctrine of
the Trinity in the fourth century. The significance of the creed shifted
once again when the creed referred back to the preceding Gospel and
was considered to be the answer of the congregation to this Gospel.
With this shift, the creed's function as a demonstration of orthodoxy
faded.

In his recent address on the occasion of being awarded an honor-
ary doctorate by the University of Bonn, Rowan Williams showed that
the symbol exercised an influence—albeit a hidden one—at a different
point in the Byzantine liturgy, namely in the pre-Sanctus prayer of the
liturgy of St. Basil, which he justifiably interprets as an attempt to build
a dogmatic bridge between the Antiochene tradition of the creed and
the gradually emerging Neo-Nicene faith: 'What appears to emerge
is a careful political strategy in the composition of the prayer: Basil
is elaborating a liturgical formula which is sufficiently deeply rooted
in local theological tradition to be a plausible bridge between Nicene
Christians and the conservative majority in Asia Minor and North
West Syria' (Williams 2004, 42). It is possible that Basil was using older
liturgical models in Antioch.

Even though the, as it were, 'raised dogmatic temperature' of the
pre-Sanctus prayer is immediately conspicuous and can probably be
explained in the manner proposed by Williams, the pre-Sanctus prayer
is certainly a prayer, not a creed. However, one can see the influence on

the liturgy exerted by the creed and the dogmatic debate surrounding it in the fourth century; so much so that the principle *lex orandi—lex credendi* could almost be reversed. The text served to structure the prayer of believers to make it more precise, and to monitor it in terms of dogma.

If, therefore, the pre-Sanctus prayer already contained an adequate number of elements of the confession of faith, the introduction of the creed presented the acute risk of duplication. This is why Robert F. Taft, who has made the most thorough examination of the location and function of the creed in the Liturgy of the Mass, today considers the creed to be completely superfluous. According to Taft, the Eucharistic Prayer suffices as a confession relating, as it does the history of salvation and reminding us of the new covenant (Taft 1975, 404f). However, the question as to the function of the creed in today's Roman Liturgy of the Mass need not be explored in any more detail here.[8] That being said, from a German Protestant point of view, it is important to point out that Martin Luther attached great importance to the *didactic-pedagogical* character of the creed when rearranging the Lutheran liturgy for his *German Mass* of 1526, thereby highlighting once again its old function as part of the preparation for baptism (cf. in particular WA 19.76.1–78.24). It was now recited in the Sunday liturgy between the Gospel and the homily, thereby becoming nothing but the congregation's profession of faith in response to the proclamation of the Word of God which, because of the fact that it was intended to be sung ('We all believe in one God', *Evangelisches Gesangbuch* 183), completely lost its significance as a test of orthodoxy (cf. WA 19.95.1. For general treatment of Luther's stance on the creed, see Barth 1978, 554f; Peters 1991. For the situation of the creed in the *Formula Missae* and the *German Mass*, see Meyer 1965, 85–90 and, more briefly, Imgard Pahl in Meyer 1989, 406f).

---

[8] Today, the creed follows the homily and precedes the prayers of intercession. Three Roman Catholic scholars comment on this fact as follows: Hermann Reifenberg categorises the creed under the heading 'prayer' and speaks of a *Bekenntnisgebet* (confessional prayer). Says Reifenberg: 'These texts are an answer to the word of God insofar as they constitute an expression of agreement with the revelation […]' (1978, 90). Adolf Adam defines the liturgical meaning of the creed as follows: 'Its inner meaning is the "yes" of the congregation to the Word of God that it has heard in the readings and the sermon; however, it is also a song of praise to our saving, triune God' (1985, 144). Hans Bernhard Meyer considers the creed to be 'the response of faith to the proclamation of the word of God', in other words, in a similar way to the *Ordo of the Rhineland*. At the same time, he considers it to be 'to a certain extent a duplicate of the Eucharistic Prayer' (1989, 338).

## II

By recapitulating the fact that the creed served (initially) both as an initiation into the faith and (later more frequently) as a test of orthodoxy and a response to the Gospel,[9] we can relatively quickly answer the question as to whether the creed is a prayer or a hymn.

Is it a *prayer*? First of all, the liturgical genre of the creed suggests that it is not: it contains no salutation or invocation of God and is instead a declaration of the faith of the person reciting the creed. In this regard, the slant of the creed is neither invocative nor doxological—in other words, God is not invoked or praised—but instead affirmative or assertive—in other words, the faith is affirmed.

This is done both by the congregation and in front of the congregation: Christians—namely newly baptised Christians—who recite the creed are professing that they belong to a specific community of Christians for whom the creed is binding. This is accompanied by a double process of distinction: by professing their trinitarian faith, the Christians are distinguishing themselves from *non-Christians*. However, they also state their orthodoxy, thereby distinguishing themselves from *heterodox Christians*, i.e. those Christians who reject the faith in the tri-unity of God.

In the Middle Ages, the creed was primarily the faithful congregation's response to the proclamation of the Word of God. This function is even more evident in the Protestant churches. The Gospel that is read out to the congregation is gratefully received in faith by the congregation. Naturally, the congregation professes this faith before God. However, it does not pray to God. The slant of the creed is more a statement, an assurance, and an understanding reached by the members of the congregation amongst themselves.

Is the creed a *hymn*? The fact that hymns are a form of song and the creed, as an integral part of every mass and every liturgy, has in the past been sung and is sometimes still sung to this day (cf. Brodde 1961, 401–411; Meyer 1965, 88–90), could give rise to the assumption that the creed is a hymn. And who would not agree that the magnificent scoring of the creed in Bach's *Mass in B minor* is decidedly hymn-like? However, in the interest of the clarity of what is done in the liturgy,

---

[9] In this context, I do not consider the use of the Apostles' Creed in the monastic office of the hours. For a summary see, for example, Vokes 1978, 544f.

one must differentiate between different liturgical genres. Quite apart from all other characteristics, if at the very least a rhythmical structure is intrinsic to a hymn (on the hymn, see Walsh & Hannick 1986; Lattke 1991; Thraede 1994; Käppel, Hossfeld, Lattke, & Praßl 2000), the creed, both with regard to its origin and its liturgical use, is no more a song than the Our Father, even though both can indeed be sung,[10] while, for example, the *Te Deum*, which Luther translated into German as 'Herr Gott, dich loben wir' ('Lord God we praise you', *Evangelisches Gesangbuch* 191), was, *from the outset*, conceived as a song of praise.

Moreover, the hymn is a song of praise, the liturgical 'drive' of which is directed towards heaven: it is a song of thanks to *God*. It does not require a congregation. This character is inherent in the *Te Deum*, but not in the creed.

In short, I am sceptical about swiftly declaring the creed to be either a prayer or a hymn. There is also a danger, then, that a text, the primary intention of which is to help us memorise the key doctrines of the Christian faith, becomes an unchangeable object of faith itself.

## LITERATURE

Adam, A., *Grundriß der Liturgie*, Freiburg—Basel—Wien 1985.
Barth, H.-M., 'Apostolisches Glaubensbekenntnis, II. Reformations- und Neuzeit', *TRE* 3 (1978).
Brightman, F.E., *Liturgies Eastern and Western; Being the Texts Original or Translated of the Principal Liturgies of the Church* [vol. I], Oxford 1896.
Brodde, O., 'Evangelische Choralkunde (Der gregorianische Choral im evangelischen Gottesdienst)', *Leit.* 4 (1961).
Capelle, B., 'L'introduction du symbole à la messe', in: *Mélanges J. de Ghellinck* [vol. 2], Gembloux 1951 = id., *Travaux liturgiques de doctrine et d'histoire* [vol. 3]; *Histoire; Varia—L'assomption*, Louvain 1967.
Connolly, R.H., *The Liturgical Homilies of Narsai Translated into English with an Inroduction* (TSt 8), Cambridge 1909.
Dix, G., *The Shape of the Liturgy*, London 2nd ed. 1945.
*Evangelisches Gottesdienstbuch; Agende für die Evangelische Kirche der Union und für die Vereinigte Evangelisch-Lutherische Kirche Deutschlands*, Berlin 2nd ed. 2001.
Finkel, A., 'Glaubensbekenntnis(se), III. Judentum', *TRE* 13 (1984).
Fuhrer, Th., *Augustinus* (Klassische Philologie kompakt), Darmstadt 2004.
Gardet, L., 'Īmān', *EI* 3 (2nd ed. 1971).
Gemeinhardt, P., *Die Filioque-Kontroverse zwischen Ost- und Westkirche im Frühmittelalter* (AKG 82), Berlin—New York 2002.

---

[10] Hans Bernhard Meyer has quite rightly said that the creed is 'a profession of faith that is formulated in sentences', which does not have 'the character of a hymn, which is closely related to music, such as the Gloria or the Sanctus' (1965, 89).

Gimaret, D., 'Shahāda', *EI* 9 (2nd ed. 1997).

Heil, G., *Ps.-Dionysius Areopagita. Über die himmlische Hierarchie; Über die kirchliche Hierarchie* (BGL 22), Stuttgart 1986.

Heine, P., 'Glaubensbekenntnis', in: A.T. Khoury, L. Hagemann, & P. Heine (eds), *Islam-Lexikon* [vol. 2], Freiburg 1999.

Jacob, C., *'Arkandisziplin', Allegorese, Mystagogie; Ein neuer Zugang zur Theologie des Ambrosius von Mailand* (Theoph. 32/AM.T 32), Frankfurt/Main 1990.

Jungmann, J.A., *Missarum sollemnia; Eine genetische Erklärung der römischen Messe* [2 vols], Wien etc. 5th ed. 1962.

Kalb, F., *Grundriß der Liturgik; Eine Einführung in die Geschichte, Grundsätze und Ordnungen des lutherischen Gottesdienstes*, München 2nd ed. 1982.

Käppel, L.; F.-L. Hossfeld, M. Lattke, & F.K. Praßl, 'Hymnus' *RGG* 3 (4th ed. 2000).

Kelly, J.N.D., *Early Christian Creeds*, London 3rd ed. 1972.

Kinzig, W., '"... *natum et passum* etc." Zur Geschichte der Tauffragen in der lateinischen Kirche bis zu Luther', in: id., C. Markschies, & M. Vinzent, *Tauffragen und Bekenntnis; Studien zur sogenannten 'Traditio Apostolica', zu den 'Interrogationes de fide' und zum 'Römischen Glaubensbekenntnis'* (AKG 74), Berlin—New York 1999.

———, & M. Vinzent, 'Recent Research on the Origin of the Creed', *JThS* 50 (1999).

Kippenberg, H.G. & G.G. Stroumsa (eds), *Secrecy and Concealment; Studies in the History of Mediterranean and Near Eastern Religions* (SHR 65), Leiden etc. 1995.

Kirsten, H., *Die Taufabsage; Eine Untersuchung zu Gestalt und Geschichte der Taufe nach den altkirchlichen Taufliturgien*, Berlin 1960.

Kleinheyer, B., *Sakramentliche Feiern I; Die Feiern der Eingliederung in die Kirche* (GDK 7,1), Regensburg 1989.

Kretschmar, G., 'Die Geschichte des Taufgottesdienstes in der alten Kirche', *Leit.* 5 (1970).

Lampe, G.W.H., *A Patristic Greek Lexicon*, Oxford 1961.

Lanczkowski, G., 'Glaubensbekenntnis(se), I. Religionsgeschichtlich', *TRE* 13 (1984).

Lattke, M., *Hymnus; Materialien zu einer Geschichte der antiken Hymnologie* (NTOA 19), Freiburg, Schweiz—Göttingen 1991.

Mahrenholz, C., *Kompendium der Liturgik*, Kassel 1963.

Mayer, C., 'Confessio. Confiteri', *AugL* 1 (1986–1994).

Merkt, A., 'Symbolum; Historische Bedeutung und patristische Deutung des Bekenntnisnamens', *RQS* 96 (2001).

Meyer, H.B., *Luther und die Messe; Eine liturgiewissenschaftliche Untersuchung über das Verhältnis Luthers zum Meßwesen des späten Mittelalters* (KKTS 11), Paderborn 1965.

———, *Eucharistie; Geschichte, Theologie, Pastoral* (GDK 4), Regensburg 1989.

Meyer-Blanck, M., *Liturgie und Liturgik; Der Evangelische Gottesdienst aus Quellentexten erklärt* (TB 97), Gütersloh 2001.

Müller, K.F., 'Das Ordinarium Missae', *Leit.* 5 (1955).

Müller, Th., *Evangelischer Gottesdienst; Liturgische Vielfalt im religiösen und gesellschaftlichen Umfeld*, Stuttgart etc. 1993.

Pahl, I., 'Die Feier des Abendmahls in den Kirchen der Reformation', in: see Meyer 1989.

Peters, A. [ed. by G. Seebaß], *Der Glaube; Das Apostolikum* (Kommentar zu Luthers Katechismus, vol. 2), Göttingen 1991.

Powell, D., 'Arkandisziplin', *TRE* 4 (1979).

Reifenberg, H., *Fundamentalliturgie; Grundelemente des christlichen Gottesdienstes* [vol. 2]; *Wesen—Gestalt—Vollzug*, Klosterneuburg 1978.

Riedweg, C., *Mysterienterminologie bei Platon, Philon und Klemens von Alexandrien* (UALG 26), Berlin/New York 1987.

Ritter, A.M., 'Glaubensbekenntnis(se), V. Alte Kirche', *TRE* 13 (1984).

———, Review of Jacob 1990, *ThLZ* 119 (1994).

Schäferdiek, K. [ed. by W.A. Löhr & H.C. Brennecke], *Schwellenzeit; Beiträge zur Geschichte des Christentums in Spätantike und Frühmittelalter* (AKG 64), Berlin—New York 1996.

Taft, R.F., *The Great Entrance; A History of the Transfer of Gifts and other Preanaphoral Rites of the Liturgy of St. John Chrysostom* (OCA 200), Rom 1975.

Thraede, K., 'Hymnus I', *RAC* 16 (1994).

Vinzent, M., *Der Ursprung des Apostolikums im Urteil der kritischen Forschung* (FKDG 89), Göttingen 2006.

Vives, J., *Concilios visigóticos e hispano-romanos* (España Cristiana, Textos vol. 1). Barcelona—Madrid 1963.

Vokes, F.E., 'Apostolisches Glaubensbekenntnis, I. Alte Kirche und Mittelalter', *TRE* 3 (1978).

Volp, R., *Liturgik; Die Kunst, Gott zu feiern* [vol. 2]; *Theorien und Gestaltung*, Gütersloh 1994.

Walsh, P.G. & C. Hannick, 'Hymnen', *TRE* 15 (1986).

Williams, R.D., 'Creed and Eucharist', in: Evangelisch-Theologische Fakultät der Rheinischen Friedrich-Wilhelms-Universität (ed.), *Gratiarum actio; Reden anlässlich der Ehrenpromotion des Erzbischofs von Canterbury, The Most Revd Dr Rowan Douglas Williams*, Rheinbach 2004.

PART FOUR

RABBINIC JUDAISM AND CHRISTIANITY

# THE ANCESTORS' PRAYERS FOR THE SALVATION OF ISRAEL IN EARLY RABBINIC THOUGHT

*Uri Ehrlich*
Ben Gurion University of the Negev, Israel

The patriarchs—Abraham, Isaac, and Jacob—are key figures in the world of rabbinic prayer.[1] In the homiletical treatment of their prayers the rabbis not only express admiration for, and expatiate on, the biblical descriptions, they also ascribe additional prayer-acts to the patriarchs (e.g., Yeb 64a; GenR 39:11; NumR 18:5). One tradition identifies the basis for the thrice-daily statutory recitation of the Prayer, namely, the Amidah, in the actions of the patriarchs:

> Rabbi Joshua ben Levi said: They learned the (obligation to recite the three daily) prayers (תפילות) from the (actions of the) patriarchs. (They derived the obligation to recite) the Morning Prayer (תפילת השחר) from (the action of) our forefather Abraham...(They derived the obligation to recite) the Afternoon Prayer (תפילת המנחה) (from the action of) our forefather Isaac...(They derived the obligation to recite) the Evening Prayer (תפילת הערב), from (the action of) our forefather Jacob...(p.Ber 4:1 7a–b; Neusner trans.; see Ber 26b and parallels).

Allusions to the prayers of the patriarchs and of other prominent figures from the past were an established feature of fast-day prayers (mTaan 2:4). Several sources treat the invocation of patriarchal merit as an important precondition for prayers being answered in times of crisis; for example, the following statement from the Babylonian Talmud: 'When Israel sinned in the wilderness, Moses stood before the Holy One, blessed be he, and uttered many prayers and supplications before him, but he was not answered. Yet when he exclaimed, "Remember Abraham, Isaac, and Israel thy servants!" (Exod 32:13) he was immediately answered' (Shab 30a; Soncino trans.).[2]

---

[1] I thank Dr. Moshe Lavie for reading and commenting on a draft of this article. Dena Ordan translated the article. On the centrality of references to the patriarchs in Second Temple prayer, see Bar-Ilan 1987, 125ff.

[2] In QohR 2:16 we find the same idea expressed as follows: כיון דישראל נכנסין לידי צרה הן אומרים 'זכור לאברהם ליצחק ולישראל עבדיך'.

In the following remarks I explore the amplification and refinement of the concept of 'patriarchal merit' in the world of early rabbinic prayer. A number of sources introduce an additional component to the patriarchal role, namely, that the patriarchs 'who lie in the dust' continue to pray to God for the redemption of Israel after their deaths.

This notion already appears in several tannaitic sources. For example, in the source cited below, Rabbi Eleazar ha-Moda'i associates the granting of manna to the Israelites in the desert with the prayers of the forefathers:

> 'And When the Layer of Dew Was Gone Up.' Behold Scripture has taught you how the manna used to come down for Israel... 'scalelike (מחוספס),' teaches that it was like scales, 'as the hoarfrost (ככפור)' teaches that it came down upon the ground like sleet—these are the words of R. Joshua. R. Eleazar of Modi'im says: 'And when the layer of dew was gone up (ותעל שכבת הטל)' means when the prayer of our forefathers who lay in the earth went up (עלתה תפילתן של אבותינו שהיו שוכבים בעפר על הארץ).... 'As a pardon' (kekippur; ככפור): God stretched out His hand, as it were, and accepted the prayer of our forefathers who lay in the earth (ונטל את תפלתם של אבותינו שהיו שוכבים על הארץ), and in return sent down the manna for Israel, in accordance with what is said in the passage: 'I have found a ransom (מצאתי כופר; Job 33:24)' (Mek vayassa' L. 2:111–113; slightly revised; cf. the parallel in Mek de-R. Simeon bar-Yoḥai, 16:14 110).

This text juxtaposes two distinct approaches: that of Rabbi Joshua, who adheres closely to the plain meaning of the text, and of Rabbi Eleazar ha-Moda'i, who proposes a far-ranging exegesis of the verses (Boyarin 1986, 659–666; Kahana 1999, 289–320). Based on the shared root שכ"ב, Rabbi Eleazar first links שכבת הטל ('the layer of dew') and the patriarchs השוכבים בעפר ('who lie in the dust'), explaining the lifting of the dew metaphorically as the ascent of the 'prayers of our forefathers' and reiterating this interpretation in his exegesis of ככפור. This exegetical ideology is consistent with Rabbi Eleazar's principled doctrine endowing 'ancestral merit' with centrality in the special relationship between God and the Israelites, also found elsewhere in opposition to Rabbi Joshua's approach.[3]

---

[3] For a discussion of the dispute between Rabbi Joshua and Rabbi Eleazar ha-Moda'i regarding the topic of 'patriarchal merit', see Urbach 1975, 496–497. For a detailed commentary on the passage from the Mekilta, see Boyarin 1986, 661–662. Cf. Naeh and Shemesh 1995, 338 and n. 20.

Another tannaitic source portrays Moses as beseeching first Eleazar and then the patriarchs to pray for him to be allowed to enter the land of Israel:

> Rabbi Ḥanina bar Idi said: At that moment Moses fell at Eleazar's feet and said to him, Eleazar, my son, request mercy for me that I may enter the land of Israel as I did for your father Aaron, as Scripture states: 'Moreover, the Lord was angry enough with Aaron to have destroyed him (Deut 9:20)'. Eleazar answered Moses: You, the backer of all Israel, seek a sponsor? You, the staff of all Israel, seek support? At that juncture Moses entreated the forefathers to beg for mercy for him (באותה שעה היה משה מתחנן כנגד אבות העולם לבקש עליו רחמים). The holy one, blessed be he, said to him: Moses, Moses, have I not said, 'Never speak to Me of this matter again! (3:26)'. To what lengths will you go in your begging? I have decreed that you will not enter the land of Israel, either in your lifetime or after your death: 'The time is drawing near for you to die (31:14)' (Midr Tann; H. 179).[4]

Moses' direct entreaties having proven ineffective, according to this midrash he elects another option, well-documented in Scripture, that of asking a righteous person to pray for him (see Gen 25:21; 1 Sam 7:8–9; Jer 42:3–4). To that end, Moses first entreats Eleazar, presenting as his rationale his identical action on behalf of Eleazar's father Aaron. In refusing Moses' request, Eleazar notes the futility of additional prayers if Moses' prayers themselves were not answered. At this point Moses seeks a new conduit of prayer and implores the forefathers to pray for him. For the homilist, the prayers of the patriarchs were evidently perceived as being on a higher level than those of the living righteous. Indirect support for this understanding comes from the continuation of the midrash, which omits the patriarchs' response, and immediately continues with the divine reprimand of Moses. Reading between the lines, I submit that, as structured, the midrash conveys the homilist's belief that, had the patriarchs prayed for Moses, their prayers would indeed have been efficacious.

A greater number of amoraic sources reflect and develop new aspects of the notion that the ancestors pray for the salvation of Israel (e.g.,

---

[4] It is well known that, with the exception of a few fragments, the original Midr Tann has not survived. Hoffman's restorations are based on those sections of the MHG, which, in his opinion, match the lost portions. The first part of the text cited here is undoubtedly tannaitic, as it has a partial parallel in Mek, Amalek (Be-shalaḥ) 2 (Horowitz-Rabin 183). The second part of the homily, treating patriarchal prayer, has no parallel there.

LevR 30:3; EsthR 7:13; ExodR 15:26). Perhaps the most famous source, which itself underwent further midrashic development, is the one treating the prayers of the matriarch Rachel for the redemption of Israel:

> 'And Rachel died and was buried on the road to Ephrath (Gen 35:19).' What was Jacob's reason for burying Rachel on the road to Ephrath? Jacob foresaw that the exiles would pass by this place, therefore he buried her there so that she might pray for mercy for them. As it is written, 'A cry is heard in Ramah...Rachel weeping for her children.... Thus said the Lord: Restrain your voice from weeping...and there is hope for your future,' (Jer. 31:15f) etc. (GenR 82:10; Theodor-Albeck 988; Soncino trans.; slightly revised).

This midrash introduces a number of innovations with respect to the tannaitic notion of our theme. First of all, additional figures—in this case, Rachel—not just the three patriarchs, can pray for Israel. Later versions of this midrash hold up Rachel's prayer as the paradigm for an acceptable entreaty, in contrast to the rejected prayers of the patriarchs and of Moses (see LamR petiḥta 24, 25–28; PesR, Ish-Shalom, ba-yom ha-shemini 11b). This amplification is not surprising, as the underlying notion of ancestral merit for the prayers of the ancestors was not restricted to the patriarchs alone (Urbach 1975, 496ff). A second innovation is the bond posited between the living and the burial place of the dead. Unlike the patriarchs in the homily in the Mekhilta, Rachel does not simply pray for Israel. Nor does she pray in response to some abstract request, akin to the one Moses is portrayed as addressing to the patriarchs in Midrash Tannaim. She awakens to the task of entreating mercy for Israel precisely when the Israelites pass by her terrestrial burial place on the road to Efrat. This is the first example in rabbinic literature of a link between the ongoing spiritual connection that motivates the patriarchs to pray for their descendants and the physical burial place of the Israelite ancestors. Although Rachel's tomb is not yet identified here as a place of prayer, but a small leap separates this source from the custom of visiting ancestral graves in order to invoke the ancestors' prayers for Israel.

Indeed, from the late third century, several sources testify to a custom of turning to ancestral graves and to gravesites in general in order to implore the dead to pray for Israel, a custom primarily associated with the cave of Machpelah—the burial place of the patriarchs and matriarchs in Hebron (Gen 23; 49:29–31):

> 'And they went up by the South and he came unto Hebron (ויעלו בנגב ויבא עד חברון; Num 13:22)'. It should have read 'and they came (ויבאו)!'

> Raba said: It teaches that Caleb held aloof from the plan of the spies and went and prostrated himself upon the graves of the patriarchs (והלך ונשטח על קברי אבות), saying to them, 'My fathers, pray on my behalf that I may be delivered from the plan of the spies' (Sot 34b; Soncino trans.).

Based on the unexpected use of the singular in the verse, Raba deduces that Caleb distanced himself from the main faction of the spies and went to the cave of Machpelah to ask the patriarchs to pray on his behalf. Although Raba's remarks can be understood as a conceptual development of the existing notion of ancestral prayers as presented here, they perhaps also reflect familiarity on Raba's part with an actual practice of praying at the patriarchs' graves in Hebron.

The following source unequivocally testifies to a custom of praying at gravesites for the purpose of having the dead entreat mercy for the living:

> Why do they go to the cemetery? R. Levi b. Laḥma and R. Ḥama b. Ḥanina differ as to the reason. The one maintains that it signifies: We are before thee as dead, while according to the other it is in order that the departed ones should pray for mercy in our behalf. What practical difference is there? The difference arises with regard to non-Jewish cemeteries (Taan 16a; Malter 1967, 222–223).

In this Babylonian source two late third-century Palestinian amoraim dispute the underlying rationale for the custom of praying in cemeteries on fast days. The first opinion cites a moral reason: proximity to the dead, even to the graves of non-Jews, evokes feelings of humility. The second vests the custom of visiting cemeteries in a desire to have the dead pray for Israel in troubled times.[5] Note that, although both views are attributed to Palestinian amoraim, the second opinion is missing from the parallel in the Palestinian Talmud (p.Taan 2:10 65a), and the ascription of the purpose of the cemetery visit to asking the dead to pray for Israel is found only in the Babylonian Talmud. This perhaps reflects a further development of this conception, one in which the appeal to the dead inheres not in their special role in Jewish history but rather in their being distant from the world of the living, sinless, and therefore somewhat closer to the celestial regions (t.Yom 4:9, Lieberman 252–253; Glick 1977, 96–97). In any event, I find it more likely that the appeal in question is to the meritorious dead rather than to the dead in general. According to the existing documentation,

---

[5] On the cemetery as a communication center, see Bar-Levav 2002, 27*–33*.

the custom of visiting the graves of the patriarchs and of righteous
individuals during the rabbinic period was of limited distribution during the rabbinic period, but underwent significant development during
the Middle Ages (Reiner 1988).

The final, amoraic, source considered here is grounded in a presumed
link between the prayers of the patriarchs and the institutionalized
Jewish statutory prayer:

> Elijah used to frequent Rabbi's academy. One day—it was New Moon—he
> was waiting for him, but he failed to come. Said he to him (the next day):
> 'Why did you delay?'—He replied: '(I had to wait) until I woke Abraham,
> washed his hands, and he prayed and I put him to rest again; likewise to
> Isaac and Jacob.' 'But why not awake them together?'—'I feared that they
> would become strong in prayer and bring the Messiah before his time.'
> 'And is their like to be found in this world? (ויש דוגמתן בעולם הזה)' he
> asked.—'There is, R. Hiyya and his sons,' he replied. Thereupon Rabbi
> proclaimed a fast, and R. Hiyya and his sons were bidden to descend
> (to the reading desk). As he (R. Hiyya) exclaimed, 'He causes the wind
> to blow (משיב הרוח)', a wind blew; he proceeded, 'he causes the rain to
> descend (מוריד הגשם)', whereat the rain descended. When he was about to
> say, 'He quickens the dead (מחיה המתים),' the universe trembled, (and) in
> heaven it was asked, 'Who has revealed our secret to the world?' 'Elijah,'
> they replied. Elijah was therefore brought and smitten with sixty flaming
> lashes; so he went, disguised himself as a fiery bear, entered amongst and
> scattered them (BM 85b; Soncino trans., slightly revised).

Patriarchal prayer in this anecdote is patterned on the halakhot govern-
ing the statutory prayers. As is required in preparation for the normative
prayer, Elijah washes the patriarchs' hands and stands them upright. The
homilist also depicts Elijah as conversant with the then current practice
of having three prayer leaders during times of terrible distress.[6] That
is why Elijah makes certain that the patriarchs do not pray in unison.
In addition, the homilist was clearly inspired by the Amidah prayer,
first and foremost, the *avot* and the *gevurot* benedictions. This emerges
explicitly in the second part of the story, which describes Rabbi Ḥiyya
and his sons reciting the formulas of the gevurot benediction (Ehrlich
2004, 565–566). Pervading the first part of the story is the opening
formula of the avot benediction: בא"י אלהינו ואלהי אבותינו אלהי אברהם
אלהי יצחק ואלהי יעקב ('Praised are You, Lord our God and God of our

---

[6] For an attestation to this practice, see, for example: מכאן אמרו אין פוחתין משלשה
בני אדם עוברין לפני התיבה בתענית צבור (Mek Amalek 1 L. 146). On this practice and
its signification, see Blidstein 1971, 72–73.

fathers, God of Abraham, God of Isaac, and God of Jacob'). Perhaps exegesis of the language of the Amidah, which is not content with the general salutation 'God of our fathers', but addresses each patriarch individually in turn, inspired the motif of waking the patriarchs for prayer in succession (Rave 1999, 39–40).

I submit, however, that the storyteller makes an even more radical assumption, namely, one of parity between the formulas of prayer in the celestial and terrestrial spheres. The anecdote presumes an analogous relationship between above and below, and, moreover, that the lower region can model itself on the upper one. This analogy underlies the appointment of Rabbi Ḥiyya and his sons to lead the prayers jointly, as the patriarchs could have but were prevented from doing. Rabbi Ḥiyya and his sons unmistakably recite the normative Amidah prayer. The storyteller invites the reader of the anecdote to imaginatively envision the analogy between the upper and lower regions and to picture the patriarchs reciting the Amidah prayer, just as Rabbi Judah the Prince appointed prayer leaders to do so on earth. This extension of the analogy is not surprising; after all, our discussion opened with a tradition attributing the setting of the recitation of the Amidah to the patriarchs.

Even this brief consideration demonstrates the significant role the ancestors of Israel play in the rabbinic world of prayer. One offshoot of this function is an explicit or implicit appeal to the notion of ancestral merit when entreating divine mercy. The sources cited here show that ancestral merit is not simply accounted to Israel's credit when they approach God in judgment, but also that 'ancestral responsibility' for their descendants is an ongoing process, even after the ancestors' death. The ancestors are envisioned as continuing to pray for the redemption of Israel throughout the generations, until its final realization. First developed in the context of sporadic individual and public prayer in times of trouble, at a later stage this concept became institutionalized on special occasions, and eventually on a daily basis. The traces of this process are particularly distinct in the Babylonian Talmud.

## LITERATURE

Bar-Ilan, M., *The Mysteries of Jewish Prayer and Hekhalot*, Ramat Gan 1987 [Hebrew].
Bar-Levav, A., 'We Are Where We Are Not: The Cemetery in Jewish Culture', *JewSt* 41 (2002) English section.
Blidstein, G., 'Sheliach Tzibbur: Historical and Phenomenological Observations', *Tradition* 12 (1971).

Boyarin, D., 'Analogy vs. Anomaly in Midrashic Hermeneutic: Tractates Wayyasa and Amaleq in the Mekilta', *JAOS* 106 (1986).

Ehrlich, U., 'An Early Version of the *Gevurot, Kedushat ha-Shem*, and *Da'at* Blessings According to a New Text from a Palestinian Siddur', *Tarb.* 73 (2004) [Hebrew].

Glick, S., *Light Has Dawned; The Relation between Marriage and Mourning Customs in Jewish Tradition*, Efrat 1997 [Hebrew].

Kahana, M.I., *The Two Mekhiltot on the Amalek Portion*, Jerusalem 1999 [Hebrew].

Malter, Z. (ed.), *The Treatise Ta'anit of the Babylonian Talmud*, Philadelphia 1967.

Naeh, S. & A. Shemesh, 'The Manna Story and the Time of the Morning Prayer', *Tarb.* 64 (1995) [Hebrew].

Rave, I., '*Shome'a Tefillah*: He Who Hears Our Prayer', *Jerusalem Studies in Hebrew Literature* 17 (1999) [Hebrew].

Reiner, E., *Pilgrims and Pilgrimage to Eretz Yisrael, 1099–1517* [Ph.D. diss.], Hebrew University, Jerusalem 1988 [Hebrew].

Urbach, E.E., *The Sages; Their Concepts and Beliefs*, Jerusalem 1975.

# KING SOLOMON AND PSALMS 72 AND 24 IN THE DEBATE BETWEEN JEWS AND CHRISTIANS

*Marcel Poorthuis*
Tilburg University, The Netherlands

Traditional scholarship holds it that Christianity has derived considerably from Judaism to mold its liturgy, its exegesis of Scripture, its community, ministry and sacraments. During the past decade, this model of one-sided dependence of Christianity upon Judaism had been challenged and refined. General statements have given way to meticulous research into Jewish and Christian documents in order to obtain a variety of refined models, adapted to the circumstances. In this contribution, I would like to investigate whether the exegesis of Psalms 72 and 24 can contribute to this refined model of interaction between Judaism and Christianity. Both Psalms have been applied to Solomon in Judaism and have been subjected to a Christological interpretation in Christianity. Ps 72 is even one of the central Psalms in both religions and its Messianic flavor made it a bone of contention between the two, comparable with the even more famous Ps 110. In addition, this Psalm is quoted in the oldest layers of post-Biblical Christian literature, i.e. Justin Martyr and Tertullian. The most important reason for choosing Ps 72, however, is Justin's explicit mention of a Jewish interpretation in his Dialogue with Trypho. Whether this dialogue constitutes a genuine dialogue or not and whether Trypho corresponds to a Jewish spokesman similar to those mentioned in rabbinic literature, are questions we will have to deal with. Ps 24 is no less important for our inquiry into the interdependence of Judaism and Christianity. The application of this Psalm to Christ's descent into the netherworld or to his ascension can be attested as early as the second century C.E. In Judaism, this Psalm has been extensively debated in rabbinic literature, again applied to king Solomon. Hence it seems that both in their Messianic/Christological interpretations and in their application to king Solomon, these two Psalms are appropriate for joint comparison. The relevance of this choice is enhanced by the fact that the figure of Solomon has not yet been given its due in research on Messianism in Judaism and Christianity.

Nonetheless, the methodological problems in such a comparison are considerable.

Firstly, there is the problem of the dating of the rabbinic sources, which is notoriously difficult. Suffice it to say that the date of redaction of a given midrash collection such as Midrash Tehillim does not constitute the date of each single midrash quoted in it, but only the terminus ante quem. The redaction process at work in such midrashic collections might be more important than has been realized in the past. In addition, we will have to deal with the interpretations of the two Psalms as quoted in both talmuds and the paraphrase of it in the targum.

Another methodological problem is the kind of Judaism presented in the Christian sources, such as Justin Martyr's Dialogue with Trypho, which treats Ps 72 quite extensively. Leaving unresolved for the moment, the issue of whether Justin's dialogue really contains an account of a genuine debate with a Jew named Trypho (the identification of this Trypho with Rabbi Tarfon being abandoned), or that Justin here and there molded the Jewish protagonist according to his rhetorical needs, it is in any case evident that Justin did not wholly fabricate Trypho's Judaism (Remus 1986, 74–75).[1] However, Trypho's Judaism, although closer to rabbinic Judaism than to Philo, should not be equated with the latter, as earlier scholars such as Goldfahn thought (1873; 49–60, 104–115, 145–153, 194–202, 257–269), be it only because rabbinic sources are generally later than the Dialogue. Justin did not know Hebrew, according to Rokéah, but this may apply even to Philo as well and does not say much about Justin's knowledge of Judaism as such. The picture of early Judaism, when perceived from the perspective of rabbinic literature, is much more Hebraicizing than appears to be the reality, even in the land of Palestine.

The way rabbinic literature deals with Christian opponents by making their opinions anonymous poses still another methodological problem. It is hard to prove that rabbinic texts actually react upon Christian opinions in such cases. Nevertheless, we will develop some criteria that allow us to ascertain such rabbinic reactions upon Christian opinions with a high probability.

---

[1] Rokéah (2002, 22–43), surveying the evidence, demonstrates that Philo is not the source for Justin's knowledge of Judaism, but tannaitic exegesis is, although communicated orally.

First we will deal with Justin's treatment of Ps 72 (chapter 1), to be followed by the Jewish interpretations of the same Psalm up to the time of Justin (ch. 2).

The influence of Christian interpretations of the Psalm from the second century onward will be traced in Jewish literature from that period on (ch. 3). Extolling the figure of king Solomon appears to be the major exegetical key to this Psalm on the Jewish side.

Finally, we deal with the Christian application of Ps 24 to Christ and the subsequent Jewish application of this Psalm to king Solomon as well, but in a highly derogatory way (ch. 4). This latter device is explained by us as a clear indication of Christian influence upon Jewish exegesis.

## 1    The Context of Justin's Dealing with Psalm 72

In chapter 34 of Justin's Dialogue with Trypho, Justin debates Ps 72 after dealing with the book of Daniel and Ps 110 in the previous paragraphs. Trypho's objection that Jesus' fate does not correspond to the glorious image of the coming of the Son of Man on the clouds of heaven is countered by Justin by pointing to a twofold coming: one in humility, as described by Isaiah as the Suffering Servant, the other in glory. Ps 110 then is taken by Trypho to refer to king Hezekiah. Justin takes this historicizing approach to this Psalm to the effect that the Psalm cannot refer to a future Messianic figure at all, according to Trypho. Curiously, this does not need to be the case in view of contemporaneous Jewish exegesis. Trypho may have been acquainted with the significance of king Hezekiah in contemporary Jewish Messianic expectations. King Hezekiah removed idolatry from Israel (2 Kgs 18:3–4) and waged wars for Israel against its enemy Sanherib (2 Kgs 19:35). In rabbinic perspective, this king, full of justice and humility, spread knowledge of the Torah and hence the prophecies of Isaiah about "a child born to us" (Isa 9:5), would be applicable to him. According to a talmudic dictum, if king Hezekiah had sung Psalms like David, he would have been the Messiah (Sanh 94a). Although David did sing Psalms, he is not the Messiah either, one may object. Both kings are figures from the past. It seems, however, that this dictum merges the past king Hezekiah with the future Messiah, such as happened to David himself. The Messiah is both the 'son of David', someone like David, or David himself (cf. Sanh 98b). In this respect, the way the Jew Trypho (in

Justin's rendering!) points to Hezekiah as a figure from the past does not reflect rabbinic usage of Biblical persons in Messianic expectations. There, Jewish interpretations of king Hezekiah cannot be limited to a historical figure in the past, on the contrary: the famous dictum of rabbi Johanan: 'prepare a seat for Hezekiah, the king of Judah, who is coming' (Ber 28b), clearly refers to a future coming of king Hezekiah! We do not need to enter into the debate whether the name Hezekiah might be a veiled reference to contemporary figures such as rabbi Judah Hanasi (Aberbach 1983/84, 353–371; in addition there is the messianic name of Menachem ben Hezekiah). Suffice it to say that Hezekiah's role cannot be limited to a historical person of the past in rabbinic interpretations. Although Justin takes Trypho's interpretation to be precisely such a historical interpretation, it is on the contrary far more probable that the name of Hezekiah could serve as a model for contemporary Messianic interpretations as well.

Although it is clear that Trypho meant to refer to the past king Hezekiah as the key to Ps 110, we may conclude that Jewish interpretations of Hezekiah are not restricted to a mere historical reference, but may still contain Messianic overtones and contemporary expectations.

Justin counters that king Hezekiah was not a priest and that Jesus should be considered the everlasting priest of the uncircumcised. In addition, the twofold appearance, one in humility, one exalted, is referred to at the end of Ps 110.

A little further, king Hezekiah is again the subject of the debate. In chapter 66, (resuming the debate from chapter 43), the well-known passage from Isa 7:14: 'See, a young woman shall conceive and give birth to a son', is the bone of contention. According to Trypho, this verse refers to king Hezekiah, whereas Justin, rendering the young woman (*neanis*) as virgin (*parthenos*), sees a reference to Christ.

Let us now turn to Ps 72, where we will encounter a similar debate, this time about king Solomon.

In ch. 34, Justin deals with Ps 72 for the first time. A debate takes place similar to the one about Hezekiah, but now regarding the person of king Solomon, to whom reference is made at the heading of the Psalm. The Hebrew *lishelomo*, can mean 'by Solomon', or 'for Solomon'. Against attributing the Psalm to Solomon's authorship would argue the fact that the Psalm ends with the statement: 'Here the Psalms of David, son of Jesse, end'. The LXX (Ps 71) translates *eis Solomon*, which should be interpreted as: 'for Solomon', implicitly assuming David's authorship. Both Justin and Trypho agree with that: David is the author of the Psalm (Dialogue 34). Justin renders Trypho's opinion later on as follows: 'The words of David quoted earlier [i.e. Ps 72], which you foolishly affirm, refer to Solomon' (Dialogue 64). Apparently, Justin agrees with Trypho that the superscription does not indicate authorship ('from'), but the subject of the Psalm ('for'). However, Justin interprets the name *Solomon* in a different way. He quotes Trypho in the understanding that the latter states that since Solomon was king, the Psalm refers to him (Dialogue 34). Justin continues: 'However, the words of the Psalm expressly proclaim that reference is made to the everlasting king, i.e. to Christ' (see Goldfahn 1873, 59). He wants to refute explicitly Trypho's opinion that the Psalm deals with Solomon. In order to do so, Justin readily admits that Solomon was a renowned king, who built the temple, but argues that the things described in the Psalm are not applicable to him. Neither did all kings worship Solomon, nor did he reign to the ends of the earth, nor did his enemies fall before him, licking the dust. Justin continues with rehearsing what is stated in the book of Kings, namely that Solomon worshipped the idols of Sidon due to a woman's influence. And Justin concludes: 'This is strictly forbidden even for the gentiles who have got to know Christ even when they have to face torture'.

Alongside the argument of the allegedly unworthy behavior of Solomon, Justin adduces another argument to underline the supernatural status of the person described in Ps 72. Justin states: 'Christ is the one who was before the sun', apparently referring to Ps 71:17 (LXX): 'before the sun his name endures' (Dialogue 64). This cannot be applied to a mortal being, Justin states, hence the reference cannot be to king Solomon.

Again Justin interprets Trypho to say that for him, as for all Jews, the meaning of this Psalm points to the past, to the historical figure of king Solomon: 'You (plural) say it refers to Solomon who was also your king. But it refers also to our Christ' (Dialogue 34.1). The phrasing reveals an interesting perspective. Justin realizes that Trypho does not bring forward his own personal conviction but that he refers to a shared Jewish interpretation with historical foundation. Solomon was indeed king of the Jews. It even seems that Justin is ready to accept this historical interpretation of the Psalm 72 as valid. At the same time, he brings forward his Christian interpretation: 'our Christ', being true as well.

Now we will address the question whether Trypho's viewpoint (in Justin's rendering) can be correlated with known Jewish interpretations (ch. 2) and whether a subsequent influence of Justin's interpretations upon Jewish interpretations can be traced (ch. 3).

## 2   JEWISH INTERPRETATIONS OF PSALM 72 BEFORE JUSTIN AND TRYPHO

It is quite probable that even before Justin, Jewish Messianic interpretations of Ps 72 were known. The figure of king Hezekiah, who served Trypho as a key to Ps 110, already has its echo's in portrayals of the ideal future king in the Hebrew Bible. After the wicked king Ahaz, Hezekiah is finally a king who acts like David himself (2 Kgs 18:3) and keeps the law of Moses. Provan convincingly argues that Hezekiah contributed to the portrayal of the ideal Messianic king (1995, 77–78). In the eyes of the prophet Isaiah, he is really the ideal king: 'Hezekiah was no doubt Isaiah's first Messiah' (Schibler 1995, 98–99).

And so was Solomon, despite his faults. His wisdom, the extent of his kingdom and the peaceful period of his reign are described with conscious overtones of fulfillment of the promises made to Abraham (1 Kgs 5:1–20; Provan 1995, 76). Solomon spoke 3000 parables, 1005 songs and taught about plants and talked to animals. 'His wisdom surpassed the wisdom of all the people of the East and all the wisdom of Egypt' (1 Kgs 5:10). Solomon's unworthy behavior is no less an impediment to his role as ideal king as was David's unworthy behavior in the eyes of later generations. It is clear that later Hellenistic Jewish literature, such as the Septuagint, the Wisdom of Solomon (7:15–21) and Josephus Flavius' Antiquities 8.2.5 embellished this favorable portrayal of Solomon as a wise king and as 'son of David', even adding his astrological knowledge and exorcist abilities (Duling 1975, 237–248 and see Feldman 1995, 103–167). Especially Solomon's building of the Temple made him an appropriate model on which to pattern the future Messianic king, who indeed was expected to rebuild the Temple. The New Testament seems to have preserved some elements of Solomon as an exorcist where it states: 'More than Solomon is here', to continue with the return of the unclean spirit (Matt 12:42). The evangelist Mark's portrayal of Jesus as a worker of miracles and exorcist may have been influenced by the Solomonic portrayal as well.[2] Solomon seems to have contributed both

---

[2] Duling (1975, 249ff) debates the title of Son of David as applied to Solomon as well. Kreitzer (2005, 484–512) claims to have discovered Solomonic imagery in Paul's Letter to the Ephesians 2:12–22.

in his royal status as 'son of David' and in his exorcist capacity to the Messianic expectations in the first century C.E.

This means that the rabbinic reference to Solomon as the key to Ps 72 should not be viewed as a mere reference to the Biblical portrayal of Solomon. Nor should it be viewed as to someone merely from the past—as opposed to a Messianic interpretation of Scripture and without any implications for the future.

Ps 72 itself was read as a charter of the ideal Messianic era well before Justin. The New Testament already contains quite a few messianic motifs—such as the adoration of the Magi (Matt 2:11), the blessing of the God of Israel and the performance of 'redemption for his people' (Luke 1:68; cf. Ps 72:14 and 18)—which seem to be derived from Ps 72.

Another early attestation of a Messianic interpretation of Ps 72 can be found in the Psalms of Solomon, generally dated in the first century C.E. This document anticipates the reign of the Lord Messiah, the son of David, who will lead his people with righteousness and will judge the tribes of the people (Ps Sol 17:26), echoing Ps 72:2: 'May he judge your people with righteousness'. Likewise this Psalm of Solomon states: 'He will have gentile nations serving him under his yoke' (17:29–30), echoing Ps 72:11: 'May all nations serve him' (cf. Broyles 1997, 28–34).[3]

This information makes it clear that juxtaposing a Messianic interpretation with historical figures was perfectly feasible in Judaism before Justin, without being hampered by allegedly morally deficient behavior in the case of Solomon (and of David). An interpretation of Ps 72 as referring to the Messiah and to Messianic times was prevalent as well. The solution first offered by 'Strack-Billerbeck' and adopted by Martin Hengel, takes recourse to chronology to solve this dual exegesis of a historical figure and a Messianic figure within Judaism. Dealing with Ps 110, they argue that the historical interpretation (i.e. Abraham) would precede the Messianic interpretations by several centuries.[4]

However, when viewed in a broader perspective, this does not seem to hold water. The historical interpretation (e.g. Solomon) remained

---

[3] Hengel (1995, 100) claims a possible reference to Solomon as ideal figure in the Dead Sea Scrolls (4Q534). In any case the terminology: 'his wisdom will extend to all people' is similar.

[4] Hengel (1995, 178) argues under reference to Strack & Billerbeck that Ps 110:1 could be interpreted as referring to a historical figure and an eschatological figure side by side in the first centuries C.E. Rabbinic reference to the Messiah arose not earlier than from the 3d century on, due to polemics with Christianity. But the distinction between a historical figure and the Messiah is not as clear as he suggests.

in force simultaneously with a Messianic interpretation, as we shall see. The distinction is sometimes not even clear: king Hezekiah, king Solomon and king David may function both as historical and as Messianic figures.[5]

How then, should we evaluate Trypho's exegesis (as rendered by Justin)? Apparently, we should not regard Trypho's exegesis as a reliable or exhaustive Jewish exegesis of his time.

Although Trypho's interpretation is only known to us via Justin's rendering of it, we still may discern its Jewish shade. However, by adducing Jewish interpretations before Justin, we discovered that reference to a historical person did not detract from a future Messianic interpretation at all. How can we explain the discrepancy between these Jewish interpretations and Trypho's? I would suggest the following: Justin himself is influenced by Jewish Messianic interpretations of Ps 72, be it only based on its distillate in the New Testament. For him as a Christian reader, it is obvious that the Messianic elements of Ps 72 have materialized in Jesus of Nazareth. Trypho realizes that by admitting the Messianic contents of Ps 72 (or of Ps 110, for that matter), he may weaken his standpoint, although he will be familiar with those interpretations within his Jewish milieu. Trypho then cites interpretations known to him, such as king Hezekiah as the key to Isa 7:14 and Ps 110, and Solomon as the key to Ps 72—but in a highly reductive way due to the exigencies of the polemical situation. Although realizing the Messianic connotations of king Hezekiah and Solomon, Trypho presents them as mere historical figures, hereby implying that for Judaism, the meaning of the Scriptural verses had already been exhausted in the past. This latter implication seems to be prompted by the polemical situation and cannot be warranted by other Jewish interpretations, on the contrary. A historical reading of Ps 72 as well as other Psalms can be attested to within Judaism, but can hardly be isolated from Messianic readings and connotations.

Justin's interpretation of Solomon is no less influenced by the polemical situation: He degrades Solomon for his unworthy behavior and for his idolatry that would be forbidden even for a new Christian from paganism. This negative interpretation of Solomon does not reflect all

---

[5] Cf. for this double function of Melchisedek and Enoch as heroes from the past and future ideals, contributing to Messianic expectations and to rivalry between Judaism and Christianity, my study 2004, 97–120.

of Christianity: Solomon's ring was venerated as an important relic in 4th century Jerusalem, as we learn from Egeria's travels (37.3; around 381 C.E.). This was undoubtedly due to the important role of the ring as a magical tool in the Testament of Solomon (2nd–4th centuries C.E.). Solomon's role as a magician became increasingly prominent within Christianity. As we shall see, it is only when Jewish opponents attribute Messianic passages to Solomon (that Christians believe Jesus fulfills), that the Christian writers become critical of Solomon (cf. Duling 1983, 951).

### 3　Jewish Interpretations of Psalm 72 after Justin

As we are interested in possible interaction between Judaism and Christianity, the question arises as to whether the Christological interpretations of Ps 72 by Justin and later Christian writers under his influence, such as Tertullian (Adversus Marcionem 5.10), affected Jewish interpretations of it.[6]

In the Altercatio Simonis et Theophili (5th century), Ps 72 is debated as well. The Jew Simon argues from the superscript that the Psalm deals with Solomon, not with Christ. Theophilus retorts that both the limited proportions of Solomon's kingdom and his unworthy idolatrous behavior at the end of his life, prevent him from being the subject of the Psalm. This dialogue does not seem to add much to what we already know from Justin's Dialogue.[7]

This is different in the Greek Dialogue of Timothy and Aquila (5th century). The Christian Timothy applies Ps 2:7: 'You are my son, today I have become your father', to Jesus as the Messiah. The Jew Aquila, however, says the passage refers to Solomon. Upon the objection that Solomon committed idolatry, Aquila wonders whether Solomon actually sacrificed locusts to idols. This detail is not told in the book of Kings (1 Kgs 11:3–6), but is dealt with in the pseudepigraphic Testament of

---

[6] Tertullian seems to have had exchanges with Jews on this Psalm independent of Justin. Augustine follows and develops Justin further (Enarrationes in Psalmos 72). Theodor of Mopsuestia denies the Christological interpretation of Ps 72, in line of the Antiochene school, and advocates a historical reading of the Psalms (Devreesse 1939, 469–477; I owe this reference to father Isaac Majoor). However, Jewish influence does not seem to be decisive here.

[7] Prigent (1964, 91–93) argues that both Tertullian and the Altercation depend upon Justin, but whereas the former corrects the quotations of Justin's Dialogue, the latter follows the Syntagma of Justin, now lost.

Solomon, already mentioned earlier (Duling 1983, 940). The Jew proposes a more favorable reading Testament of Solomon 26.5: Solomon
may not actually have sacrificed the locusts, but unwillingly crushed
them in his hand.[8] The curious thing is that the Christian fully accepts
the authority of this document. Now this document, replete as it is
with magic, portrays Solomon as the outstanding master of spirits and
demons and as the adversary of major devils as Beelzebub. Solomon's
downfall is only referred to in the last few lines of the document.

Although both dialogues are already highly formalized and derive
from earlier documents, notably Justin's Dialogue, belonging as they
do to the Adversus Iudaeos literature, an original argument from the
Jewish side seems to resonate in the latter dialogue, dealing with Psalm
2, not Psalm 72. Interestingly enough, both the Jew and the Christian
accept the positive, (not the Messianic) role of Solomon as a magician,
of which the Testament of Solomon provides such eloquent testimony.
Apparently the Jewish reference to Solomon as the subject of Ps 2 and
as the 'son of God' in the Dialogue of Timothy and Aquila does not at
all intend to counter the Christian Messianic interpretation by alluding
to a figure on a more human level. The religious and cultural proximity
of the Testament of Solomon to both spokesmen proves this. Aquila's
Judaism views Solomon as no less supernatural than Christianity views
Jesus.[9] In addition, the Jewish preference for the historical figure of
Solomon as the subject of certain Psalms does not at all detract from
the Messianic flavor of the Psalms for Judaism. The sole point seems
to be that in claiming Solomon as the subject of certain Psalms, a
Christological reading is prevented. It is only within the context of a
Jewish-Christian polemic that the Jewish interpretation of Solomon
receives its historicizing coloring, as if by pointing to the figure of
Solomon in the past the meaning of the Psalm would be exhausted.
Again, this Jewish argument can only be found in a polemical context,
not in rabbinic literature itself. There Solomon and the Messiah can
figure side by side as the subject of Ps 72 and Solomon's ideal kingship
supplies considerable elements for Jewish Messianic expectations.

---

[8] See Duling (1983, 986 n. d) quoting a variant version that reads: 'Take these
grasshoppers and crush them together in the name of the god Moloch and I shall go
to bed with you. This very thing I did.'

[9] Note the difference with Justin's *Dialogue*: Justin seems to defend a supernatural
Messiah, Christ, against a human king, Solomon.

How then can we ascertain a decisive influence of Christological interpretations upon Jewish interpretations of Solomon? In general, we should distinguish between three different strategies put forward by the Jewish side:

1. Referring to a Biblical figure from the past as the sole key to the Psalm, devoid of Messianic overtones and remote from the pre-Christian Jewish Messianic interpretations of Ps 72. We saw this in Trypho's interpretation of Ps 72 and in Aquila's interpretation of Ps 2, both referring to Solomon. Rabbinic literature does not seem to contain such explicitly historical readings, thereby excluding Messianic connotations.
2. Referring to a Biblical figure from the past (i.e. king Solomon), not as a mere human, but as someone at least equal to Christ. This line of interpretation asserted by the Jewish side, shows continuity with the pre-Christian Messianic interpretations (i.e. of Ps 72).
3. Rebuking a Biblical figure (i.e. Solomon) for assuming divine authority and presenting him as only too human, which would serve as camouflaged criticism of Christological claims.

We have dealt with examples of the first strategy above. We will now deal with the latter two. To begin with, we have to establish criteria for ascertaining certain Jewish interpretations of king Solomon as polemical against Christological claims, given the fact that rabbinic literature hardly mentions Christian interpretations explicitly. We propose the following criteria:

– In a polemical rabbinic portrayal of a Biblical person, there should be a striking deviance from usual Biblical or post-Biblical portrayals.
– That deviance should be meaningful in the light of anti-Christian polemics.
– A historical context of that rabbinic statement relevant to Jewish-Christian relations may offer additional corroboration for an anti-Christian polemic (cf. for the last criterion, Poorthuis 2004).

*Solomon as equal to Christ (elaborating no. 2 above)*

Rabbinic literature contains a wealth of interpretations of Ps 72, linked to both a Biblical figure and to a Messianic figure, often side by side.

The first line: 'For Solomon. Give, o God, your judgments to the king and your justice to the son of the king', receives the following rabbinic comments:

The Midrash on Psalms (72.2) puts David forward as the author of the Psalm, who expresses the wish that the 'son of the king', i.e. Solomon, may be able to judge as impartially as the king (David) has done. God grants that wish by placing Solomon on God's throne: 'Solomon was seated upon the throne of the Lord' (1 Chr 29:23). An imaginary opponent who wonders whether a mortal can sit upon God's throne, receives the answer: 'Till thrones were placed and the Ancient of Days sat down' (Dan 7:9, 'thrones' is used in the plural!).[10] Solomon's renown as judge is well-known. Solomon's glory and throne are compared to God's glory and God's throne. Solomon's royal dynasty meant peace to the people. The power of the kings diminished only after Solomon's lifetime (ExodR 15.26).

The extent of the reign described in Ps 72:8: 'from sea to sea, from the river to the ends of the earth' is a traditional Christian argument against Solomon as the subject of the Psalm. Justin states: 'neither did all kings worship him, nor did he reign until the ends of the earth' (Dialogue 34), implying that the Psalm must refer to the Messianic figure of Christ. The following midrash flatly denies these arguments and compares Solomon's throne to God's throne! 'Solomon sat on the throne of God' (2 Chr 9:23–24). Is it possible for man to sit on God's throne? No, but just as God rules from one end of the world to the other and has dominion over all kings, Solomon rules from one end of the world to the other and has dominion of all kings as it is said: 'All the kings of the earth sought the presence of Solomon and they brought him presents' (2 Chr 9:23–24; cf. ExodR 15.26, where the comparison of Solomon's throne with God's throne is elaborated upon;[11] CantR 1.10). Patterned after the imperial court of the Byzantine era, Solomon's throne increases in grandeur even further, receiving its zenith in the miraculous descriptions of the Targum Sheni to Esther. In several poems there Solomon is extolled. And again, Ps 72 plays a role here: 'That Solomon, the great king, whom the Holy One, blessed

---

[10] This same verse was used by rabbi Akiba to argue that one throne was for God and the other for David (Hag 14a). Rabbi Josi ha-Gelili rebuked him for this view (Hengel 1995, 181ff Segal 1977, 44ff).

[11] The elaborate description of Solomon's miraculous throne in 2 Chr 9 is further embellished in later midrash; see Jellinek 1967, 34–39 and Salzberger 1912.

be he, appointed to rule from one end of the world to the other end.' Further on, this targum states: 'All kings loved him. All rulers trembled before him.' Again Psalm 72 serves as the utopian pattern to describe Solomon (see Grossfeld 1991, 106–107 and Ego 2001, 57–73 who fails to acknowledge the role of Psalm 72 however). This argument is not only divergent from what Scripture states about the extent of Solomon's reign, but does not seem to restrain itself in any way to keep Solomon within merely human dimensions, as Trypho does. On the contrary, Solomon is viewed as a Messianic king whose throne resembles God's throne. Hence we may detect an anti-Christian polemic here. What we have here is a rivaling Jewish interpretation using a Biblical figure with Messianic overtones, fit to counter Christological claims.

The same can be said of the intriguing rabbinic dictum: 'Whoever says that Solomon sinned makes an error' (Shab 56b), which tries to make Solomon's idolatry vanish via interpretation. The context of this talmudic debate even argues that Solomon did not commit idolatry at all. His only mistake was that he allowed his wives to do so. This may well be directed against Christian interpretations such as Justin and his followers and runs entirely along the same lines of the whitewashing of Solomon by the Jew Aquila in the debate with Timothy, as quoted above.

This increasing aggrandizement of Solomon does not prevent an application of Ps 72 to the Messiah. Solomon's ideal reign seems to go hand in hand with Messianic expectations.

### Jewish Messianic Interpretations of Psalm 72

In the same midrash on Psalms that seemed to confine the protagonists of Ps 72 to David and Solomon, another explanation applies the 'give your justice to the king' to the king Messiah. To buttress this identification, the midrash quotes Isa 11:1–4, where the Messianic figure possesses the same moral attribute of justice: 'A sprout from the stem of Isai (…), he judges (Hebrew: *shapat*) the poor in righteousness' (MidrPss 72.3).

Rabbi Hiya (280 C.E.) likewise interprets the ideal description of Ps 72:16: 'He will be as rich cornfield in the land', as the Messianic future (GenR 48.10). By implication, the Psalm as such would deal with the Messiah, not with Solomon, in an interpretation already attested to at the beginning of the third century: 'They shall fear thee with the sun' (Ps 72:5) is interpreted as 'awe for the Messianic king', who is compared to the sun (Sanh 99a, in the name of Rabbi, 200 C.E.). Verse 17:

'His name shall endure forever; before the sun, his name flourishes', is interpreted as an indication of the premundane name of the Messiah (Sanh 98b and parallels, again to be dated at the beginning of the third century C.E.; see Goldberg 1979, 77ff. Besides the numerous rabbinic parallels, Goldberg refers to the pseudepigraphic apocalypse 1 Henoch 48:2–3). The list of attributes that were created before the world varies both in number and in contents, but the name of the Messiah is seldom lacking among them. Whether the Rabbis from the early third century really distinguished between the premundane name of the Messiah and the actual preexistence of the Messiah, remains the question; it may well be that this question reflects later debates.

Based upon the same Psalm verse, 72:17, the name of the Messiah is reckoned among the six persons whom God called by their names even before they were born: Isaac, Ishmael, Moses, Solomon, Josia and the name of the Messiah (PRE 32, note that the name of Solomon figures among them).

Some interpretations revolving around Solomon idealize the past, using it as a model for Messianic times. Although referring to the past, there is no trace of a historicizing reading of the Psalm by reducing its subject to a mere human king from bygone times. Admittedly, the name of Solomon is not mentioned as a Messianic name, but the name Shalom or 'Sar ha-Shalom' ('prince of peace') is, although primarily in later sources.

There is yet another connection between Solomon, the Messiah and Ps 72, according to rabbinic hermeneutics. The expression 'Lebanon' (72:13) is taken by the rabbis to refer to the Temple, which washes white the sins of the people (Git 56b; Yoma 39b; cf. Vermes 1961, 28ff). It was king Solomon who built the Temple.

Rabbi Oshaiah (300 C.E.) said: 'When king Solomon built the Sanctuary, he planted therein all kinds of [trees of] golden delight, which were bringing forth their fruits in the seasons, and as the wind blew at them, they would fall off, as it is said: "May his fruits rustle like Lebanon" (Ps 72:16), and when foreigners entered the Temple, they withered, as it is written: "And the flower of Lebanon languishes" (Nah 1:4), and the Holy One, blessed be he, will in the future restore them, as it is said: "It shall blossom abundantly and rejoice, even with joy and singing; the glory of Lebanon shall be given unto it" (Isa 35:2)' (Yoma 21b).

The promise of the restoration of the Temple is one of the features of the Messianic times. The miraculous atmosphere of the Solomonic temple was destroyed by foreigners (which may actually refer to the destruction of the Second Temple by the Romans in 70 C.E.), but will be restored in the messianic age by God himself.

In a very early dictum, the talmud interprets Psalm 72:16: 'they [read: the righteous] shall blossom forth out of the city', in Messianic perspective as well. It hints at the resurrection, which will take place in the city of Jerusalem (Sanh 90b, in the name of Rabbi Meir, 150 C.E.; see Ket 111b, in the name of the Amora Rabbi Hiyya ben Joseph; see Bacher 1890, 69, who does not seem to doubt the attribution to Rabbi Meir who speculated more often about the Messianic age).

An important testimony of the Messianic reading of Ps 72 can be found in the Targum to Psalms (see Levey 1974, 115–118). While integrating elements from the midrash, the targum offers new elements as well, be it only for the reason that it has to order the motifs in a coherent paraphrase, without being able to resort to different opinions (as the midrash does). The targum solves the problem of the two addressees in the first line in a determined fashion, choosing Solomon as the author: 'By the hand of Solomon, spoken through prophecy. O God, give the king Messiah the laws (halakhot) of Thy justice, and Thy righteousness to the son of king David'. Solomon by prophetic foresight appears—in marked distinction with the midrash—to be the author of the Psalm which is now wholly Messianic. The 'king' and the 'son of the king' (Ps 72:1) are one and the same person: the Messiah, who is, incidentally, involved in rabbinic halakha!

It is interesting to see how the 'gold given to the ruler' (Ps 72:15) is interpreted in an altruistic Messianic way as: 'he will give to the poor of the gold which they shall bring him from Sheba'. The premundane nature of the name of the Messiah is underlined as we saw in the midrash as well: 'His name which was prepared before the sun came into being' (Targum on Psalms 72:17).

Obviously the targum does not need to adapt the description of the Psalm to the reign of Solomon as we noted in some of the midrashim quoted above, as from the viewpoint of this targum, the Messianic era is the subject of this Psalm. This does not detract from the fact, however, that other targums do apply the Psalm to Solomon as we saw from the Targum Sheni on Esther above.

It is clear that especially in later sources, the figure of Solomon and the figure of the Messiah go hand in hand, sharing the same royal honor in their reign extending from one end of the earth to the other. There is no trace of any rivalry between the two. Apparently, the aggrandizement of Solomon in rabbinic interpretations of Psalm 72 does not prevent a rabbinic Messianic reading of the same Psalm but serves the polemical aim to counter Christological interpretations of that Psalm.

## 4   SOLOMON AND CHRIST IN PSALM 24

Although there might be ample reason to criticize the figure of Solomon for his leanings toward idolatry and women, we found little trace of criticism in the rabbinic sources quoted above. Rabbinic literature, however, does present vehement invectives against Solomon as well. Sometimes this sharp rebuttal is explained at the basis of his magical proclivities. Indeed, rabbinic literature has an ambiguous attitude to magic, more so than, for example the pseudepigraphic Testament of Solomon. The widely attested popularity of the name of Solomon in amulets and incantation bowls seems to fit more to the latter document than to rabbinic literature as such. Magic and idolatry are intrinsically connected, according to the rabbis, who note with satisfaction that king Hezekiah 'hid the Book of Cures' (Ber 10b), a book sometimes attributed to king Solomon.[12] Despite the many similarities between the Testament of Solomon and rabbinic literature—cf. the talmudic account of Solomon's building of the temple with the aid of spirits and in battle with Ashmedai/Asmodeus (Git 68b)—one rabbinic opinion suggests that Solomon was first king, reigning over the higher world, but ended as a commoner reigning over the lower world only (Sanh 20b).[13] Another rabbinic opinion, however, emphasizes Solomon's reestablishment in his former glory. It seems to me though that the utterly negative portrayal of Solomon in the rabbinic sources to be quoted hereafter, nearly exclusively confined to the interpretation of Ps 24, cannot be explained as a mere extrapolation of his Biblical idolatry, nor as a veiled polemic against magic.

What we have here is another device to counter Christological claims: Jewish criticism of Solomon as a veiled criticism of Christ. We mentioned this type of rabbinic apologetics against Christianity as the

---

[12] Several Church fathers quote this rabbinic dictum, such as Anastasius Sinaites, in the name of Eusebius Pamphilus, see Preisendanz 1956, 660–704.

[13] Cf. the question whether Solomon should be reckoned among the kings who have no share in the World to Come: p.Sanh 10.2 29b. The question of Solomon being saved became central in Christian literature from the Middle Ages: see Mishtooni Bose (1996, 2.187–210) to receive an affirmative answer quite often.

third form (p. 267). Whereas Justin's negative portrayal of Solomon seemed to contrast with the positive account of Solomon in Judaism, now matters appear to be more complicated. The rabbinic interpretations of Ps 24 accuse Solomon of assuming divine authority. This may come as a surprise, given the Biblical rendering and post-Biblical Jewish embellishments of Solomon. This utterly negative reading of Solomon in conjunction with Ps 24 cannot be explained as simply rabbinic reservations against magic, but should be viewed as a veiled reaction against Christological claims. Adding more weight to this argument, one should consider the fact that this Ps 24 is a major testimony, according to the early Christians, of Christ as a supernatural Messianic figure.

In Ps 24, the gates (of the Temple) are commanded to raise, in order to give entrance to the king of glory. The gates, however ask: 'who is the king of glory?' (Ps 24:8). The answer given in the Psalm itself is: 'The Lord of Hosts is the king of glory'! Rabbinic interpretation inserts a small dialogue: Solomon assumed divine authority when entering the Temple, acting as if he himself was the king of glory. The gates refuse to give entrance and even threaten to devour or crush Solomon, until he finally admits: 'The Lord of hosts is the king of glory'! According to this midrash, Solomon's arrogance is such that he assumes divine authority (NumR 14.3; 15.13; Tan beha'alotkha 9). The talmudic parallels, however, felt the need to come to the defense of Solomon. They shift the blame from Solomon to David who only after his death and by the aid of Solomon, obtains divine forgiveness. It is only then that Solomon can enter the gates of the Temple (MQ 9a, Shab 30a). Apparently we have here two distinct and hardly compatible motifs to explain Solomon's initial inability to enter the Temple: on the one hand his arrogance, on the other hand his intercession on behalf of his father David. The talmud clearly opts for the second, highly favorable interpretation.[14]

Some other versions combine the two motifs (Sanh 107b; MidrPss 24:10; Tan wa'era 7). It is hard to decide which of the two is the more original, although I am inclined to see the talmudic versions as conscious

---

[14] For some different versions, see Salzberger (1912, 22–28). The talmud seems to have mitigated the midrashic criticism of the divinization of Solomon by connecting it to his plea for forgiveness on behalf of David. Perhaps here is a difference between the Palestinian milieu of the midrash close to Christianity, where rabbinic criticism of Christological interpretation may be expected, and the Babylonian context of the talmud.

redactions in opposition to a negative portrayal of Solomon. For our purpose, it is sufficient to conclude that the motif of Solomon being accused of arrogance cannot be explained wholly out of the refusal of the gates to let Solomon pass. On the contrary, Solomon's divine arrogance is a surprising element, given the general appreciation of Solomon in rabbinic literature. It should be noted that the rabbinic treatment of Ps 24 shows a remarkable distortion of its plain meaning as well. Whereas a plain interpretation clearly suggests that it is the 'king of glory' who is entering the gates, these rabbinic explanations are forced to admit that not the king of Glory, but only Solomon is the one to enter. This striking distortion may also be an indication of a polemical context.

If then we are correct about a veiled Jewish criticism of Christological claims of Ps 24 by rebuking Solomon for his arrogance, then by implication the midrash considers Christ's divinity an infringement upon God's majesty. This explanation of Solomon's arrogance becomes even more plausible considering the fact that in spite of his many faults, including idolatry, Solomon's idolatry did not consist in megalomania, as was the case with Nimrod and others.

In addition, Christological interpretations of Psalm 24 are attested in the earliest layers of Christian exegetical literature from the second and early third centuries C.E., offering ample food for rabbinic polemics in dealing with the same Psalm. Like Solomon, Christ addresses the gates to raise and to open up, whereas the location significantly has been transferred from the Temple to the netherworld (Acts Pil. 21; Schneemelcher & Wilson 1991, 524). Christ conquers death by opening the gates and descending into the Sheol. In another setting, Christ addresses the gates of heaven to open up at the moment of his baptism in the Jordan (Hippolyt, On the holy theophany 6 ANFa 5.236) or at the moment of his ascension to heaven (Justin, First Apology 51; Hippolyt, Fragments from commentaries, on Psalm 24; ANFa 5.170).[15] In each of these different interpretations of calling the gates to raise their heads, Christ's divinity is underlined and the connection of the Psalm with the Temple severed. Justin is even aware of previous Jewish interpretations that connect this Psalm to king Solomon or to king

---

[15] Note the interpretation of entering the gates as the victory over mortal existence in gnostic circles; Hippolyt, Refutation of all heresies 5.3, ANFa 5.53. The opposition of the rulers of heaven against the entering of Christ does contain gnostic overtones.

Hezekiah. He argues though that only Christ is appropriately called 'Lord of Hosts' in this Psalm, not Solomon (Dialogue 36, 83, 127). The rulers of heaven did not recognize Christ's divine status because of his uncomely appearance and had to be admonished by the Holy Spirit to open the gates of heaven for the 'Lord of Hosts' (Dialogue 36).[16] However, Justin does not seem to be aware of a strongly negative role assigned to Solomon in the Jewish interpretations of Ps 24, nor of king Hezekiah. This corroborates our claim that the strongly negative portrayal of Solomon in rabbinic interpretations of Psalm 24 occurs later and should be regarded as a Jewish polemic against Christological interpretations of the same Psalm.

By introducing Solomon as assuming divine authority (within the context of entering the Temple) and being rebuked for that by the Holy One himself, rabbinic literature contests Christian claims of Christ's divinity. The Temple itself remains the undisputed holy place, capable of judging Solomon's spiritual level.[17] The Temple gates as it were, correct Solomon's arrogance of assuming divine status, according to this rabbinic interpretation.[18]

Here we detect a specimen of the above-mentioned third rabbinic device to counter Christological interpretations: by introducing a well-known Biblical figure who behaves in a way similar to Christ and is rebuked for his arrogance. Although Christ is not mentioned explicitly, this rabbinic criticism of Solomon in Psalm 24 is intended to criticize Christological claims.

In contrast with that, we noted in other Jewish interpretations of Ps 72 a tendency to aggrandize the figure of Solomon in order to counter Christological claims as well, again without mentioning Christ. It is only

---

[16] Addressing the 'rulers' instead of the gates themselves may have been influenced by the LXX, where the Hebrew word *rosh* is not interpreted as 'head', but as 'ruler'.

[17] Note the difference with Gnostic-Christian perception of Solomon who associates himself with demons to build Jerusalem (Testimony of Truth, Nag Hammadi Codex IX.3.70). This motif, taken from Jewish midrash, but utterly transformed, explains, according to the author, the demonic character of Jerusalem, of the Old Testament king Solomon and of his god; see Giversen (1972, 16–21 esp. 16). This utterly negative portrayal of Solomon in connection with the Temple, is continued in the 'holy Rood' traditions: Solomon is unable to use the holy wood from Paradise, which is to become the cross, as a beam for the temple. See Quinn (1969, 51ff) and my study (1998, 231–264).

[18] Curiously, the Gnostic tract The second Treatise of the Great Seth (NHC VII.2.62), likewise accuses Solomon of considering himself Christ, possibly under the influence of Jewish sources, but here of course transformed to contrast with the real Gnostic Christ.

in medieval Jewish literature that anti-Christian Jewish polemics dealing with Ps 72 mention Christian interpretations explicitly (cf. Berger 1975, 287–303 esp. 296, who refers to Jacob ben Reuben, Nahmanides and the Nizzahon Vetus). But this is another story.

## Conclusion

The initial picture of a favorable Jewish interpretation of Solomon contrasted with a negative Christian interpretation of him, such as we found in Justin's Dialogue and in later Christian dialogues, needs to be refined. The full picture seems to be as follows:

Ps 72 already had its Jewish Messianic interpretations before the advent of the New Testament. The figure of Solomon received Messianic connotations as well, both in Jewish sources and in the New Testament, even influencing the picture of Jesus in the gospels.

Prompted by Justin's Christological reading of Ps 72, in which Solomon as a candidate is excluded, the Jew Trypho felt obliged to refer to Solomon in a historicizing fashion, hereby excluding a Messianic significance of Ps 72. This Jewish voice appears to be influenced by the polemical situation, as Jewish Messianic interpretations of this Psalm remained in force well after the Christological readings by Justin and later Christian writers. Justin and Christian writers after him likewise tended to downplay Solomon in debates with Jews, which did not reflect the generally high appreciation of Solomon as a wise king and magician in Christianity. In addition, on the Jewish side, Solomon was promoted as a competitor with Christ regarding Messianic and divine status. In this process, the human status of Solomon receded more and more into the background.

In marked contrast with that, the Jewish polemic against a Christological reading of Ps 24 (itself a transformation of Jewish interpretations of that Psalm revolving around Solomon or Hezekiah), in which Christ's entrance through the gates as the King of Glory was described, painted a highly critical portrait of Solomon, rebuking him for his divine aspirations. This development, more apparent in Palestinian midrash than in the Babylonian Talmud, should be regarded as a veiled but no less conscious Jewish polemic against Christianity. In this Jewish polemic, Solomon played the role of Christ and was rebuked for that. Possibly in later times, in the period of the later midrash and of the Targum Sheni, which both paint such a lofty portrait of Solomon, the urge to downplay Solomon as part of the polemic against Christology, was no longer felt.

This interaction between Jewish and Christian interpretations of Biblical figures is a promising field for further research, rendering any study that remains within the confines of one religion, or claiming a one-sided influence only, somewhat naive. The Christological debate can benefit from this interaction as well, as it demonstrates the intrinsic connection of the divinity of Christ with other divine Biblical figures, such as king Solomon.

## LITERATURE

Aberbach, M., 'Hizkiah, King of Juda and Rabbi Jehuda Hanasi', *Tarb.* 53 (1983/84) [Hebrew].

Bacher, W., *Die Agada der Tannaiten* [vol.] 2, Straßburg 1890.

Berger, D., 'Christian Heresy and Jewish Polemic in the Twelfth and Thirteenth Centuries', *HThR* 68 (1975).

Broyles, C.C., 'The Redeeming King: Psalm 72's Contribution to the Messianic Ideal', in: C.A. Evans & P.W. Flint (eds), *Eschatology, Messianism and the Dead Sea Scrolls* (Studies in the Dead Sea Scrolls and Related Literature 1), Michigan 1997.

Devreesse, R., *Le commentaire de Théodor de Mopsueste sur les Psaumes* (StT 93), Rome 1939.

Duling, D.C., 'Solomon, Exorcism and the Son of David', *HThR* 68 (1975).

———, 'Testament of Solomon', in: J.H. Charlesworth (ed.), *Old Testament Pseudepigrapha* [vol.] *I*, New York 1983.

Ego, B., 'All Kingdoms and Kings Trembled Before Him: the Image of King Solomon in Targum Sheni on Megillat Esther', *Journal for the Aramaic Bible* 3 (2001).

Feldman, L., 'Josephus' Portrait of Solomon', *HUCA* 66 (1995).

Giversen, S., 'Solomon und die Dämonen', in: M. Krause (ed.), *Essays on the Nag Hammadi Texts in Honour of Alexander Böhlig* (NHS 3), Leiden 1972.

Goldberg, A., 'Die Namen des Messias in der Rabbinischen Traditionsliteratur. Ein Beitrag zur Messianologie des rabbinischen Judentums', *FJB* 7 (1979).

Goldfahn, J., 'Justinus Martyr und die Agada', *MGWJ* 22 (1873).

Grossfeld, B., *The Two Targums to Esther* (The Aramaic Bible 18), Edinburgh 1991.

Hengel, M., *Studies in Early Christology*, Edinburgh 1995 [esp. the chapter: 'Sit at my right hand. The enthronement of Christ at the Right Hand of God and Psalm 110:1'].

Jellinek, A., 'Salomo's Thron und Hippodrome', in: idem, *Beth Hamidrasch* [vol.] V, Jerusalem 3rd ed. 1967.

Kreitzer, L.J., 'The Messianic Man of Peace as Temple Builder: Solomonic Imagery in Ephesians 2:13–22' in: J. Day (ed.), *Temple and Worship in Biblical Israel*, London—New York 2005.

Levey, H., *The Messiah: an Aramaic Interpretation; The Messianic Exegesis of the Targum* (MHUC 2), Cincinatti 1974.

Mishtooni Bose, 'The Medieval Solomon', *MAe* 65 (1996).

Poorthuis, M., 'Moses' Rod in Zipporah's Garden', in: D. Houtman, M. Poorthuis, & J. Schwartz (eds), *Sanctity of Time and Space* (Jewish and Christian Perspectives Series 1), Leiden 1998.

————, 'Enoch and Melchisedek in Judaism and Christianity. A study in Intermediaries', in: idem & J. Schwartz (eds), *Saints and Role Models in Judaism and Christianity* (Jewish and Christian Perspectives Series 7), Leiden 2004.

Preisendanz, K., 'Salomon', in: *PRE.S* 8 (1956).

Prigent, P., *Justin et l'Ancien Testament* (EtB), Paris 1964.

Provan, I.W., 'The Messiah in the Book of Kings', in: P.E. Satterthwaite et al. (eds), *The Lord's Anointed; Interpretations of Old Testament Messianic texts* (Tyndale House Studies), Carlisle 1995.

Quinn, E.C., *The Quest of Seth for the Oil of Life*, Chicago 2nd pr. 1969.

Remus, H., 'Justin Martyr's Argument with Judaism', in: P. Richardson & D. Granskou (eds), *Anti-Judaism in Early Christianity* [vol.] 2; *Separation and Polemic* (SCJud 2.2), Waterloo, Ont. 1986.

Rokéah, D., *Justin Martyr and the Jews* (Jewish and Christian Perspectives Series 5), Leiden 2002.

Salzberger, G., *Salomos Tempelbau und Thron in der semitischen Sagenliteratur* (Schriften der Lehranstalt für die Wissenschaft des Judentums 2.1), Berlin 1912.

Schibler, D., 'Messianism and Messianic Prophecy in Isaiah 1–12 and 28–33', in: see Provan 1995.

Schneemelcher, W. & R.McL. Wilson (eds), *New Testament Apocrypha* [vol.] *I*, Cambridge 1991.

Segal, A.F., *Two Powers in Heaven; Early Rabbinic Reports about Christianity and Gnosticism* (SJLA 25), Leiden 1977.

Vermes, G., 'Lebanon', in: idem, *Scripture and Tradition* (StPB 4), Leiden 1961.

# PARODY AND POLEMICS ON PENTECOST: TALMUD YERUSHALMI PESAḤIM ON ACTS 2?

*Daniel Stökl-Ben Ezra*
Centre National de la Recherche Scientifique,
Aix en Provence, France

Liturgy[1] and especially festivals offer a convenient vantage point to analyze collective identities providing access to collective mentalities rather than individual ideas of intellectuals often more or less confined to ivory tower (e.g. Assmann 1991, 13–30). Ritual addresses the whole human being, the intellect, emotions, and the body and it does so in establishing and defining relations between the individual, its in-group and the out-group (cf. Bell 1992 and 1997). Every collective identity is built and rebuilt in a continuous process encompassing exchange with as well as distinction from other optional collective identities in the vicinity. Sometimes, this construction of a 'we' in distinction to a 'them' takes place in more explicit, sometimes in rather clandestine and encrypted fashions. Both approaches are relevant to this article.

Many studies have been written on the emergence of Pentecost among the Christian festivals in the first two centuries (cf. Rouwhorst 2001, 309–322; Cocchini 1977, 297–326; Erez 1993, Potin 1971, Cabié 1965, Kretschmar 1954/1955, 209–253). However, research on the interrelationship of Christian and Jewish festivals *after* the second century when both religions were already separate entities has largely concentrated on Pesaḥ/Easter and Sabbath/Sunday (e.g. Yuval 2006, Bauckham 1982, 221–250). In this paper on Shavuot and Pentecost, my focus shall therefore be not so much on the early times, but rather on their less researched interrelationship in the fourth and fifth century, making

---

[1] I would like to thank the organizers of the conference, Clemens Leonhard and Albert Gerhards, for the invitation and the participants for their comments. Tali Artmann, Oded Irshai, Clemens Leonhard, Ophir Münz-Manor, Israel Yuval and especially Michael Kohlbacher provided most helpful comments. Holger Zellentin kindly sent me a chapter from his Princeton dissertation in progress on parody in Rabbinic literature. I would also like to thank Avital Erez for making a copy of her unpublished M.St. thesis (2003) available to me. My research assistant, Avi Perrodin was very helpful in the preparations and during the search for bibliography.

three points: After a short introduction on Shavuot in the Bible and the Second Temple and tannaitic periods, I shall discuss some patristic references on Pentecost/Shavuot that show that Christian religious leaders were acquainted with post-biblical Jewish Shavuot traditions. Then, I will argue that Jewish sources as well wrestle with the challenge posed by the Christian Pentecost by demonstrating that a passage from *Toledot Yeshu* on the Christian festival calendar can be dated to the early Byzantine era and is acquainted with the Christian Ascension/Pentecost festival. Finally, in light of this, i.e. bearing in mind that the Christian Pentecost was not unknown to (some) rabbinic Jews, I want to suggest reading a story from the Palestinian Talmud as a polemical parody of the foundational story of the Christian Pentecost.

In the Bible, Shavuot—one of the three pilgrimage festivals—is a harvest festival considered a particularly suitable day to offer first fruits in the Temple (cf. Num 28:26; VanderKam 1992, 895–897). At some point, this festival became connected to revelation, to the covenant and to the giving of the Torah, a crucial point for the understanding of the relation between the Jewish and the Christian Pentecost. It is, however very difficult to say when and to which extent—i.e. how widespread—this conception of Shavuot was. In addition to the well known passage in the book of Acts, hints can be found in at least three pre-rabbinic texts (van Goudoever 1967; 95–100, 170, 199–206). For Jubilees, which uses a different calendar, Shavuot falls on the 16th of the third month and is the day of revelation (and covenant) par excellence: for Abraham, for Jacob and for Moses (Jub 1:1; 15:1–3; 44:1–5; cf. also 4Q266 11.17 and 4Q275 1.3 and [the late] Targum to 2 Chr 15:8–15; cf. VanderKam 1992, 896). The *Liber Antiquitatum Biblicarum* dates the covenant of Joshua on Shavuot.[2] In 2 Enoch, according to the oldest manuscript, Enoch ascends to heaven on the sixth of Sivan, i.e. Shavuot.[3] In addition, a story in Josephus about a kind of voiceless Bat Kol (φωνῆς ἀθρόας, Bell 6.299) in the Temple on Shavuot might possibly reflect an ancient connection between this festival and revelation. In

---

[2] LibAnt 23.2. The reading is uncertain and could be either sixth or sixteenth day of Sivan. Despite the ambiguity, 'it is nonetheless quite clear that the dating of Joshua's covenant to the month of Sivan must be due to the parallel with the Sinai covenant.' Jacobson (1996, 2.711).

[3] 2 Enoch 68:1–3 according to ms P and J. Ms R has Pamovousa (i.e. Tammuz). The former reading is preferred by Andersen (1983, vol. 1, 196), while Böttrich (1996, 1002) favors the latter one.

Qumran, the festival of Pentecost probably commemorated the yearly covenant renewal ceremony described in the Community Rule.[4]

According to the consensus, the revelation motif was less prevalent in the early tannaitic times. In general, the festival becomes somehow elusive in rabbinic literature, especially in the early compositions (cf. Tabory 1995, 146–155). Unlike the other principal holidays, Pesaḥ, Sukkot, Yom Kippur, Shabbat, even Rosh Hashanah, no tractate is dedicated to the discussion of Shavuot—despite the fact that it had been one of the three pilgrimage festivals. Amoraic literature provides little information on this festival either.[5] The central ritual in the transitory period after the destruction of the Temple seems to have been a discussion of the sacrifices (t.Meg 3.5). The oldest extant list of readings for the festivals in the Mishna suggests Deuteronomy 16:9ff (the description of the offerings of Shavuot) for reading (Meg 3.5). The Tosefta is the first to attest the comeback of the revelation motif by including Exodus 19, the Sinai covenant, as an alternative liturgical reading (t.Meg 3.5). In principle, this tradition in the Tosefta might be at least as early as the Mishna or describe an alternative early practice. However, being closer to the later liturgical usage, it is the *lectio facilior* in comparison with the Mishna. Therefore, the absence of any reference to revelation texts among the readings in the Mishna seems to have been the more prevalent practice in rabbinic circles of tannaitic times. While the connection of Shavuot and the giving of the Torah appears also in *Seder Olam Rabba*: 'In the third [month] | on the sixth of the month, the Ten Commandments were given to them | and it was a Friday,'[6] the early dating of this text to the tannaitic period remains controversial (Stemberger 1996, 362f and Milikowsky 1981).

---

[4] 1QS I 16–II 28. The oldest fragments of the Damascus Document date the covenant renewal ceremony to the third month. 4Q266 11.16–18 = 4Q270 ii 11; cf. also the very fragmentary 4QCommunal Ceremony (4Q275) 1.3. Cf. Eiss (1997, 165–178) and Elgvin (1985, 103–106), but see Schreiber (2002, 58–77 esp. 68).

[5] The main name for Shavuot in the Rabbinic literature is עצרת (or עצרתא in Aramaic), probably emphasizing the aspect of the festival as the conclusion of the paschal period. Cf. already Josephus, Ant 3.253. According to Tabory (1995, 146 n. 3), the term עצרת appears 24 times in the Mishna, 39 times in the Tosefta and 16 times in Sifra, never שבועות (but see חג השבועות in t.Hag 1.6). In the amoraic literature חג השבועות appears many times. According to the Bar Ilan CD Rom (Responsa), it appears on 6 pages of the Bavli and on 2 of the Jerusalem Talmud.

[6] SOR 5.49–51. Other textual witnesses read 'Sabbath.' For the translation and discussion of the various textual witnesses, see Milikowsky (1981, 2.465).

It was only in the amoraic period that the association of Shavuot with
the revelation at Sinai becomes frequent.[7]

## A) Jewish and Christian Views on Pentecost as Recorded by the Church Fathers

At least from the second half of the fourth century onwards, some
Church Fathers are aware of the Jewish tradition that ascribes the giving of the Torah to Shavuot. Typically, Christian theology contrasted
the giving of the Spirit on Pentecost in a typology with the giving of
the Torah on Shavuot. To the best of my knowledge, the first attestation can be found in *Quaestiones veteris et novi testamenti* by Ambrosiaster
(366–384), who is well known for his acquaintance with many Jewish
traditions:[8]

> The Law has been given on the very same day, on which also the Holy
> Spirit descended upon the disciples in order that they may obtain author-
> ity and know to preach the evangelical law, i.e. on Pentecost (Geerlings
> 2002, 18f).

Beyond this text, Jerome, Augustine, Leo the Great, and Chrysostom
also demonstrate that this typology became widespread from the end of
the fourth century to the mid fifth century. In a tractate on the camps
of Israel in the desert dedicated to Fabiola, Jerome writes:

> The law was given on the summit of Mount Sinai on the fiftieth day of
> the Exodus of Israel from Egypt. Whence both the festival of Pentecost
> is celebrated, and afterwards through the descent of the Holy Spirit the

---

[7] The tradition from SOR is quoted explicitly in Shab 86b with the naming of
'Seder Olam' (דתניא בסדר עולם 88a). In Pes 68b, a similar expression is put into the
mouth of R. Eliezer. Cf. also Shab 86b 'The Sages say: on the sixth of the month,
the Ten Commandments were given to Israel. Rabbi Jose says: on the seventh of it';
cf. also Taan 28b (in the context of a list of bad things that happened to Israel on
Tammuz 17) and PRE 45.5 as well as the Aramaic statement in Shab 129b (Israel
would have been destroyed on Shavuot had it not received the Torah). Cf. also PRK
12.4. According to a passage in p.RH 4.8 [7] 59c attributed to R. Mesharshaya, the
description of the offerings on Shavuot differs slightly from that of other festivals since
Israel received the yoke of the Torah, presumably (but not unambiguously) on Shavuot.
Liturgically, the connection of the festival to revelation was further reinforced when
Ezekiel 1 became one of the Haftarot in Meg 31a.

[8] CSEL 50.168.6–9 cf. PL 35.2289. This statement is followed by a complicated
calculation. Those Christian traditions supporting their typology with a calendrical
calculation arrive at Pentecost based on grounds differing from the Jewish calculations
in Shab 86b–88b or SOR 5.

revelation of the Gospel is fulfilled, in order that just as previously on the fiftieth day, a true Jubilee and true Sabbath year and through the true 550 dinars which are given away to debtors, the law has been given to the people, [now] also to the apostles and those who were with them ([their] number [of 120 people, cf. Acts 1:15] being constituted in the 120 years of Moses' age) the Holy Spirit would descend and through many languages of the believers the whole world would be filled by the proclamation of the Gospel (ep. 78, cf. Newman 1997, 163, text: PL 22:707D–708A).

Around 400 C.E., Augustine writes in the long *Epistle* 55 to Januarius explaining the reasons behind various ecclesiastical celebrations and liturgical customs, among them Pentecost:[9]

> The fiftieth day is also commended to us in Scripture; and not only in the Gospel, by the fact that on that day the Holy Spirit descended, but also in the books of the Old Testament. For in them we learn, that after the Jews observed the first Passover with the slaying of the lamb as appointed, 50 days intervened between that day and the day on which upon Mount Sinai there was given to Moses the Law written with the finger of God; and this 'finger of God' is in the Gospels most plainly declared to signify the Holy Spirit: therefore one evangelist quotes our Lord's words thus, 'I cast out devils with the finger of God,' another quotes them thus, 'I cast out devils by the Spirit of God'.

In his first *Sermon on Pentecost* dated to May 23, 443, Leo the Great states that

> For as of old, after the Hebrew nation had been released from the Egyptians, on the fiftieth day after the sacrificing of the lamb the Law was given on Mount Sinai, so after the suffering of Christ, wherein the true Lamb of God was slain, on the fiftieth day from His Resurrection, the Holy Ghost came down upon the Apostles and the multitude of believers, so that the attentive Christian may easily perceive that the beginnings of the Old Testament were preparatory to the beginnings of the Gospel, and that the second covenant was founded by the same Spirit that had instituted the first. [An exegesis of Acts 2 follows] (Sermon 75.1; Dolle SC 74bis, 2nd ed. 1976, 286–289; I amended the translation in NPNF).

Chrysostom opens his first Homily on Matthew with the following highly polemic typology of the giving of the Torah and the descent of the Holy Spirit:

---

[9] Ep 55.16 (29) NPNF, cf. also On the Catechising of the Uninstructed 23. Intriguing is Dialogue with Faustus 12 where Augustine ascribes to Pentecost forgiveness as a central element, similar to Qumran's covenant renewal festival.

How then was that law given in time past, and when, and where? After the destruction of the Egyptians, in the wilderness, on Mount Sinai, when smoke and fire were rising up out of the mountain, a trumpet sounding, thunders and bolts of lightning, and Moses entering into the very depth of the cloud. But in the new covenant not so,—neither in a wilderness, nor in a mountain, nor with smoke and darkness and cloud and tempest; but at the beginning of the day, in a house, while all were sitting together, with great quietness, all took place. For to those, being more unreasonable, and hard to guide, there was need of outward pomp, as of a wilderness, a mountain, a smoke, a sound of trumpet, and the other similar things: but those who were of a higher character and submissive and who had risen above mere corporeal imaginations, [had no need of anything of these] (First Homily on Matthew 3, PG 57.15, NPNF 1.10.12).

Of course, the *Sitz im Leben* and the contexts of these texts differ widely. Leo's text is the only one directly related to the liturgy of Pentecost. Nevertheless, it becomes immediately clear that for Christian ears the typology proved at once the authenticity of the descent of the Spirit, the identity of God at Sinai and God at Pentecost as well as its superiority. For Christian spiritual leaders, Pentecost is closely related to Shavuot but utterly different in that it supersedes it.

## B)   An Ancient List of Festivals in Toledot Yeshu

Just as the Jewish tradition linking the giving of the Torah to Shavuot did not remain hidden from Christian writers who exploited the similarity ideologically, likewise the Christian Pentecost and its traditions were not unknown to Jews. An explicit reference to Christian Pentecostal traditions is found in some recensions of *Toledot Yeshu*, a Jewish anti-Christian romance or kind of anti-Gospel (see Newman 1999, 59–79; di Segni 1985; Krauss 1902. Cf. Krauss and Horbury 1996 on the history of motifs as well as Howard 1988, 60–70). Dating *Toledot Yeshu* is notoriously difficult and this question is further complicated by the fact that there exist numerous recensions and the literary development is rather complex.[10] The Pentecost-tradition appears in the recension

---

[10] See the nice introduction in Newman (1999) as well as di Segni (1984, 83–100) and (1985, 29–42, 216–219). Most manuscripts are late medieval or modern and, indeed, some details are best explained as medieval or even modern embellishments. However, single traditions appear as early as Origen's Contra Celsum, Tertullian, and the Talmudic literature. Agobard in the ninth century seems to be the first witness for a full fledged story (cf. Krauss & Horbury 1996, 68–71): Agobard, De iudaicis supersti-

customarily called the Helena-Group, the sole recension to include a kind of 'anti-Acts'.[11] The following argument will demonstrate that some Jews were acquainted with the Christian Pentecost as early as the fourth or beginning fifth century. The passage in question appears in a speech given by a certain Elijah, a code-name for Paul, to the Christian Jews:[12]

> Jesus said to you: Everybody in my power shall desecrate the Sabbath (that already the Holy One, may he be blessed, hated) and keep the First Day [Sunday] instead since on this day the Holy One, may he be blessed, enlightened his world; and for Pessah, which Israel does, make yourself a festival of the resurrection (מועדה דקיימתא),[13] since he rose from his tomb; and for Shavuot (עצרתא) Ascension (סולקא), and this is the day on which he ascended to heaven; and for Rosh Hashanah the invention of the Cross (אשכחתא דצליבא); and for the Great Fast [Yom Kippur] the Circumcision (גזורתא); and for Chanukkah Calenda.

This text represents a sort of Jewish perspective on the parting of the ways. It gives considerable space and detail to the question regarding the development of an independent Christian festival calendar. Apparently, it matters greatly to the Jewish authors, the redactors, copyists and readers of this tractate to distinguish the Christian festivals from their all too similar Jewish counterparts. The birth of the Christian calendar is dated extremely early, another sign for the fundamental importance attributed to its establishment.

Samuel Krauss dated the list of festivals early in the history of *Toledot Yeshu*, emphasizing that the festival names are in Aramaic while the rest of the text is in Hebrew. Yet, he also regarded it as confused or imprecise (Krauss 1902, 271f). He complains, e.g. that Shavuot is compared to the Ascension instead of Pentecost and Rosh Hashanah to the

---

tionibus et erroribus 10 (PL 104.77–100 = MGH Ep. V.185–199); cf. also the Epistula contra Iudaeos of Agobard's successor Amulo (PL 116.141–184) and several Aramaic witnesses from the Genizah which give the earliest direct attestation (Newman).

[11] The three main recensions have been named according to the protagonists supervising the trial of Jesus (Pilate, Helena, and Herod). On the 'Anti-Acts', see Legasse (1974, 99–132) and (1974/1975, 121–139), als well as di Segni (1985, 203–215).

[12] ישו אמר לכם כל מי שיהיהה בחזקתי יחלל השבת שכבר שנא אותו ה"ק"ב"ה וישמור יום ראשון תחתיו כי בו האיר הקב"ה עולמו ובשביל פסח שעושין ישראל עשו אותם עדה [או מועדה:] דקיימתא שעמד בו מקברו ובשביל עצרתא סולקא והוא יום שעלה בו בשמים ובשביל ראש השנה אשכחתא דצליבא ובשביל צומא רבא גזורתא ובשביל חנוכה קלנדא. Manuscript Strassburg according to Krauss (1902, 48) with the variants according to Krauss (1933, 44–61).

[13] According to a better manuscript mentioned by Krauss (1933, 47).

Invention of the Cross in May instead of the Exaltation of the Cross.
Krauss is correct from the perspective of the modern liturgy. However,
if we consider Christian liturgical practice at the end of the fourth or
the fifth century, the confusion vanishes and the Jewish text emerges as
being informed about Christian festivals including Pentecost.

In the fourth and early fifth century, Pentecost commemorates *both*
the Outpouring of the Spirit on the Apostles *and* the Ascension of
Jesus (Cabié 1965, 127–142; Kretschmar 1954/1955, 209–253). A
separate festival of Ascension developed only slowly from the late fourth
century onwards as we can learn from Egeria and even from the Old
Armenian Lectionary, reflecting the Jerusalem liturgy from the early
fifth century, where Ascension seems to be a rather recent development
(Egeria, Itinerarium 43.5; cf. Renoux 1971, nos LVII [Ascension] and
LVIII [Pentecost] 336ff, esp. n. 1 and 5 to LVII). This prima facie
impression is reinforced by further observations regarding the other
festivals mentioned.[14]

This passage from *Toledot Yeshu* about Christian festivals demonstrates
the centrality of heortology beyond Pesaḥ in the Jewish dispute with
Christianity even as early as in late antiquity, shortly after the redaction
of the Palestinian Talmud (or even parallel to it). The following section is
an attempt to elaborate on a rabbinic passage from the Yerushalmi that
mentions Shavuot and possibly polemicizes and parodies the Christian
Pentecost and its tradition.

C)   A Parody/Polemic on Pentecost in the Yerushalmi

One of the few rabbinic texts mentioning Shavuot tells a short story
of a Rabbi who is (falsely) accused of being drunk and justifies his
strange appearance by referring to the effect of wisdom. This recalls
the account in Acts 2 where the disciples are (wrongly) accused of
being drunk on Shavuot when the Holy Spirit descends on them. As I
mentioned above, Shavuot appears rarely in the rabbinic corpora. If
one of these few texts seems to be close to the fundamental story of
the Christian Pentecost, this is all the more noteworthy. Let me add

---

[14] I will deal more extensively with this passage in a paper for the conference
'Between Syncretism and Independence Models of Interaction between Judaism and
Christianity' (Bar Ilan in 2007). I would like to express my deep gratitude to Michael
Kohlbacher whose detailed and erudite comments greatly enhanced my interpretation
of this passage.

that in both cases, the accusation comes from an outsider, a 'Matrona', a rich Roman lady here, a non-Christian Jew there. In both stories, the claim is rebutted by referring to the source of authority as cause for the unusual look, not the spirit but learnedness in the Torah. But let us look at the text first:[15]

> [A] When Rabbi Yona drank four cups during the night of Pesaḥ, he held his head until Pentecost.
> [B] Rabbi Yuda son of Rabbi Elai drank four cups in the night of Pesaḥ and held his head until Sukkot!
> [C1] A Matrona saw his face glowing.
>> [C2] She said to him: Old man, old man, one out of three things is in you:
>> [C3] Either you are a wine drinker, or a usurer or a pig farmer.
> [D1] He answered her: May the spirit leave this woman!
>> [D2] None of these three things is in me but my learning as is written
>> [D3] 'the wisdom of a man makes his face shine' (Eccl 8:1c).

This difficult but fascinating story appears in the tractate *Pesaḥim* and emerges from a discussion of the question of which kind of wine is suitable to be used for the four cups during the Pesaḥ Seder. It is, of course, a piece of literature reflecting social history, not the account of an actual encounter. The absurdity of a hangover longer than one month reveals a grain of rabbinic humor.

Before we pursue our comparison with Acts 2, however, we have to respond to the question whether we can be sure that Shavuot is the pivotal point of the story, not Sukkot. Quite clearly, the only phrase referring to Sukkot, sentence [B], about Rabbi Yuda's six-month hangover from Pesaḥ to Sukkot seems to be an addition to the original folkloristic account by the redactor of this part (or a later figure). It does not appear in the parallel in the Bavli. Moreover, Rabbi Yona belongs to the Palestinian amoraim in the mid fourth century and Rabbi Yuda, son of Rabbi Elai, to the tannaim of the mid second century. Had the story grown according to chronological order starting with R. Yuda, it would have been very strange indeed to supplement the six-month hangover with a one and a half month long period. The opposite process is much more plausible from a literary standpoint.

---

[15] My translation of p.Pes 10.1 37c. Cf. the verbal parallels p.Shab 8.1 11a and p.Sheq 3.2 47b. Related versions appear also in EcclR 8.1 (22a); TanB Huqqat 19 (58a); PesR 14 (62b–63a); PRK 4.4 (68), Ned 49b, cf. also Ber 55a.

Finally, the supposedly tannaitic fragment, is not written in Hebrew but in Aramaic. It simply continues the story in the same language and is even phrased in exactly the same words as the first sentence ascribed to an amoraic speaker.[16] Clearly, the phrase on Sukkot fulfills a literary function—to exaggerate the already absurdly long hangover of Rabbi Yona *in extremis*: Not just a mere one and a half months, but six. The Matrona therefore, primarily responds to Rabbi Yona on Shavuot as mentioned in the opening phrase [A].

There are further connections to Shavuot beyond the explicit mention in the opening sentence [A]. The shining face [C3] recalls, of course, Moses' face glowing from the divine *kavod* upon his descent after the giving of the Torah in Exodus 34. The connection to the *imaginaire*[17] of Shavuot is a strong argument since the shining face motif is otherwise not very widespread in rabbinic literature. Furthermore, the prooftext [D3] quoted from Eccl 8:1c, appearing rarely in amoraic and never in tannaitic literature, seems to be particularly closely related to the concept of revelation. In the talmudim, all four attestations can be found in this story and its parallels, all dealing with revelation. Among the midrashim, *Pesiqta deRav Kahana* is the earliest composition to mention this verse several times: all of them in an anthology containing practically all the exegeses of this verse that can be found in the other amoraic and medieval midrashim (PRK 4.4 Mandelbaum 1.65–69). One of these links the verse with Israel at the giving of the Torah at Sinai, another one with Moses, and another one is a direct parallel to the Yerushalmi story. (The other traditions relate the verse to Adam, the prophets and the *talmid ḥakhamim*. At least the second is again clearly connected to revelation.) All of them demonstrate the close relation of this verse to the *imaginaire* of Shavuot.

After assessing the explicit and implicit motifs connecting the story to Shavuot, we can proceed to the comparison with the account in Acts 2. As mentioned above, both narratives depict an outsider (wrongly) accusing the protagonist(s) of intoxication and both relate this event to Shavuot/Pentecost. The Matrona is clearly a code, not a historical

---

[16] The Tanna R. Yuda replaces the amora R. Yona as protagonist in the parallel accounts in EcclR, the Bavli and PRK. In the Yerushalmi, R. Yona is the anchor of the story in the halakhic discussion in the immediate context. Possibly, the story about the faces of R. Yosi and R. Yona appearing in the vision of Ursicinus in p.Ber 5.1 37b played an important role in the attribution of the shining face to R. Yona, here. I would like to thank Oded Irshai for this suggestion.

[17] For a definition of *imaginaire*, cf. Stökl Ben Ezra (2003, 8–10).

person. Though she does not belong to the group, she is potentially interested in it. This is true for the non-Christian Jews in Acts and the non-Jewish Roman Lady in the Yerushalmi.[18] In the parallel tradition in EcclR, the outsider status of the interlocutor is emphasized, being explicitly called a *goy*. The *sugya* is therefore clearly dealing with boundaries and a traversing between the Jews and others.

And it is in this context, in opinion, that we are able to understand a real crux in the text, the awkward tripartite combination of accusations against R. Yona uttered by the Matrona: to have a shining face as a drunkard, a usurer or a pig breeder [C3]. (These accusations reappear in all parallels, not always in the same order, but nevertheless with intoxication as the acme.) The accusations clearly have widely varying degrees of plausibility. While the imbibing of alcohol certainly may influence facial expression and color, pig breeding and usury simply do not. The traditional explanation that pig breeding and usury are professions generating high profits which cause the face to shine seems rather fanciful. I do not know of any clear-cut rabbinic proof-text for the arguments of financial profit causing the face to shine and that pig breeding was particularly lucrative (though usury was). A symbolic interpretation as a literary function seems more plausible. Similarly as with intoxication though even more so than it, usury and pig breeding define the boundaries between insiders and outsiders. Rabbinic traditions liken both usury and pig breeding to apostasy. The biblical distinction between the interdiction of usury of fellow Jews and the permission to outsiders already demonstrates the connection of usury to definitions of boundaries. A clear connection to apostasy is found in the following quotation from the Tosefta:

> Said R. Yose: Come and see how blind are the eyes of those who lend at usurious rates. A man calls to his fellow to serve an idol, have unlawful sexual relations, or shed blood, [for] he wants him to fall [into sin] with him. But this one brings a scribe, pen, ink, document, and witnesses, and says to them: Come and write concerning him that he has no share in the One who commanded concerning usury. And he writes the document and registers it in the archives, and so denies him who spoke and thereby brought the world into being, blessed be he. Thus you have learned that

---

[18] מטרונא and מטרוניתא do not appear very often in the Talmudim (15 times in the Bavli, 6 times in the Yerushalmi) but very often in the aggadic midrashim (333 times, of these 71 in the earlier collections, e.g. 17 in GenR). On the Matrona, see Artmann (2002) and Gershenzon (1985, 1–41). The anthology by Ganan (2002, 131–150) is not helpful.

those who lend at usurious rates deny the principle [of divine authority].
R. Simeon b. Eleazar says: More than they make they lose. For they treat
the Torah like a fraud, and Moses like a fool. They say: Now if Moses
knew how much money we would make, he would never have written
[the prohibition of usury] (t.BM 6.17)!

Transferring the rationale of this story to ours, the Matrona is accusing
Rabbi Yona of behaving like a non-Jew or an apostate. The next accusation, pig breeding, a forbidden profession according to the Mishnah,
is not one of the favorite topics of the rabbinic literature. Yet wherever
it appears, there is a clear connection between pigs and the non-Jewish
world, between pigs and apostasy. Diocletian is called a swine herdsman
(p.Ter 8.11 46b) and the Roman kingdom is called a pig:

> R. Phinehas and R. Hilkiah, in the name of R. Simeon, said: Out of
> all the prophets, only two, namely Asaph and Moses, named it (i.e. the
> fourth beast). Asaph said: The boar (חזיר) out of the wood does ravage
> it (Ps 80:14). Moses said: And the swine (חזיר), because it parts the hoof,
> and is cloven footed, but does not chew the cud, he is unclean to you (Lev
> 11:7). Why is it (i.e. Edom or Rome) compared to a חזיר (swine or boar)?
> To tell you this: Just as the swine when reclining puts forth its hooves
> as if to say: See that I am clean, so too does the empire of wickedness
> (Edom/Rome) boast as it commits violence and robbery, under the guise
> of establishing a judicial tribunal. This may be compared to a governor
> who put to death the thieves, adulterers, and sorcerers. He leaned over
> to a counsellor and said: I myself did these three things in one night
> (LevR 13.5 Margulies 291f).

Famous is the following tradition from the Bavli where the study of
Greek wisdom as well as (raising) pigs are connected to treachery:

> Our Rabbis taught: When the Kings of the Hasmonean house fought
> one another, Hyrcanus was outside and Aristobulus within (the city wall).
> Each day (those that were within) used to let down (to the other party)
> denars in a basket, and haul up (in return) animals for the daily offerings.
> An old man there, who was learned in Greek wisdom, spoke with them in
> Greek wisdom, saying: As long as they carry on the Temple service they
> will never be delivered into your hands. On the morrow, they let down
> denars in a basket and hauled up a pig. When it reached halfway up the
> wall, it stuck its claws into the wall, and the land of Israel was shaken
> over a distance of four hundred parasangs by four hundred parasangs. At
> that time they declared: Cursed be the man who rears pigs and cursed be
> the man who teaches his son Greek wisdom (Men 64b, Sot 49b)!

Also the third accusation, intoxication, is not a frequent topos in rabbinic
literature, and, unlike the Bible, it does not even appear many times as
a narrative element with non-Biblical figures (cf. Git 57a, 68a). In Rab-

binic literature, we find frequent declarations against drunkenness (cf. Ber 31b; Er 64a–65a; Pes 113b; Taan 17b; Sanh 22b, 42a), yet much less compared to other offences such as incest. Likened to apostasy e.g. in Hos 4:11–12, intoxication, too, belongs to the characteristics of a gentile.[19] The only well known exception is, of course the commandment to get drunk on Purim (Meg 7b).

In this light, I would like to suggest that we might understand the crux of the intention of the Matrona's accusations as follows: 'Your face shines since you are like one of those pig breeders and usurers, those apostates, those who became Christians who appeared on Pentecost as having drunk too much.' The outsider accuses the insider of being closer to being an outsider than she herself is. The rabbi's answer is 'None of this is true! I am not like one of those apostates who falsely claim that the Spirit is enlightening them. I belong to God's people and it is my learning of God's Torah that makes my face shine just like Moses at Sinai who was truly inspired by God on the authentic, original Pentecost. I adhere to the Torah and its commandments and therefore I drink four cups of wine on Pesaḥ as commanded. Those Christians and we Jews look similar to outsiders like you, but we are utterly different.' The redactor of the Talmudic story then parodied this polemic by exaggerating the already absurd 50 days of the hangover to 180 days without changing the character of the episode as a humorous self-definition narrative, a polemical parody. Finally, R. Yona's curse [D1] 'May the spirit leave this woman', fits extraordinarily well to a polemical anti-Christian function in the context of Pentecost. While it is clearly not a rare formula in the rabbinic corpus, many other expressions could have been used instead.

To be sure, there are differences between Acts 2 and the Yerushalmi story.[20] Yet we should not expect a full-fledged typology. It is the nature of parody to choose a specific set of elements to make fun of.

---

[19] See e.g. LamR 3.5 on Lam 3.14: 'I have become a derision to all my people.' It is written, They that sit in the gate talk of me (Ps 69:13). This refers to the nations of the world who sit in theatres and circuses. 'And I am the song of the drunkards.' After they sit eating and drinking and become intoxicated they sit and talk of me, scoffing at me and saying: We have no need to eat carobs like the Jews!

[20] While in Acts 2 it is the expression of the disciples' mouth, the strange talk, that causes attraction. Here, it is the expression of R. Yona's face. There, many are accused, here only one. The only possible 'convert' mentioned in the Yerushalmi is the Matrona herself in distinction to the masses in Acts 2. The Scriptural prooftexts differ, Joel there, Ecclesiastes here. The disciples claim not to have drunk at all, while R. Yona drank, even if 50 days ago.

## Conclusions

Numerous Christian texts polemicize against the Jewish festival of Shavuot and against exploiting Jewish traditions of this festival to ideologically justify its substitution by the Christian Pentecost. The passage from *Toledot Yeshu* shows that Jews were not apathetic vis-à-vis the Christianization of liturgical time in the Roman empire. Some rabbinic Jews were familiar with liturgical aspects of the Christian Pentecost at least in the fourth or fifth century, and the general framework of that passage attests also to some acquaintance with the story of Acts. Viewing the Yerushalmi story as parodying polemics of the Christian Pentecost plausibly solves some difficulties in traditional understandings of this passage. It offers a glimpse of the Jewish perspective on the Jewish-Christian rivalry—a rivalry regarding the implementation of biblical festivals and the liturgical calendar that clearly was not limited to Pesaḥ.

## Literature

Andersen, F.I., '2 (Slavonic Apocalypse of) Enoch' in: J.H. Charlesworth (ed.), *The Old Testament Pseudepigrapha* [2 vols], New York etc. 1983.

Artmann, T., דיאלוג, מיתוס ויצוג דמוי היסטוריה: קריאה בשבעה מפגשים בין מטרונה לר' יוסי בבראשית רבה, [unpublished M.A. thesis, Hebrew University] Jerusalem 2002.

Assmann, J., 'Der zweidimensionale Mensch. Das Fest als Medium des kollektiven Gedächtnisses' in: idem (ed.), *Das Fest und das Heilige; Religiöse Kontrapunkte zur Alltagswelt* (Studien zum Verstehen fremder Religionen 1), Gütersloh 1991.

Bauckham, R., 'The Lord's Day,' in: D.A. Cardon (ed.), *From Sabbath to Lord's Day; A Biblical, Historical, and Theological Investigation*, Grand Rapids/Michigan 1982.

Bell, C., *Ritual Perspectives and Dimensions*, New York—Oxford 1997.

———, *Ritual Theory—Ritual Practice*, New York—Oxford 1992.

Böttrich, C., *Das slavische Henochbuch* (JSHRZ 5:7), Gütersloh 1996.

Cabié, R., *La Pentecôte; L'évolution de la cinquantaine pascale au cours des cinq premiers siècles* (Bibliothèque de liturgie), Tournai 1965.

Cocchini, F., 'L'evoluzione storico-religiosa della festa di Pentecoste', *RivBib* 25 (1977).

Eiss, W., 'Das Wochenfest im Jubiläenbuch und im antiken Judentum', in: M. Albani et al. (eds), *Studies in the Book of Jubilees* (TSAJ 65), Tübingen 1997.

Elgvin, T., 'The Qumran Covenant Festival and the Temple Scroll', *JJS* 36 (1985).

Erez, A., *The Evolution of Shavuot; From a Temple Oriented Festival to a Commemoration of the Giving of the Torah* [unpublished M.St. dissertation in Hebrew and Jewish Studies] Oxford 2003.

Ganan, M., 'Matrona', *Shana be Shana* (2002) [Hebrew, also: http://www.daat.ac.il/daat/kitveyet/shana/ganan-1.htm].

Geerlings, W., 'Ambrosiaster' in: idem and S. Döpp (eds), *Lexikon der antiken christlichen Literatur*, Freiburg—Basel—Wien 3rd ed. 2002.

Gershenzon, R. & E. Slomovic, 'A Second Century Jewish-Gnostic Debate: Rabbi Jose ben Halafta and the Matrona', *JSJ* 16 (1985).

Goudoever, J. van, *Fêtes et calendriers bibliques* (ThH 7), Paris 3rd ed. 1967.

Howard, H., 'A Primitive Hebrew Gospel of Matthew and the Tol'doth Yeshu', *NTS* 34 (1988).

Jacobson, H., *A Commentary on Pseudo-Philo's Liber Antiquitatum Biblicarum with Latin Text and English Translation* [2 vols] (AGJU 31), Leiden 1996.

Krauss, S., *Das Leben Jesu nach jüdischen Quellen*, Berlin 1902.

———, 'Neuere Ansichten über "Toledoth Jeschu"', *MGWJ* 77 (1933).

———, & W. Horbury, *The Jewish-Christian Controversy from the Earliest Times to 1789; Volume I. History. Edited and Revised by William Horbury* (TSAJ 56), Tübingen 1996.

Kretschmar, G., 'Himmelfahrt und Pfingsten', *ZKG* 66 (1954/1955).

Legasse, S., 'La légende juive des Apôtres et les rapports judéo-chrétiens dans le haut Moyen Age', *BLE* 75 (1974).

———, 'La légende juive des Apôtres et les rapports judéo-chrétiens dans le Moyen Age occidental', *Yearbook of the Ecumenical Institute for Advanced Theological Studies* (1974/1975).

Milikowsky, C., *Seder Olam; A Rabbinic Chronography* [2 vols, unpublished Ph.D. Diss.] Yale 1981.

Newman, H., *Jerome and the Jews* [unpublished Ph.D. Diss, Hebrew University] Jerusalem 1997.

———, 'The Death of Jesus in the *Toledot Yeshu* Literature', *JThS* 50 (1999).

Potin, J., *La fête juive de la Pentecôte* [2 vols] (LeDiv 65), Paris 1971.

Renoux, Ch./A., *Le Codex arménien jérusalem 121; Tôme 2: Édition, comparée du texte et de deux autres manuscrits* (PO 36.2), Turnhout 1971.

Rouwhorst, G., 'The Origins and Evolution of Early Christian Pentecost', *StPatr* 35 (2001).

Schreiber, S. 'Aktualisierung göttlichen Handelns am Pfingsttag. Das frühjüdische Fest in Apg 2,1' *ZNW* 93 (2002).

Segni, R. di, 'La tradizione testuale delle Toledoth Jeshu: Manoscritti, edizioni a stampa classificazione', *RasIsr* 50 (1984).

———, *Il Vangelo del Ghetto*, Rome 1985.

Stemberger, G., *Introduction ot the Talmud and Midrash*, Minneapolis 2nd ed. 1996.

Stökl Ben Ezra, D., *The Impact of Yom Kippur on Early Christianity* (WUNT 163), Tübingen 2003.

Tabory, J., *Jewish Festivals in the Time of the Mishna and Talmud*, Jerusalem 1995 [Hebrew].

VanderKam, J.C., 'Weeks, Festival of' in: D.N. Freedman (ed.), *Anchor Bible Dictionary* [vol. 6], New York, 1992.

Yuval, I., *Two Nations in Your Womb; Perceptions of Jews and Christians in Late Antiquity and the Middle Ages*, Berkeley 2006.

# THE ROOTS OF THE EARLY CHRISTIAN EUCHARIST: JEWISH BLESSINGS OR HELLENISTIC SYMPOSIA?

*Gerard Rouwhorst*
Tilburg University, The Netherlands

## INTRODUCTION

The origins of few early Christian rituals have been debated as intensively as those of the Eucharist. From the mid-twentieth century to this day, liturgical scholars have devoted a flood of articles and books to the subject, sparked off by Gregory Dix's *The Shape of the Liturgy*, which appeared in 1945, just before World War II came to an end.

If one attempts to chart the main lines of thought that emerge from the vast amount of secondary literature, one is struck by the fact that approaches have changed conspicuously in recent decades. After the appearance of Dix's extensive and influential monograph, scholars turned at length to the Jewish roots of the Eucharist in their search for parallels with Jewish meal traditions. Certain Christian Eucharistic prayers and Jewish prayer texts were believed to be similar. They included blessings pronounced before and after meals (especially the 'birkat ha-mazon', the grace after meals) and blessings, thanksgivings and supplications said on other occasions (the blessings before and after the Shema and the benedictions of the Amidah). Scholars concluded from such parallels that the early Christian Eucharist could be traced back largely to Jewish meal traditions, which would have been transformed by Jesus and the first generations of Christians. Outspoken exponents of this approach were Louis Bouyer (1966), Louis Ligier (cf. esp. 1968, 19–57 English translation: 1970, 113–150; 1972, 181–202 English translation: 1973, 161–185), Thomas Talley (1976, 11–39; 1984, 404–420; 1992, 15–43), Herman Wegman (1980, 263–278; 1991, 193–216) and Enrico Mazza (see esp. the articles collected in 1992 and 1996 [French and English translations 1999]).[1]

---

[1] I myself have tried to sketch the development of the Eucharist and the Eucharistic prayer of early Syriac Christianity (the first four to five centuries), starting from the *birkat ha-mazon* as reconstructed by Louis Finkelstein and the Eucharist underlying Did

In the past two decades, however, this approach has been increasingly criticised. The main objection, voiced particularly by Paul Bradshaw, concerns an uncritical examination of Jewish liturgical traditions which, moreover, are often attributed to a far too early period. (See in particular his book 2002. See further Bradshaw's monograph on the origins of the early Christian Eucharist 2004 and his article 2003, 21–36.) At the same time, several scholars have explored new paths by drawing attention to similarities between the early Christian Eucharist and Greco-Roman banquets. The latter, often designated as symposia, were a common phenomenon in the Mediterranean world; they cut across religious and ethnic boundaries (Jews, Greeks and Romans) and usually followed a general pattern involving a number of customs and rituals. It has been proposed that the Christian Eucharist originated and developed as a variety of this symposium. (See in particular Klinghardt 1996; de Jonge 2001, 209–237 and 2006; Smith 2002. See also McGowan 1999, esp. 45–60; Bradshaw 2004, 43–44. See for the symposia also: Leyerle 1999, 29–61.)

Unlike scholars investigating Jewish origins of the Eucharist, most adherents of the symposium theory are less interested in liturgical *texts* than in the social dimensions of the early Christian Eucharist. Rather than analysing prayers, blessings and thanksgivings and their theological significance, they examine social structures and internal hierarchies, and non-verbal, material aspects such as the architectural setting, the compilation of the menu and the choice of food. Some scholars draw their main inspiration from social theory, derived from sociology or cultural (social) anthropology. A typical example of this emphasis on the social and material aspects of the early Christian Eucharist is Andrew McGowan's study *Ascetic Eucharists*, which deliberately leaves aside prayer texts to focus on meanings encoded in food and drink (esp. McGowan 1999, 1–9).

In this paper I would like to offer a brief critical evaluation of theories regarding the pre-Christian origins of the Eucharist. I shall consider objections to the Jewish roots of the Christian Eucharist and the early dating of Jewish liturgical traditions. I shall also assess the symposium

---

chs. 9 and 10, which in my view is based on Jewish meal customs (see: Rouwhorst 1980, 211–240). For a survey of the research of the Eucharistic Rites, see Bradshaw 2002, 118–143.

thesis and the extent to which early Christian ritual meals were based on Greek and Roman symposia.

Before proceeding, some observations should be made on the development of the early Christian Eucharist itself. In recent decades, apart from the investigation of pre-Christian roots, there has been a tendency to study the emergence and early history of the Eucharist from a new perspective. This has involved a different way of selecting relevant sources and the questioning of theological views previously considered self-evident. Since these two aspects are interconnected, they cannot be considered separately. Moreover, they have repercussions with regard to the pre-Christian roots of early Christian ritual meals, and in particular the Eucharist.

## THE DEVELOPMENT OF A NEW PARADIGM FOR THE STUDY OF THE EARLY CHRISTIAN EUCHARIST AND THE SELECTION OF SOURCES

One of the principal convictions underlying the traditional view of the early Christian Eucharist is that, from the very beginning, it was the continuation of the Last Supper (which many scholars believed to have taken place in the setting of the annual Jewish Passover ritual).[2] The early Christian Eucharist would have followed the pattern of the Last Supper, with the blessing of the bread preceding that of the wine, the institution narrative recited during the Eucharistic prayer, and the ritual as a whole primarily commemorating the death of the Lord. This approach was based on a selection of source material that legitimated it and thereby contributed to the exclusion of contradictory sources. The principal sources taken into consideration were the New Testament institution narratives, the description of the Eucharist by Justin (150 C.E.), and the Eucharistic prayer encountered in the so-called Apostolic Tradition, usually ascribed to Hippolytus of Rome at the beginning of the third century. On the basis of Justin in particular, it was generally accepted that the main ritual elements of the Eucharist

---

[2] One of the most important and influential representatives of this traditional view is again Gregory Dix, who has assumed the existence of an original, pristine and 'apostolic' core of the Eucharist, which would have evolved from a 'seven-action' form, attested by the New Testament institution narratives, into a 'four-action' pattern. For a discussion of this hypothesis, see Johnson 2006, 32–75 esp. 44–50. On questions raised by this traditional view proposed by Dix and held by many other scholars, see also Rouwhorst 1993, 89–112.

had been dissociated from the meal (originally held in the evening, as was customary in the Mediterranean) and had been amalgamated with the Jewish synagogue's 'liturgy of the word'. This would account for the general dual structure of the Eucharistic liturgy in practically all liturgical traditions of the east and west: the liturgy of the Word preceding the preparation and offering of the gifts (1), blessing and thanksgiving (2), breaking of the bread (3) and communion, i.e. the ritualised eating and drinking of bread and wine (4) 'eucharistised' by the prayer of blessing and thanksgiving. The so-called anaphora of the Apostolic Tradition (ch. 4) was seen to support the view that the Eucharistic celebration included the recitation of the institution narrative. Incidentally, this text played an important role in 'proving' continuity between the New Testament period and the golden age of the Church Fathers (4th and 5th centuries). It served as a kind of stepping stone, allowing scholars to jump from the 'apostolic' era to the patristic period. Sources not fitting into this pattern were considered to describe other types of ritual meals, particularly the agape, or to derive from heterodox or at least marginal circles. They include the Didache (chs. 9 and 10), apocryphal Acts of the Apostles such as those of Thomas and John, and descriptions of common meals found in Tertullian (especially in his Apology, ch. 39) and in the Apostolic Tradition (chs. 25–29; ed. of B. Botte 1989; Bradshaw, Johnson, & Philips 2002).

Today, this traditional approach is being abandoned by more and more scholars. In a sense, a complete reassessment of the sources has taken place: those ignored or marginalised by adherents of the traditional paradigm now take pride of place in reconstructions of the development of the early Christian Eucharist (see Bradshaw 2004 and also Rouwhorst 1993; 1996, 177–200; Klinghardt 1996, 499–522; McGowan 1999). The reliability of the institution narratives as testimonies of early Christian liturgical practice is increasingly questioned. (In addition to the literature given above, see Johnson 2006, 45–48.) Conversely, the Didache now occupies a key position in the argumentation (Rouwhorst 2005a, 143–156. Cf. McGowan 1999, 21–22 and Mazza 1992, 19–50 and 77–109). Attempts to fit it into the traditional pattern by the Procrustus method—by removing or adding elements that are not in the text—are rejected by most scholars. Further, contrary to what was generally believed, McGowan and Bradshaw have argued that the supper described by Tertullian in his Apology, and designated as an 'agape', was a Eucharistic celebration. They have also produced persuasive evidence that the gatherings before daybreak, at which the faithful received 'the sacrament of the Eucharist' 'from none but the hands of the presidents' (De corona militis, ch. 3, 3; cf. De oratione 19,4), were not 'Eucharists', but a sort of communion service at which Christians received Eucharistic food consecrated beforehand at an evening meal, called *agape* in Apology ch. 39 (McGowan 2004, 165–176; Bradshaw 2004, 96–103. Cf. for Apology, ch. 39 also Kinghardt 1996, 514–517). At the time of Cyprian, the Eucharist had already been transferred from evening to morning, but according to McGowan and Bradshaw this innovation gave rise to disputes echoed in Cyprian's famous sixty-third letter about the water-drinkers (McGowan 2004, 173–175; Bradshaw 2004, 108–114). As for the so-called Apostolic Tradition, its attribution to Hippolytus, its Roman origin and its date are now open to discussion (see for instance Bradshaw, Johnson, & Philips 2002, 1–15). In the context of this paper it is noteworthy that several scholars have voiced serious doubts about the homogeneity of the anaphora of chapter 4, suggesting that some passages, including the epiclesis and the institution narrative, might have been added in the fourth century (see esp. Bradshaw, Johnson, & Philips 2002, 44–46; Bradshaw 1997, 1–18, esp. 10–14). Although I am rather sceptical about attempts to split the text into older and younger sections, I do have doubts about the dating of the prayer as such (Rouwhorst 2005b, 337–340). In fact, I would suggest that the entire anaphora of chapter 4, rather than parts of it, might have been added to the Apostolic Tradition at a considerably late stage in the development of these documents, and that the earliest practices concerning the celebration of the 'Eucharist' in this source are to be found in chapters 26–29, which contain descriptions of ritual suppers remarkably similar to the 'agape' described by Tertullian in his Apology.

If all of this is true, it has far-reaching implications for the reconstruction of the development of the early Christian Eucharist. It means that the separation of the Eucharist from the context of an evening meal occurred at a much later date than is often assumed—in Africa at least, but probably in other regions too. As for the Eucharist described in Justin's Apology, assuming that it was actually held in the morning (which is indeed likely, though difficult to prove; cf. Kinghardt 1996, 500–509), its case was rather exceptional, and it did not simply constitute the norm from which other communities would have deviated. More important still, the influence of the Last Supper and the New Testament institution narratives on early Christian practice was less than has often been believed, and became stronger only in the course of time. (This observation may give rise to numerous questions which I have discussed elsewhere and which I will therefore leave aside here.)

This new approach obviously has repercussions for the various theories on the roots of the Christian Eucharist. In general, it seems quite clear that scholars who have tended to find these roots primarily in Jewish liturgical traditions have depended considerably on the 'traditional paradigm'. This is certainly true of Dix, and to some extent also of Ligier and Talley. (Mazza's view, on the other hand, contains many elements of the new paradigm.) However, this does not imply that the theory must be discarded for this reason alone, to be replaced by one attributing the origins of the Christian Eucharist to a so-called Hellenistic symposium. Theoretically, one can even imagine that the proponents of Jewish roots could find some support in the new paradigm. Moreover, the plausibility of the symposium theory is not enhanced purely by the fact that it fits better in the new paradigm sketched here. A critical assessment of the two approaches on the basis of other criteria remains necessary, and particular attention should be given to the manner in which available sources are interpreted.

## THE JEWISH ROOTS THEORY RECONSIDERED

The most decisive argument against the Jewish roots theory, as stated at the beginning, is that it is based on uncritical use and incorrect dating of Jewish liturgical sources. The question therefore arises as to how this argument stands in the light of our knowledge of the development of Jewish liturgical traditions in the early centuries of the Christian era, or, put differently, in the Amoraic and particularly the Tannaitic periods. Should we conclude that the whole theory is untenable?

This question, I believe, is too complex to be answered with a categorical 'yes' or 'no'. Firstly, it cannot be denied that a number of scholars, some of whom have already been mentioned, have drawn undiscerningly on rather late Jewish sources. Some have rather naively interpreted any parallel between Jewish and Christian liturgical practices or texts—often irrespective of region or date—as an indication of the dependence of the Christian tradition on the Jewish. Furthermore, some may be blamed for making hasty and sweeping generalisations, often based on a very limited number of sources. An example is the tendency to trace back all early Christian Eucharistic prayers to the pattern of *birkat-ha-mazon*. While it cannot be denied that some surviving Christian prayer texts fit comfortably in this pattern, many others do not, or are only faintly similar to this Jewish prayer (which, incidentally, is attested by rather late sources; see for instance Bradshaw 1997, 9–10). It should also be admitted that certain widespread theories about the Jewish roots of specific aspects of the early Christian Eucharistic prayer have become entirely obsolete. An example is Ligier's attempt to explain the insertion of the institution narrative in the Eucharistic prayer by comparing it to the practice of inserting so-called embolisms in the *birkat ha-mazon* during the great Jewish festivals (see Ligier 1972/1973). Apart from the fact that it is difficult to know precisely when this practice originated in Judaism, the entire argument is founded on the problematic assumption that the insertion of the institution narrative occurred at a very early date, when the first Christian rituals emerged in a predominantly Jewish environment. If there is one assumption that has become questionable, it is precisely this one. Another widely accepted theory that has become increasingly problematic is that of the dependence of the early Christian Eucharist on the Jewish Passover celebration. Here again, two objections can be raised. On the one hand, most versions of this argument exaggerate the role of the institution narratives, which indeed constitute the principle basis of the hypothesis. On the other hand, with regard to the reconstruction of the Last Supper and its alleged Passover context, the proponents tend to draw uncritically on Jewish sources of a much later period than the New Testament (cf. Jeremias' influential study 1967 and in this connection the critique of this theory advanced by Stemberger 1987, 147–158 = 1990, 357–374). This holds for the Mishnah and the Tosefta, and without doubt for the Babylonian Talmud. (On the development of the Pesachhaggada from the destruction of the Second Temple until the beginning of the first millennium, see Leonhard 2003, 201–231 and 2004, 151–166.)

This being said, it would be premature to reject outright the entire thesis of the Jewish roots of the Christian Eucharist. A number of facts should prevent us from drawing such a drastic conclusion.

1. In spite of all objections to the Jewish origins of Christian liturgy, the fact remains that Christianity and its earliest rituals emerged and developed within the variegated world of Judaism at the beginning of the Common Era. Obviously, this fact cannot be used uncritically to prove the Jewish origin of any early Christian ritual remotely similar to some sort of Jewish Christian tradition. Nonetheless, one must realise that the earliest Christian liturgical practices were not

invented out of thin air. This goes to support the hypothesis that the earliest Christian rituals had their origins in Jewish traditions.

2. In so far as the new view on the early Christian Eucharist, as I have described it, allows for a variety of ritual practices not necessarily based on the uniform pattern of the Last Supper, it may support the assumption that early Christian rituals such as the Eucharist have their origins in Jewish traditions. If evidence indicates that some early Christian Eucharists were based on Jewish meal traditions rather than the pattern of the Last Supper, this cannot simply be refuted by claiming that the early Christian Eucharist was not a Eucharist at all unless it followed the pattern of the Last Supper.

3. Although liturgical scholars of the past were often rather naive in attributing Jewish origins to certain aspects of the early Christian Eucharist a number of facts cannot be denied. The prayers in Did 9 and 10 exhibit striking parallels with Jewish meal berakhot, in particular the *birkat ha-mazon* (See for instance: Rouwhorst 2005a, esp. 149–151. See also Rordorf & Tuilier 1978, 175–181; Wengst 1984, 47–53; van de Sandt & Flusser 2002, esp. 310–313), even if the oldest known Jewish versions date from a much later period. Klinghardt and others, who have made little of these facts, argue that the author or editor of the Didache did not employ written texts, but was dependent on an oral tradition in which texts were subject to variation (1996, 407–427). Although this is a valuable conclusion in itself, it fails to refute the thesis of Jewish origins. Apart from the case of the Didache, it can hardly be ignored that there is strong evidence that at least some aspects of early Christian Eucharists and ritual meals had Jewish roots. Suffice it to mention parallels between the structure and some parts of the anaphora of Addai and Mari and various Jewish texts, including the *birkat ha-mazon* (Wegman 1979, 15–43; Rouwhorst 1980, 231–239), the so-called *ya'aleh we yavo* (Rouwhorst 1980, 235; a prayer inserted in the *birkat ha-mazon* on festivals), and the blessings preceding the Shema (see Spinks 1977, 146–161 = 1993, 21–36; Vellian 1982, 201–223). Last but not least, we should bear in mind the prominent place occupied by thanksgivings and blessings in early Christian Eucharists and ritual meals, a phenomenon unique to Jewish ritual meals—and Christianity—and apparently unparalleled in Greek and Roman traditions. This can only be explained, I believe, by a certain dependency of Christian texts on orally transmitted Jewish models, even if the degree of dependency remains difficult to establish.

## THE SYMPOSIUM THEORY ASSESSED

Having discussed the question of Jewish sources, let us turn to the alternative approach, in which the early Eucharist is viewed as a Christian variety of the symposium. The latter is assumed to have been common practice in the Mediterranean, and known to both Greeks and Jews, as well as to the followers of other religious and ethnic traditions.

Generally speaking, this theory has the advantage of fitting in well with the new approach to the early Christian Eucharist sketched above. More specifically, it is favoured by an increasing number of liturgical scholars who wish to draw on the broadest variety of sources, putting into perspective the one-sided focus on the Last Supper and the institution narrative. From another point of view too this theory is most revealing, in that it opens our eyes to the sociological dimensions of the early Christian meal traditions which were often neglected by scholars who, in their search for Jewish roots, were absorbed primarily by texts. We may become more aware, therefore, of the communal nature of early Christian ritual meals and their relation to the identity of certain social groups. There were rules for the admission of non-members, and hierarchical patterns inside the groups, and these could be adopted or abandoned in early Christian meals. Finally, the study of Greco-Roman community meals may tell us much about dining customs and material aspects such as the selection of menus; as McGowan has demonstrated (1999), the social and religious significance of these traditions will escape us if we continue to focus exclusively on texts.

In spite of the merits of this approach, however, several limitations or even risks are evident which, in my view, are not always taken sufficiently into consideration. I shall limit myself here to two brief observations.

1. Adepts of the 'search-for-Jewish-roots' approach are frequently accused of drawing rather uncritically on sources whose range is too wide and whose geographical and historical backgrounds are too diverse. In my view, a similar objection may be made to the manner in which some scholars employ Greco-Roman meal customs to explain the origin and development of the early Christian Eucharist. They do not hesitate to combine data derived from sources as heterogeneous as the writings of Plato, Plutarch, Petronius, Philo of Alexandria, and sources derived from the Qumran community or rabbinic milieus (see for instance Klinghardt 1996, 21–249; Smith 2002, 13–172). Despite the fact that meal customs were probably

less susceptible to change than the prayer texts to which proponents of the Jewish-sources theory appeal, the vast range of periods and regions from which data are drawn should make us wary of hasty generalisations. Further, the question may be raised as to whether differences between various types of banquets are taken sufficiently into account. One wonders, for instance, what philosophical banquets have in common with sacrificial banquets, or with banquets held by all sorts of guild-like groups, let alone the Qumran-communities or the Jewish havurot. It is surely relevant to consider whether a symposium was mainly for socialising and amusement, or had a particularly religious atmosphere (even allowing for the fact that religion had a different function in Antiquity than in modern Western society, and that it is not always easy to distinguish between the sacred and the profane). One may even pose the question whether the symposium pattern was much more than a general model on which a great variety of meals—whether religious or not—were based, but which, in itself, provides little insight into the specific character of each type of meal.

2. As I have remarked, one of the principal merits of this theory is that it makes us alert to the sociological aspects. Precisely here, however, the danger of one-sidedness looms once more. Whereas scholars in search of Jewish roots run the risk of focusing exclusively on the religious significance of texts, adherents of the symposium theory are in danger of going to the other extreme, emphasising social practices and related social codes at the expense of religious meanings. Unless one wishes to follow Emile Durkheim in reducing God or the sacred to nothing but a reflection or projection of society, it is necessary to develop a well-balanced approach that does justice to both the religious and social dimensions of rituals, without reducing one to the other. This implies that research into early Christianity and its meal traditions should involve both non-textual and textual elements, and their pre-Christian roots, whether Jewish or non-Jewish.

## Final Remarks: the Christian Appropriation of Jewish and Greco-Roman Traditions

It will be clear from the foregoing that the two theories discussed each have their own validity. Both shed light on important aspects of the development of early Christian meal practices and the early

Christian Eucharist in particular. The overall conclusion is that the two theories are not mutually exclusive, but rather complement each other, each focusing on important aspects of early Christian ritual meal traditions.

Both theories, however, have their limitations. This holds for the more traditional approach, which, as opponents did not hesitate to emphasise, concentrated on the Jewish roots. It also applies, however, to the symposium hypothesis, which, developed and increasingly accepted only in recent years, has yet to be critically assessed.

Moreover, both theories have a limitation in common that is inherent in the concept of a search for origins. Given the fact that they are primarily concerned with the dependence of early Christian ritual meals upon pre-Christian traditions, whether Jewish, Greek or Roman, it is easy to overlook specifically Christian dimensions. It is therefore important to bear in mind that practices are never simply copied, but rather appropriated and transformed. Once a particular tradition has been transmitted from one community to another, it will be restructured and adapted. As it begins to fulfil new religious and social functions, new meanings will be ascribed to it and new elements will be added. The full significance of a specific tradition, ritual or otherwise, cannot be discovered only by laying bare its antecedents. This applies to the ritual meals of early Christianity just as it does to the Passover Seder or the rabbinic ḥavurot, which were doubtlessly influenced by the Greco-Roman symposium tradition.

The question remains what happened to the Jewish and Greco-Roman elements that became incorporated in the ritual meals—Eucharists or otherwise—of early Christian communities. It is not possible to discuss this at length here; indeed, the question requires a fresh and critical re-examination of all early Christian sources that refer or allude to any sort of ritual meal practiced by groups of Christians. I shall therefore limit myself to two suggestions for further research.

Firstly, in the transformation of pre-Christian meal practices, the role played by the introduction of the institution narrative and elements derived from the Last Supper tradition has been overstated. As will be clear from this paper, the process by which the early Christian Eucharist incorporated and indeed gave a central place to the Last Supper tradition, and particularly the recitation of the institution narrative, was slower and more gradual than has been assumed.

Secondly, the transformation of pre-Christian elements related to meal customs, as they became incorporated in the early Christian

Eucharist, cannot be studied only in terms of texts. We must bear in mind that non-textual elements, for instance *gestures*, too may have acquired new significance in early Christianity. An interesting example might be provided by the 'breaking of the bread'. The importance given to this gesture from the very first days of Christianity (1 Cor 10:16; Luke 24:30, 35; Acts 2:42, 46; 20:7; Did 14:1; Apocryphal Acts of the Apostles, esp. those of Thomas; Ephrem the Syrian; cf. for the Apocryphal Acts of Thomas and the works of Ephrem the Syrian: Rouwhorst [forthcoming]) appears to be unparalleled in Greco-Roman and Jewish sources. In the Jewish tradition, the emphasis lies on the blessing accompanying the breaking of the bread rather than on the breaking itself. In early Christianity, this ritual gesture gained an intensity it had never had in Jewish or non-Jewish symposiums.

Needless to say, these concluding observations in no way deny the importance of tracing and mapping the pre-Christian roots, Jewish or otherwise, of early Christian ritual meals, in particular those of the early Christian Eucharist. Although the study of these pre-Christian roots alone is insufficient to gain a better understanding of the ritual meals of early Christianity, it cannot be denied that it is an indispensable precondition in order to achieve that goal. It is a first step in that direction, but a very important one.

## LITERATURE

Botte, B., *La Tradition apostolique de Saint Hippolyte* (LQF 39), Münster 5th ed. 1989.

Bouyer, L., *Eucharistie; Théologie et spiritualité de la prière eucharistique*, Tournai 1966, reprinted 1990.

Bradshaw, P.F., 'Introduction: The Evolution of Early Anaphoras', in: Idem (ed.), *Essays on Early Eastern Eucharistic Prayers*, Collegeville 1997.

————, *The Search for the Origins of Christian Worship; Sources and Methods for the Study of Early Liturgy*, London 2nd ed. 2002.

————, M.E. Johnson, & L.E. Philips, *The Apostolic Tradition* (Hermeneia), Minneapolis 2002.

————, 'Parallels between Early Jewish and Christian Prayers. Some Methodological Issues', in: A. Gerhards, A. Doeker, & P. Ebenbauer (eds), *Identität durch Gebet; Zur gemeinschaftsbildenden Funktion institutionalisierten Betens in Judentum und Christentum* (Studien zu Judentum und Christentum), Paderborn 2003.

————, *Eucharistic Origins*, Oxford 2004.

Dix, G., *The Shape of the Liturgy*, London [1st ed., January] 1945 [2nd ed. August 1945; reprinted 1946, 1947, 1949, 1952, 1954, 1960, 1964, 1970, 1975, 1978, 2005]

Jeremias, J., *Die Abendmahlsworte Jesu*, Göttingen 4th ed. 1967.

Johnson, M.E., 'The Apostolic Tradition', in: G. Wainwright & K. Westerfield Tucker, *The Oxford History of Christian Worship*, Oxford 2006.

Jonge, H.J. de, 'The Early History of the Lord's Supper', in: J.W. van Henten & A. Houtepen (eds), *Religious Identity and the Invention of Tradition*, Assen 2001.

————, *Zondag en sabbat; Over het ontstaan van de christelijke zondag*, Dies-oratie University of Leiden, 2006.

Klinghardt, M., *Gemeinschaftsmahl und Mahlgemeinschaft; Soziologie und Liturgie frühchristlicher Mahlfeiern* (TANZ 13), Tübingen—Basel 1996.

Leonhard, C., 'Die älteste Haggada: Übersetzung der Pesachhaggada nach dem palästinischen Ritus und Vorschläge zu ihrem Ursprung und ihrer Bedeutung für die Geschichte der christlichen Liturgie', *ALW* 45 (2003).

————, 'Die Ursprünge der Liturgie des jüdischen Pesach und das christliche Osterfest', in: A. Gerhards & H. Henrix (eds), *Dialog oder Monolog?; Zur liturgischen Beziehung zwischen Judentum und Christentum* (QD 208), Freiburg 2004.

Leyerle, B., ' Meal Customs in the Greco-Roman World', in: P. Bradshaw & A. Hoffman (eds), *Passover and Easter; Origin and History to Modern Times* (Two Liturgical Traditions 5), Notre Dame 1999.

Ligier, L., 'De la Cène du Seigneur à l'Eucharistie', *ASeign* 1 (1968) [English translation: 'From the Last Supper to the Eucharist', in: L. Sheppard (ed.), *The New Liturgy*, London 1970].

————, 'Les origines de la prière eucharistique: de la Cène du Seigneur à l 'Eucharistie', *QLP* 53 (1972) [English translation: 'The Origins of the Eucharistic Prayer: From the Last Supper to the Eucharist', *StLi* 9 (1973)].

Mazza, E., *L'anafora eucaristica; Studi sulle origini* (BEL.S 62), Roma 1992; esp. 'La "dottrina dei dodici apostoli" o "Didache"' [19–50] and 'L'eucaristia di 1 Cor 10,17 in rapporto a "Didache" 9–10' [77–109].

————, *L'eucaristia nella storia*, 1996 [French translation: *L'action eucharistique*, Paris 1999; English translation: *The celebration of the Eucharist*, Collegeville 1999].

McGowan, A., *Ascetic Eucharists; Food and Drink in Early Christian Ritual Meals* (Oxford Early Christian Studies), Oxford 1999.

————, 'Rethinking Agape and Eucharist in Early North African Christianity', *StLi* 34 (2004).

Rordorf, W. & A. Tuilier, *La Doctrine des douze Apôtres (Didachè)* (SC 248), Paris 1978

Rouwhorst, G., 'Bénédiction, action de graces, supplication. Les oraisons de la table dans le Judaïsme et les célébrations eucharistiques des Chrétiens syriaques', *QuLi* 67 (1980).

————, 'La célébration de l'Eucharistie dans l'Eglise primitive', *QuLi* 74 (1993).

————, 'Didache 9–10: A Litmus Test for the Research on Early Christian Eucharist', in: H. van de Sandt (ed.), *Matthew and the Didache; Two Documents from the Same Jewish-Christian Milieu?*, Assen—Minneapolis 2005 [quoted as 2005a].

————, Review of Bradshaw, Johnson, & Philips 2002, in: *VigiChr* 59 (2005) [quoted as 2005b].

————, [The article announced on p. 306 will be published in the series Quaestiones disputatae in 2008 (conference volume)].

Sandt, H. van de & D. Flusser, *The Didache; Its Jewish Sources and its Place in Early Judaism and Christianity*, Assen—Minneapolis 2002.

Smith, D., *From Symposium to Eucharist in the Early Christian World*, Minneapolis 2002.

Spinks, B., 'The Original Form of the Anaphora of the Apostles: A Suggestion in the Light of the Maronite Sharar', *EL* 91 (1977); reprint in: Idem, *Prayers from the East*, Washington 1993.

Stemberger, G., 'Pesachhaggada und Abendmahlsberichte des Neuen Testaments', *Kairos* 29 (1987); reprint in: Idem, *Studien zum rabbinischen Judentum* (SBAB 10), Stuttgart 1990.

Talley, T., 'De la *berakah* à l'eucharistie. Une question à réexaminer', *MD* 25 (1976).

————, 'The Literary Structure of Eucharistic Prayer', *Worship* 58 (1984).

————, 'Structures des anaphores anciennes et modernes', *MD* 191 (1992).

Vellian, J., 'The Anaphoral Structure of Addai and Mari compared to the Berakhoth Preceding the Shema in the Synagogue Morning Service contained in the Seder R. Amram Gaon', *Muséon* 85 (1982).

Wegman, H., 'Pleidooi voor een tekst. De anaphora van de apostelen Addaï en Mari', *Bijdr.* 40 (1979).

——, 'Généalogie hypothétique de la prière eucharistique', *QuLi* 61 (1980).

——, 'Genealogie des Eucharistiegebetes', *ALW* 33 (1991).

Wengst, K., *Didache (Apostellehre), Barnabasbrief, Zweiter Klemensbrief, Schrift an Diognet* (SUC 2), Darmstadt 1984.

Winkler, G., 'Weitere Beobachtungen zur frühen Epiklese (den Doxologien und dem Sanctus). Über die Bedeutung der Apokryphen für die Erforschung der Entwicklung der Riten', *OrChr* 80 (1996).

# BLESSINGS OVER WINE AND BREAD IN JUDAISM AND CHRISTIAN EUCHARISTIC PRAYERS TWO INDEPENDENT TRADITIONS

*Clemens Leonhard*
Westfälische Wilhelms-Universität Münster, Germany

Judaism[1] and Christianity developed rituals that change the religious status of certain foods—either as a sanctification of symbolic food at special occasions or as an indispensable prerequisite for proper eating in general. The following paper calls into question the assumption that these rituals derive from common origins.

The question of what a 'berakha' is, can be answered by means of a description of the literary form(s) of specimens of its genre. Although it is important for the reconstruction of the development of rabbinic berakhot, it does not help in understanding phenomena in Christian traditions; for the few similarities that are sometimes claimed to exist between Christian and rabbinic blessings do not explain the *function* of these texts within the rituals. The most salient common feature of the wording of early rabbinic and Christian (e.g. Didache 9f) prayer texts is that they do not reveal their function(s) within the ritual frame of the meal.

In this context, it is necessary to rely on texts of the same epochs which explain the purpose and structure of the rituals. t.Ber 4.1 18 is the best interpretation of rabbinic birkhot ha-nehenin:

> 4.1 (a) It is forbidden for a man to taste anything before he recited a berakha. For, i(t is said): 'The land (הארץ) and its contents are Y's" (Ps 24:1aα).
> (b) Everyone who enjoys this world (העולם הזה) without a berakha is like someone who makes improper use of sacred property, before the (fulfillment of) all commandments allowed him (to do so). [?]
> Everybody must use his face, hands, and feet to the honor of his creator only; for (it is said): 'Y' has made everything for himself' (Prov 16:4).

---
[1] I am grateful to Günter Stemberger for many important remarks on a draft of this paper. The work on this paper was made possible by a generous grant of the Alexander von Humboldt-Foundation.

4.2  Over syrup of dates, wine of apples, vinegar of late figs, he recites the same berakha as over *muries*.

4.3  Over unmixed wine, he recites the berakha: '…who creates the fruit of the tree' and they wash the hands with it. But if he put water into it, they recite over it the berakha: '…who creates the fruit of the vine' and they do not wash the hands with it. These are R. Le'azar's words.

But the sages say: This way or the other, they recite the berakha '…who creates the fruit of the vine' over it and they do not wash their hands with it.

4.4  They served him (different) kinds (of food as a) dessert…

Being carried away by similarities between these paragraphs and 1 Cor 10:26, 31; Eduard Lohse (1956, 277–280) sees in Ps 24:1 a proof-text for the function of berakhot in Judaism and Christianity. Yet, t.Ber 4.1 uses Ps 24:1 in a way that is the opposite of how Paul does. According to 1 Cor, the 'strong ones' may eat meat from pagan offerings. Having 'rendered thanks' (1 Cor 10:30), it is clear that they do not intend to partake in the food of idol worship. Paul does not use Ps 24:1 as a scriptural basis for a kind of 'thanksgiving', but wants to emphasize that pagan cults cannot change the quality of the food, because nothing can override God's ownership of the universe. The divine owner-ship of the world erases the difference between sacred and profane (cf. Rom 14:6). For Christians, there is no sacred food. Ps 24:1 allows the Christians—but forbids the rabbinic Jews—to eat anything. Early Christianity did, however, not abide by this conclusion (1 Tim 4:4f, Didache 9f; cf. Maier 2004, 375–390 esp. 388).

One could argue that R. Le'azar regarded undiluted wine as food (*on behalf of which* one would wash one's hands with water) while diluted wine was the most important beverage in the symposium. Yet, p.Ber 6.1 10a shows that the Tosefta should be read as implying that the wine is used for washing the hands. While this is probably more a halakhic example than a practical problem, this was imaginable. Plu-tarchus mentions the use of wine with spices (ἀρώματα) for the wash-ing of the feet at a luxurious meal (Pocion 20.2f; Kötting & Halama 1972, 747f). The sages of the Tosefta regard wine in any form not as liquid for washing one's hands. In R. Le'azar's first case, the berakha does not make (the undiluted) wine sacred (in the Christian sense of 'eucharistized' wine)—in a sense that excludes that one should wash one's hands with it.

The tannaim knew that Ps 24:1 does not provide a sufficient basis for the argument that food is generally forbidden for humankind. Thus, they supplied a paraphrase of this rule. Baruch M. Bokser (1981, 557–574) interprets the change of concepts from 'taste' to 'enjoy' in sections (a) and (b) as an indication of different sources that were combined in this text. He shows (563), however, that 'enjoy' (= 'derive benefit from') belongs to the legal context of me'ila. Whoever wanted to explain the use of Ps 24:1 by means of the concept of me'ila, would use 'enjoy' as a legal term. 4.1 (b) is, therefore, better understood as a periphrastic explication of the genuine sense of 4.1 (a).

The assumption that God's property must be handed over to the Temple personnel can be gathered from laws about tithes and teruma and the like. God foregoes his rights to portions of certain agricultural products for the benefit of the priests and Levites (Numb 18:8). If everything is God's property, it must by analogy be given to the Temple. Therefore, any profane use constitutes an infringement of the rights of the Temple. The laws of tithes and teruma are *not* quoted as proof-texts. Having provided Ps 24:1 as a proof-text for the custom to recite berakhot, the Tosefta stops its discussion and leaves the two following questions open. These are discussed and partly answered in the talmudim.

First, large portions of the order of Zeraim are concerned with the question of how to handle those portions of agricultural products that are actually God's property, that belong to the Temple, but which cannot be handed over to it any more. The rabbis assemble a plethora of solutions for many problems posed by the clash of the biblical laws with the Greco-Roman society in which they live. It is, therefore, curious that two paragraphs of massekhet berakhot construct an easy and inexpensive parallel structure of handling God's rights to the agricultural products (cf. Bokser 1981). Why did the Tosefta and the Mishna go on to discuss the minutiae of rabbinic life and their handling of agricultural products if they had already solved all problems by the rule that everything belongs to God and is redeemed by the recitation of a few words before eating and drinking? One possible answer to this question may be that it is Israel's *privilege*—not burden—to fulfill the commandments of the Tora. One should, however, expect an increase of agricultural laws because of this concept. Yet, the straightforward system of berakhot became the universal standard without being the fulfillment of a single commandment of the Tora against many laws of the Tora—which became obsolete. For Babylonians, who could not apply the system of tithes and teruma, birkhot ha-nehenin would have been highly attractive as a means to keep the agricultural laws (cf.

Bokser 1981, 566f). Birkhot ha-nehenin are, however, a given for the tannaim, who tried hard to keep the agricultural commandments, too. The theological and legal relationship between the system of birkhot ha-nehenin and the laws of the handling of agricultural products remains an open question.

The second question that is not answered by the Tosefta concerns the legitimization of the berakha as a solution for the problem that one must not actually eat anything for fear of me'ila. How can a few words of praise that acknowledge God as the creator of the food upon one's table do away with God's ownership thereof? This is one of the problems of any Formgeschichte approach to birkhot ha-nehenin. The reason for is that the text of these berakhot does not indicate that it intends to loosen the bond of property between the creator and his creation.

These questions are partly answered in the talmudim. Thus, the PT associates the text of the Tosefta to Ber 6.1, the short list of coined berakhot (9d–10a) in this context:

> (Catchword of the Mishna) 'How does one say a berakha over fruits,' etc.
>
> (a) 'The land and its contents, the world and its inhabitants are Y's'; (implying that) whoever enjoys anything from the world, before the (fulfillment of the) commandments allows him (to do so), makes improper use of sacred property.
>
> (b) R. Abahu said: it is written, 'lest all of it both the (produce of the) seed that you sowed as well as the yield of your vineyard become sacred' (Deut 22.9). The whole world and its contents are regarded as the vineyard. What is its redemption? A berakha.
>
> (c) R. Ḥizqiya, R. Yirmeya, and R. Abun (said) in the name of R. Shim'on ben Lakish: 'You said to Y': you are Y'. My good (i.e. my property) is not upon you'[2] (Ps 16:2). If you ate and blessed, it is as if you ate from your own.
>
> (d) A(nother) i(nterpretation). 'My good is not upon you'. I use up my good in your body.[3]

---

[2] The verse can hardly be translated. The Septuagint understands it in a similar way as the rabbis: 'I said to the Lord. You are my Lord. You do not need any of my goods (טובותי instead of טובתי).' Resh Lakish either implies something like: 'mine (mankind's) is not yours (God's)' or as God speaking: 'mine (God's) is not upon you (so that you ate your own)'. The interpretation only explains birkat ha-mazon *after* the meal as it alludes to Deut 8:10—not birkhot ha-nehenin.

[3] Horowitz (1975, 158 n. 5): this is said in God's name. בל is interpreted as belonging to the root בל״י.

(e) A(nother) i(nterpretation). 'My good is not upon you'. All the goods are mixed together and come upon you.[4]

(f) Said R. Aḥa: What does 'not upon you (*bal alekha*)' mean? (It means) that I do not bring a good upon the world without you (*mibil'adekha*), co(rresponding) to the (verse) that s(ays): 'Nobody will lift up his hand without you' (Gen 41:44).

(g) R. Ḥiyya taught (as a tannitic rule): 'a holiness of praises' (Lev 19:24) teaches that it requires a berakha before and after it. From this (verse), R. Akiva said: nobody may taste anything before he recited a berakha (Sifra kedoshim par. 3 § 9 Weiss 90b, cf. Bokser 1981, 559f).

The redactors of the PT are even less interested than the Tosefta to standardize the words that should be used to bless fruits. They prefer to discuss the raison d'être of the custom. Thus, rabbi Abahu provides the missing verse from the Tora (b): the law about forbidden mixtures regarding the vineyard. If the whole world is taken as one vineyard, it is definitely 'mixed' and hence in a state of sacredness. It cannot be used by human beings. The produce of the mixed vineyard must be burned (Ter 7.5). The Bible does not provide a ritual to 'separate' or redeem forbidden mixtures. Yet, there is a remedy in the case of the whole world: a berakha.

(c) and (d) are concerned with birkat ha-mazon (after the meal). The mixed vineyard issue seems to be taken up in again, (e). This links the quotation from the Psalms with the Tora. Spoken in God's name, the statement reveals the tension between the laws of agricultural dues and berakhot.

May the raw and undetermined status of tevel (a lot of untithed products of agriculture) be compared with the mixed vineyard? (Biblical) Israelites are forbidden to eat tevel, because teruma in an undeclared status is still an indistinguishable part within it. As it is forbidden to eat teruma (unless one is a priest, in a status of purity, etc.), because teruma belongs to God, the mixed status of tevel makes it forbidden as a whole. If 'the whole world' should *resemble* tevel, this statement could suggest nothing less than that the berakha transforms something like tevel into permitted food. The rabbis were careful, however, not to confound the systems of tithes and birkhot ha-nehenin. Thus, the Mishna (Ber 7.1a) can rule that persons who ate 'tevel' should not be invited to birkat ha-mazon *afterwards*. Note that the Interpreters (cf. the Maimonides and the Bertinoro and t.Ker 1.5 Zuckermandel 561)

---

[4] יכללו is read as יבללו Nifal of בל"ל (lemmatization: Maagarim).

explain this as tevel as a 'rabbinic'—as opposed to a biblical—category; that grew in flower-pots and not in the earth of the Land of Israel. Although this is not mentioned, a berakha *before* eating does not remove that kind of state of the food as tevel. The sacred portions *within* tevel can only be declared, separated, and subsequently destroyed (if there is no proper recipient available), but never made profane. (BM 4.8, that speaks about the a posteriori redemption by 120% of its value of teruma, bikkurim, etc., must imply someone who ate those priestly portions unwittingly.)

Ps 24:1aα in t.Ber 4.1 must be read as a catchword and not as a full quotation. Ps 24:1b, which speaks about the earth/universe, תבל, is evoked, too; for this is the basis for the term 'world', עולם, in the following paraphrase. Birkhot ha-nehenin are not restricted to the Land of Israel, because they are not built upon the system of tithes and teruma.

The BT begins the discussion at the point where the PT ended it (g; Maier 2004, 381) and departs from Lev 19:24: 'In the fourth year, all of its fruits are a holiness of praises for Y' (cf. Bokser 1981, 572 for the low age of this passage). The association of the concept of neta reva'i is appropriate, because the Mishna (Ber 6.1) begins the discussion with the fruits of the *trees*. Lev 19:24 itself rather enacts that the fourth year's fruits of trees (and by derivation from that, also vines) must be treated like second tithes in some respects: they may be redeemed—i.e. their holiness can pass onto an amount of money corresponding to their value (+20%; MSh 5.4f; BM 4.8). That money must (at least in theory) be disposed of (e.g. cast into the Dead Sea, t.Naz 3.16 134) as long as there is no Temple available where it can be converted into food again and be consumed.

The Tora does not prescribe a *verbal* component of the ritual of separation (and declaration) of teruma and other agricultural products. This was supplied by analogy in t.Ber 6.14 37. The commandments of the agricultural dues are fulfilled by means of their correct handling by the correct person in the correct situation. In the BT, birkhot ha-nehenin are understood as a *verbal* act of 'praise' (of God) and require, hence, a different biblical basis. The phrase 'holiness of praises' in the law of neta reva'i is a good choice. Furthermore, the neta reva'i actually belongs to the Temple according to the Bible. It corresponds neatly to the concept of me'ila which is already used in the Tosefta as a legal principle for the understanding of birkhot ha-nehenin. Fruits of trees in the land of Israel (not in Babylon) in their fourth year are, however, not redeemed by an act of 'praising' God, but by the evaluation and the declaration of redemption money (MSh 5.4f). Nonetheless, neta reva'i comes very close to what the Babylonian sages need: a precedent for the transformation (by means of 'praise') of foodstuffs from their being God's (i.e. the Temple's) property to a commodity that can be eaten by all Israelites. Like the PT, the BT also adds a few details to the tradition (Ber 35a–b):

> Our masters taught (as a tannaitic tradition): It is forbidden for a man to enjoy this world without berakha. Everyone who enjoys this world without berakha made improper use of sacred property. What is its remedy? Let him go to a sage! What is he going to do for him? He has (already) done what is forbidden for him.[5] But Rava said: May he go to a sage beforehand and let him teach berakhot, in order that such a case of improper use of sacred property should not happen.
>
> Rav Yehuda said in the name of Shmu'el: Everyone who enjoys this world without berakha is like someone who enjoys the holy things of heaven (i.e. God's property), because it is said: 'The land and its contents are Y's' (Ps 24:1).
>
> R(abbi) Levi pointed out a possible contradiction. It is written: 'The land and its contents are Y's' and it is written: 'the heaven is Y's heaven. He gave the land to humankind' (Ps 115:16). How can this (be reconciled)? Here (in Ps 24, he speaks about the situation) before the berakha and there (in Ps 115, he speaks about the situation) after the berakha.
>
> R(abbi) Ḥanina bar Pappa said: everyone who enjoys this world without a berakha is like someone who steals (גז"ל explaining מע"ל) from the (property of) the Holy One, may he be blessed, and the community of Israel, because it is written: 'He who steals from his father's or his mother's and says: this is no crime...' (Prov 28:24). (In this verse,) 'his father' is the Holy One, may he be blessed, because it is said: 'Is he not your father?' (Deut 32:6). 'His mother' is the community of Israel, because it is said: 'do not reject your mother's Tora' (Prov 1:8). What does it mean: 'he is a colleague of the man of destruction' (Prov 28:24)? He is a colleague of Jeroboam, the son of Nebat, who destroyed all of Israel for their father who is in heaven (because Jeroboam made Israel sin, Rashi).

The sages are aware that the function of birkhot ha-nehenin does not have a basis in the Tora (cf. Maier 2004, 380 and p.Meg 4.1 74d–75a). Bokser (1981, 557 and cf. 560 n. 4) quotes 1 Sam 9:13 as a proof for the antiquity of the custom to recite a blessing before eating. The verse

---

[5] This alteration of the discussion in the PT and the Tosefta seems only intended to explain the past tense of מעל. If someone has already transgressed, there is no remedy a posteriori.

is quoted in p.Ber 7.1 11a (p.Meg 4.1 75a; Mek pisḥa 16 Lauterbach 137), a context that discusses the problem that berakhot before the meal do *not* have a basis in the Tora. 1 Sam 9:13 speaks about a meal at a sanctuary. There is no reason to assume that it had any formal, functional, or genetic connection to the rabbinic birkhot ha-nehenin, because Samuel is obviously expected to sanctify the offering—not to make it profane (Maier 2004, 383 and ff). Likewise, Bokser's quotation of Deut 26:15 does not explain the function of berakhot. That God is the giver of the land and deserves to receive thanks from human beings is a theological truism and not a ritual.

The BT explicitly associates this kind of berakha with an instance of 'praise' in the Bible. Now, the berakha is the remedy for this status of foodstuffs. This kind of berakha is neither what interpreters of Christian liturgies (rightly) understand as 'anamnesis' (of a piece of salvation history) nor an 'epiklesis', which asks God to get involved in the ritual processing of the food. Ber 38a–b (p.Ber 6.1 10a) discusses the question of whether ה־מוציא in the berakha over bread implies the past ('who brought forth') or present ('who is bringing forth') tense in the berakha. The majority holds the opinion that the past tense is meant. Nevertheless, God does not seem to be praised in commemoration of something like 'creation' at 'the beginning' but for his continued sustenance of mankind that is manifest in his having procured the raw material for the bread in front of the person who speaks the berakha.

The difference between Didache 9.5 and the rabbinic approaches is glaring:

> Nobody may eat or drink from your Eucharist except for those who are baptized in the name of the Lord. For, the Lord said about this: 'Do not give the sacred to the dogs' (Matth 7:6).

'Your Eucharist' are either (as in later texts) the cup and the pieces (κλάσματα) upon which the (Christian) blessings have been recited or those together with the whole meal. The Christian blessing makes formerly profane food sacred, whereas the rabbis think that a kind of sacredness of the food is removed by the berakha. This change of the quality of the food is also perceived very differently than in Christianity (cf. Maier 2004; 382, 386–390). Thus, berakhot must be recited again if the meal had been interrupted (e.g. t.Ber 4.19 24f) whereas as early as the mid-2nd cent., Justin tells his readers that 'deacons' bring portions of the food (as ἀποφόρητα, although he does not use this term) to the absent members of the community (2nd Apology 65.5; 67.5 cf.

Bradshaw 2004, 67f; and 87 for Ignatius' perception of the sacredness of eucharistized bread).

The function of the berakha is much more flexible and rather designed to establish a correct relationship between God, the food, and oneself. The rabbinic declaration and separation of agricultural dues developed in the same way. Thus, the rules about handling demai—products whose status regarding tithes and teruma was doubtful—imply that the same commodity could be tithed several times. The status of 'tevel' versus 'tithed correctly and ready to be used' is apparently more significant for those relationships than for the material quality of the food.

The rabbinic Jews create a distinction between sacred and profane, and remove the sacred parts of the commodity, in order to make the rest of it free for profane use. The tannaim are anxious to *reduce* the extent to which sacredness intrudes into the world in the context of food. They devise sophisticated means in order to be able to keep some biblical laws and to lead normal lives at the same time.

The Christians are interested in the opposite. Their rituals create sacred food and the theologians soon begin to explain its significance while the people cherish its spiritual or even magical powers.

In order to facilitate abiding by these commandments, the tannaim establish associations of people who may be trusted to handle the sacred and profane parts of the food correctly. The majority of them (not being priests) creates an inner-rabbinic identity that incorporates those who do *not* eat the sacred parts of the food. Christians build 'Christ's body'—also the 'body' of the corporation—by means of those who eat the sacred food and who distinguish themselves from the rest of the world, who do not.

As soon as the quality of the Eucharist is explained in the sources, it is clear that it is something different than the ritual of the contemporary rabbinic berakha. It may now be asked whether the Christians or the Jews altered an originally 'common' understanding. The chances that such a common root would be detectable are quite low, because there are hardly any formal or functional parallels between the two. It is difficult to identify such berakhot in earlier material unless one is content with the observation that some kind of invocation is performed before eating (cf. Maier 2004 for Qumran and Bokser's references above).

In the search for common origins, the decisive question is when birkhot ha-nehenin and their understanding emerged in Rabbinic Judaism. Alan Jeffry Avery-Peck (1985) has shown that hardly any of the laws regarding agricultural dues goes back to second Temple times. The rabbinic handling of tithes and teruma has a different agenda and purpose than what can be learnt from the Bible. It is, moreover, unclear to which extent the biblical laws were actually kept in Second Temple times. One of their practical consequences (if not their raison d'être) was the support of the Temple and its personnel. In exchange for that, the Temple rendered its services as a center for the creation of a Judaean identity (cf. Schwartz 2001, esp. 59–66). Most of this system, that the rabbis made applicable for a situation without the Temple, was apparently no longer practiced in later amoraic times[6] and was only applicable in Palestine in any case.

A conditio sine qua non for the invention of common principles for birkhot ha-nehenin and the laws of agricultural dues is the rabbis' expansion of the applicability of biblical laws. These laws are apparently based on a principle of *opus operatum*. Thus, tithes (etc.) must be separated from agricultural goods as closely as possible to the context of the harvest—hence under the eyes of the fellow farmers and possibly the future recipients—and handed over to certain persons in order to make the product permissible for further use. The first stages of the processing of the food like the unbaked dough (ḥalla) could be included. Even if Deut 12:17; 14:23 speaks of 'cereals, (unfermented?) must or new wine, and Oil' (דגן, תירוש, יצהר) as well as the firstlings of animals, one would not remove tithes from the roasted veal cutlet in wine-sauce. The intention of the individual is irrelevant. A category such as agricultural products whose status is doubtful (demai) is impossible in such a system. If this was ever applied as written, a single farmer would not have had many opportunities to break the law.

When the rabbis re-invented the system, they could not—or did not want to—base this system on memory fragments of a social and economic reality from the times of the Second Temple. Neither could they just implement the laws as written, because they did not exert any control over the circumstances regarding farming in Palestine. Thus, they shifted the responsibility of the performance of these laws from

---

[6] The Reḥov Inscription (7th cent.?, Sussmann 1973/74, 154ff) is apparently the result of an increasing rabbinization of Palestinian Judaism (Stemberger 1998, 213). p.Dem 2.1 22c, רבי התיר בית שאן, does not appear in the inscription, although it exempts the area from certain obligations regarding the Sabbatical year (cf. Sussmann 99f and n. 74f). The halakhic implications cannot be assessed here (cf. Schwartz 2001, 260 n. 50). The text does not prove that Palestinian Jews kept these agricultural laws in Late Antiquity.

the biblical farmers to themselves—the only ones whom they could trust to keeping the laws.

This move overturns the system. It includes many products and many situations in the scope of the laws that were excluded in biblical times. The handling of the holy portions became less important now, although it is still discussed in great detail. The system *almost* always keeps its link to the material reality. Nevertheless, the rabbis explore the boundaries of this system. This ushers in its collapse.

For the tannaim, the dietary and many of the purity laws have one aim and focal point: the symposia of their associations. The identity of the ḥaver, the member of the rabbinic collegium, is established and maintained by his abidance by some of those laws. If he invites his fellows to a dinner party, they may be sure that he carefully chose and processed the food that is served and supervised the handling of furniture, vessels and implements. They would not worry about the removal of parts of the food as teruma at the meal, because this has already been done. This is not a remnant from biblical times but a highly innovative invention of an archaizing way of life.

As a small minority even among the Jews in Greco-Roman Palestine, haverim of such collegia could not and did not want to restrict their company to themselves all the time. Like the Christians (1 Cor 8 and 10), rabbis took part in social events such as symposia that were given by Jews who did not care about tithes and purity—perhaps even by pagan[7] hosts. Two passages of the Tosefta clarify the ritual and halakhic implications (t.Dem 3.6–8 74f):

> 3.6 (a) A ḥaver may only serve at the symposium and at the dinner of an am ha-areẓ, if (the food) that is passing through his hands is tithed, even if it should only be a single scoop of wine.
> (b) Therefore, a ḥaver who serves at the symposium and at the dinner of an am ha-areẓ creates a (justified) presumption regarding tithes (i.e. that the wine that he serves is made from tithed grapes etc.).
> 3.7 (a) A ḥaver who sits (ms. Erfurt: reclines) at the symposium and at the dinner of an am ha-areẓ does not create a (justified) presumption regarding tithes (i.e. that the food that he eats is tithed), even if he is seen taking (food) and eating (it) immediately and drinking immediately; for he could have tithed (food and drink) in his heart.

---

[7] The following texts of the Tosefta imply that the host is a Jew who does not care about certain halakhot. t.Ber 5.21 28 suggests that non-Jews could recite berakhot at meals. The law makes sure that rabbis would not say 'amen' to pagan religious utterances. It is difficult to know whether or not R. Ammi's prohibition of pagan symposia (p.AZ 1.3 39c) may be generalized.

(b) If his son is reclining with him, he tithes for him.

(c) If someone else (is reclining with him), he does not tithe for him.

(d) If his son is reclining at another place (apparently at another couch at the same symposium of an am ha-arez), he (i.e. the ḥaver) tithes for him.

3.8 (a) The son of a ḥaver who sits (ms. Erfurt: reclines) at the symposium and at the dinner of an am ha-arez, does not create a ( justified) presumption regarding tithes (i.e. that the food that he eats is tithed), even if he is seen taking (food) and eating (it) immediately and drinking immediately; for he could have tithed (food and drink) in his heart.

(b) All of this (is acceptable), although (people) say that these (rules of behavior) are a snare for others.

The ḥaver of these lines finds himself at the dinner party of a host who does not pay any heed to tithes and purity laws. 3.6 clarifies the background. Perhaps, the guests chose a symposiarchos from among them. He would supervise the drinking and pass out wine. The ḥaver cannot accept this position, because he must refuse to serve untithed wine to the other guests. His fellows would assume that the wine which he distributes is tithed.

Each ḥaver watches his peer's behavior. One of them takes food and eats. Here, the Tosefta seemingly changes the rules. In this situation, there is no presumption of the fact that he knows the food is tithed. The rest of the laws (3.7 and 3.8 a) explain this situation.

One must *and can* tithe only one's own property. Thus, the ḥaver, who eats food from his plate can have tithed it 'in his heart' whereas the elected symposiarchos distributes wine that was provided by the host for the guests. No scoop of that wine belongs to him at any moment during the meal. Therefore, he *cannot* tithe it 'in his heart'. He would be forced to distribute what he should never distribute to others, let alone to members of his group: untithed wine. Under this legislation, his colleagues can be absolutely sure that *he* knows that the wine has been tithed by the host when he pours it into their cups. The Tosefta advises ḥaverim to avoid this situation. The same principle is also applied to the ḥaver who becomes a collector of alms (t.Dem 3.4 74):

> At first they used to say that they remove from the association a ḥaver who becomes a collector (of alms). Later, they said that he is not (regarded as) trustworthy (in cases of tithes and purity) as long as he is collector. As soon as he leaves his collectorship he is (again regarded as) trustworthy.

To this, one may quote Dem 3.1 for further clarification:

One (distributes) demai as food to the poor. One (distributes) demai as food to the guests of the hospice. Rabban Gamli'e(l) used to (give) demai as food to his workers.

(Regarding the) collectors of alms, the Shammaites say that they give tithed (food) to those who do not tithe and (food) that has not yet been tithed to those who tithe. (The result of this entirely fantastic procedure is) that every person is eventually eating tithed (food).

The sages said, however: (the collectors of alms) collect just as they get it and distribute it just as they got it and everybody who wants to tithe, will tithe.

The collector of alms is an important functionary of the community and ḥaverim must not refuse an appointment to such a position. Yet this creates a huge problem for their 'trustworthiness' in the eyes of the members of their collegium, even if they were appointed to that office because of their 'trustworthiness' in the eyes of the people of the town. For, the collector of alms by definition takes in untithed products *and distributes* untithed products. Even the totally impracticable suggestion of the Shammaites that the collector of alms store tevel and tithed food separately and hand it out according to the way of life (or religious affiliation, p.AZ 1.3 39c and par.—a text that is embedded in matters of the symposium) of the people who receive it, presupposes that certain people take untithed food from his hands. Again, he simply cannot provide a remedy for the situation, because the goods that he is handling are not his property and because property is a conditio sine qua non for the obligation and ability to separate tithes.[8] Therefore, the ḥaver's membership in his collegium is suspended as long as he is a collector of alms. This is not a kind of punishment for his acceptance of the office, but the consequence of the principle that ḥaverim are trustworthy with regard to the products that leave their possession.

The last sentence of the Tosefta (t.Dem 3.8 b 75.29) indicates what Paul's letter to the Corinthians discusses at length, that all those rules are written into a grey area of behavior that may easily lead to problems in the community, especially when not all of its members share one and the same approach to their solution.

While all those rules can be decoded within the tannaitic network of halakha, the idea that the ḥaver might have tithed his food 'in his

---

[8] The Tosefta apparently regards the food that the ḥaver's son is eating at the symposium as his father's property, even if he does not eat it from the same table as his father whereas another person who shares the table with the ḥaver acquires the food for himself alone and cannot rely on the ḥaver's tithing; cf. Krämer 1971, 49f.

heart' destroys the system. For, the possibility to 'tithe in one's heart' renders all legal constructions of the correct handling of agricultural products null and void. Everybody could take any food at any stage of processing from the land of Israel, 'tithe it in his heart'—and eat (store or sell) it.

Commentators wonder *how* the ḥaver 'tithed in his heart' and quote another text of the Tosefta (t.Dem 8.4f 101f; cf. Krämer 1971, 3–142 esp. 49 n. 43):

> 8.4 Somebody invites his colleague (ḥaver) to eat at his house, but he is not trustworthy with regard to the tithes. He (the ḥaver) says before the evening of the Sabbath: Whatever I am going to eat is tithed. These are the tithes separated (lit. made) from it (lit. on it) and the rest are the tithes (lying) close to it. I made this (portion) to be the tithes and the teruma of the tithes (lying) close to it. The second tithes (lying) north of it or south of it, are herewith profaned by means of the coins.
>
> 8.5 (a) Said R. Yehuda: how can this one tithe anything that is not his property (lit.: did not come into his hand)? But R. Yehuda admits (the whole procedure, in the case that) he takes at the place where this one takes (implying that he buys food at the same place as his host in which case the prospective guest may separate tithes from the 'same' commodity as the host, but from things that are in his possession, because he bought it at the same place as the latter).
> (b) They mixed (and filled) him the cup and he says: Whatever I am going to leave on the fringes of the cup these are the tithes and the rest are the tithes (lying) near it[9]—this (portion) is what I made to be the tithes and the teruma of the tithes (lying) close to it. The second tithes (lying) north of it or south of it, are herewith profaned by means of the coins.

Thus, the ḥaver in the former passage of the Tosefta (3.6) should have related the 'tithing in his heart' to this formula which he allegedly pronounced beforehand. This explanation is false. It is false because no reason is given why the ḥaver should 'tithe in his heart' at all, if he could do the same by means of this formula or even by means of his *action* of post-buying after his host and pre-tithing according to rabbi Yehuda's suggestion. Dem 4.1 constructs a case of post-tithing after the Sabbath, which implies that one should not tithe on a Sabbath.

---

[9] The text (וא<ה>שאר) may be disturbed here; cf. Krämer 1971, 127f and n. 16. The wording of the formula is not relevant in the present context.

t.Shab 2.19 10 implies that it is possible to separate tithes and teruma on the Sabbath, although it is definitely forbidden.

t.Dem 8.4f 101f speaks about the case of an invitation to a meal that takes place on the Sabbath. Separating tithes and teruma on the Sabbath is forbidden. Therefore, the ḥaver in t.Dem 8 cannot 'tithe in his heart' during the meal at the Sabbath. The Tosefta allows the performance of the ritual of tithing *before* the Sabbath for this occasion only. Rabbi Yehuda restricts it again on the basis that the ḥaver cannot *yet* tithe his future meal, because it is still his host's property. Only if he manages to buy enough from the same lot, he may separate tithes from that commodity.[10] In t.Dem 3, 'tithing in one's heart' is the standard procedure but may apparently be applied on weekdays only. t.Dem 3 does *not* indicate that the ḥaver performs a ritual as it is described in t.Dem 8.5 (b). On the contrary, the point of t.Dem 3 is that his action of tithing is performed on the spot but it is *invisible* and *inaudible* for the ḥaver reclining next to him. If he separated certain pieces of his food, his colleague could observe the tiny ritual action or listen to the formula of the declaraion of tithes and realize that he does not regard the served food as tithed. He 'eats immediately' according to the Tosefta—exactly as if he knew that the food was tithed properly and hence without any further manipulation. t.Dem 3 invented spiritual tithing—a point that is well understood by the PT, which cannot but reject it. p.Dem 7.1 26a stipulates that the ḥaver must at least *whisper* a declaration of the pieces on his plate as tithes. In general, the replacement of ritual actions by words or even thoughts was known and interpreted as spiritualization by the rabbis. Thus, p.Ber 4.1 7a calls the Amidah a 'sacrifice of the heart' (עבודה בלב cf. Langer 2003, 127–156 esp. 313). The context interprets Hannah's prayer, that is performed *silently* (2 Sam 1:13).

This casts some light upon the situation of the ḥaverim within the society. Ḥaverim cannot perform rituals which might reveal their attitude towards the food that is served. Neither can they enter a conversation about the status of the food during the symposium among themselves. Ḥaverim are supposed lead double lives. Yet, even if there were spiritual solutions to practical problems in the margins of the system, this kind of behavior was eventually bound to vanish along with the whole

---

[10] Therefore, the continuation of the paragraph, 'they mixed (and served) him...' (b), cannot refer to the same situation, because the ḥaver must not tithe on a Sabbath. Yet, he can in any case use this procedure during other days of the week.

system. It resembles, however, the system of birkhot ha-nehnin. A verbal (or mental) activity performed before eating serves to make food that is actually forbidden allowed—in both cases.

Then what does t.Ber 4.1 (b) 'before all commandments allow him (= declare it permitted for him)' (עד שיתירו לו כל המצות) mean? It may imply that the recitation of the berakha is the fulfillment of the last link in a chain of commandments that are connected with this particular food. If this chain of commandments includes the separation of agricultural dues (as it is not said explicitly by Lieberman 1955, 56 who reads the text through the eyes of much later material), this does not fit the context; for the performance of *all* ritual obligations regarding the food has but one purpose, to make it clear that the food no longer contains sacred parts (that belong to God). After 'all commandments' have been fulfilled, it is the prospective eater's property entirely. It would be absurd to declare all of that to be God's property *again* and that it must be redeemed by an additional kind of ritual once more.

Thus, Bokser (1981, 559) is probably right in suggesting that the Tosefta implies the meaning: 'he makes improper use of the property of the Sanctuary (or of God) before all the commandments permit him (which is done by the berakha only)'. The abbreviated language of the Tosefta does not allow certainty on this point. Yet, taken in conjunction with the first paragraph, it is more logical to assume that the birkat ha-nehenin eventually replaces the fulfillment of all the commandments of agricultural dues already according to the Tosefta—in the Land of Israel as well. This is what happened in the history of the rabbinic berakhot.

Birkhot ha-nehenin and the interpretation of their function may have been developed simultaneously with the rabbinic reconstruction of the agricultural laws. The construction of the latter eventually led to a very similar principle: 'tithing in one's heart'. Birkhot ha-nehenin and the handling of agricultural dues are mutually exclusive, although rabbis appear to have practiced both of them for some time. They exclude each other, because they solve the same problem: to sever a link of possession between God and some of his creatures—or between God and the fruits of the Land of Israel.

The system of birkhot ha-nehenin does not have any precedents in biblical times and presupposes the destruction of the Temple. Yet, it seems to have emerged within the same environment of the same rabbinic activity as the (rabbinic) laws of agricultural dues. Moreover, it is hardly older than the latter because the complicated system of tithes and teruma would not have been invented if its commandments could have been fulfilled in such an easy way as a berakha.

The customs of Greco-Roman symposia and the patterns of organization of associations were well established in Palestine long before 70 C.E. (Klinghardt 1996, 227–249). However, the ḥavura as an association that is centered on the keeping of the laws of tithes (and purity) is dependent upon the creation of the rabbinic laws and is therefore a post-destruction phenomenon. Birkhot ha-nehenin likewise emerged in the context of the symposium. They are discussed in t.Ber 4f, which is a piece of sympotic literature.

The rabbis' attempts to find precedents for these berakhot in the Bible show that they are not evident, even in the larger canon of the Hebrew Old Testament. Blessings after eating were well known in antiquity while blessings before eating were not customary among the Greeks (Klinghardt 1996, 58ff). Expressions of gratitude towards the deity after the meal need to be assessed on a different basis. Yet, invocations of the deity before drinking wine (after the meal) and the removal and offering of certain portions of foodstuffs during their processing was well known and widespread. Thus, a libation of a drop of wine or the invocation ἀγαθοῦ δαίμονος or Διὸς Σωτῆρος comes closer to the ritual function of '... who creates the fruit of the vine' than the rabbis might have wanted to admit. While such customs certainly suggested themselves for the creation of Jewish replacements in the context of the symposium, it cannot be proven that the rabbis created the system of birkhot ha-nehenin as precisely this kind of replacement.

The system of tithing (etc.) is a more realistic precedent for the rabbinic invention of birkhot ha-nehenin than polytheistic libations. Even if it is performed as 'tithing in one's heart', it precedes the consumption, makes actually forbidden food allowed, and honors God by the fulfillment of a commandment of the Tora. Birkhot ha-nehenin have most of the advantages of the rituals of the declaration and separation of tithes (etc.) while they do not share any of its disadvantages. They make goods that are actually God's property free for human use. They make one remember one's identity as a Jew in the context of each meal. They do not resemble pagan libations in any way. Furthermore, they are independent of Palestine and applicable to any food, although bread and wine are singled out and retain the special importance that they already had in the Jewish modification of the Greek symposium. This also explains the significance of birkhot ha-nehenin within the ritual of the meal. Conceived in analogy to the laws of tithing (etc.), they must be performed *before* the consumption of wine and bread.

Is the Christian Eucharist related to the rabbinic birkhot ha-nehenin? Among other features, the position of the Eucharistic prayer within the fourth century celebration of the Christian mass (before the consumption of the elements) shows that it is not related to grace after meals. Birkat ha-mazon designates the point after which no bread may be eaten (t.Ber 4.14 21; 5.12 27), although the drinking of wine is still permitted. The custom of reciting a berakha over food in order to release it for profane use cannot antedate the rabbinic system of tithes (etc.). In the long run, it replaces the agricultural laws. This implies that it emerged in the second century. Therefore, birkhot ha-nehenin cannot have been a model for first and early second century Christianity because of their date of origin and because of their liturgical function.

## LITERATURE

Avery-Peck, A.J., *Mishnah's Division of Agriculture; A History and Theology of* Seder Zeraim (BJSt 79), Chico 1985.

Bokser, B.M., '*Ma'al* and Blessings over Food: Rabbinic Transformation of Cultic Terminology and Alternative Modes of Piety', *JBL* 100 (1981).

Bradshaw, P.F., *Eucharistic Origins* (An Alcuin Club Publication), Oxford 2004.

Horowitz, C., *Berakhoth* (ÜTY 1.1), Tübingen 1975.

Kötting, B. & D. Halama, 'Fußwaschung', *RAC* 8 (1972).

Krämer, W.-F., 'Demai', in: idem & P. Freimark, *Die Tosefta; Seder I: Zeraim. 2: Demai—Schebiit* (RT 1 Die Tosefta I.2), Stuttgart etc. 1971.

Langer, R., 'The 'Amida as Formative Rabbinic Prayer', A. Gerhards, A. Doeker, & P. Ebenbauer (eds), *Identität durch Gebet; Zur gemeinschaftsbildenden Funktion institutionalisierten Betens in Judentum und Christentum* (Studien zu Judentum und Christentum), Paderborn etc. 2003.

Lieberman, S., *Tosefta Ki-Fshutah; A Comprehensive Commentary on the Tosefta; Order Zera'im, Part I*, New York 1955 [Hebrew].

Lohse, E., 'Zu 1 Cor 10 _{26. 31}', *ZNW* 47 (1956).

Maier, J., 'Psalm 24,1: rabbinische Interpretation, jüdische *b°rakah* und christliche Benediktion', in: idem, *Studien zur jüdischen Bibel und ihrer Geschichte* (SJ 28), Berlin—New York 2004 [updated version of an article that appeared 1988 in Italian in *Aug.* 28].

Schwartz, S., *Imperialism and Jewish Society; 200 B.C.E. to 640 C.E.* (Jews, Christians, and Muslims from the Ancient to the Modern World), Princeton—Oxford 2001.

Stemberger, G., 'Juden', *RAC* 19 (fasc. appeared 1998).

Sussmann, Y., 'A Halakhic Inscription from the Bet-Shean Valley' [Hebrew], *Tarb.* 45 (1973/74).

# INDEX OF NAMES

The asterisks indicate pages with full bibliographic references.

# INDEX OF SUBJECTS

Entries in Italics refer to texts.